Eden's Garden

Eden's Garden

Rethinking Sin and Evil in an Era of Scientific Promise

Richard J. Coleman

ROWMAN & LITTLEFIELD PUBLISHERS, INC.
Lanham • Boulder • New York • Toronto • Plymouth, UK

ROWMAN & LITTLEFIELD PUBLISHERS, INC.

Published in the United States of America
by Rowman & Littlefield Publishers, Inc.
A wholly owned subsidiary of The Rowman & Littlefield Publishing Group, Inc.
4501 Forbes Boulevard, Suite 200, Lanham, Maryland 20706
www.rowmanlittlefield.com

Estover Road
Plymouth PL6 7PY
United Kingdom

Copyright © 2007 by Rowman & Littlefield Publishers, Inc.

All rights reserved. No part of this publication may be reproduced,
stored in a retrieval system, or transmitted in any form or by any
means, electronic, mechanical, photocopying, recording, or otherwise,
without the prior permission of the publisher.

British Library Cataloguing in Publication Information Available

Library of Congress Cataloging-in-Publication Data

Coleman, Richard J.
  Eden's garden : rethinking sin and evil in an era of scientific promise / Richard J. Coleman.
    p. cm.
  Includes bibliographical references and index.
  ISBN-13: 978-0-7425-5238-8 (cloth : alk. paper)
  ISBN-10: 0-7425-5238-1 (cloth : alk. paper)
  ISBN-13: 978-07425-5239-5 (pbk. : alk. paper)
  ISBN-10: 0-7425-5239-X (pbk. : alk. paper)
  1. Good and evil. 2. Fall of man. 3. Sin–Christianity. 4. Religion and science. I. Title.
  BJ1401.C59 2007
  170–dc22   2006017583

Printed in the United States of America

∞ ™ The paper used in this publication meets the minimum requirements of American National Standard for Information Sciences—Permanence of Paper for Printed Library Materials, ANSI/NISO Z39.48-1992.

*Dedicated to my grandchildren:
Grace, Zoe, Xavier, Jasmine, and Cole.*

*May they bring as much joy to the world
as they bring to me.*

Contents

	Foreword	ix
Introduction		1
Part 1	**Science's Coming-of-Age Story**	
Chapter 1	Knowledge Too Powerful to Be Ignored: The Good and Noble Scientist	45
Chapter 2	Knowledge Too Good Not to Be Exploited: The Compromised Scientist	79
Part 2	**The New Occasion for an Original Temptation**	
Chapter 3	Sin of the Common Variety: Distinguishing Sin from Evil and Sin from Sins	129
Chapter 4	Sin Uniquely Christian: A Fresh Interpretation of "The Fall"	161
Chapter 5	Sin's Genealogy: The Emergence of Sin	189
Chapter 6	Science as the New Occasion for Sin: When Humans Overreach	223
Part 3	**Science and Theology in Counterbalance**	
Chapter 7	What Can We Expect? So Much Depends on How We Answer	249

Selected Bibliography	285
Subject Index	295
Author Index	297
About the Author	301

Foreword

Midway through the twentieth century, in the midst of a terrible war, scientists created the most destructive weapon known to humanity. Six months into a new millennium President Clinton, with Francis Collins and Craig Venter at his side, announced the mapping of three billion "letters" of the human genome. The age we leave behind—the triumph and epitome of physics—generated pessimism and the ever-present threat of unthinkable cataclysm. The promise of the twenty-first century is no less than the prospect of ending our evolutionary fate as determined by our genes. With the power to create life after our own likeness, the last stronghold of fate is breached. But what if that likeness is itself flawed? This question is exceedingly important when the human species is on the cusp of becoming the subject rather than the object of its own evolution.

The future could not be more auspicious: effecting biomedical miracles, dazzling us with new reproductive technologies, making ourselves better than well. And where in all of this do we locate sin and evil? We sense that they reside somewhere in the vicinity of Promethean aspirations of pursuing the technological vision of perfection; and we are downright certain sin and evil play a critical role in the multitude of ethical decisions thrust upon us by biotechnology. But, still, we can't quite put a finger on the vital spot.

The ancient story of sin (Genesis 3) directs us to look at the original or fundamental temptation: the desire to be like God by knowing all things, both good and evil. The pursuit of knowledge, unbounded and highly prized, is also the story of science's coming-of-age. Secluded away at Los Alamos, scientists began to appreciate that they are the gatekeepers to knowledge both good and evil. Between the atomic age and the DNA era, scientific knowledge went from being too potent to be ignored to being too good not to be exploited. As the Cold War receded and science feasted on new appropriations, another dynamic comes into play. Profit-sharing contracts and market shares displace the acquisition of knowledge for the good of humanity. Scientists themselves are troubled by the positive synergy between science and the marketplace, torn between doing good science and selling that science to the highest bidder. Again we sense the presence of sin and evil but are not quite sure how to identify them in the midst of so much knowledge for so much good. *We live in a virtual garden of delight and for this reason alone we shadow Adam and Eve as they romped through Eden, also known as "garden of delight" or paradise.*

I often see myself dragging sin and evil into the postmodern era in order to restore some sanity to what otherwise is a future seen through rose-tinted glasses. As such, the book is a theological gloss on the posthuman debate about the nature of being human. Sin and evil are not usually given a place at the table of critical ideas. Apart from the "world" of conservative theology, and the occasional mention of evil by a president of the United States, sin and evil are dismissed as irrelevant and antiquated. A rethinking of sin and evil is required if anything is to change. Reinhold Niebuhr took the initial step toward emancipating sin from a literal past and the notion that we sin because of one defining moment in history. The task he left undone is to provide sin with its own evolutionary history.

Just as we are reaching the pinnacle of our evolutionary development—the moment we begin manipulating genes to be our friends rather than surrendering to their fate—science is blissfully unaware of how biotechnology is the new occasion for sin. Science has advanced far beyond making a better mousetrap. Now it is a better human being. But can the creator create anything except what he or she already is, and what if we are already flawed? Look not for the sinister scientist hidden away in a laboratory but to science as an indispensable component of a capitalistic culture. Keep an eye on what the heart desires and the good we intend, for embedded within them is the ancient urge to know all things—a new version of an ancient temptation. And Yahweh said: "Do not desire to know all things, both good and evil," for in the reaching you will overreach—an itch that is inflamed by the unbridled optimism of an over-promising science.

The potent and complex issues of a new century are distilled by the question of whether we can trust ourselves. It's the same question Adam and Eve neglected to ask. If we can, there is little we will not attempt. If we cannot, we should be wary of what we might do to our planet and ourselves.

Introduction

> Our civilization has chosen machinery and medicine and happiness. That's why I have to keep these books locked up in the safe. They're smut.
>
> —Mustapha Mond, Resident World Controller for Western Europe, from Thomas Huxley's *Brave New World*

> Science is the measure of the human race's progress. . . .
>
> —Scientist in a letter to Congress and the National Institutes of Health calling for the government to make all taxpayer-funded research papers freely available

> It's a big opportunity. We are in the life science moment of research on this planet.
>
> —Senator Edward M. Kennedy replying to Governor of Massachusetts Mitt Romney's proposal to ban the cloning of embryos for stem cell research

An introduction sets the stage within a larger context. On the stage the actors will speak their lines: the arguments I defend and the writers I engage. The stage itself is the corpus of the book, but neither the stage nor the book exists in isolation. Surrounding us are the larger events of world history, the prevalent presumptions, both accepted and questioned, and my own life story. This introduction charts the flow of ideas and arguments, but it does so with an eye toward mapping the terrain that is our present moment in history.

The perspective is theological, drawing on the Christian understanding of sin and evil, and the task is to rethink sin and evil in such a way that they are recognized as necessary for the understanding of the human condition. The book's outline is straightforward. Part 1 tells the story of science's coming-of-age—how the creators of knowledge too powerful to be ignored become the engineers of knowledge too good not to be ignored. Part 2 turns theological in order to explore the depths of sin and evil. The concluding chapter of part 3 raises issues of what we can realistically expect. The book succeeds to the extent sin and evil become credible in this age of scientific promise.

The bookend chapters of part 1 are meant to provide some historical perspective. At one end is the science of the atomic bomb. At the other end is the science of reproductive biology, genetic enhancement, robotics, artificial intelligence, and virtual reality. When it comes to science proper, it isn't easy to say where sin and evil reside. Because of its aura of objectivity, science is regarded as exempt from culpability. But is the knowledge that scientists discover and develop inherently good, and what if that knowledge can kill a million people or be sold to make a profit? Apart from Robert Oppenheimer's mention of having blood on his hands during a postwar discussion with President Harry S Truman, the language of guilt is blatantly absent.[1] The scientists who created "the Bomb" had few regrets—few at first and more in time—for they had done what was necessary, the right thing at the right time. And perhaps as scientists they did. In either case their story is more complex. What we forget or don't know is the uncommon way they dedicated themselves to the common good of the nations. They became politically involved in a way we haven't seen since. The reason for a historical perspective is to remind us that the science of the atom is very different from the science of the cell and to understand both in their own unique situations. Theologians, however, will not retreat from the claim that human nature hasn't changed whether the knowledge we reach for is good or evil. But embarking on an age of technological promise presents its own singular challenges to understand sin as original and perennial.

In an era where knowledge is the most important currency, the relevancy of sin is immediately appreciated once it is construed as the inevitable overreaching that accompanies the human desire to know all things. The first four chapters of part 2 have the rather ambitious agenda of restoring a level of credibility to sin and evil so they might be taken seriously by skeptics in general, and the scientifically minded in particular. The issue is whether sin and evil can make it out of the pew and into the laboratory. It simply will not do to think the connection between sin and science is the rogue scientist who creates a monster and lets it loose in society. Instead, think of sin as what happens when our best intentions are vitiated with unbridled optimism and visions of perfection.

My approach to rethinking sin and evil is to lay aside the ethical ramifications of the new sciences in order to concentrate on the most fundamental aspects of the human condition. For this reason you will not find an up-to-date interpretation of sin and evil in realms personal and societal (such as Ted Peter's *Radical Evil in Soul and Society*), or a retrieval of a primordial awareness that confirms the orthodox and neoorthodox doctrine of sin (such as *A Breviary of Sin*, by Cornelius Plantinga, Jr.), or a detailed analysis of the scriptural evidence for original sin (such as Henri Blocher's *Original Sin*). Nor will you find a reworking of sin and evil within a sociobiological framework (such as Patricia A. Williams' *Doing Without Adam and Eve: Sociobiology and Original Sin*). In fact, I question the value of trying to make sin or evil empirically tenable though I confess that there are moments when I am tempted to do just that, and it may appear that is what I am doing. The distinction I make is between a reasonable claim that we have a genetic disposition toward good (altruism) or evil (violence),[2] and turning this argument into the sole warrant for finding sin and evil acceptable in a postmodern context. To make the move toward empirically valid is important but it should not be allowed to either predominate or denigrate a theological understanding.

In the process of rethinking sin and evil, I make three interlocking arguments: (1) begin with sin as a dimension of self-transcendence, (2) emphatically separate sins from sin, and sin from evil, and (3) draw the connection between sin and the evolutionary emergence of certain human capacities. Although there are many ways to interpret sin, only one meets the critical criteria of being truly perennial. Only when sin is understood to be a dimension of human consciousness will it persist in and through the next stage(s) of human development. Because sin is a dimension of self-transcendence, we do not trump it by becoming more intelligent or more morally sensitive. Similarly, we must focus on the fundamental dynamic of sin and not allow ourselves to be sidetracked by cataloging our sins of omission and commission. The only effective way to address the deeper sin of desires, ideals, good intentions, and promises ultimately perverted is to look for them in the narratives we write (the stories that are written by the lives we live and the history we make). Finally, if we do not move beyond biblical depictions and venture into the landscape of evolution and biology, skeptics will not listen because they have heard it all before and are not convinced.

Part 3 explores the human condition from the perspective of expectations. We are going to tinker with our biology, just as the physicists at Los Alamos had the time of their lives playing with the secrets of the atom. Expectations are running high. Joel Garreau, author of *Radical Evolution*, is almost euphoric thinking about "a curve of change unlike anything we humans have ever seen," and he is more restrained than most of the gurus he writes about. That the future is promising is an understatement. Laying aside irrational exuberance, the trajectory of sin and evil is more difficult to follow if you are only cautiously optimistic. Bill McKibben of national bestseller *The End of Nature* fame wants to know if we will learn to say enough is *Enough* (the title of his 2003 book). "In societies where most of us need storage lockers more than we need nanotech miracle boxes," he writes, "we need to declare that we have enough stuff. Enough intelligence. Enough capability. Enough" (*Enough*, 109). If only it were so simple or easy. The science I will write about is the scratch for the human itch to know everything. It lives by racing to the next "Big Thing," and only the first one there is declared the winner. But in the end scientists only do what we expect them to do: give us more not less, keep us safe, and keep us happy. And where is the sin in that? If you ask the question, you are doing more than most.

Much is expected of religion and science. If both play according to the rules, religion will be the guardian of our most cherished values. Science will push forward to the limit while enjoying doing the next technically sweet thing. It seems inevitable that their respective raisons d'être are counterpoised. This may not be such a bad thing, much in the same way our government works by a separation and balance of powers, but it is the kind of argument that rests squarely on expectations. It is often said that science has no moral compass; it merely proceeds driven by market needs and the possibility of a theoretical breakthrough. But why shouldn't we expect scientists to be more responsible for the knowledge they mine and turn into something useful? And why should theologians be restricted to the role of border guards? To the degree that theology and science are "to thine own self be true," they operate with distinctive methodologies, sources of authority, and ultimate loyalties. What is not helpful, however, is to confine each to its own domain. I would rather have them constructively confront each other and have them serve the common good by being effective at what they each do best.

The question coursing its way throughout is why sin and evil are not afforded a place at the table of critical thinking. I would like to think I have answered the question, removed some long-standing obstacles, while securing more acceptable underpinnings.

What's at Stake

What's at stake is the end of fate. So much depends on whether we think we have reached that place in history where we have the means to choose our destiny. In essence, this is the promise of a new era of scientific discovery. The breakthrough happened by cracking the universal code of life. Once having gained access to the fundamental unit of life, as once we broke open the fundamental unit of matter, the possibility exists to clone human life and manage it according to our desires. As such, we seem poised to fulfill the modern dream of doing better than allowing the fickle hand of fate to rule our lives. The sociologist Peter Berger succinctly identified the modern consciousness as the movement from fate to choice (*The Heretical Imperative*, 10). His prime example was the advent of modern forms of birth control and the resulting liberation from fate long associated with sexuality and pregnancy. But modern history does not tell an even story of progress toward ending contingencies we did not ask for, such as cancer, or ending horrendous crimes against humanity. Alongside birth control let us set the AIDS pandemic and thereby see a truer picture. Science is doing what it does best: discovering a vaccine against the virus. Humanity does what it does best: continuing to demonstrate that it cannot rise to the occasion and practice abstinence, use condoms, or find a just way to distribute drugs that have proven effective. The lesson to be learned is obvious. While science provides fate-ending technological advances, it does not ensure the rational and responsible use of those technologies. But the promise of this new century is unlike any other: reshape human beings genetically so that we are not only healthier and live longer, but are in every way the persons we dreamed ourselves to be. Fate will at last meet its match when genes become our friends.

Have we not evolved from the brutish ape that lived from moment to moment oblivious of any distinction between good and evil? Our species has tamed every environment and reached unimaginable achievements. There are strong indicators pointing to a long evolutionary trajectory toward an international world order, a universal recognition of basic human rights, a stable world population, a higher standard of living. At the close of the twentieth century, Francis Fukuyama, who is both professor of international political economy at the Johns Hopkins School of Advanced International

Studies and former director of the U.S. State Department's Policy Planning Staff, boldly predicts the culmination of history in liberal democracy (*The End of History and the Last Man*). If we do indeed stand at the brink of self-determination—people prepared to choose a form of government that permits the maximum freedom—why shouldn't we think in terms of a gradual evolutionary path toward greater freedom and greater self-determination? The logic of this scenario leaves us with the singular sin of not seizing the day and not using our knowledge to make for ourselves a better tomorrow. And this is exactly what Sir Francis Bacon urged. For too long we have foolishly relinquished control of our lives by putting our trust in ancient myths, the entrails of oracular predictions, the coincidences of the stars. They were our gods, writes Matt Ridley (*The Agile Gene*, 249). From his perspective and position at Princeton University's Departments of Molecular and Evolutionary Biology, Lee Silver thinks this tyranny of fate ends when we let go of religious notions of a predetermined goal for the evolution of humankind—that we live in the best world possible because it was created by God—and the belief that "this goal can only be achieved by the current random process through which our genes are transmitted to our children" (*Remaking Eden*, 218). Even if a reasonable argument could be mounted to counter this unbridled optimism, would it make any difference? Are we so committed to a promising future and the prospect of creating a better human being that sin and evil are simply naive beliefs of a bygone era?

As far as anyone can see, the science that matters is biological. Nothing is more personal and matters more than knowledge of how we perpetuate our species: how we have babies, what will be their genetic makeup, who will count as our parents, how long we live. Because it will be possible, we will elect to change how we look, moderate and attenuate our moods, commingle the biological with the robiotic, blend the natural with the artificial, add in a few nanotechnological enhancements, and we will be on our way to being a new person. And rising to the surface is the burden of your own life as well as that of generations to come. That may be part of the bargain we did not ask for. And with this crescendo of possibilities, the pot of discontentment is agitated and the need to get what your heart desires is stirred. If this is not a recipe for sin and evil, then I do not know what is.

What is at stake is the Christian teaching that sin and evil are ubiquitous and continuous. There never was a time and never will be a time when humans do not make a mess of things, even when their intentions are good. And the universe itself is somehow caught in a parallel struggle between good and evil. In its traditional form this teaching is a hard pill to swallow by anyone with a modern consciousness. Yet it is equally difficult to deny the destructive and self-destructive nature of our species. The universe itself is not exactly a bed of roses. An honest reading of history must account for the stark reality that, as far as we know, sin and evil are truly universal in scope, in every place and time. This means, if there is any doubt, that if we were to encounter a self-conscious extraterrestrial being, we should expect that he or she, or whatever, has experienced its own struggle with good and evil. What we do not know, in part because this is the issue we face at this moment of our own evolution, is whether there is a way out, a way not merely to tame our destructive impulses but to transcend to a higher level of existence.

Humans are what humans are. But what exactly is our human nature and is this nature fixed? In the Western philosophical tradition, the pendulum has swung this way and that way. Until Darwin, the Pauline-Augustinian notion of original sin prevailed. As a species set apart by our capacity to know right from wrong, we are powerless to consistently exercise that capacity for the good. When that tenacious bulldog for Darwin's theory of evolution, Thomas Henry Huxley, gave a lecture to a crowded auditorium in Oxford, England, in 1893, he placed humans in the animal kingdom, where might makes right and survival is the only game that matters (see his *Evolution and Ethics*). The hope of humankind, as Huxley presented his case, is to fight nature with morality, but it is a slim hope at best because nature usually wins. Not a century passes without some great thinker having something to say about human nature. Jean-Jacques Rousseau was convinced of the basic goodness of humans while others, such as Thomas Hobbes, argued for the basic nastiness of human nature. The reasonable conclusion is that we are both, basically good and basically nasty. But no matter how reasonable this conclusion, it has had no abiding power because it seems to be an impossible contradiction.

Let's leave it at that—it is a puzzle that we exhibit both unthinkable depravity and sublime self-sacrifice. What we cannot and will not leave alone is the other enduring question: Is our nature fixed? In a book that judiciously argues that it is not nature or nurture but both working together, Matt Ridley identifies the bone of contention between philosophers and theologians:

> During most of the twentieth century "determinism" was a term of abuse, and genetic determinism was the worst kind of term. Genes were portrayed as implacable dragons of fate, whose plots against the damsel of free will were foiled only by the noble knight of nurture. This view reached its zenith in the 1950s, in the aftermath of the Nazi atrocities, but in some corners of philosophical inquiry it took hold much earlier. (*The Agile Gene*, 98)

Nazism, along with every ideology of supremacy and superiority, flourishes and flounders on the premise that humans can be molded in spite of their genes, can supersede because of their genes. What never changes is the belief that we are malleable—a virtual blank slate—and can become whatever we darn well please. But not if we are irredeemably sinful.

In modernity's hell-bent drive to eliminate fate, determinism is the enemy. Our genetic nature stands in the way, as does any notion of a sinful condition. Insofar as sin is associated with determinism, it too is the enemy. But we have entered a new era. Genes are not immutable. While the science of this century acknowledges the extent to which we are genetically predisposed, it will not matter ultimately if we can modify our genes. Are we not the species that can modify anything? Or is reality the fact that no matter how much we become the subject rather than the object of evolution, no matter how much knowledge we accumulate or how smart we get, the likelihood that we will mess up (sin) does not change. Sin will only put on a new face. What's at stake is this matter of how much to trust ourselves. If we put our undivided confidence in the promise that we can handle this tantalizing knowledge of how life works, and not mess it up, then we should seize the day without hesitation. On the other hand, if humans will do what humans have always done, sometimes choosing good and sometimes choosing evil, then we should expect more of the same dubious form of progression with a upside and a downside.

Of course science will promise us a better future and the future will be better, in some ways but not in all ways. The progress we have known is two steps forward, one step backward. Why should we believe we will be able to eliminate the one step backward? Perhaps we just can't help being the optimistic rather than the pessimistic. After all, only the former attracts friends. Those who believe sin and evil are inescapable realities are thought to be pessimists on the way to being useless cynics. But the diehard optimist can be accused of ignoring the past. A glass seen as half full is a glass that will be filled to the brim, and science is anxious and ready to do just that. A glass seen as half empty is a glass in need of safekeeping lest it be completely emptied. This makes us cautious and conservative. But rather than being forced to choose between reckless optimism and cynical watchfulness, I ponder a realism concerning human nature that exceeds our capacity for both good and evil.

What is at stake is whether religion will be sidelined as belonging to the old order while positivists pursue whatever is technically possible. We have a good idea what science is good for. But what is religion good for? Congressmen still consult religious leaders when a particular sensitive boundary is about to be crossed but for the most part matters of this kind are reduced to ethics. There is a difference, however, between the ethics of what is right for this situation and how everyone is caught up in sin. Only the latter is sufficient reason to expect the worst and plan accordingly. Ethics, as in medical ethics, can dispense with sin and ignore evil. Judgment, grace, forgiveness, and atonement have no place when ethical guidelines are being drawn up. The focus of ethical protocols is immediate and practical: Will anyone be harmed, have the standards been followed, has consent been obtained, is there any future liability? Traditional religion is good at standing guard over the sacred and inviolable and this is no small matter. But even as those guards stand watch, the values beneath their feet are being swept away. All religions are confronted by a host of difficult challenges, the likes of which they have never seen before. It will be a new era for religion or, as the vernacular puts it, religion will be history.

The opportunity presents itself to re-examine the relationship between science and theology. How should science and theology serve the common good vis-à-vis their own interrelationship? While this is the primary subject of the last chapter, a thumbnail sketch is appropriate. Over the centuries theology and science have behaved like rival siblings (philosophy is the third sibling).[3] Each jockeyed for status and the right to claim, "I know more than you and my knowledge is more important than yours." Through the Middle Ages and into the Renaissance, theology ruled the roost as queen of the sciences, but as science claimed its own identity as a distinct and separate methodology, the tables were turned. Science showed itself to be the creator of knowledge most relevant and ever accumulating, and in doing so it gained dominance while theology struggled to demonstrate a credible methodology for itself. In the end, a truce was reached where each claimed a domain of competence for itself.

Presently, theology and science are engaged in a form of rapprochement. Some traditional boundaries are falling away and others are becoming interdisciplinary. The byword is not so much corroboration or collaboration but consonance. Scientists and theologians are mostly interested in finding points of contact and seeing connections where a shared understanding emerges.[4] To the degree that each discipline can acknowledge the other as utilizing a methodology particularly suited to its domain, the old rivalry will dissipate. But when religion dons the mantel of science and presents an alternative theory of intelligent design, a clash of methodologies is inevitable. To the extent theology and science are constituted by different governing interests and care deeply about different matters, the present rapprochement has its limits. How each regards sin and evil is thoroughly illustrative. When theologians discuss sin, they are making truth claims about human nature. Evil opens another door to the nature of the universe. As long as sin and evil are strictly theological understandings, only a minimal form of intersection can be expected. But once empirical status is sought—sin and evil describe the way things are—a different and less congenial, but more fruitful, conversation begins. Complicating matters is the predisposition of theology toward truth already revealed and science toward truth yet to be discovered. What is at stake is how science and theology will support and counter each other when both persist in their conviction that they know something the other is ill prepared to know. Should we be looking for compromise or some kind of comprehensive integration? Or is this asking too much?

Why, then, this odd conjunction of sin, evil, and science? The oddity is intriguing, isn't it? It also speaks volumes because of the discomfort we feel. The protests begin with shunning the implication that science is sinful and continues with asking religion to stick to its own business. Empiricism is objective; religion is personal. In the long history of their relationship, scientists and theologians rarely find themselves engaged on opposite sides in the struggle of good and evil. But it is difficult to get past the notion that science and religion are like oil and water. Our inner protesting will continue until the frame of reference is changed. Begin by recasting sin as the desire to know all things and the connection with science is at least viable. The desire to know is a good thing but that desire pursued without limits and responsibly is a different matter. The sin and evil I hope to expose is hidden within the promises of making nature serve us. For individuals or a nation weaned on assurances the future is what we choose to make it, sin is a downer. But so are Auschwitz and a world of sovereign states armed with atomic bombs. As we insert microchips into almost everything mobile and immobile, and recombine genetic information to produce something we believe is superior, we had better ask what it means to be human. If we do not ask, there is little hope that we will preserve the integrity of the human species. For whatever truth contained in the Christian teachings about sin and evil, any truth that alerts us to the human propensity for self-deception is paramount. There is a reason the confession from the Book of Common Prayer reads—"If we say that we have no sin, we deceive ourselves, and the truth is not in us" (I John 1:8)—and if the reason for our denial is not evident, our culture has "done a job on us."

Throughout this book science and theology are personified and generalized. They represent two disciplines with distinct contours. The scientific discipline I have in mind is bounded by its methodology. To be scientific or empirical means to seek truth in regard to the nature of the universe and living organisms by utilizing a method of supportable evidence and verification. It is simpler to say what science is against: speculation, unwarranted suppositions, superstition. The theological partner in this conversation is not easily identified by way of its methodology. What does stand out is a discipline shaped by a history of ecumenical councils, the authority of Scripture, and well-defined traditions which are Roman Catholic, Orthodox, and Protestant in character. When theology and science lock horns, as they often do in this volume, it is never a question of superiority but only truth-seekers who understand things from different perspectives, and we are better off because of it.

I have not tried to make careful distinctions between science and technology but have assigned science two definitions. It is both an academic discipline and the generalized cultural phenomena driven by a particular kind of knowledge derived from a methodology we know as empiricism. Technology also bears two meanings: (1) the forces of production associated with machines and organized labor and the larger socioeconomic components generated, (2) an ideological underpinning characterized by philosopher and statesman Vaclev Havel as the dominant reflex of modern civilization, whether capitalist or socialist, intended "to address all social problems by amassing more scientific knowledge and technological power in order to construct better systems of control."[5] The meaning I have in mind is usually clear from the context and as a rule this formula will work: technology is the practical handmaiden of science.

The Swirl of Intellectual Ideas[6]

The water doesn't get much muddier than when you mix sin and evil into the postmodern, now posthuman debate. Taken separately they are a head full. Together they bring on a headache. While the terminology can be oblique, there is a substantial worthiness that should be looked at. Postmodernism is essentially a philosophical reexamination of the foundational suppositions of the Enlightenment: objectivity, realism, universal truths, rationalism, the blank slate, essences, meta-narratives (socialism, liberalism etc.). Posthumanism is an inquiry into matters biological, as thinkers grapple with the repercussions of genetically enhancing life. If philosophy followed a logical sequence, the postmodern is giving way to the posthuman because just as postmodernism barred the last road laid down by the Enlightenment, so the posthuman is meant to pave the way to an new era of biotechnology. While postmodernists deconstruct the idealism of the Enlightenment, posthumanists explore what it means to become human. Many of us are left wondering what is left to guide a posthuman science after the postmodernists are done discrediting the values that have undergirded Western civilization for lo these many years. The demise of sin and evil belong to the same changing of the guard. Sin and evil are replaced by secular notions of immaturity, superstition, irrationality, and false pretense. But as with all translations, something is lost when the framework for a theological appraisal of history and personal responsibility is cast aside as a harmful meta-narrative.[7] Where the postmodern and posthuman do converge is over the thorny issue of human nature. With considerable justification, then, Steven Pinker's *The Blank Slate* is subtitled "the modern denial of human nature" and he declares that "[a]n honest discussion of human nature has never been more timely" (xi).

Pinker, a psychologist at MIT and relentless sleuth of modern ideas, finds us clinging to a trinity of ideas which have served their usefulness: the Blank Slate (the mind has no inherent structure), the Noble Savage (people are born good but corrupted by society), and the "Ghost in the Machine" (each of us has a soul that makes choices independent of our biology). No doubt about it, even as the importance of our genetic makeup is revealed, we continue to believe we can shape the lives of our children, that we are basically good and endowed with an immortal soul. The reason why we should renounce these particular intellectual resources rests with the growing scientific consensus that we are hardwired from birth. In a previous book, the *Language Instinct*, Pinker argues convincingly that we are hardwired for language; that is, children can learn any particular language because they already have a capacity for language itself. Like many things scientific, it is beyond me how grammar is somehow encoded into our genes. But I can accept it along with Pinker's rag on Blank Slate psychology, but the philosophical debate about human nature is far from finished just because it has met its genetic, evolutionary master. Pinker is perfectly at home discussing human universals, such as empathy, snake wariness, and thumb sucking, but cannot force himself to consider whether sin is something more than a misdirected construct derived from a myth.[8] If hardwired for language and a host of universal behaviors, then why not for values? What is so terrible about giving human nature a theological interpretation and even some notion of original sin? If we are prepared to allow for a level of hardwiredness or genetic disposition without going off the deep end of determinism, then the same rationality holds for a deep-seated, persistent human nature that struggles with good and evil. The good and evil we do are not entirely separate from our chemistry and biology but they are not identical with our physiological constitution. Are we not human because of our capacity to transcend the fate of genes and the present moment? Pinker is typical of those biologists or evolutionary philosophers, such as Daniel Dennett (*Freedom Evolves*), who take us to the brink of biological determinism and then pull back.[9] And for good reasons.

When you put the recent interest in human nature in historical perspective, it goes against the standard rule laid down by philosophers and scientists who disallow making any connection between what *is* and what *ought* to be (what David Hume derisively labeled the naturalistic fallacy). It is a refrain heard too often: that human nature is too complex, that it is culturally conditioned, genetically determined, or not uniquely differentiated from animals to set us apart. Fukuyama remarks that John Rawls in his very influential *A Theory of Justice* does not find it necessary or desirable to appeal to human nature in order to establish a set of minimal moral rules that would govern a just society. Fukuyama then points out, as does H. Allen Orr (below) that whenever you begin discussing human rights or a just society, you "cannot escape making certain judgments about what is *naturally* best for human beings" (*Posthuman Future*, 120–22, emphasis added). Fukuyama is definitely swimming against the prevailing current with his remark that "the common understanding of the naturalistic fallacy is itself fallacious and that there is a desperate need for philosophy to return to the pre-Kantain tradition that grounds rights and morality in nature" (*Posthuman Future*, 112).[10]

When in the swirl of relevant ideas two heavyweights voice the same sentiment, it cannot be ignored. Moreover, it is an attractive sentiment—one we want to believe is true. Peter Singer, a philosopher who has devoted a career to interrogating ethical assumptions, speaks of an "expanding circle" of the human concern while Pinker contends that we are riding "a moral escalator."[11] The evidence is of various kinds:

> Customs that were common throughout history and prehistory—slavery, punishment by mutilation, execution by torture, genocide for convenience, endless blood

feuds, the summary killing of strangers, rape as the spoils of war, infanticide as a form of birth control, and the legal ownership of women—have vanished from large parts of the world. (*Blank Slate*, 166)

Singer's argument for a steadily expanding circle of compassion identifies another trend. By nature or nurture the circle of our concern has grown outward from family to village to clan to tribe to nation, and most recently to all of humanity. As a global community, we have written a Universal Declaration of Human Rights and convened international courts to hear cases of crimes against humanity. This is progress but what does it imply about human nature? Is it possible that we are becoming more sensitive in some ways and more subtle in our inhumanity in other ways? If so, the metaphor of an escalator or a pyramid is unfortunate because it infers that our sinfulness is slowly yielding to the progress of rationalization and greater moral sensitivity. Perhaps the reason I am uneasy with the progress Pinker identifies is the omission of a discussion of sin and evil. Take a second look at the state of the world and one can see how easily we fall back into barbarism even as we grow in moral sensitivity.

Where in this or any optimistic picture do we fit the assault on human dignity so prevalent at the turn of a new millennium? Is nothing sacrosanct, not even the joy of a marriage or the solemnity of a funeral? Are there no innocents, not even children doing their lessons in a classroom? Whether bodies that litter the tracks in Madrid or children who have their throats piously severed in the classrooms of northern Nigeria, the question of nature or nurture seems irrelevant—totally irrelevant if you are standing in the blazing sun waiting for a United Nation's forensic team to hand over body parts, but not if you are responsible for what happens next in Darfour or asking yourself if peacekeepers can stem the tide of evil. Liberia, a beautiful country on the east coast of Africa founded by freed American slaves but plagued by a total collapse of rule and characterized by a relentless campaign of wanton violence, looks very much like a real-life enactment of William Golding's *Lord of the Flies*. "Is the spiral of antihumanism now unstoppable?" asks Wole Soyinka, recipient of the Noble Prize in Literature.[12] His question, like all questions that return us to fundamental notions, will only be answered adequately when a theological dimension is considered.

According to Pinker's analysis, reciprocal altruism (distinct from kin altruism) is the driving dynamic behind an expanding moral circle. The circle expands when the network of reciprocity expands and retracts when the sympathy knob is turned down. There are cultural and economic reasons for a changing climate. It is very foolish, for example, to kill someone with whom you trade. I have no argument against the claim that our moral sense is itself a product of evolution. Pinker and Singer, along with those who think of themselves as sociobiologists, are probably right for the same reasons I argue our sense of sinfulness emerged over time. But saying something is part of our evolutionary history does not entitle someone to single out moral sensitivity and project a progressive trajectory. According to H. Allen Orr, there is little justification to explain everything in terms of a crude morality that gets better with time. Why is it, Orr asks, that "once kings but not women once had rights, but now women but not kings do."[13] This was scarcely a reciprocal trade-off whereby kings and women decided both would be better off if they exchanged rights. When human nature does not yield to justice—as it rarely does—a political struggle or the imposition of a court ruling is required. What seems evident is that when a theological understanding of human nature is omitted, human nature becomes much less of a paradox than it really is.

Perhaps I misjudge Pinker and Singer but I do not think I am amiss in detecting a culture that prefers to be naive, maybe even childish, and surely expectant. "No one after a certain age has the right to this kind of innocence, of superficiality, to this degree of ignorance or amnesia," writes Susan Sontag. Her comment comes after a moving meditation on the imagery of suffering and horror in photography, painting, and media. "There now exists a vast repository of images," as Sontag documents, "that make it harder to maintain this kind of more defectiveness." And just who is she indicting?

> Someone who is perennially surprised that depravity exists, who continues to feel disillusioned (even incredulous) when confronted with evidence of what humans are capable of inflicting in the way of gruesome, hands-on cruelties upon other humans, has not reached moral or psychological adulthood. (*Regarding the Pain of Others*, 114)

Also qualifying as a heavyweight, Francis Fukuyama wrote a book at the close of the twentieth century titled *The End of History*. More than a few regard his thesis to be outlandish.[14] History will reach its end when it culminates in liberal democracy and capitalism. Sounding a lot like Hegel, Fukuyama believes history has its own coherent, evolutionary process beginning with simple tribal societies based on subsistence agriculture, moving through various monarchies and feudal aristocracies, and ending with a form of government and economy that best enhances self-determination. The evidence he marshals is impressive. It will not happen immediately or smoothly but over time, Fukuyama is convinced, people will choose self-determination and nation-states will learn to cooperate with each other for the larger (global) good.

From almost every angle Fukuyama's book looks to be a perfect venue for considering the realism of sin and evil. Fukuyama does not neglect an account of human nature but this only makes his analysis more frustrating. He comes close but never quite gets there, and so it goes with nearly every analysis of who we are. The human condition is not a struggle over choosing good or evil but "the struggle for recognition." From his learned perspective the motor of human history is the struggle for recognition, and the reason progress has not been steady is our nature to dominate others, to enforce homage or require obedience. Fukuyama would affirm that "man does not live by bread alone," since we are more than a bundle of desires and more than the rational animal par excellence. Whether on the battlefield or the economic field of competition, it is not just the territory or the pay scale but the respect we are due. The dark side of our nature is ambition and the desire for glory. The bright side is "an innate sense of justice," and as such it is the "sea of all the noble virtues like selflessness, idealism, morality, self-sacrifice, courage, and honorability" (*The End of History*, 171). We can hope for the withering of the oppressive state, but if it never comes we will know why. Human nature hasn't changed.

My question to Fukuyama is the same: Is the human condition such that eventually the dark side will diminish along with all forms of megalomania? If sin and evil are real, are they sufficient to derail the movement toward democracy and capitalism where justice prevails across the globe? At the end of the book Fukuyama strikes a more cautionary note, almost as if he had a premonition of Rwanda and September 11th. Both horrors, nevertheless, fit into his argument of what happens when humans are not shown the respect they feel they are due by virtue of being human. Nevertheless, something is missing here. Stephen King would have something to include, if only at the personal level, regarding the way evil magnifies the smallest human desire. If Fukuyama is less optimistic because he recognizes how difficult it will be to shift the basis of human societies from unlimited desire to a just sharing of natural and material resources, and how easy it is to fall back into barbarism, then shouldn't he be a realist because modern history is replete with demonstrations that we cannot plan for contingencies that mock our good intentions?[15]

I am undecided whether Leon Kass is an alarmist or right as right can be.

As the president's appointment to chair the Council on Bioethics, his opinions carry considerable weight. In both his *Toward a More Natural Science* (1985) and *Life, Liberty and the Defense of Dignity* (2002), Kass expresses concern that "our society is dangerously close to losing its grip on the meaning of some fundamental aspects of human existence" (*Life, Liberty*, 99). He writes about "the price of progress," "the perversities of cloning," "the permanent limitations of biology," and "the tragic meaning of 'right to die.'" "Everything," Kass declares, "depends on rejecting the rationalist and utopian dream of perfecting human beings by re-creating them, and on remembering that richer vision of human liberty and human dignity that informs the founding of our polity" (*Life, Liberty*, 50). For Kass, biotechnology is a particular peril because it threatens to weaken the time-honored restraints enshrined within traditional values of family, marriage, legitimacy, and lineage. "These time-honored restraints," Kass writes, "implicitly teach that clarity about who your parents are, clarity in the lines of generation, clarity about who is whose, are the indispensable foundation of a sound family life, itself the sound foundation of civilized community" (*Life, Liberty*, 99–100). But alas, Kass does not write about sin or evil either. The danger he explicates exists in a culture of technology rather than the human heart.

It's more than coincidence that two centuries ago Mary Shelley wrote a horror story of a young philosopher-scientist who creates a creature who does not know who he is or where he has come from and so becomes a monster (see below). It's important to note that Shelley herself stood on the cusp of science's coronation as queen of all knowledge. Whether you side with Kass or think he is overreacting, it is difficult not to affirm the moral crisis enveloping us because we stand on the brink of another scientific era. I use the word "crisis" in the minimal sense that we will be confronted by ethical questions that strain the traditional personal ethic of every religion. Spider-man learns that with great power comes great responsibility and that responsibility is all about making good decisions. Our technological future will force us to make decisions by the basketfull. That much is a given, but what is undecided is whether we will make them carefully and deliberately or inadvertently and thoughtlessly.

Sin and Evil in Need of an Overhaul

Speaking of sin, has anyone notice its blatant absence? The good news is that after a long hiatus sin and evil have reentered our common vocabulary.[16] The right time has arrived—philosophically, culturally, and politically—to

> **Dateline *New York Times*, 5 March 2004**
> ## Companies Face Ethical Issues as Drugs Are Tested Overseas
> Dr. Louis G. Lange, a cardiologist and the chief executive of a small biotechnology company, has a new drug that, if approved, will be the first new treatment for angina in a quarter-century.
> Like many drug companies, Dr. Lange's, CV Therapeutics of Palo Alto, Calif., tested its new product overseas, where studies go faster because it is easy to find patients who are eager to participate.
> But the company's testing is nearing its end, and Dr. Lange is faced with an ethical quandary: Is his company obliged to make the drug available to the patients in poor countries like Russia who took part in the studies? The issue is especially difficult when it comes to drugs, like Dr. Lange's, that do not save lives but can vastly improve the quality of life (Gina Kolata, NYTimes.com 2004/03/05/science).

speak of sin in the public domain. The bad news is the deep-seated reluctance, even among theologians, to say anything relevant in a postmodern, posthuman era. Sin may be "the only empirical verifiable doctrine of the Christian Faith," but outside of the religious right it is regarded as merely a theological construct.[17]

I am not surprised, but dismayed, that sin hasn't been invited to the intellectual party of human nature and common good.[18] So, battered and bruised by the currents of secularism and empiricism, sin is barely breathing. Its identification with sectarian voices (belonging to a particular religion) makes it unacceptable among pluralistically minded contemporaries. Evil is a different matter. Presidents Ronald Reagan and George W. Bush did not shy away from denouncing nations and individuals as evil.[19] We seem to know what evil is and where to find it. But why evil and not sin? Have we confused the two, collapsed one into the other in order to tar others while wearing our white hats banded with the colors of good intentions? Any conversation about sin and evil will therefore have to carefully untangle the two.

The task of resurrecting sin as valid and convincing requires much more (three chapters in fact). My broader hope rests with the conviction that a theological perspective focused on evil and sin brings something vital and necessary to the table where the future of our species is being addressed. All explanations, scientific and otherwise, are dangerously incomplete and seriously flawed if they pass over a three-thousand-year-old tradition supported by a history equally as long of a world unable to right itself. Sin and evil are realities we must take into account if our posthuman future has any hope of being something other than a repeat performance of knowledge (as in the Tree of Knowledge) too tempting to resist.

A different way of looking at what I am attempting is to think of the conjunction of science and human nature as a test case for sin. In other words, can sin "hack it" in the world of white coats and test tubes? Dogging us from cover to cover is the simple question: Where is the sin? If Robert Oppenheimer had the courage to raise the possibility that "the physicists have known sin,"[20] then it behooves us to ask the same question about matters biological. An immediate burden of this book, then, is to make a cogent argument for sin's viability as socially and politically cogent. The timing could not be better. If every parent wants to enhance their child's intelligence, then every child will be smarter than his parents but no smarter than his peers. But that won't do. The commencement of genetic warfare—who will have access to genetic enhancements—is still warfare. Imagine the political intrigue, the opportunity for graft, the legal battles over intellectual property, the money to be made, the widening gap between gene-rich and gene-poor. But then in a posthuman world we might find a way to share the wealth of information so justice is served and equality is achieved. The odds that this will come to pass are directly tied to what one believes about sin and evil.

We are in the midst of a biological revolution and sin will remain banished from academic and public forums unless it too becomes biological and evolutionary. Fair warning is issued here. If we think of sin as genetically determined we are no better off than when everyone's sin is predetermined by Adam and Eve's sin. If Adam and Eve's historicity is made pivotal, we as theologians might as well pack our bags and go home. The scientific community will have none of it. The universality of sin is, however, a different matter. It is non-negotiable for Christians. The task is to reaffirm sin's universality while explaining how this happens, and it is exactly the lack of any credible explanation that has plagued its secular-public acceptance.[21]

In order for sin to be received into the market place of ideas, a number of smaller projects are required. Chapter 3 separates sin from evil and sin from sins, removes the sectarian stigma associated with sin, and gives it a human face as the narrative truth about ourselves we really don't want to know. Chapter 4 provides a conceptual reworking of sin rooted in our need to know but invariably ending with overreaching. The next chapter undertakes an evolutionary account of sin. The last chapter in part 2 returns to science and the ways it tempts us to overreach.

There are specific reasons for each chapter. When I discuss the common variety of sin, I am referring to more than those human transgressions we associated with commandments. Even in the friendly environs of Christianity, the terrain is difficult. Surely sin is preached "mightily" in certain regions of the United States. The airways are filled with preachers warning us of our sinful ways. But whether sin is always on our minds or hardly at all, it is becoming an ever-larger pill to swallow. A recent *New York Times* poll revealed that 73 percent of the respondents believed people are born good, and 85 percent thought "they could pretty much [become] anything they wanted to be."[22] Of course if we believe that we are born good and are capable of just about anything, sin is a relic. We want to think of ourselves as good people who, for the most part, live good lives. It offends our sense of justice to be told we are going to hell forever even though we tried to do our best. A literal reading of Genesis 3 does not really explain why the ungrateful disobedience of ancestors from the distant past should doom all of us to an eternity of fire and brimstone. Only theologically speaking is the symmetry attractive: one rejection of the gifts of God is matched by a second divine gift, the death and resurrection of Jesus Christ (Rom. 5). For Augustine it made perfect sense: infinite punishment for infinite guilt. This may fit into a Calvinistic doctrine of double predestination, but it offends our sense of fairness when you are damned if you do and damned if you don't. It may not matter much whether the congregation is gathered in Waco, Texas, or Harvard Square, Cambridge, when the depth and width of sin is reduced to the sins of transgression, there are good Christian people wondering what they have done to deserve the passion of Christ. As I understand the good news of Jesus Christ and its Pauline interpretation, conversion means that those sins of the flesh no longer rule in us (Rom. 8:12–14). Christians are not impervious to relapse or temptations but they should not have a litany of personal sins to confess every Sunday. Nor do a lot of other people, with no religious affiliation. Undoubtedly this halo of goodness is sin deceiving us but, by golly, Miss Molly, the sins of the Bible and Christian tradition are more than transgressions. And if more than transgressions, they scorch life and history leaving their embers signaling our helplessness.

Does anyone under the age of forty, or anyone living in our secular society, think "sin" when they see the film *Mystic River* or read *Ethan Frome*? And yet everyone recognizes that a new story begins when eleven-year-old Dave gets into the car of two men claiming to be policemen, or when Ethan's hand almost brushes against the forbidden fruit of the live-in servant, Mattie. Dave's two companions (Jimmy and Sean), who are relieved and thankful they did not join Dave, do not know that their lives are about to change when twenty-five years later David is implicated in the death of Katie, Jimmy's nineteen-year-old daughter, and the arresting detective is Sean; any more than Zeena, Ethan's cold-hearted wife, can know that she will become the caretaker for her husband and his lover. Sin is like that: a transgression stirring the emotions, spreading out like a smoldering fire, causing shock waves to radiate into a future of unthinkable entanglements. Sin is the narrative we did not want to begin but happens in spite of our best intentions. Sin is the story that begins when we say, "it's no big thing." It is the stories we are afraid to tell or can't tell, the stories that re-create a world without innocence.

By disentangling sin and sins, sin and evil, we are well on our way toward a more viable understanding of both realities. And while the "sins of the fathers" and the greed of some corporate executives are not our daily fare, there is a common, everyday understanding of sin. But it will never see the light of day unless it is narrated. The great novelists have understood and portrayed this better than any theologian.[23] The everyday understanding of sin which wakes us up in the morning and puts us to bed each night is animated in Stephen King's story of *Needful Things*. King has no particular philosophical or theological ax to grind. He has a story to tell and it happens to be about human nature. When Leland Gaunt hangs his open-for-business sign, everything is already in place for him to do his devilish thing. When is temptation sweeter than to have your heart's desire for such a small price? King snares us once again and by the time we put the book down we wonder what price we have paid and what benefit we thought we would get for such a small indiscretion or unkindness.

Stephen King's story takes us just so far but never enters the perennial debate about why we are the way we are. Still within the narrative framework of sin, I remember two classics from my university days: Jean-Jacques Rousseau's *Emile* and Golding's *Lord of the Flies*. Although I read them separately for different reasons, when placed side by side they represent a fork in the road. A little background is necessary. Rousseau's *Emile* was reviled in his lifetime because it was understood as a veiled attack on original sin. Immanuel Kant's opinion was quite different. He regarded Rousseau as another Newton because he suggested a natural connection between sin and suffering. We suffer the consequences of our own actions but not at the hand of God disbursing divine retribution. Before Rousseau, Susan Neiman writes, there were just two alternatives: either sin and evil are genuine and defy explanation, or they aren't real and can be explained (*Evil in Modern Thought*, 41–42). The first alternative means we live in a world where tragedy and suffering are just the way it is. In other words, "shit happens." David Hume went to great lengths to show us the world as it is and not as we would like it to be. In *Candide*, Voltaire was content to describe the consequences of sin and evil without explaining it. If the first alternative is hard to stomach, the second alternative is something of a farce. Sin and evil are explained—biblically or otherwise—so that even the worst that happens is part of a divine plan. But a world of such awful tragedies does not reflect well on its Creator. By making God ultimately responsible for everything that happens, defending God becomes a never-ending burden. Given two unsatisfying alternatives, something had to give.

First came the separation of natural and moral evil. Next came the shift in responsibility. God is first exonerated of natural disasters (natural evil) and then relieved of the burden of moral evil. Neiman argues that a new and modern understanding of evil begins when natural and moral evil are separated, which was provoked by the Lisbon earthquake of 1755. It sent shock waves throughout the intellectual world. What kind of moral evil could be responsible for this kind of natural evil? Rousseau provides a straightforward answer. Natural evils, such as earthquakes, are genuine and need no further explanation. Rousseau's theology has no need to defend God against the charges of incompetency or callousness. That leaves moral evil. Rousseau undertakes to educate Emile to demonstrate that we are not born inherently perverted. The historical and conceptual line back to Rousseau is clear. There are no bad people, innately speaking, only individuals who have been corrupted by bad learning. Such is the optimism of the behaviorist B. F. Skinner in his depiction of life in *Walden Two* where a carefully designed environment shapes the individual and everyone lives in harmonious cooperation. Knowledge, not penance, is our salvation. Optimism and not pessimism should inspire us to be responsible for our actions and stop crying over spilt milk. The outcome is to disempower God by making God less responsible while empowering humans to be more responsible for their own actions, and no one defended this argument with more vigor than Nietzsche.[24]

Time, however, has shown that even the suggestion of a world not under God's loving protectorate is intolerable for many. Remember the offense of Alfonso X, king of Castile, in 1252. After several years of intensive astronomical studies, the king declares: "If I had been of God's counsel at the Creation, many things would have been ordered better." "This little sentence, or some variation of it," Neiman writes, "expressed the essence of blasphemy for close to half a millennium" (*Evil in Modern Thought*, 15). By way of contrast, no amount of injustice seems to disturb the theology of the Psalms. Everything that looks like evil, or looks as if injustice has won the day, is in fact part of a larger good (Rom. 8:28). Anything, it seems, would be better than an amoral world or a world without design. We are conflicted, nevertheless, because the bombing of the World Trade Towers constitutes a moral evil that mocks a world of our own making, just as the horrific tsunami in Asia mocks a natural world supposedly in the hands of God. It matters not that we have learned to distinguish natural evil from moral evil—for both are meaningless in that they destroy the innocent—but that we sense nevertheless that sin and evil are entangled in some way beyond our comprehension.

For Rousseau, sin brings its own misery and evil is a supernatural mystery of little importance. In *Lord of the Flies* William Golding introduces another thought experiment to parallel Rousseau's presumption that entrusted with a child he could educate him to be a civilized gentleman. Given an island and a group of "civilized" English boys, what would we learn about human nature? Golding, who served in the Royal Navy during World War II and encountered a world ripped apart by evil, leads us toward the opposite conclusion. Even with an ideal education and all the benefits of civilization, we are who we are, and even worse when thrown together collectively. Their rescue happens when a British cruiser passes by. A proper naval officer interrupts a savage boy hunt in progress, only to take them on board a warship engaged in its own manhunt. The officer is puzzled by what he sees: "A semicircle of little boys, their bodies streaked with colored clay, sharp sticks in their hands, were standing on the beach making no noise at all." The officer inquires, "Fun and games." As the warship "sails" away, Golding wants us to weigh, "And who will rescue the adults?"

The overhaul I have in mind is incomplete unless it includes the posthuman imperative to make the biological connection. This is the work of chapter 4 and my effort in this regard is not entirely original. Reinhold Niebuhr made an important contribution at a particular historical juncture. His *The Nature and Destiny of Man* (1941 and 1943, 2 volumes) pivots around the theme of human destiny as rooted in human nature. It reflects both a world where superpowers clash and a literal reading of Genesis is being discredited. Niebuhr and Paul Tillich, along with a number of other revision-minded theologians, were interested in shifting the basic ontology from a static to a process orientation.[25] Stanley Hauerwas makes the comment that "Niebuhr's account of original sin is his attempt to do natural theology," with the expectation that "Christians may not be able to convince agnostics and non-believers that God exists, but Christians can convince non-believers that sin exists" (*With the Grain of the Universe*, 120).

However successful Niebuhr was in his effort to makes sense of the human condition in the light of sin, it does not go far enough. The liberal argument for the veracity of sin is simply this: there never has been a human being who has not known sin. Niebuhr shows sin to be a universal experience embedded in history but manages, at best, to historicize and socialize sin without giving it a true past. The empiricism liberal theology evoked is the observed behavior from time immemorial. While conservatives argue from past to present (we sin because Adam and Eve sinned), liberals reverse the argument from present to past (we sin because we are born into a world where sin is our history). Both explanations lack any real causal connections. There is a presumed biological link, especially with fundamentalists, but for the most part Christians acquiesce to a less than coherent explanation. The biological connection, whether past or present, is a no-man's-land where angels fear to tread because it implies genes and genes imply determinism. Hiding in the background is the fear of relieving us of our moral responsibility by adding sin to the genetic arsenal of "not me but my genes made me do it." The danger is manifestly real, even more so when sociobiology enters the picture. There is a price to pay when no reasonable account is given to account for our human condition, but to biologize sin is inviting another set of difficulties. The thrust of chapter 5 is to make sin credible without reducing it to the level of genetic predisposition. This crucial disentanglement is always close at hand. To contend that sin is thoroughly biological and evolutionary is not the same as saying it is genetic or deterministic. We do have genetic dispositions and our biology equips us with neural systems wired for language and self-differentiation, but not for lying and pride since these kinds of traits are one of many manifestations of a larger human capacity. The gift of language, for instance, can be used for both truth telling and deceit. The process of coming to know oneself apart from others lays the groundwork for both empathy and pride. That nebulous human quality we know as "will" determines whether we choose good or evil. (And if we follow MacIntyre's reading of Augustine, it was his understanding of the will as the ultimate determinant of human action that corrected something missing in Plato and Aristotle *Whose Justice?*, 154–59.) Over an extended period of time a host of specific dispositions, such as cooperation, altruism, empathy, and self-denial emerged and developed, and in so far as they emerged and developed they are biological. But sin is a theological construct meant to language some very complex human behaviors.[26] Idolatry, pride, envy, lust, covetousness, and deceit do not come packaged with a soul dropped from heaven into a body from earth.

Above all else, the holistic nature of sin must never leave our sight. Sin will forever elude a precise location on the DNA helix, because sin corrupts our human capacities for thought, emotion, intention, speech, and disposition. It is a moving target.

My conceptual overhaul begins with a fresh interpretation of Genesis 3 as the prototypical act of overreaching. Adam and Eve already possess the capacity to freely make decisions for good or evil, otherwise the snake's offer to become all-knowing like God would be implausible. In the Garden of Delights (Eden), they are free to pick freely of the fruits of the other trees. What they are warned against is not to overreach by thinking they are entitled to unlimited access to the Tree of Knowledge of Good and Evil. Eating the fruit of this Tree means their eyes will be opened and they will see with complete clarity all there is to know. Because we stand poised to reach and take of the knowledge that will make us like God, this Tree becomes the quintessential symbol for our historical moment. We want to know how to re-create ourselves in whatever image we choose. We want to know everything, that is, we want to partake of the fruit of Good and Evil. We are the creature par excellence who inquires, explores, and creates. Whatever the limit—the edge of the earth, the highest mountain, the mysteries of the universe—we think of it as a challenge. And this very capacity to reach out constitutes the possibility of overreaching.

Dateline *Boston Globe*, 29 June 2000

Scottish Scientist Create Gene Alteration Procedure for Sheep

In a step toward creating healthier livestock and using animals as organ banks, scientists have developed a way to alter and insert new genes into sheep with unprecedented precision.

"For some of us, this was sort of the Holy Grail, the ability to achieve this kind of modification," said Alan Colman, research director at PPL Therapeutics in Edinburgh—the same laboratory that helped produce Dolly the cloned sheep in 1966.

PPL Therapeutics hopes to use the gene targeting process to create genetically altered pig clones to provide organs for transplant into humans (Callahan, A29).

Just as chapter 3 is a non-theological portrait of sin, chapter 4 is a thoroughly Christian understanding of sin where the language is necessarily theological. It does not have to be technical since the fundamental concept is straightforward. Sin is not only universal, it has a "no escape" clause. (Of course the allusion is to Sartre's *No Exit*.) Our human predicament is nothing less than being in a room with no exit. But being the creature we are—clever, inventive, bold, restless—we will give it our best shot to make an exit and claim that we have the right to do what is best for ourselves. The Christian understanding of the way out, unlike the description of our predicament, is paradoxical. No one can understand what sin does to us by analyzing the situation from within the room. Only in light of God's grace can we begin to fathom how helpless we really are, how far we have actually "fallen." When the only thing you know is darkness, a ray of light is how you realize what darkness is. As the prodigal son begins his journey home, he prepares a litany of confession and repentance in order to win back his father's love. What he discovers is a father waiting to embrace him and tell him that he never was an unloved son. Then, and only then, does the son "wake up" to the limitless nature of God's grace. Then, and only then, does the son understand that he had it all wrong: that he had to renounce his father's love in order to find himself, that he was perfectly able to write his own destiny without anyone else's help.[27]

When sin tries to swim in the larger ocean of secular ideas, it has little to no chance of making it to the surface. Its language of limits, human predicament, universality, and no exit offends our sensibilities and those of science in particular. Sin is an irritant in the modern conceptualization of human nature. Modernity's song is to worry less about the way the world "ought" to be and get with the program of transforming it. Progress is forever the invitation to seize the day and make the most of it. Given this picture, sin looks like the pessimistic drag who won't be invited to the party. Sin and evil constitute the reality check to our habitual overreaching and unbridled optimism.

Anyone who feels compelled to advocate for the innateness of sin might as well shoot himself in the foot. All those noble ideas clustered around the blank slate—the rational being, the self-made person, the perfectibility of human beings—serve as a bulwark against anyone or anything that would diminish our freedom and right (in some countries) to dream the impossible dream. This quote from the founder of behaviorism, John B. Watson (1878–1958), sounds familiar to everyone because it encapsulates the staunch resistance to anything resembling innateness.

> Give me a dozen healthy infants, well-formed, and my own specified world to bring them up in and I'll guarantee to take any one at random and train him to become

any type of specialist I might select—doctor, lawyer, artist, merchant-chief, and yes, even beggar-man and thief, regardless of his talents, penchants, tendencies abilities, vocations, and race of his ancestors. (quoted from *Blank Slate*, 19)

Such is the generation of cultural anthropologists who would not rest until they had convinced all of us that human nature is almost unbelievably malleable. Whatever innateness exists is secondary to the culture, for it is culture that shapes the individual. (It takes a village to raise a child.)

The pendulum has now swung the other way and nurture takes a back seat to heredity.[28] We know the pendulum has swung this way when someone committed to defending evolution writes a book about freedom in order to offset the drift toward genetic determinism. I am referring to Daniel C. Dennett's book *Freedom Evolves*. But regardless of whether one favors environment or heredity to explain human nature, explaining sin becomes even more difficult. If sin is too closely associated with instinct, then human beings are sinful because of the way they are genetically programmed. If sin is something that is culturally and historically learned, then we should be able to unlearn the evil we do. So, if we are neither a blank slate nor a slave to instinct then what is our essential nature? Well, that leaves something in between hardwired and master of our lives. We know the course we need to steer but it is anything but easy or straightforward.

The last chapter in part 2, "Sin as the occasion for sin," is presumptuous on my part. Presumptuous or not, science receives no "get out of jail" pass from me. Chapter 6 inquires if there are methodological reasons why science is the occasion for being tempted by the voice that invites us to know all things. Science itself is not sinful or evil, and neither are scientists any more sinful or evil than the rest of us. But modern science, especially in its biotechnological form, is both transforming and intensifying both good and evil. Time and time again I will refer to the subtle way science packages obvious benefits with covert harms. The point of concern is acute. If science is handing us the tools to reconstruct human life, it becomes imperative that we have a clear understanding of what makes us distinct as a species. Leon Kass is more picturesque with his metaphor of an operating table: "Human nature itself lies on the operating table, ready for alteration, for eugenic and psychic 'enhancement,' for wholesale design" (*Life, Liberty*, 4). But there is little reason to think we will re-engineer ourselves into something much more than what is expedient, normative of the dominant culture, and self-serving of an elite few. And within the confines of science there is barely a whiff of the possibility that theology might be the counterweight to the excesses of science (discussed more fully in the last chapter).

From science we expect a flow of disinterested knowledge, that is, knowledge supported with public monies for the good of the commonwealth. What we are getting—and here is the rub—is the corrosion of values and the commercialization of knowledge. We expect religion to protect our moral traditions and embody the good we value. What we are getting is religion so identified with the culture that it has no space to be prophetic. The intriguing question is whether the common good is better served when science and theology (as distinct from religion) counterbalance each other. This would allow science and theology to do what they each do best and what the other is ill prepared to do.

Scientists are miners of knowledge. This is their passion and vocation. They satisfy our need as humans to invent and create, to explore and discover. On the other hand, religion creates communities of believers that honor sacred places and times. Theologians, who bring to expression the beliefs we hold, often feel obliged to raise the yellow flag—not red or green, but the cautionary flag of "not so fast." As socially responsible miners, scientists should at least keep better watch over knowledge that is ultimately not theirs, and knowledge with the potential for good and evil. We do not expect scientists to be prophets for justice because that obligation falls on men and women who dedicate their lives to remaking a world where justice and peace embrace.[29] Archbishop Oscar Romero rightly makes the connection between the absolute desire of having more and the selfishness that destroys the communal bonds of all God's children.[30] Romero indicts the idolatry of riches as preventing the majority from sharing the goods that the Creator has made for all, but he would have been equally justified to call out the misuse of knowledge and the idolatry of trusting ourselves to do the right thing.

No setting of the stage is complete without a personal note about the author. I am a non-scientist theologian writing about science with the gall to suggest I know something they don't. I know the feeling when a non-theologian wants to teach me something about theology. What can I say except that I write about science in the most general sense, where it becomes philosophical, introspective, and political. I admit that science is where the action is, and you better not arrive late. But in the end, the reason I write is my conviction that something is gained when one discipline is set over against another discipline in order to gain a new perspective. This is the argument I introduced in *Competing Truths: Science and Theology as Sibling Rivals* and pursue here by rethinking what sin and evil mean in a postmodern setting. In describing science as desperately seeking perfection and infected with unbridled optimism (chapter 6), I am knowingly stirring the pot hoping for a reaction. There have been periods when theology and science have gone their separate ways or have been openly antagonistic toward each other.[31] This is not the situation now and what we should expect is fruitful engagement.[32]

A book about sin and evil vibrates with negativity. In addition, a critical look at science is easily read as hostility. A broader Christian perspective is informed by several theological tenets, and I ask the reader to keep them in mind even though they are only implicit. The goodness of creation and common grace are dear to my heart but never really discussed.[33] The goodness of the creation points to something empirical about the universe, such as the way the earth feeds itself or the way the universe is delicately balanced between creative and destructive forces. Whether you see the universe through the eyes of faith or not, this law-abiding, life-bearing, awe-inspiring cosmos is good. Because of creation's goodness, our understanding of the universe becomes a good thing. And this creature who knows and communes with creation and its Creator belongs to this goodness. The goodness of creation is prior to evil. Sin and evil are unoriginal in that they disrupt preexisting goodness.[34] Deep within all of us is the sense that "this isn't the way it should be." We know intuitively what is good, right, and beautiful. It is our nature to procreate, plant, heal, laugh, dance, build, embrace, love (Eccles. 3), and to this common grace, the Christian adds, to glorify and enjoy God forever. Likewise, we know when we sin because it is a perversion, corruption, and destruction of what is good. We know what is evil because it too is a disruption of the natural order of things. Sin and evil, then, are the perversion of the good, the goodness of a gracious Creator whose longs for the "day" when all things raise an everlasting hymnody (Ps. 96). Whether evil exists apart from good is arguable but our knowledge of what is evil is surely dependent on its dialectic with the good. Scripture does not try to explain the origin of evil but is patently forward in ascribing to God an original goodness.

Besides the Christian doctrine of created goodness and the grace common to all of us to taste and know this goodness, the Reformed tenet of *simul justus et peccator* ("at one and the same time righteous and sinner") is always present. Both Christians and those who stand outside of faith are guilty of collapsing human nature into a single dimension. I have no intention of entering into any of the long-standing debates about sanctification, free will, or how to interpret Romans 7. (Is this Paul's lamentation over life before or after being made right with God?)[35] Whenever we dare enter into the topic of sin or good and evil, the notion of *simul* must prevail. If I have tilted the balance in this book toward the negative, it is only because we live in a culture that overestimates our nature to be good when in fact we are at the same time good and sinful, just as the world staggers between good and evil.

Prophetic Admonitions

It seems that many who are interested in our posthuman future feel some compulsion to revisit the fictional classics which anticipate its coming. And I think I know why. Mary Shelley, Aldous Huxley, George Orwell, and B. F. Skinner had the exceptional acuity to disclose the future based on what was unfolding before them. Each engages us by way of a narrative thought experiment by asking what would it be like to live in a world of our own creation, and then to reflect on how good intentions might go so terribly wrong; or in the instance of *Walden Two*, why shouldn't we follow a perfectly reasonable blueprint toward utopia? With the exception of Shelley's *Frankenstein*, the other writers are preoccupied with issues of personal freedom, control, behavioral conditioning, monopoly of information, progress, utopia—and understandably so against a backdrop of totalitarianism and socialism. If the brave new world is a hell we didn't see coming, then *1984* is the hell we would resist with all our strength. We acknowledge the horrors of totalitarianism. Big Brother is watching you, a camera in every bedroom. It's reality television where you don't get remunerated with big hugs and large sums of money but with a torture chamber. Huxley's *Brave New World*, published in 1932, has received the most attention because he anticipated the means of our dehumanization as biotechnological. We have become somewhat jaded about the inevitable wheel of progress and yet find ourselves embracing technological innovation as our salvation. These stories endure because they pose enduring issues.

The epicenter of Huxley's *Brave New World* is the conversation between the Resident World Controller for Western Europe, Mustapha Mond, and the Savage, who like Tarzan has been reintroduced into civilization from the confines of primitive isolation. The two men represent the proverbial fork in the road.[36] They stand apart from the herd because of their heightened self-awareness, that is, they understand the future is a matter of trade-offs. Huxley concludes his foreword with these words: "You pays your money and you takes your choice." On one side of the balance sheet is happiness in the form of freedom from want, danger, chaos. In this brave new world people are happy because "they get what they want, and they never want what they can't get." They are well off, safe, never ill, and not afraid of death. What else could anyone want? The price includes the loss of art, religion, and pure science. These are deemed superfluous because in a new world of advanced technology there is no place for anything antiquated. They are also forbidden because they are subversive. They excite passion and independence, nobility and heroism, and these promote instability. Pure science must be chained and muzzled and permitted to continue solely to produce goods for a consuming populace. Religion is superfluous because it no longer fulfills a felt need. When every one has youth and prosperity, why perpetuate the religious sentiment? And if anything should go wrong, the Controller reassures the Savage, there's *soma* (the ever-present dream drug supplied by the government to take all your cares away). The Savage is not persuaded. "But I don't want comfort," he exclaims, "I want God, poetry, real danger, I want freedom, I want goodness. I want sin." You can have them, Mustapha responds, and along with them you can have the right to grow old and ugly, the right to live in constant apprehension of what may happen tomorrow, the right to have syphilis and cancer. "I claim them all," the Savage says at last.

Mustapha and the Savage have made their choices and they are willing to live with the consequences. The others in the brave new world are not so fortunate. They are the unenlightened ones: they do know what came before—the past is irretrievably gone as it is for the residents of *1984*—and so is their freedom to choose. The Savage is alive, rather than *soma* deadened, because his rough edges have not been filed away by artificiality; the very artificiality which numbs the savage in us because of its machinelike quality, and machines are everything we are not—robotic, dead, indistinguishable, replaceable, dependable (if properly oiled). The Savage has nightmares of rows of identical midgets at the assembling tables, those "human maggots swarming round Linda's [his mother's] bed of death." Mustapha feels the need to explain. "They're the gyroscope that stabilizes the rocket plane of state on its unswerving course." The Savage, on the other hand, is savagely alive because he still has convictions and passions. And the price he pays is to be conflicted. He is very much alive because he cannot reconcile passions of the flesh (his passion for Lenina) with his deepest held beliefs about marriage and sex (they go together), and because they cannot be resolved he commits suicide alone in a lighthouse. Huxley ends his story with the somber picture of what we "buy into" when passions of the body and passions of the heart abide in the same soul.

The process of dehumanization depicted in *1984* and *Brave New World* seem far-fetched and highly unlikely for citizens of a democracy who value personal freedom above everything else. Nevertheless, Huxley and Orwell invite us to contemplate the possibility that gradually, one trade-off at a time, we lose consciousness of what we once most valued. With uncommon clarity they understand the disposition of science toward the mindless offering of one technical advance after another without regard to its value. Huxley in particular underscored the value of art and religion to foster independent thinking, self-denial, human virtues such as nobility and heroism, and the kind of passionate (savage) love that makes you unmanageable. As perceptive observers of history, Orwell and Huxley depict for us a world where comfort and happiness have become the highest good.

B. F. Skinner is the only scientist among the four storytellers. His *Walden Two* (written in 1945 and published in 1948) is a very different account, because he is deadpan serious. His vision is frightening, because it lacks irony, and Skinner the individual is prophetic, because he is oblivious to the way he embodies an unqualified confidence in what men of science can do. Like the brave new world, Skinner's *Walden Two* looks like a nice place to live. In his experimental society I am neither somatized nor imprisoned. Every day is a picture of harmony. Everyone is empowered. Any constraints to my freedom are for the common good. But there is a hitch. I would have to abide a know-it-all. Something tells me the designer-engineer, T. E. Frazier (Skinner incarnate), is not finished with his experiment and I am not going to have much to say about its design. I may not be the rat being trained to run the maze for its reward, but it feels as though I am a human being trained to run someone else's maze. For Skinner this is not a horror story of a mad scientist. Frazier is entirely confident that "men are made good and bad and wise or foolish by the environment in which they grow." The only original sin observable is the one identified by Hobbes: "Each of us has interests which conflict with the interests of everybody else." This however is a defect redeemable by the science of behaviorism. "We have no truck," says Frazier, "with philosophers of innate goodness—or evil for that matter. But we do have faith in our power to change human nature." Therein lies a truth easily missed. We do not have to take seriously any theology of original sin because we have complete confidence in our power to shape human nature.

Augustine Castle visits *Walden Two*, as do Professor Burris and friends, but Castle refuses the invitation to join the community. He represents Skinner's ultimate challenge. He is wary because he cannot shake the feeling his personal freedom will be compromised. He is mistaken, Frazier informs him, if he thinks personal freedom is the deciding issue. No matter where you live, even in a democracy, freedom is a myth. To cite the frightful misuses of behavioral technology (or the potential frightful misuse of biotechnology) only illustrates what happens when technology ends up in the wrong hands. My question to you, Frazier asserts, is whether you have "the courage to take up and wield the science of behavior for the good of mankind?" Castle needs more time to consider the question, but Burris is fed up with the do-nothing attitude of academia. For those who side with Frazier, there is no alternative to seizing the day.

> It is now widely recognized that great changes must be made in the American way of life. Not only can we not face the rest of the world while consuming and polluting as we do, we cannot for long face ourselves while acknowledging the violence and chaos in which we live. The choice is clear: either we do nothing and allow a miserable and probably catastrophic future to overtake us, or we use our knowledge about human behavior to create a social environment in which we shall live productive and creative lives and do so without jeopardizing the chances that those who follow us will be able to do the same. Something like a *Walden Two* would not be a bad start. (From the preface of *Walden Two*)

Why not seize the technological day? It's a valid question which has been around for a very long time. Mary Shelley (below) and the Greeks (the myth of Prometheus) were intrigued with the consequences of playing with fire. But Shelley occupied herself with a thoroughly modern question: Why should scientists be wary if there are no gods or God from on high prepared to punish those who dare usurp the role of all-knowing? Without sin's dark shadow over human nature, there are no limits or no reasons to think something might go terribly wrong. Humility does not always mean a permanent end to a particular course of experimentation—but it might. It has more to do with the pace and style of science. Another kind of thought experiment would consider a science tempered by humility and sensitive to the human touch. It would have to be a story of scientists who blend together a passion for truth and justice. I wonder what that would look like?

Is there any story more befitting our moment in history than Mary Shelley's *Frankenstein*? Published in 1818, it is prophetic in its own circumstances. The novel's subtitle—*The Modern Prometheus*—indicates that Shelley understands the book's main theme to be a critique of the aspirations of modern masculine science. Around her swirls the Romantic idealism mobilized by faith in man's creative powers. More immediate than the protagonists who defy the gods by stealing fire is the experimental work of Dr. Erasmus Darwin (Darwin's eminent grandfather) whereby the galvanizing effect of electricity stirs what was once dead. In the novel, the young Dr. Frankenstein is entranced by the momentous "panegyric on chemistry" delivered by Professor Waldman. Mary Shelley is well acquainted with Humphry Davy's *Elements of Chemical Philosophy* (1812) and only slightly exaggerates Davy's claim that science possesses "unlimited powers" to unfold the deepest mysteries of creation. In her own household, Mary is surrounded by Romantics writing about overreaching heroes—namely her husband Percy Shelley and Lord Byron, both of whom encourage Mary, one dark and stormy night, to write a horror story. From her journal we learn that she is more comfortable with power tempered with kindness, compassion, and softness, a not so subtle rejection of the aggressive masculine ambition of the males around her.

> "Some have a passion for reforming the world; others do not cling to particular opinions. That my parents and Shelley [her husband] were of the former class, makes me respect it. I respect such when joined to read disinterestedness, toleration and a clear understanding. . . . But since I had lost Shelley I have no wish to ally myself to the Radicals—they are full of repulsion to me—violent without any sense of Justice. . . ." (Quoted from the introduction to *Frankenstein* by Maurice Hindle, xli)

What exactly is Dr. Frankenstein's sin? What went wrong? He begins with the best of intentions. He would be willing to sacrifice his fortune, his life, and every hope if it were possible to "banish disease from the human frame and render man invulnerable to any but a violent death!" One man's life or death, he exclaims, would be a small price to pay for such knowledge. His is a noble cause pursued by a noble person. Is sin, then, his creation, the nameless monster who is usually portrayed as evil incarnate? The one-dimensional monster of movie fame—rendered to elicit screams of horror—obscures the nobleness of the creature. Here is a creation capable of sorrow, moved to empathy, and given to repentance. He is not unlike his creator who reflects on the events that have brought both of them so low.

> When I run over the frightful catalogue of my sins, I cannot believe that I am the same creature whose thoughts were once filled with sublime and transcendent visions of the beauty and the majesty of goodness. But it is even so; the fallen angel becomes a malignant devil. Yet even that enemy of God and man had friends and associates in his desolation; I am alone. (*Frankenstein*, 213)

Both Frankenstein and his creature seem unable to escape the destiny imposed upon them. But then that's the nature of sin: to deceive us into thinking we know how to handle power and make it serve the good and thereby reverse the dismal failures of the past. From hindsight both creatures begin to understand what went wrong. Frankenstein knows that his initial enthusiastic frenzy blinded him to the possible consequence of probing the mysteries of Mother Nature. Rejecting the counsel of his father to maintain familial affections, Frankenstein pursues his conquest in splendid Los Alamos–type isolation. We have every reason to think the creature is made in accordance with a Rousseauian "unfallen state of innocence." But the good doctor abandons him immediately, not even willing to look upon the face of the one he has made. As a result the Creature wants to know, just as everyone wants to know, where he has come from and why he is here. He knows no loving father or friends, for all have averted their eyes and abhor him as inhuman. One who is unloved becomes one who hates in spite of himself. Frankenstein tempts fate—rashly setting into motion a "machine over whose progress I had no control"—and is subsequently run over by it. The Monster murders the doctor's dearest friend and beloved wife, and both creator and creation are left desolate.

The story is told through the eyes of Captain Walton who has himself embarked upon a similar pursuit of glory. His quest is to be the first to discover the North Pole. In the wasteland of ice and cold they meet, and Frankenstein at once undertakes to tell his tale, much like the Ancient Mariner does, hoping to convince the Captain not to go down the same road. Telling his tale is Frankenstein's way of seeking absolution, atoning in some small way for all the grief he has brought upon his family. Here at the end of his life he can ask: How does science pursue noble ends without imparting the kiss of death? Shelley gives us not only a narrative but images to convey a nightmarish possibility. When Frankenstein dreams of meeting his beloved Elizabeth in the bloom of health, walking in the streets of Ingolstadt, he hears himself saying, "Delighted and surprised, I embraced her, but as I imprinted the first kiss on her lips, they became livid with the hue of death." Shelley's prose may be overly Romantic to our ears but such is the manner of any talk of sin and evil, fate, and destiny. Having gained some assurance that we aren't going to end the world in a cloud of radioactive dust, we are wont to think fate and destiny are in our hands. We no longer see films being made about mad scientists; they are instead confidently overly optimistic as is the professor of *Jurassic Park* fame. But even this scenario may be overly dramatic, for we might just extinguish a great number of lives slowly and imperceptibly with industrial smoke and millions of cooking fires fueled with dried cow dung.

> **Dateline *Wall Street Journal*, 6 May 2003**
>
> ## A Dirty Discovery over Indian Ocean Sets Off a Fight
>
> Using planes, ships, balloons and satellites, his [Indian scientist Veerabhadran Ramanathan's] multinational team of 200 scientists traced a gritty brown blanket of soot, dust and smoke that was nearly two miles thick. It hung over an area of the Indian Ocean roughly the size of the United States.
>
> This February at a meeting in Nairobi, Kenya, T. R. Baalu, India's Environment and Forests minister, backed by diplomats from Pakistan and Indonesia, asked the United Nations Environment Programme to reject a request by Dr. Ramanathan and other scientists for more money to broaden their research to cover all of Asia. . . . After the objections, further research funds were removed from UNEP's core funding activities . . . (John J. Fialka, A1).

My method of documentation is a bit unorthodox but follows one simple rule: when documentation is simple the book and page number are placed in parenthesis in the text. As a reader I like to know the source without having to hunt it down. When the documentation is more complex and further remarks of a more academic nature are added, look for notes at the end of each chapter. A selected bibliography provides the full reference for cited sources.

Both in content and style the skeptic is my constant dialogue companion. In this I am reminded of Friedreich Schleiermacher, who was something of a skeptic writing to skeptics who were struggling with the growing chasm between the dogmas of the church and science of the Enlightenment. Skeptics may be the best kind of interlocutor, because they press the author to make muddy water clear. Skeptics come in many varieties. There are Christian skeptics who need to be convinced, once again, that they are in bondage to sin and that I am no exception. They include parents seeking baptism for their newborn who cannot understand why someone so cute and loveable needs to be immersed in the water of forgiveness; and the pastor who once again is at a loss for words to explain that while the infant has committed no sins of her own, she is burdened with a history of sin not of her own doing. I hope the scientist and the scientifically minded, like myself, will be intrigued by a chapter titled "Science as the New Occasion for Sin" and find there none of the usual cliché arguments. In my imagined audience there will be skeptics who can find no reason to refer to the language of sin and evil when the issue of the human condition is brought to the public forum, reluctant even though they acknowledge a reality that is both malevolent and perdurable. Wherever the skepticism is coming from, I hope that skepticism includes a nagging sense that something is missing in almost everything being written about our posthuman future. Skeptics and cynics that we are, there is a great distance between the burdensome reality of sin and evil and falling into nihilism.[37] Hope is what separates the two, and the hope the Christian lives by, myself included, is not dependent on human achievement but the grace of God.

> In hope, we already have salvation; in hope, not visibly present, or we should not be hoping—nobody goes on hoping for something which he can already see. But having this hope for what we cannot yet see, we are able to wait for it with persevering confidence. (Rom. 8: 24–25, The New Jerusalem Bible)

Most books of any substance have a history behind them. My first introduction to the dynamics of sin and evil did not come from a class of systematic theology but a course on the book of Romans taught by the late Professor J. Christiaan Beker of Princeton Theological Seminary. From Dr. Beker we, since I know I am not alone, learned the dynamics of sin and evil through the inner struggles of St. Paul. More recently, a weekly reading group of ministers and retired professors provided me with encouragement and stimulation, and together we read through most of the manuscript. During the course of a lifetime sin and evil become our teachers. My own life and the lives of others I have been privileged to share as friend and pastor are no exceptions, and together with all humanity we struggle to do the good we intend but come to learn that grace and forgiveness make us truly whole.

Notes

1. The meeting between Truman and Oppenheimer probably took place on October 25, 1945. Truman recalls that "he spent most of his time ringing [sic] his hands and telling me they had blood on them because of the discovery of atomic energy." From remarks Truman made after the meeting, Oppenheimer was allowing his guilt to get the better part of valor.

2. See for example Marjorie Hewitt Suchocki, *The Fall to Violence: Original Sin in Relational Theology* (New York: Continuum, 1994). Suchocki reconfigures sin by looking at our propensity to a "violence-engendered anxiety" rather than a Niebuhrian "finitude-

engendered anxiety." In *An Examined Faith*, James M. Gustafson makes a valid distinction between those approaches that accommodate science by *inviting* them to inform theology, *limit* theology, or *authorize* theology. My own approach is to afford science the role of limiting what theology can claim regarding human nature in order not to be judged unreasonable; and while this concedes a fact of life that theological truth claims are credible when they are scientifically informed, science does not authorize or legitimate those truth claims. I find myself most attuned to Gustafson's discussion of Karl Barth (pp. 59–66).

3. See Coleman, *Competing Truths: Theology and Science as Sibling Rivals*, for an in-depth interpretation of their history as truth seekers belonging to same family, making them sibling rivals.

4. See Ted Peters, ed., *Science and Theology: The New Consonance*. For a more diverse approach see Gregersen and van Huyssteen, eds., *Rethinking Theology and Science*, where six models are discussed; and Paul Kurtz, ed., *Science and Religion: Are They Compatible?*

5. See Rosalind Williams, "The Political and Feminist Dimension of Technological Determinism," in *Does Technology Drive History?* eds. Smith and Marx, 231; as well as a similar discussion by Holton, *Einstein, History and Other Passions*, 34–37.

6. Each chapter is a dialogue with particular thinkers. The introduction grapples with, and is indebted to, Steven Pinker, Francis Fukuyama, Leon Kass, and Susan Neiman. The chapter about "knowledge too powerful" appreciates Schweber's book, *In the Shadow of the Bomb*. In "knowledge too good not to be exploited," Daniel Greenberg (*Science, Money, and Politics*) and Sheldon Krimsky (*Science in the Private Interest*) play a major role, as well as Lee Silver (*Remaking Eden*). I like to think part 2 is primarily my own original, creative effort but one that begins with Reinhold Niebuhr's *Nature and Destiny of Man*. The last chapter focuses on expectations by engaging Joel Garreau's stimulating *Radical Evolution*, and more indirectly Bill McKibben's *Enough*.

7. Merold Westphal's article is a summary of the shortcoming of a postmodern critique. See her "Blind Spots: Christianity and Postmodern Philosophy," *Christian Century*, 14 June 2003, 32–35.

8. In Pinker, *The Blank Slate*, 2, 435–39. Pinker includes an appendix listing human universals complied by Donald D. Brown in his *Human Universals*. While scientists may prefer to study humans in terms of their behaviors, these behaviors bear values. Why shouldn't we think of ourselves as distinctive by the values we hold dear?

9. An exception among biologists is Richard Lewontin. For example, see his *The Triple Helix: Gene, Organism, and Environment* (Cambridge, Mass.: Harvard University Press, 2000).

10. The philosopher Hilary Putnam takes dead aim at Hume's naturalistic fallacy in *The Collapse of the Fact/Value Dichotomy* (Cambridge, Mass.: Harvard University Press, 2002).

11. See Singer, *The Expanding Circle*, and Pinker, *The Blank Slate*, 165–69, 188. For a similar sentiment by another philosopher, see Michael Shermer's *The Science of Good and*

Evil, concluding chapter and 224, and the zoologist, Frans de Waal, in his *Good Natured*, 213.

12. Soyinka, *Climate of Fear*, xxi. Three adventurists who signed on for a "tour" with the UN peacekeeping efforts during the 1990s undoubtedly asked the very same question. Hedi is a New York social worker, Andrew a young doctor, Ken fresh from Harvard Law School. They see the worst of the latter half of the twentieth century as it transpires in Cambodia, Somalia, Haiti, and Bosnia, and their idealism is shaken to the core by the atrocities of a new kind of warring. Read their stories in *Emergency Sex and Other Desperate Measures* (New York: Hyperion, 1991).

13. H. Allen Orr's review of *The Blank Slate* in *New York Review of Books*, 27 February 2002, 20, and the exchange of letters in *New York Review*, 1 May 2003, 48–49. For a parallel observation regarding the impediment of Enlightenment ideals, see Kass, *Life, Liberty and the Defense of Dignity*, 29–36, 50–51.

14. For a sustained (nearly four decades) counter-assessment of Western history, see the writings of William Pfaff. His most recent book, *The Bullet's Song: Romantic Violence and Utopia* (New York: Simon and Schuster, 2005), is nothing less than a long essay on utopian violence propelled by the Western faith in progress, and this would include the liberal belief in democracy, technology, free enterprise, globalization as ideals worthy to save humanity from violence and chaos.

15. Since Hegel's understanding of history is the springboard for Fukuyama's thesis that history is directional, see Susan Neiman's sharp jab at the future of Hegelianism where she quotes Arendt, whose only kind word for the philosopher was to regard him as the last of the old philosophers who managed to evade the important questions. See her *Evil in Modern Thought*, 260.

16. In *The Death of Satan: How Americans Have Lost the Sense of Evil*, Andrew Delbanco chronicles the way we have lost the ability to language evil, noting that the "old language of evil has become a collection of what George Orwell called 'dead metaphors (p. 11).'" While his effort is very different from mine, the goal is the same. We want to provide intellectual resources for understanding the presence of a reality we cannot deny.

17. The originality of this assertion is uncertain. Reinhold Niebuhr makes reference to it in *Man's Nature and His Communities* (New York: Scribner, 1965), 24. G. K. Chesterton is a more likely candidate.

18. Phyllis A. Tickle may disagree with my assessment. She detects a contemporary fascination with the age-old sins, writing about one of the seven deadly sins at the request of the New York Public Library and Oxford University Press. See her book, *Greed*, 9, 69, n. 35. Sin and evil have gained a level of currency—evil in academic circles and sin in the popular press—but I am not deterred from my argument that neither is taken seriously when science speaks about human nature.

19. See, for example, Peter Singer's *The President of Good and Evil: The Ethics of George W. Bush* (New York: Dutton, 2004). When President Jimmy Carter spoke of sin (the lust in his heart), he caused waves of shock and dismay. It would seem that it is safer to talk

about evil, when it is the evil "over there," than to mention sin because sin is something for which I am personally responsible.

20. Oppenheimer, *Physics in the Contemporary World*, 10.

21. The acceptance of sin and evil as genuine knowledge in the public square is part of a larger problem, namely, that theology is no longer regarded as a field of knowledge, neither in the university nor the public square. For a discussion of the reasons and what should be done to reinstate theological truth claims, see the discussion of "Theology as Knowledge" by James R. Stoner, Jr., Stanley Hauerwas, Paul J. Griffiths, and David B. Hart in *First Things* (May 2006): 21–27.

22. Ellingsen, *Blessed Are the Cynical*, 31.

23. With only contemporary writers in mind, is there a story without sin and evil? While they intertwine sin and evil without much thought given to how they differ, Steven King and Dean Koontz, and more subtly with J. M. Coetzee and John Updike, to mention just a few, show us the dark side of human nature.

24. Neiman is her usual astute eloquence when depicting Nietzsche in *Evil*, 203–27.

25. See Roy D. Morrison, *Science, Theology and the Transcendental Horizon: Einstein, Kant and Tillich* (Atlanta, Ga.: Scholars Press, 1994). A good overview of recent treatments of original sin is found in Tatha Wiley, *Original Sin: Origins, Developments, Contemporary Meanings* (Paulist Press, 1989). Henri Blocher's *Original Sin* (Eerdmans, 1997) interacts with scientific and literary insights, while Patricia A. Williams is more interested in providing original sin with an empirical foundation in *Doing without Adam and Eve: Sociobiology and Original Sin* (Fortress Press, 2001). For a social analysis see Cornelius Plantinga, Jr., *A Breviary of Sin* (Eerdmans, 1995); Ted Peters, *Sin: Radical Evil in Soul and Society* (Eerdmans, 1994); and Marjorie Hewitt Suchocki, *The Fall to Violence: Original Sin in Relational Theology* (Continuum, 1994).

26. There is an empirical parallel to the complex human behavior I am explaining. Among those trying to explain consciousness, the word "qualia" represents those features of consciousness that give it depth or color. How to account for the redness of red, the sadness of melancholia, the trembling before what is awfully holy, the gratitude of a life reborn, a sense of oneness with the cosmos, and so forth? Qualia constitutes a major challenge for any researcher who wants to provide a fully naturalistic account of consciousness based on the neurochemistry of the brain. Surely sin falls into this category of the difficult to explain empirically because it refers to matters of the will and heart, and relationships gone bad.

27. Two insightful expositions of the story of the Prodigal Son play an important role in a number of places in this book. See Henri Nouwen, *The Return of the Prodigal Son*, and Miroslav Volf, *Exclusion and Embrace*, 156–65. The prodigal son is not the only one who has it all wrong. In the parable of the talents (Matt. 25:14–30), the servant is asked: "You knew, did you, that I reap where I did not sow, and gather where I did not scatter?"

28. Two short but good summaries of how the pendulum has swung between innateness and malleability, between heredity and environment can be found in Ridley, *Agile Gene*, chapter 1, and Pinker, *Blank Slate*, chapter 2.

29. One of the finest expositions of the biblical understanding of *shalom* is Nicholas Wolterstorff, *Until Justice and Peace Embrace*—and no better example of *shalom* than the life so dedicated, Archbishop Romero.

30. See James R. Brockamn, *The Word Remains: A Life of Oscar Romero* (New York: Orbis Books, 1983).

31. See, for example, John Hedley Brooke, *Science and Religion: Some Historical Perspectives* (Cambridge: Cambridge University Press, 1991).

32. See John F. Haught, *Deeper than Darwin* (Westview, 2003), as an example of engagement between science and theology without compromise.

33. See Daniel Migliore, *Faith Seeking Understanding*, chapter 5, "The Good Creation," and Richard J. Mouw's treatment of common grace in *He Shines in All That's Fair*. At times Mouw seems limited in what he counts as common grace and this is the consequence of his effort to be faithful to the Evangelical-Reformed tradition. I prefer a broader interpretation and that leads me to think the Evangelical-Reformed tradition is deficient in some way regarding common grace. For a broader discussion of the common good, see Dennis P. McCann and Patrick D. Miller, eds., *In Search of the Common Good* (New York: T&T Clark, 2005).

34. See Cornelius Plantinga, Jr., *A Breviary of Sin* (Grand Rapids, Mich.: Wm. B. Eerdmans, 1995), chapter 1, "Vandalism of Shalom." In Garry Wills's discussion and translation of Saint Augustine's expositions of sin, both the words "un-making" and "disordering" are used. In *The City of God*, Augustine writes of Adam's sin that it is the first act of an evil intent that is "more an un-making [*de-fectus*] of God's work to make something of its own, rather than a thing made in itself. That is what constitutes its evil—the will's substitution of its own working for God's work." See Wills, *Saint Augustine's Sin*, 87.

35. Luther understands Paul to be describing the life of the Christian, justified but still doing battle with sin. Luther believes Christians are and remain throughout their whole lives sinners before God; yet through God's grace the sinner is now justified. I read Romans 7 as the divided life still under the Law. If we have been made right with God and accept the lordship of Jesus Christ, our lives are no longer divided and we are free "to be a sinner and sin boldly," to use Luther's own words. In other words, the Christian no longer lives under the tyranny of sin and is able to do the good God expects of us. If God's spirit dwells in us, sin will visit but will not stay. The difference between Luther and myself is that Luther is more pessimistic concerning the human condition, and reading about his life and times I can understand why.

36. Robert Frost expressed it poetically but science fiction has its own fascination with moments of momentous decision. Consider *The Matrix* cycle, where Neo must choose between good and evil, love and hate while also choosing to claim his mission.

37. See Robert Jenson's discussion of "our culture of nihilism" in *Sin, Death and the Devil*, 1–6. For a broader analysis of western philosophy, notably postmodern philosophy, as an ontology of nihilism, see John Hart, *The Beauty of the Infinite*, 125–51.

PART ONE

SCIENCE'S COMING-OF-AGE STORY

While the introduction places the arguments into a larger framework and charts the flow of ideas and arguments against the present posthuman context, part 1 lends a historical perspective by recounting science's coming-of-age story, a story of how science mutates from the keeper of knowledge too powerful to be ignored to the purveyors of knowledge too good not to exploit.

We do ourselves a considerable disservice if we see science as monolithic. If measured from Robert Oppenheimer's farewell speech to his colleagues at Los Alamos at the end of World War II to the sequencing of the human genome, science is a transformed quasi-establishment. Those who created the first atomic bomb accepted without question the premise that knowledge is inherently good but as the enormity of what they had done began to unfold, they became more and more self-conscious and socially responsible. They felt they could not not be politically active. In hindsight this generation of scientists were good and noble, with a vision and practical ideas of how to "build" a peaceful world. As the Cold War receded and science feasted on new appropriations, another dynamic comes into play. Both the science and the knowledge it handles changes again. The lethal knowledge of atom splitting is displaced by the promises of biological intervention.

CHAPTER ONE

Knowledge Too Powerful to Be Ignored: The Good and Noble Scientist

It is not possible to be a scientist unless you believe that the knowledge of the world, and the power that this gives, is a thing which is of intrinsic value to humanity, and that you are using it to help in the spread of knowledge, and are willing to take the consequences.

—Robert Oppenheimer (farewell speech to colleagues at Los Alamos, November 2, 1945)

The new powers that science had conceived and engineering had delivered had destroyed the innocence and the sense of freedom of the scientist. Henceforth the scientist could never profess a lack of responsibility for the fate of society.

—Don Price, eulogy for Oppenheimer

When you see something that is technically sweet, you go ahead and do it and you argue what to do about it only after you have had your technical success. That is the way it was with the atomic bomb.

—Robert Oppenheimer

How to characterize the twentieth century? Was it a good century? Did humankind show itself to be the one species capable of being the subject rather than the object of its own evolution? That is, did we do the good we intended or did we once again act as our own worst enemy? While this century had its very dark episodes—some of the darkest in our entire history—it did end on an optimistic note. Regardless of the spiral of destruction and self-destruction, the one beacon of hope was the steady advancement of science toward a comprehensive understanding of the universe. The epitome of this culmination was comprehending the basic building blocks of matter to the place where we could release its power. The scientific revolution beginning at the turn of the century and associated with Eddington, Planck, Heisenberg, Bohr, and Einstein was brought to fruition when a magnificent scientific fraternity at Los Alamos tested the theories of modern physics and demonstrated they "had it right."[1]

Almost every coming-of-age story is about the maturing use of knowledge: our sexuality, our place in the world, the consequence of our actions. The same was true for science insofar as it learned how to handle knowledge too powerful to be ignored. After the detonation of the first two atomic bombs during August 1945, the nations of the world viewed science in a different way and scientists understood themselves in a different light. The realization that scientific knowledge is not simply about improving life but changing the entire political landscape served to awakened anyone who previously regarded science as ancillary. The world would have to grapple with the twin truths that science is both our best hope for a better future and potentially our worst nightmare. As someone who likes to reflect on the broader questions science raises, Richard Feynman relates a wake-up experience of his own:

> Once in Hawaii I was taken to see a Buddhist temple. In the temple a man said, "I am going to tell you something that you will never forget." And then he said, "To every man is given the key to the gates of heaven. The same key opens the gate of hell." (Feynman, *The Meaning of It All*, 7–8)

Nothing Will Ever Be the Same—Robert Oppenheimer's Farewell Speech

On a rainy evening of 2 November 1943, only three short months after the dropping of the first atomic bomb, Robert Oppenheimer gave a remarkable speech to some five hundred friends and colleagues crowded into the auditorium at Los Alamos.[2] Oppenheimer had a clear understanding that nothing would be the same, that a decisive moment in history was upon them, and that both peril and hope lay ahead.

What has happened to us—it is really rather major, it is so major that I think in some ways one returns to the greatest developments of the twentieth century, to the discovery of relativity, and to the whole development of atomic theory and its interpretation, in terms of complementarity, for analogy. These things, as you know, force us to re-consider the relations between science and common sense. (*Letters and Recollections*, 315–16)

But the knowledge they harvested was not like relativity or complementarity. This kind of knowledge came with the immediate potential for goodness and evil. It was contracted for a specific purpose, under dire circumstances, coordinating the efforts of many scientists at different locations. There was really nothing like it, ever before.

I am not interested in turning this book into a historical study. My primary concern is to defend the thesis developed in the next chapter that we find ourselves in a radically different situation. In order to do this I must first establish a baseline constituted by scientists who had to learn how to broker knowledge everyone wanted. I have lifted up Robert Oppenheimer as my primary example because his status as "statesman for science" made him a leading architect of America's nuclear policy. Oppenheimer was the director of the Los Alamos Laboratory overseeing all aspects of the bomb's development. After the war he declined an invitation to return to the University of California at Berkeley in order to be the foremost liaison between the worlds of science and politics. In 1947 he accepted the post of director of the Institute for Advanced Study in Princeton, where his extraordinary career ended with his death in 1967. Although there were many distinguished scientists surrounding him, Robert Oppenheimer chose for himself the role of interpreter and conscience at a time when both science and the world were being transformed by Cold War politics.

During this period of coming of age, an implied agreement was being written among science, government, and the commonwealth. To serve the common good is the expressed purpose of both science and government, but we know that is not the entire story. Nevertheless, it is interesting to examine how the quasi institution of science and the entrenched system of politics worked out their mutual needs to the satisfaction of both. My focus is on atomic science because those who created the most destructive force the world had ever witnessed felt the initial change in self-awareness. And while it was politicians who made the decision to employ the Bomb, there would be no going forward without the technical expertise of science. The new social contract being written rested squarely on these six factors.

1. The self-conscious scientist
2. The socially responsible scientist
4. The visionary scientist
5. Knowledge is a good thing
6. Autonomous but beholden.

The Self-Conscious Scientist

The morning of Monday, 16 June 1945 was a defining moment for science. When he saw the mushroom cloud rising over the New Mexican dessert, the Harvard physicist in charge of the Trinity test, Kenneth Bainbridge, made the trenchant remark: "Well, now we're all sons of bitches."[3] The morning began with the question: Will it work? It ended with the question: What have we done? The enormity of the Trinity test meant that henceforth scientists would have to be more mindful of the consequences of the secrets they unlocked.

While the part scientists played in the development of radar might have been more decisive in determining the outcome of the war, Oppenheimer had no doubt that here was something that shook them to the core of their being. It also isn't difficult to understand why scientists, but especially those working on the Bomb, became deeply reflective about the political and moral implications for the world. Robert Oppenheimer, Leo Szilard, Enrico Fermi, Eugene Wigner, Arthur Compton, Ernest Lawrence, Edward Teller, Hans Bethe, and Victor Weisskopf, to name a few, shed their images of ivory-tower theorists. Gone were the days when the scientist could neatly separate pure, autonomous research from its application. It quickly became apparent that the way science was to be done was unalterably changed. Oppenheimer spoke of "this troubled sense of responsibility" nowhere more poignantly than "among those who participated in the development of the atomic energy for military purposes" (*Open Mind* 87; lecture delivered on 25 November 1947 at MIT).

The epicenter of this new self-awareness was knowing that what a scientist does can affect all of humanity. Science was no longer a minor player. It was on its way from orphan to establishment (see next chapter). In a lecture in 1954, as part of Columbia University's Bicentennial, Oppenheimer had time to realize that it wasn't simply splitting the atom that had changed everything but the nature of change inherent in scientific knowledge. "What is new is new not because it has never been there before, but because it has changed in quality. One thing that is new is the prevalence of newness, the changing scale and scope of change itself" (*Open Mind*, 140–42).

More so than most of his colleagues, Oppenheimer felt a sense of remorse and responsibility for the death of so many civilians and the possibility of so many more. On one occasion he spoke of sin and much has been made of it. The occasion was an address at MIT in 1947.

> The physicists felt a peculiarly intimate responsibility for suggesting, for supporting, and in the end, in large measure, for achieving the realization of atomic weapons. Nor can we forget that these weapons, as they were in fact used, dramatized so mercilessly the inhumanity and evil of modern war. In some sort of crude sense which no vulgarity, no humor, no over-statement can quite extinguish, the physicists have known sin; and this is a knowledge they cannot lose.[4]

Most likely Oppenheimer was not thinking of sin in the traditional Christian sense, for his understanding had little to do with Jesus Christ, the cross and resurrection. Taking into account his Enlightenment education, and more specifically the German tradition of the *humanistisches Gymnasium* and *Bildungsträger*, where the education of the whole person was central, sin fell into a moral category. His education would have exposed him to the Kantian moral philosophy and the categorical imperative to treat every person as an end and not as a means.[5] For those who accepted the mission to build an atomic bomb, the moral imperative was to save American lives and to end the war. In the heat of the moment there were no feelings of sin and guilt. Paramount was a sense of patriotism and fear of what the Germans might be doing. Once the first test proved successful and the bomb's terrible devastation had been seen with their own eyes, there was room for other feelings. Oppenheimer's suggestion of sin should be taken as the mature reflection of someone who was living in a world where scientists were building ever more powerful weapons. The confessional door Oppenheimer opened was quickly shut because it is difficult for scientists, as it is for all of us, to second-guess our motives, and especially so when you believe what you are doing is for the good of the nation or the world.

I must confess that a superficial reading of the history of the Bomb led me to conclude that here were scientists cloistered in splendid isolation doing what they loved best, the pursuit of fundamental scientific knowledge. "It would be expecting too much," I wrote, "to think these scientists could distance themselves from their duty to the 'national interest.' The only voices to be heard were those of males doing masculine science" (*Competing Truths*,

195). In the heat of the moment and during the excitement of discovery, their world had become very constricted and detached. What is remarkable, especially so when the working environment imposed a rigid division between science and policy, that even before the Trinity test voices of a new self-consciousness were raised.[6] It wasn't a sense of sin or guilt that motivated them, but a forward-looking stirring of a future filled with great peril and hope. The stirring of these feelings were apparent in the weeks preceding the Trinity test and immediately afterward when it was clear that deployment was very near. At all three principal sites of the Manhattan Project—the Metallurgical Lab in Chicago, the Clinton Labs at Oak Ridge, and Los Alamos—reservations were starting to surface. The two most vociferous and deliberate protests against immediate use on human beings came from the Franck Report of 11 June 1945, emanating from the Met Lab, and the Szilard petition. The former was prepared for the Interim Committee on Social and Political Implications, established by Secretary of War Henry Stimson in early May 1945 to consider the postwar role of atomic power (peaceful and otherwise). Among several petitions circulated at Chicago, the strongest was Szilard's. It was addressed to President Truman himself dated July 17 and signed by sixty-four scientists representing a majority voice at Chicago.[7] The Franck Report, a thirteen-page document, was forthright about the prospects of an arms race, the necessity for international control and mutual trust, the highly unlikely prospect that nuclear bombs could remain a "secret weapon" of any one nation, the call for broad public support and debate, and the development of a long-range national strategy. It took as its premise the conviction that "we cannot hope to avoid a nuclear armament race either by keeping secret from the competing nations the basic scientific facts of nuclear power or by cornering the raw materials required for such a race." It went so far as to urge that the best way to create a conductive atmosphere for an international agreement would be a visible demonstration of the power of atomic weapons "before the eyes of representatives of all the United Nations, on the desert or a barren island."[8]

The most vivid memories of the scientists of the Manhattan Project congealed around feeling of collegiality, and this is far more than just an interesting historical footnote. In his eulogy for Oppenheimer at the Institute for Advanced Study in the spring of 1967, Hans Bethe highlights Oppenheimer's leadership at Los Alamos in this way:

> But I never observed in any one of these other groups quite the spirit of belonging together, quite the urge to reminisce about the days of the laboratory, quite the feeling that this was really the great time of their lives. (Schweber, 106)

The awakening of Oppenheimer's conscience seems to be linked to the incongruity of having the best time of their lives while creating the most destructive weapon on the face of the earth. Freeman Dyson, a brilliant physicist with a predilection toward introspection, makes this observation:

> The sin of the physicists at Los Alamos did not lie in their having built a lethal weapon. To have built the bomb, when their country was engaged in a disparate war against Hitler's Germany was morally justifiable. But they did not just build the bomb. They enjoyed building it. They had the best time of their lives while building it. That, I believe is what Oppy had in mind when he said they had sinned. And he was right. (*Disturbing the Universe*, 52–53)

Whatever the sin of the physicists who created the Bomb, it did not become the kind of confessional of any lasting value. Oppenheimer's use of the word became a minor footnote and the nations of the world proceeded to ring themselves with ever more destructive weapons made possible by scientists who enjoy doing the technically sweet thing.[9]

The Socially Responsible Scientist

The outcome of these last-minute protests and requests for further consideration is much discussed. In the end, the Franck Report, the Szilard's petition, and Compton's poll of scientists all failed to reach President Truman but did provide a valuable lesson: in order to be effective scientists would have to be better organized. Their first obstacle would be to overcome the perception that scientists were incompetent outside their narrow area of expertise. On 3 October, President Truman sent to Congress his message on atomic energy, and on 4 October a bill to establish an atomic commission was introduced in Congress. The May-Johnson bill became the focus of their attention. It was eventually defeated and in its place the McMahon Act was passed establishing the Atomic Energy Commission. Just how vocal and organized did these atomic physicists become? In an article for *Life* titled "The Atomic Scientists Speak Up" (29 October 1945), Arthur Compton took notice of some eight hundred scientists who made it known that they rejected the position that the application of their work was something they should leave to others. In meeting after meeting, conference after conference, resolutions were discussed, voted on, and referred to the proper person or committee. Alice Smith reports, for instance, that "on October 23, sixty leading scientists, educators, and civic leaders wired Truman, Patterson, General Marshall, and Representative May urging withdrawal of the May-Johnson bill on the grounds that it granted unprecedented powers to an administrator responsible neither to the President nor to Congress" (*Peril and a Hope*, 181). Two insiders, James Newman and Byron Miller, recall how "[t]he scientists swarmed down from their ivory towers 'and with energy, fervor, passionate conviction, and a somewhat unexpected talent for organization threw themselves into the battle.'"[10]

Practically simultaneously with the deployment of the first two atomic bombs the scientists of Chicago, Oak Ridge, and Los Alamos formed associations or federations. They spearheaded the initial political activity of socially agitated and morally awakened scientists. In December 1945 these three upstart federations and the Manhattan Project laboratory at Columbia University, code name "Substitute Alloy Materials" (SAM), established the Federation of Atomic Scientists (FAS). The new organization had the distinction of being led by younger scientists representing labs and universities spread across America. Whether or not it was a historical first, FAS was something new in that it was a congregation of scientists for non-scientific ends. In its constitution six goals were enumerated. In the field of atomic energy, members are to urge the United States to initiate a workable system of control among all nations, to counter misinformation with scientific fact, to safeguard the spirit of free inquiry and interchange, to promote those public policies which will secure the benefits of science to the general welfare, and to strengthen international cooperation tradition among scientists. The very heart of FAS is expressed in their second mandate: "In consideration of the broad responsibility of scientists today, to study the implications of any scientific developments which may involve hazards to enduring peace and the safety of mankind" (A. Smith 236–37). Both within the immediate context and global threats to follow, one is struck by the prophetic voice of scientists aware of their "broad responsibility" for scientific discoveries and how that might impact "the peace and safety of mankind."

A socially aroused and responsible scientific community made possible a new question: To whom is the scientist ultimately accountable—himself, his government, the good of society (the commonwealth), or the good of humanity (the commonweal)? Where does one draw the line between the scientist speaking about science and the scientist speaking as a concerned and informed citizen? The easy answer would be to separate scientific fact from interpretation and both from implementation. When he was appointed to the Interim Committee's scientific panel in the spring of 1945, Oppenheimer sensed the trap with his comment, "Now we are in for trouble." The difficulties arise on two fronts. The scientist as politician is something of an oxymoron, for politics is something they are ill suited and ill prepared to do. Second, only an obscurantist with his head in the sand would miss the writing on the wall: the interpenetration of research and application was inevitable.

As the hot war became the Cold War, scientists of the Manhattan Project found their conviction put to the test concerning their next paycheck. No one could plead ignorance or innocence this time. The prospect of an arms race was hard upon them and every personal decision was intensified by the burden of moral responsibility. The two titans, Oppenheimer and Teller, represented polar opposites and each gave moral reasons for the paths they took. Though in favor of exploring the feasibility of a fusion bomb, Oppenheimer argued against its actual creation because it would undermine the vision of world peace through openness and international control. Edward Teller, a principal architect of the hydrogen bomb, the guiding force of the Livermore weapons laboratory, and passionate advocate of an antimissile defense system, reasoned it was either us or them, and so he dedicated himself to an overwhelming American military superiority. Not every scientist—most in fact—felt so strongly or acted so decisively. Hans Bethe found himself sitting on the fence and distressed that he was not more resolute. My "inner troubles stayed with me," he recollects, "and are still with me and I have not resolved the problem" (Schweber 166). He confesses that he wishes he had been a more consistent idealist. Bethe did join the scientists at Los Alamos near the end of their work on the hydrogen bomb in February 1952 and witnessed once again the destructive forces of nature manipulated by human minds. The first hydrogen bomb was tested on 1 November 1952 with a yield eight hundred times more powerful than the Hiroshima bomb. Bethe was wary from the beginning and the more removed from 1952, the more he agreed with Andrei Sakharov that what we were doing was a great tragedy. In 1954 he called its development a calamity (Schweber 169).

Teller wasn't an immoral man and Oppenheimer wasn't a saint. What separated them was not only their judgment call whether overwhelming military advantage or sufficient military strength would promote peace. What should disturb us is Teller's reluctance to allow himself to be troubled. Teller not only advocated a strong defense but also sold it by way of exaggeration.[11] Oppenheimer, on the other hand, remained constantly watchful of the corrupting power of knowledge and cognizant of growing isolation of science from the commons. What Teller lacked and Oppenheimer possessed was a sense of humility (though both had very large egos). Knowing what each of these scientists knew and their experience with totalitarian governments, the least one would expect is an awareness of how evil corrupts good intentions.

Still within the realm of remarkable is the initiative taken by scientists to affect world events. It was not President Franklin Roosevelt who approached the scientific community to commence the development of an atomic bomb. Roosevelt did not even know such a thing was possible and even nuclear scientists themselves were not of one mind. He was alerted to the possibility by a letter from Albert Einstein, drafted by Szilard and literally delivered by Teller to be signed by Einstein at his summer residence on Long Island. (Szilard lacked an operator's license.) This critical event took place at the end of July 1939, and was by no means the end of the story. The president was willing to proceed but reluctantly. Acting on the urging of Einstein, Roosevelt appointed an Advisory Committee on Uranium in the summer of 1939 and in June 1940 issued an executive order creating the National Defense Research Committee, which one year later become part of a new and more comprehensive Office of Scientific Research and Development. This would never have happened if it were not for the initiative of two college presidents with scientific credentials, James B. Conant of Harvard and Karl (brother of Arthur) Compton of MIT, along with Frank B. Jewett, president of both the National Academy of Sciences and Bell Telephone Laboratories, and Vannevar Bush, an educator and political insider. Thus began the official entanglement of science and government. It took leaders of the scientific community to push for the establishment of an administrative framework. As scientists they became proactive because they believed in the feasibility of using uranium fission to make a bomb of enormous destruction. But these were also individuals who were motivated by an uncommon sense of moral responsibility. They were not going to sit idly by and watch the world be overrun by dictators.

The Visionary Scientist

More than any other scientist Niels Bohr anticipated the necessity for a new framework for the world dropped into an atomic age. His constant refrain was, "We are in a completely new situation that cannot be resolved by war," and he took this refrain to Los Alamos, to President Roosevelt, and Prime Minister Winston Churchill. Bohr was our first contemporary visionary scientist. In December 1943, nineteen months before the Trinity test of 16 July 1945, and again in January 1944, Bohr visited Los Alamos. His visits included a discussion of technical matters but Bohr, who was living in Sweden in the autumn of 1943 after escaping from Nazi-occupied Denmark, was not privileged to classified information. As the grip of war widened, Bohr increasingly undertook the prophetic task of opening a new horizon on a world moving toward mutual destruction. As the father of atomic fission, Bohr was one of the first to understand that an atomic bomb was not like any other bomb or any other weapon of destruction. It would be a weapon that any nation with sufficient resources could build and would build. Nuclear weapons would spread and no one would be able to win, because no nation would be able to defend itself. What Bohr also saw with unusual clarity was how this unprecedented threat could be an unprecedented opportunity. If all nations were equally threatened with thermonuclear destruction, all nations would be motivated toward international control and regulation. In the first part of 1944 Bohr tried to convince Churchill, then Roosevelt, to begin arms-control discussions with Stalin before an atomic bomb was used. He reasoned that if Stalin could witness a spirit of openness in matters of science, then perhaps he also could in the matter of weapons. In June 1945 Compton, Fermi, Lawrence, and Oppenheimer put before Colonel Stimson, the secretary of war, the suggestion that in addition to Britain, Russia, France, and China be advised and consulted about the use of an atomic bomb with the hope that of laying a new foundation for international cooperation.[12]

For various political reasons it wasn't to be, but it is noteworthy that prominent and informed scientists stepped forward with an alternative worldview. At this juncture both Bohr and Oppenheimer are usually considered politically naive, and both readily confessed they were neither in a position to be informed nor knowledgeable about such matters. As other scientists became acquainted with Bohr's vision—principally through Oppenheimer—this Achilles' heel was discussed at depth. They may have been politically uninformed but not naive. Listen to the premise of the Franck Report of 11 June 1945: "Given mutual trust and willingness on all sides to give up a certain part of their sovereign rights, by admitting international control of certain phases of national economy. . . ." (A. Smith, 569). The latter was referring to the limitation of raw materials. The report continues by saying, "One thing is clear: any international agreement on prevention of nuclear armaments must be backed by actual land efficient controls" (A. Smith 570). The critical issue, then as now, is how to engender mutual trust to the level that states would be willing to sacrifice some of their sovereign rights. What actually happened at Potsdam was entirely the opposite. On 24 July 1945, Truman relates, "'I casually mentioned to Stalin that we had a new weapon of unusual destructive force. The Russian premier showed no special interest. All he said was that he was glad to hear it and hoped we would make 'good use of it against the Japanese.'"[13] Bohr was justifiably concerned that a window of opportunity was closing. The Yalta Conference in February 1945 proved to be symptomatic. On 12 April 1945, Roosevelt died. Truman was of the mind that it was too late for the initial exercise in trust building—a view held by Churchill. Bohr however did not give up. He continued to plant seeds turning to the United Nations just as it was being organized. In an "Open Letter to the United Nations," he proposed once again the hope that the progress of science might initiate a new era of cooperation between nations.

The initial test bans and subsequent missile treaties eventually slowed the arms race. The even more recent reduction of atomic weapons by America and Russia are predicated upon mutual trust coupled with checks and balances. How quick we are to conclude that the end of World War II was not the historical moment for a spirit of openness and trust. The core of Bohr-Oppenheimer's vision cannot be so easily dismissed. The vision held out to us was a world of increasing openness between societies beginning with treating atomic energy as an international problem. In an era of globalization, a spirit of openness makes eminent good sense. Will scientists, who depend on the free and open exchange of research, lead the way or will they fall prey to the other dynamic of globalization—selling knowledge for what the market will bear?

Oppenheimer's farewell speech returns again and again to the hope that the existence of such a massive means of destruction would compel a "new spirit of international affairs."

> If atomic energy is to be treated as an international problem, as I think it must be, if it is to be treated on the basis of an international responsibility and an international common concern, the problems of secrecy are also international problems. (*Letters and Recollections*, 321)

In the years to follow, Oppenheimer would persistently and untiringly give this vision a voice.

> It is a new field, in which the role of science has been so great that it is to my mind hardly thinkable that the international traditions of science, and the fraternity of scientists, should not play a constructive part. It is a new field, in which just the novelty and the special characteristics of the technical operations should enable one to establish a community of interest which might almost be regarded as a pilot plant for a new type of international collaboration. (*Letters and Recollections*, 319–20)

As the Cold War deepened, issues of secrecy and freedom from political constraints intensified. In both Germany and Japan, scientists had no choice but working for the interests of the government. The Manhattan Project was another model, one that was unique. At Los Alamos, Chicago, and Oak Ridge, scientists had been invited by other scientists, perhaps recruited is more accurate, to participate in creating a new weapon of mass destruction. Some chose not to involve themselves. At their respective labs the scientists governed themselves but with the one proviso that what they learned was to be kept secret. The role of the military, in the person of Gen. Leslie R. Groves, was not to tell scientists how to do science but to ensure that what they discovered would be available to the military, and there was no suggestion that President Truman alone would decide how the bomb would be employed. Nevertheless, the scientists of the Manhattan Project tactfully and openly declared their independence. Oppenheimer was more than a little sensitive to the inherent tension between military procedures and the empirical tradition of openness.

> There has been a lot of talk about the evil of secrecy, of concealment, of control, of security.... I think that the talk has been justified, and that the almost unanimous resistance of scientists to the imposition of control and secrecy is a justified position, but I think that the reason for it may lie a little deeper. I think that it comes from the fact that secrecy strikes at the very root of what science is, and what it is for. It is not possible to be a scientist unless you believe that it is good to learn. (*Letters and Recollections*, 317)

What might have been tolerated while the war raged on was fodder for heated discussions as soon as the outcome was decided. Within days after Hiroshima and just as scientists from the three Manhattan Project sites were about to issue nearly identical statements of principles and purpose regarding the need to establish a system of international control that would avoid an atomic arms race, President Truman issued a directive forbidding any disclosures without his personal permission. Oppenheimer was not alone in regarding the issue of secrecy and control as cutting into an even more critical question.

> But what is surely the thing which must have troubled you, and which troubled me, in the official statements was the insistent note of unilateral responsibility for handling of atomic weapons. However good the motives of this country are—I am not going to argue with the President's description of what the motives and the aims are—we are 140 million people, and there are two billion people living on

earth. We must understand that whatever our commitments to our own views and idea, and however confident we are that in the course of time they will tend to prevail, our absolute—our completely absolute—commitment to them, in denial of the views and ideas of other people, cannot be the basis of any kind of agreement. (*Letters and Recollections*, 324)

Oppenheimer had given considerable thought to the question whether there is something in the methodology of science itself, or in the spirit of science, that could justify the intrusion of science into other domains, such as politics and philosophy. He begins by professing that for himself, and like-minded colleagues, scientists do not make very good philosopher-kings. "It [the study of physics] almost never makes fit philosophers—so rarely that they must be counted as exceptions" (*Open Mind*, 92). As Oppenheimer pursues the question, he is more positive. He specifies several qualities that are important when we take up "the affairs of men." Science demonstrates a critical and open mind, that is, a willingness to examine questions impartially, to weigh the relevant evidence, and to even welcome the detection of error. He speaks of the importance of error, as one would expect of a scientist, and also connects error with the open mind. "In physics the worker learns the possibility of error very early. He learns that there are ways to correct his mistakes; he learns the futility of trying to conceal them. For it is not a field in which error awaits death and subsequent generations for verdict—the next issue of the journals will take care of it" (*Open Mind*, 93).

Oppenheimer added another perspective in his vision of science as a model for the world. The spirit of science teaches us the benefits of a freedom of inquiry as it operates independent of authority. "In the place of authority in science," Oppenheimer writes, "we have and we need to have only the consensus of informed opinion" (*Open Mind*, 115). By example, then, scientists promote a conducive attitude by the reliance on persuasion and their dedication to communicate evidence in such a way that any interested person can understand and evaluate. Since 1945 there has been no backing off from the principle of openness. Chet Raymo writes in his weekly science column in the *Boston Globe*: "There is no such thing as American science or Chinese science, Buddhist science or Islamic science, capitalist science or socialist science" (5 November 2002). In other words, the empirical model of consensus building is laudatory behavior for politicians and generals. Bohr and Oppenheimer lived their lives as a testimony to their conviction that a window of opportunity had opened to write a covenant with implications for "the affairs of men."

The issue of secrecy and sharing is once again front and center as the Pentagon moves to implement the administration's policy of "Full Spectrum Dominance," the military strategy that we must dominate space before they do. The counterargument says that by sharing our technology the military playing field is leveled and no nation feels compelled to escalate or enter the arms race. When all nations feel secure, then no one nation must race ahead. If our nation acts unilaterally by testing and arming weapons in space, we know for certain what will happen because we know the nature of technology is to never stand still. Jack Hitt sees a logic behind the decision by our government to allow open access to the Global Positioning System (GPS) of satellites to download maps with an accuracy of one meter even when GPS is also a cornerstone of our precision-guided missile system. Why did the Pentagon open it up to the public in 2001? Hitt believes the logic goes like this: If everyone were permitted to use the system, no one would feel compelled to launch a competing system. And no one has and everyone has become dependent upon GPS for cell phones and a host of other location gadgets. By sharing GPS and allowing it to become ubiquitous internationally, "any country that damaged it would provoke a global fury." Of course there are ways our military can encrypt messages and block a belligerent nation's access to GPS.[14] Anyone with a sense of history knows it is repeating itself. The reason history repeats itself is no mystery. The same human nature persists through time and unfortunately it chooses to dominate rather than uplift everyone at the same time.

Knowledge Is a Good Thing

The oxygen feeding our faith in technological progress is the premise that knowledge is intrinsically good. This was the message America broadcast from the moon: "One small step for man, a giant step for mankind." We proceed as if scientists are miners who bring to the surface nuggets of knowledge, putting aside the question whether these are pure nuggets of gold. In their blood and in their discipline, it is their nature to believe knowledge is a good thing. In his farewell address Oppenheimer spoke for the fraternity of scientists.

> But when you come right down to it the reason we did this job [building the atomic bomb] is because it was an organic necessity. If you are a scientist you cannot stop such a thing. If you are a scientist you believe that it is *good* to find out how the

world works; that it is *good* to find out what the realities are; that it is *good* to turn over to mankind at large the greatest possible power to control the world and to deal with it according to its lights and its values.

It is not possible to be a scientist unless you believe that it is *good* to learn . . . unless you think that it is of the highest value to share your knowledge, to share it with everyone that is interested. (*Letters and Recollections*, 317, emphasis added)

The source of scientific optimism comes from the belief that pure knowledge is good and by sharing it that good will be enlarged. For the moment let us put aside the difficulties attached to the phrase "pure knowledge" and focus on knowledge as something inherently good. This conviction does not stand alone but is sublimely connected with several other core values, such as the physical universe is comprehensible and therefore describable, reason overcomes superstition, scientific knowledge is apolitical, knowledge will lead to progress. Oppenheimer believed with all his heart that scientific knowledge is intrinsically good. It is not merely neutral but good. He continued in the next sentence.

And, therefore, I think that this resistance which we feel and see all around us to anything which is an attempt to treat science of the future as though it were rather a dangerous thing, a thing that must be watched and managed, is resisted not because of its inconvenience—I think we are in a position where we must be willing to take any inconvenience—but resisted because it is based on a philosophy incompatible with that by which we live, and have learned to live in the past. (*Letters and Recollections*, 317–18).

Time and time again this optimism becomes expressed in the form of two confidences: (1) the doing of science is an organic necessity and (2) it is inherently good because knowledge is intrinsically good. As the embodiment of a new social awareness among scientists, Oppenheimer faced squarely the tension between scientific knowledge and its application, between his participation in making it possible for nations to wage a new kind of horrific war and the promise of a new world order. A world that endured Hitler and Stalin required internationally monitored inspections. Oppenheimer understood this to be a political fact but it did not shake his confidence that pure science must be pursued (an organic necessity) and that ultimately it will lead to the good. It was an idealism that would soon be tested by a new set of facts: globalization, science as big business, the commercial exploitation of discoveries, the diminishing concern for the common good. If it is true that science will reach for the next technologically sweet thing, then it is imperative that knowledge be intrinsically good.

But not all scientific knowledge is the same. Einstein's remarkable insight that $E=mc^2$ is different from the discovery of the DNA. The difference is partly physics versus biology, the inanimate versus something very personal. Both discoveries are about fundamental knowledge but no one thinks of trying to patent Einstein's revelation. The nature of the pursuit tells us something important. Everything about the Human Genome Project reeks of patents, profits, and market shares. Knowledge of our DNA is the key and every biologist understood this from the beginning. It has proven to be a great motivator: get your hands on the key and you can open an unlimited number of doors. The Senate and House hearings of 1989 and 1990 provoked heated discussions about national interests and international justice, that is, how to ensure that those who funded the research would receive their fair share of the benefits.[15] It is difficult to imagine a similar scenario for Einstein's formula even if it had taken place in a similar climate, because not all scientific knowledge stirs the same motivation. By its very inherent nature, some knowledge is lethal and other curative, some incendiary and other temperate, some innocuous and other toxic, and most if not all scientific knowledge is a mixture of both good and evil.

Consider another kind of knowledge. Computer-assisted geographic information, or "geographic information systems (GIS)," has come a long way. In the age of sailing ships geographers were highly respected but once a reliable system of navigation and maps were in place, they fell into near obscurity. "The newest road to fame and fortune is mapping the world," writes *Wall Street* reporter Lee Gomes. "You can taunt physicists or make fun of chemists but don't mess around with geographers." Their smart maps can show rare big-leaf mahogany trees in South America, endangered chimpanzees in West Africa, migration patterns of almost anything, and Saddam Hussein's palaces.[16] Global information systems may be just another tool in the information age and as valuable as computer spreadsheets or atomic fission, but is it objective or neutral? Some information more than other forms cries out to be co-opted. A cartographer may say she is only interested in producing an accurate map, but what she maps depends on who is paying her, where the information finally resides, and what details are included or excluded. These are hardly disinterested questions. Even if we agree with Steven Weinberg's argument that scientific knowledge in its mature form is culture free and permanent, we have not settled the question whether fundamental truth about the nature of the universe is inherently good.[17] It cannot be neutral and good at the same time. And why is knowledge inherently good and not inherently evil? Or is it both, tilted in various degrees in one direction or the other? Let's agree, at least, that knowledge possesses the *potential* for good or evil.

Scientific knowledge has this peculiar characteristic: it has the explosive potential for both good and evil. Understanding the physics of the atom resulted in nuclear reactors and nuclear bombs. The same knowledge used to fly you to a family reunion was used to firebomb Tokyo, killing more than a million Japanese and more than both atomic bombs.[18] Dual uses constitute an old quandary but in today's world it is intrusive and ubiquitous. The Food and Drug Administration has cleared the way for a Florida company to market implantable chips providing easy access to an individual's medical records. Applied Digital Solutions claims its devices could save lives and limit harm from errors in medical treatment. Because the chip does not contain any records and does not emit a signal—Applied Digital's handheld radio scanner reads a code number that grants access to the records—there is no danger that it could be used as a tracking device. But the path from a passive chip to an active tag is straight and broad, and the ramifications for mischief are endless.[19]

Is this a technology deserving the label "good" or "evil?" Not exactly, but neither is it neutral. And in the same way good and evil adhere to both the technology of a gun and the human who holds it, sin will find a way to tilt the balance.

Dateline *Wall Street Journal*, 6 May 2002
How Hunch May Have Hindered the Nuclear Ambitions of Iran

A successful inventor, he [Frank Behlke] has designed such things as a camper bus with a drive-in garage for his Ferrari as well as a high voltage switch that can be used for disintegrating kidney stones or triggering a nuclear explosion. He had never sold more than two of the switches in a year until recently when his company had shipped a batch of 44. But as he sat in his office that night, rummaging through files, his doubts about the way his company had handled the sale only increased. What Mr. Behlke didn't know was that he had just sent enough switches to detonate a nuclear bomb to two businessmen with ties to Iran (David Crawford, A1).

Autonomous but Beholden

Entering the nuclear age had a radical impact on the way scientists would relate to the powers and authorities of government. Writing in the second issue of the *Bulletin of the Atomic Scientists*, Eugene Rabinowitch, one of the journal's creators, stated succinctly what had changed: "The revolutionary fact of the present situation is that military have ceased to be experts on security."[20] The context of the statement was one of the many amendments to the McMahon bill and the extent to which the military would share control with the Atomic Energy Commission. Whatever role the military would have—as a liaison committee or as sitting members on the committee—they were no longer the experts and in matters of atomic fission that was significant. As one of its primary tasks during the first seven months of 1946, the recently formed Federation of Atomic Scientists undertook a campaign to support legislation favoring civilian oversight. They favored the McMahon bill over the May-Johnson bill because the latter had loopholes and fuzziness around the role of the military and its emphasis upon secrecy. Scientists of the Manhattan Project understood from the beginning that their research would be classified and the "property" of the U.S. government. It was a condition they could live with during the war but once they observed politicians formulating national and foreign policy, they asserted their independence and right to become politically active. They had no idea what was to come: a new kind of cold war coupled with the hysteria of McCarthyism. Both their political and moral will were tested again and again: the wisdom of a crash program for an H-bomb, issues relating to security and declassification, passport and visa restrictions, technical aid to underdeveloped countries, and defending members of their profession—the most celebrated being Oppenheimer himself in 1954.[21] The mood of the nation swung from adulation to a peak of anti-scientific feelings in 1955. Along the way came the salutary feelings of disenchantment with public affairs and the realization that this was not what scientists do naturally. The shine may have been off the apple, but the parties to a new contractual agreement knew with certainty it would be impossible to return to simpler days. The scientific community and the politicians had no choice but to work through a difficult situation without sacrificing what mattered most to each and to both.

The contract being written went something like this. Science would agree to a level of secrecy and classification as long as the restrictions were not overly stringent and unreasonable and did not impinge upon their work as scientists. As the two bills were debated and amended, the decisive distinction was made between basic or technical information against military application with the thought that only the latter would be classified. The distinction made its way into the McMahon bill, and the Atomic Energy Commission was entrusted with oversight of restricted data, defined as "all data concerning the manufacture or utilization of atomic weapons, the production of fissionable material, or the use of fissionable material in the production of power" (A. Smith, 410). In the best of all worlds, scientists would be free to do basic research and civilian authorities, in liaison with the military, would decide on the application. It proved to be a model that became increasingly difficult to sustain because technical information so readily becomes militarily valuable and that is the reason why technical information is quickly classified. Scientists, on the other hand, continued to publish and otherwise disseminate what they considered to be basic empirical information—information that is objective in nature, verifiable by a scientist in any country, and belonging to the human commonwealth.

Scientists have argued persistently that secrecy stifles scientific progress. Thus, Michael Polanyi expresses a common sentiment among scientists:

> The pursuit of science can be organized . . . in no other manner than by granting complete independence to all mature scientists. They will then distribute themselves over the whole field of possible discoveries, each applying his own special ability to the task that appears most profitable to him. The function of public authorities is not to plan research, but to only provide opportunities for its pursuit. (quoted from Greenberg, *The Politics of Pure Science*, 5)

The reality of postwar science is something else. While this example from a FAS press release in 1946 is outdated, it nevertheless exposes the myth of pure science. Suppose that the M1 rifle had involved fundamental scientific discoveries in metallurgy. Would it be proper to keep the research secret if the metal were of such a new and marvelous nature that it would be revolutionary if used in airplanes and motorcars? Would the military be justified in insisting that this metal could be used for guns but not for automobiles?[22] During the subsequent years we have been given a better appreciation of how basic research is driven by its application. It is not simply a matter that those who fund scientific projects influence the research from the beginning. Most often research and development are integrally one because discovery is dependent upon testing and testing requires more research. Polanyi speaks of the ideal and the ideal is dependent upon a linear model where technology is the offspring of basic research. Whether it is the invention of the M1 rifle, the development of radar, or research conducted for the cancer-fighting drug Velcade, the pursuit of pure science independent of its profit or use is a longstanding myth. Science is undoubtedly impeded by secrecy, but the need to produce something useful has driven scientific discoveries from the beginning and secrecy has been part of the process. A threshold had been crossed, though, because the level of secrecy and its importance had become a matter of life and death for everyone.

In 1946 the reality of independent but beholden was only beginning to sink in. From hindsight we recognize how complex everything has become, but we should not overlook the fundamental insight that scientific research is always influenced by a particular historical and cultural context. Scientists do not want to be beholden to anyone except to their ideal of free pursuit of knowledge for the good of humanity, but there is no escaping the age-old question: Who will pay the bills? The Manhattan Project was a military operation funded by the government. The money flowed through many channels but the military was the ultimate paymaster. As those scientists pursued their careers in new settings and under new auspices, how would they maintain their ideals and still be paid? Nothing sobered them faster than their foray into politics. They soon learned their obligations to the commonweal included justifying what they were doing and what they proposed to do. As for those putting up the money, they too were caught in conflicting interests and compromises.

Postmortem

Undoubtedly something new transpired at the end of the Second World War between science, government, and the public. The parties involved did not use the language of contract or covenant but an agreement had been struck between science and government with the public as the intended beneficiary. At least two authorities describe this contract as one of mutual need. From her unique advantage point as assistant editor of the *Bulletin of the Atomic Scientists* from 1946 to 1948, Alice Smith concludes that "science and government have been drawn together far more by mutual need—for technical advise, on the one hand, and for research money, on the other—than because scientists have demanded a voice in determination of policy" (*Peril and a Hope*, 532). As a journalist who has covered the politics of science for some forty years, Daniel S. Greenberg affirms the motivation of mutual need but derides scientists for their lack of ethical concern and their withdrawal from public affairs and political participation except when it served their own interests. "The impression of a scientific presence in politics is a leftover from the Cold War days when scientists were summoned to the high councils of government to provide advice on the creation and control of new weapons" (*Science, Money, and Politics*, 4–5). The next chapter will examine this dynamic in greater detail, but let me first draw together some conclusions concerning the implied contract born in the idealistic passion of a new window of opportunity, tried and tested during the Cold War, found wanting as globalization took hold and as the biological sciences moved to the fore. This can be done by evaluating each one of the original tenets.

Self-conscious scientists of the postwar era would no longer allow themselves to be cloistered in ivory towers of academia with the luxury of "feeling that this was really the great time of their lives" (Bethe). By their own creativity and diligence they had been thrown into an arena of high expectation. What they did and what they promised constituted headline news. They quickly understood that much was expected of them and much was dependent upon their rocket-science minds. The circumstances of war, hot and cold, threw into sharp relief their decision to work for the government and to contribute their unique talent for military purposes, or to walk away from it. What had changed was the awareness that what they did mattered and it mattered greatly.

How could they possibly shun their responsibility, which extended far beyond the classroom and peer review? They had to ask themselves if they could be socially responsible without being compromised. On the other side of the implied agreement, elected officials asked how they could give what scientists demanded—autonomy to pursue scientific truths without interference—and require accountability. Scientists were not asking for a free ride but the right to conduct science the only way they knew how: to be trusted to do the right thing. And for this reason the scientific community banded together and spoke with one voice whenever its integrity was questioned. In part, because scientists speak the same language worldwide and because empirical truths are not the intellectual property of one nation, their social responsibility extends to all of humanity. This has been their mandate since Bacon called them to "the conquest of nature for the relief of man's estate."[23] For Bacon there is a direct link between knowledge gained by a scientific methodology and the common good, and this meant the conquest and mastery of nature for the benefit of humankind.

We are reminded of another historical moment when early in the twentieth century nuclear physics was coming into its own and Werner Heisenberg, Alfred North Whitehead, and Bertrand Russell felt compelled to explore the wider philosophical ramifications of theoretical physics. But the moment had come to do more than think. Atomic physics came of age when terrifying weapons of mass destruction defined what it meant to be a superpower. Bohr, Oppenheimer, and Einstein, among others of their generation, became *visionaries* because their understanding of ethics went beyond the personal to the global. Nevertheless, taking on the role of philosopher or prophet does not seem to come easily for scientists. When Percy Bridgman, the respected Harvard physicist who had just been awarded the Noble Prize in physics, presented his view on these matters in a lecture titled "Scientists and Social Responsibility," he limited responsibility to what the individual scientist does. Responding and concurring with Bridgman, I. I. Rabi defined their responsibility as "to do good, sound, honest science and to publish the results as clearly and objectively as we know how."[24] This is the work of science and it has changed little over the centuries, and so it is almost with a certain longing that we remember a time when genius saw the bigger picture. This was a social responsibility emboldened by a vision of what the world could be, and resolutely given teeth by seeking out heads of states and formulating political strategies. They had this in common with the Old Testament prophets: to forewarn and hope at the same time.

And if there was a philosophical belief, a deep-seated conviction, pushing them forward into places they had not gone before, it was the pursuit of truth because *truth is a good thing*. Unlike the affairs of politics, the truth they pursued was not the result of messy compromises. The nature of the universe just *is* and therefore it can be methodologically described in an objective manner. (While considerable criticism has been heap upon this attitude, it still serves to contrast empiricism with other methodologies.) It is easier to be socially responsible, even visionary, when you believe knowledge of the universe is inherently good. To their consternation, however, scientists found themselves in the company of those who saw objective truths as bargaining chips and considered the inherently good to be a matter of perception.

The defining issue of this consensual agreement was how to balance science's *autonomy* with the public's need for some form of *accountability*. Scientists understood themselves to be *beholden* to their own conscience, to the public at large (the commonwealth), and the good of the public (the commonweal). They were also slowly but surely understanding the difficulties and conflicts of serving more than one master. With the rising level of expectations and the reality of undertaking large-scale projects, it became increasingly advisable to earn a doctorate, find a suitable teaching position and do nothing else. In "the good old days" the naturalist was the amateur or the artisan who dabbled in science for the joy of it.[25] What had changed by the end of the World War II was the level of self-consciousness due to the intensity and gravity of the knowledge. The truth that knowledge is power had not gone unnoticed by scientists of any age—after all, it was the only leverage they possessed—but holding the key to knowledge that no one dared to ignore meant that for the first time science was granted the status of "partner."[26]

In 1945 Vannevar Bush proposed a contractual agreement whereby the federal government would assume fiscal responsibility for postwar science, and in return science would provide the technology to keep us safe, healthy, and economically prosperous. Bush was the consummate scientist-politician, fully at home at the Pentagon or up on the Hill. During and after the war he served as the president of the Carnegie Institute in Washington, D.C., one of the most respected non-academic research organizations in the country. President Roosevelt commissioned a report and Bush delivered it to Truman in July 1945, a little more than a month before the surrender of Japan. *Science: The Endless Frontier* represents the mature form of the contract between science and the commonwealth. Bush believed basic research was the key to everything. From it would flow the technical applications necessary for the nation's security and prosperity. In return for a continual flow of scientific discoveries, scientists would be granted "complete independence and freedom." The idealism behind Bush's blueprint for the future surfaces in the assumptions. First, "the scientist doing basic research may not be interested in the practical application of his work." Second, there would need to be "a wall of separation consisting of private citizens not otherwise connected with government." As each of the key organizational pieces fell into place—the Atomic Energy Commission and the Department of Energy (both direct descendants of the Manhattan Project), the National Aeronautics and Space Administration, the National Institute of Health, and the National Science Foundation—the idealism of separating matters civilian from matters military was exposed. In the end, Bush's linear model of basic research leading to application could not withstand the onslaught of complexities science and society were to experience. As the wall of separation came down and research and application merged, the common good became one of the compromises aspiring scientists would face.

No contract will be executed unless both parties enjoy a benefit and are willing to surrender something in order to receive that benefit. Science traded a degree of autonomy for a constant stream of funding, the opportunity to work on cutting-edge technology for a level of secrecy. It accepted, sometimes willingly and sometimes reluctantly, a modicum of accountability to generals, politicians, and bureaucrats. The commonwealth gave science the benefit of the doubt. Universities and industries opened their doors to a new level of cross-fertilization, and together they would share in the profits and rewards of turning knowledge into something good. But I am getting ahead of myself for this is the direction science was headed by the end of the Cold War. The conclusion I want to press here is the potential for this original, baseline agreement to implode because of inherent and unresolved contradictions. This is the justification for a conclusion titled "Postmortem."

To speak of the self-conscious scientist implies a global awareness joined with a deeper sense of responsibility. In a remarkable passage Oppenheimer verbalized the obligation to seek a truth broader than discovering the laws of the universe.

> These are things [truths of a broader scope] that have rather a normative or a *thematic* quality. They assert the connectedness of things . . . the priority of things; and without them there would be no science, without them there would be no order in human life. But they do not have this possibility of being tested by reference to nature by an experimental method, nor do they follow from such things by the rigorous application of logic or its derivative, the various forms of mathematics. . . . One does not need to insist that the poet speaks the truth; he does sometimes; most of the time he is doing something equally, perhaps more important. He speaks meanings, and he speaks order, and this *thematic*, as opposed to *proposition*, discourse is the typical function of the public section of our lives. (*Some Reflections on Science and Culture*, 11–12; emphasis added)

Bohr and Oppenheimer were extraordinary human beings because they kept asking questions about the consequences of their research. We easily overlook the courage it took to be a public representative advocating for the value of thematic truth and its place in the marketplace of public discourse, because we forget that the likes of Bertrand Russell and A. J. Ayer ridiculed anyone who mingled factual truth with poetic meanings.

How can you be responsible for what you do unless you anticipate what might happen, both good and bad? You can, of course, wait until the shoe drops and try to pick up the pieces. The prophet belongs to those with foresight. The other lesson that wants to knock some sense into us is the episodic or hard-to-sustain character of the prophetic. We took notice how difficult it was for individual scientists, not to mention the scientific community, to sustain a commitment to issues of peace and justice. I assert here and defend later the proposition that scientists are not equipped to be the moral conscience of a nation. A sustained commitment to matters of justice requiring political action requires a sustaining community of individuals dedicated to that singular purpose. One thinks of the "Union of Concerned Scientists" and "Doctors without Borders" but surely this is the exception not the rule. Making a more generalized assessment from his extended experience as editor of *Science & Government Report*, Greenberg observes the reluctance by scientists to be politically engaged except when there is some direct benefit to themselves.[27] As knowledge too dangerous to ignore becomes knowledge too good not to exploit, the more difficult it becomes to be both visionary and socially committed. It is far more tempting to mirror the prevailing culture and find refuge in patent and copyright law, contractual agreements, and ethics by committee.

From the Christian perspective a connection exists between self-awareness and sin, but in a peculiar way. A confession of sin requires a mature level of self-awareness, but self-awareness is not sufficient (the necessary but not sufficient argument). Otherwise, as we become more self-aware we would become less sinful. But this is wrong on two accounts. First, when Christians confess their sinful condition they acknowledge the limits of self-awareness. They are cognizant that sin deceives so that when they think they are blameless, they do not know the depth of sin that dwells within. Second, our sinful nature is not something we "manage" or overcome for that would mean that we could overcome every temptation once we became aware of it. Our experience of sin is very different. Knowing that we are tempted and knowing the evil we do not want to do is no assurance we will the right thing.

This little theological excursus is important because is sharpens the difference between hindsight and foresight. Oppenheimer was transformed by Los Alamos; he and many others became exemplars of the socially responsible scientists. What more could be asked of them? Oppenheimer the Jew not only expressed regret but also made what sounded like a Christian confession of sinfulness. Richard Feynman, who was a young junior scientist at Los Alamos, made a similar reflection in a 1981 BBC television program.

> But what I did—immorally I would say—was to *not remember* the reason that I said I was doing it [in defense of my country and before the Germans did it], so that when the reason changed, because Germany was defeated, not the singlest [sic] thought came to my mind at all about that, that meant now that I have to reconsider why I am continuing to do this. I simply didn't think, okay? (*The Pleasure of Finding Things Out*, 9–10; emphasis added)

What is missing from this picture is an understanding of sin and evil that is *already in place*—a teaching or doctrine, if you like, with a two-thousand-year history (longer if you include the Jewish understanding). Hindsight is not without value but it comes after the fact, and in an era of daily announcements of some promising advancement, hindsight will not serve us very well (it's too late and too little). When scientists are working behind closed doors, when they alone know the potential of their research, they bear the primary responsibility for what they are doing. When the barn door is open and the horse is out, the kind of ethical response that is possible is quite different. Senior statesman in the scientific community, Freeman Dyson chides the scientific establishment to begin the new century with a new beginning where technology is guided by ethics. "Too much of technology," he writes, "is making toys for the rich. Ethics can push technology in a new direction, away from toys for the rich and toward necessities for the poor" (*The Sun, the Genome, and the Internet*, 61). What would it take, I ask, to reverse an entrenched historical pattern? Dyson verbalizes a worthy sentiment but it isn't going to happen.

What might have transpired if scientists of the Manhattan Project began each morning with songs of gratitude and a confession of sin? Maybe the Bomb would have been developed and dropped as it was, maybe it was the right thing to do, but across the years and stepping into an era of great scientific promise we can at least hope that those who bear the greatest responsibility for life and death will be self-aware to the point of knowing humans do the evil they do not intend. Both Oppenheimer and Feynman spoke of a deadly forgetfulness. Jews of the Holocaust speak of it too. The place to start is with the self-awareness of who we have been and still are. And knowing that we cannot trust ourselves to overcome evil, rely less on knowledge of immediate relevance and more on archetypal truths of our creatureliness and finitude.

Moral visionaries are those who take political risks. I wonder how the public would react if scientists around the world, or from just one nation or one scientific project, mounted a work stoppage for one day to protest the research and development of weapons that kill. I think they would be surprised by the support they would receive. Religion leaders, labor unions, mothers, students would join them. On 13 February 2003, the inside lead story of the *Boston Globe* reported that India had fired a supersonic cruise missile capable of hitting major cities in Pakistan. India had developed the missile with Russia's help. Pakistan had similarly conducted a series of missile tests in recent months, most likely with the help of China and North Korea. I ponder the motives of the scientists who make all this possible—a mixed bag, no doubt. A little patriotism, a paycheck, pressure from "on high," curiosity to see if it would work, pride of the accomplishment, and rationalization that it was the right thing to do. But are they being socially responsible, political engaged, and motivated by a vision of the world as it should be?

The conflicted disposition of the first contract is evident in the inherent tension within science when it wants to influence public opinion but does not want to be distracted by political tactics. The Manhattan Project paved the way for greater participation in worldly matters. Because their technological information had become indispensable, scientists were quickly incorporated into the fabric of government. They became politically valuable. But then the inevitable happened (perhaps inevitable is not totally accurate but it suggests the problem at hand). They disengaged. They returned to the laboratory, the lecture hall, and their research. They became disenchanted when senators, congressmen, and presidents asking for their counsel and then told to get out of the way. Why was their foray into politics a historical anomaly rather than a sustained commitment? Were the likes of Bohr, Oppenheimer, Compton, and Bush the exception to the rule? Scientists should not be singled out for criticism, because any sustained effort on behalf of the common good is uncommon. There are, nevertheless, further considerations to keep in mind. Scientists guard their independence for good reasons. Sit-ins, picket lines, and professional lobbyists are not their primary concerns. They want to be left alone to think deep thoughts and publish their experiments. They believe that no one will take their recommendations seriously if they compromise the neutrality of their research by tainting it with partisan politics. And because they are without political power (no political constituency), counsel is usually all they have to offer.

Having seen it all, Victor Weisskopf, writing in the a 1969 issue of *Physics Today*, reminded his colleagues of the multilateral character of science in its relation to society. In most instances the scientist cannot avoid being drawn into the decision-making process regarding the applications of science. "In facing such problems and dilemmas," Weisskopf forewarns, "will miss the sense of agreement that prevails in scientific discussions, where there is an unspoken understanding of the criteria of truth and falsehood even in the most heated controversies."[28] Weisskopf did not hide behind a cloak of neutrality or patriotism. Nor did he separate his life into different roles, one as citizen and one as scientist. In this he was following in the footsteps of Niels Bohr who declined the safety of neutrality and carried his vision first to the scientists at Los Alamos and then face to face with President Roosevelt and Prime Minister Churchill. Oppenheimer made the deliberate choice to sacrifice his love of research in order to embark on a career of scientist with a principled agenda. Oppenheimer was acting upon a personal obligation every scientist should have—a moral obligation no less "to see to it that the uses that society makes of scientific discoveries are beneficent."[29] More recently, the story is told of Linus Pauling who had been invited to a reception for American Nobel winners by President John F. Kennedy in 1962. Pauling took this opportunity to demonstrate outside the White House to protest U.S. atmospheric nuclear tests. Then in the evening at the White House reception Pauling went through the receiving line and approached the President and Mrs. Kennedy; Kennedy turned to him and said, "Dr. Pauling, I understand you've been around here earlier today." The most remarkable story is that of Andrei Sakharov, who has the unlikely distinction of being both the father of Russia's H-bomb and recipient of the Nobel Peace Prize in 1975.[30] Like the other visionaries, Sakharov's vision expanded from individual human rights to encompass the freedom and self-determination for people in every nation.

But scientists have also made their commitment to the commonweal unnecessarily difficult. Because science presupposes an ontological world that is neutral and a methodology that is objective, the logical conclusion is to believe scientists deal with knowledge that is objective, because the data they assemble comes from a neutral universe. But the neutrality of matter and that of the observer are not the same, since matter needs an interpreter and this interpreter invariably sees what he sees for a reason. And what moves data off the page and into the realm of application is political if only because it requires a decision to spend some amount of a limited human resources on a particular question. The more consistent conclusion is to recognize knowledge to be inherently predisposed toward good or evil and therefore readily politicized.

So much depends upon the premise that knowledge is inherently good. It is a natural assumption when looking at the myriad of benefits we enjoy, the pain we are spared, the health and longevity extended to us, the fundamental knowledge of the earth and the universe we acquire. But the good that science pursues requires a more basic question: What is the historical, empirical, or philosophical basis for the premise that knowledge is intrinsically good? Science is hard pressed to provide sufficient evidence or a coherent argument. On the contrary, science has backed itself into an untenable position. Science cannot presume that knowledge of the universe is good when the world itself is without purpose and value-neutral. And if its only purpose or value is what we add, there is no escaping the cultural, political, prejudicial judgments of one's historical moment. What seems obvious to philosophers, historians, and theologians—that the acquisition and utilization of technical information is never neutral—is often beyond discussion with scientists. The reason why science finds it difficult to accept the possibility that there may be some things we ought not to know because that knowledge might not be safe in human hands is merely the mistaken conclusion that knowledge is inherently good and we can be trusted.[31] Here we are on familiar ground because some will argue it is not the gun (gun technology and its cumulative modifications) but the gun owner who must be watched. But not all knowledge is of the same kind. Some knowledge by its nature is incendiary. Research toward a vaccine for AIDS is not like the research that gives us a more lethal gun or a more powerful bomb. A handgun is "just asking" to be held and fired. Gun technology is power easily corrupted. The same is true for the first atomic bomb and its creators were among the first to understand this. The history of what happened afterward, notably the development of the hydrogen bomb, shows the ease with which scientists could rationalize their research by referring back to the premise that basic knowledge (basic knowledge of the atom) is a good thing.

Scientists have a problem with limits. Their need to know is balanced by the public's need to be informed, but scientists are quick to presume the public does not know enough to set proper limits. The consequence is a stalemate. Inherently suspicious of governmental oversight, disdainful of public opinion because it is not informed, wanting desperately to be trusted to do the right thing, scientists are likely to be impatient and wary of anything that appears to be interference with their "right" to know. Not even Oppenheimer fully understood that if the pursuit of knowledge is the kind of thing "you cannot stop" (an organic thing), limits are necessary and necessarily established by someone other than scientists themselves. Scientists live for the next big breakthrough. If you try to restrict them, you are viewed as impeding progress. The conflict is fundamental: the scientist's need to know without limits and the public's need to oversee by imposing limits.

A final element in the fragility of any contractual agreement involving the military—and much of what science does is tied to the military directly or indirectly—is the matter of conscience. The civilian control of the Atomic Energy Commission, the establishment of Brookhaven National Laboratory, and the establishment the Office of Naval Research showed the government to be a generous patron and less dictatorial than expected. With uncommon insight Smith concludes: "Then, too, scientists began more honestly to face the fact that what they had to fear was not so much the voracious desire of military men to control them as their own technological skills in devising destruction" (A. Smith, 522). We would all feel better if scientists could be heard making this kind of self assessment frequently, openly, and confessionally, and since we do not, the commonwealth is reluctant to trust science to define what is good. Only those who know something of the deluding nature of sin to corrupt and the capacity of evil to overwhelm good intentions find themselves suspicious of all human aspirations, and that in itself justifies the democratic principle of the greatest participation to ensure the greatest good.

Notes

1. For an account of this revolution resulting in modern physics, see I. Bernard Cohen, *Revolution in Science* (Cambridge, Mass.: Harvard University Press, 1985), notably 419–34.

2. For the full text of Oppenheimer's speech to the Association of Los Alamos Scientists, see Oppenheimer, *Letters and Recollections*, ed. Smith and Weiner, 315–25.

3. Schweber, *In the Shadow*, 3.

4. Oppenheimer, *Physics in the Contemporary World*, 10. This remark first appeared in a February 1948 *Time* magazine interview.

5. For a discussion of the ethical and cultural milieu of Oppenheimer's growing up, see Schweber, *In the Shadow*, 42–53.

6. Nuel Pharr Davis characterized the situation this way: "Those in Washington who knew much about the bomb did not know much about the military situation. Those who knew much about the military situation did not know much about the bomb." See his *Lawrence and Oppenheimer*, 245.

7. A full accounting of the four different attempts on the part of scientists to convey their feelings to the government regarding the social and political implications of an atomic bomb can be found in *The Bulletin of Atomic Scientists* 1, no. 10 (May 1946): 1.

8. See Smith, *A Peril and a Hope*, 560–72, for the complete text of the Franck Report; and Davis, *Lawrence and Oppenheimer*, 243–48, for a discussion of the protests. To those who ask why Chicago became the hotbed of dissent, Daniel S. Greenberg makes the interesting suggestion that scientists at the Met Lab, unlike their colleagues at the other sites, knew their task to be substantially finished and so had time to ponder postwar the moral implications of the weapon they were helping to build. See Greenberg, *The Politics of Pure Science*, 99.

9. The lure of the finding "sweet" solutions to technical puzzles seems to be a temptation peculiar to scientists. Ann Finkbeiner recounts the continuing story of the Jasons—a secretive group of independent scientists who gather in order to advise the government

on matters mostly military related. Physicist John Wheeler conceived the group in the late 1950s during a time when scientists were still riding the wave of prestige generated by the Manhattan Project. Their motives are far from sinister and have to do with serving their country, reducing the threat of nuclear war, *and* being a unique kind of power broker. See Ann Finkbeiner, *The Jasons: The Secret History of Science's Postwar Elite* (New York: Viking 2006).

10. Smith, *Peril and Hope*, 199. Smith examines the May-Johnson bill in considerable detail in chapter 4.

11. See the review of Teller's *Memoirs: A Twentieth-Century Journey in Science and Politics*, by Alan Lightman, "Megaton Man," in *New York Review*, 23 May 2002, 34–37.

12. Oppenheimer, *Uncommon Sense*, 188; and Hershberg, *James B. Conant*, 230.

13. Smith, *Peril and Hope*, 53. Smith is of the same mind as most historians who conclude that while the days at Potsdam were highly significant, the decision to deploy the Bomb had been made during the first three weeks of June. For Truman to stall would have gone against the advice of his most trusted associates (Smith, 65).

14. Jack Hitt, "Battlefield: Space," *New York Times Magazine*, 5 August 2001, 30–35.

15. See Henry Greely, "The Human Genome Diversity Project," 71–81; and Karen Lebacqz, "Fair Shares," in *Genetics*, Ted Peters, ed., 82–102.

16. Lee Gomes, "The Newest Road to Fame and Fortune Is Mapping the Road," *Wall Street Journal*, 14 July 2003, B1.

17. It may surprise the reader that I agree with Steven Weinberg, over against most philosophers and sociologists of science, that scientific knowledge is a different kind of consensus knowledge in that "it is culture-free and permanent." Weinberg makes the critical distinction between the initial discovery-formulation period and what is finally accepted as its permanent form. His argument, however, has a limited validity set within the debate of realism versus anti-realism. Move the discussion into the broader context of acquisition and application (can these really be separated?), knowledge, as distinct from data, is culturally and historically shaped. See Weinberg, "Physics and History," in *The One Culture?* ed. Labinger and Collins, 122–23.

18. For a fuller account of the firebombing of Tokyo, Nagoya, Osaka, and Kobe, see Rhodes, *The Making of the Atomic Bomb*, 591–600.

19. The story by Barnaby J. Feder and Tom Zeller, Jr., "Identity Badge Worn under Skin Approved for Use in Health Care," appeared in the *New York Times*, 18 October 2004, accessed at www.nytimes.com/2004/10/14/technology/14implant.html (18 October 2004).

20. The first six-page issue of *Bulletin of Atomic Scientists*, something of a collector's item, appeared 10 December 1945; the quote is from page 16 of the 15 March 1946 issue. See Also Smith, *Peril and Hope*, 389.

21. See Gregg Herken, *Brotherhood of the Bomb* (Henry Holt, 2002).

22. Federation of Atomic Scientists press release, 18 March 1946, cited from Smith, *Peril and Hope*, 390.

23. See Bacon, *The New Organon*, bk. 1, cxxxix. For a balanced appraisal of Bacon in this regard, see Zaforin, *Francis Bacon*, 121–23.

24. For a reprint of Bridgman's lecture and the comments of six noted scientists, see *Bulletin of Atomic Scientists* 4, no. 3 (1948): 70–75; as well as Schweber's discussion of the issue of social responsibility, *In the Shadow*, 6–9.

25. Steven Shapin explores the basis for scientific knowledge in the seventeenth century as the English experiment in "the gentlemanly constitution of scientific truth." See his *A Social History of Truth* (Chicago: University of Chicago Press, 1995).

26. The most patent evidence indicating a change in relationship between science and the commonwealth (primarily the federal government) is the number of modifications in patent and copyright laws, as well as changes in federal and state policies. It is not an overstatement to say science has been elevated to the level of partner. For details, see Krimsky, *Science in the Private Interest*, 28–33, 61–65.

27. Greenberg, *Science, Money, and Politics*, introduction. In chapter 10, Greenberg chronicles "the only large-scale involvement of scientists in national politics took place in the presidential campaign of 1964" (149). The reason for their "detour into politics" was to defeat Goldwater who was seen as trigger-happy and likely to lead America into a nuclear war. Greenberg concludes: "When the scientists successfully completed their political work in that campaign, many of them feared they had damaged the sanctity of science. Never again in significant numbers did science return to ballot-box politics" (149).

28. Victor Weisskopf, "The Privilege of Being a Physicist," is reprinted in *Physics Today* (February 2003): 48–52, accessible at www.physicstoday.org. This issue also contains a short but good biography of Weisskopf.

29. The quote is from Percy Bridgman quoted from Schweber, *In the Shadow*, 7–8.

30. See Richard Lourie, *Sakharov: A Biography* (Waltham, MA: Brandeis University Press, 2002).

31. For a rare discussion of whether there may be some things we ought not to know and whether information, independent of the manner of acquisition and utilization, can invoke moral impropriety, see Nicholas Rescher, *Forbidden Knowledge and Other Essays on the Philosophy of Cognition* (Dordrecht, Holland, and Boston: Reidel, 1987), especially page 9. Rescher thinks not but I do not agree with him, because every particular knowledge inherently tilts toward good or evil.

CHAPTER TWO

Knowledge Too Good Not to Be Exploited: The Compromised Scientist

> In fact, since World War II, science has been deeply absorbed into the nation's economy and culture. Apart from heady interludes of antispending bombast, science is indisputably regarded, at times uncritically, as essential to prosperity, national security, environmental protection, and fulfillment of our hopes for healthful longevity.
>
> —Daniel S. Greenberg (*Science, Money, and Politics*, 74)

> I believe most assuredly that the next science to find itself in moral difficulties with its applications is biology, and if the problems of physics relative to science seem difficult, the problems of the development of biological knowledge will be fantastic.
>
> —Richard Feynman in a speech given in 1964 at the Galileo Symposium in Italy (*The Pleasure of Finding Things Out*, 99)

Hope may characterize the beginning of a new century. The twenty-first is no exception but what exactly is the character of this hope? Might it be the promise of a new scientific era, biological in nature? If the defining event—scientifically speaking—of the last century was splitting of the atom, then the defining event of the present century is unraveling the universal code of life. But there is a difference between the science of the atom and the science of the gene, and this is the substance of this chapter.

Meet the New 800-Pound Gorilla

The scientists responsible for building the first atomic bomb were the first to ponder a world that could never be the same. The burning issue in America turned on who would have access to this power-laden information. The structure and composition of the Atomic Commission galvanized their concerns. On a broader level science and the commonwealth agreed to mutually support each other. Science would provide the technical knowledge and in return the public would financially support its programs of research and development and grant science an unusual measure of independence and freedom. But the "contract" began to unravel as the Cold War receded. The world was changing and so was science. We no longer think of ourselves on the brink of total annihilation. We are survivors of the Cold War and ours is a brave new world. But this brave new world has its own foreboding perils. This, though, is to anticipate what is coming before examining the remarkable transformation of science itself, a story best understood by looking at the money trail it leaves behind.

Prior to the Second World War, science was an enclave of university professors and pragmatic practitioners. Unlike the academic research science of Europe, American science was deeply rooted in the tradition of Benjamin Franklin, Eli Whitney, and Thomas Edison, a tradition of inventors and gadgeteers. The university was the primary context for basic research since science was closely related to teaching. As the most practical of the sciences, agriculture, chemistry, and engineering were dominant. The guiding principle was to reserve public monies for practical applications and to resist establishing formal links with permanent agencies or bureaus. By mutual consent a wall of separation was maintained. Scientists fiercely guarded their independence and politicians saw no reason to enter into alliances with them.

In this context science was a bootstrap affair. In the late 1930s the total monies available for scientific research in universities was about $31 million. Forty years later, research and development surpassed $3 billion—a hundredfold increase. That kind of increase mandated a change in how scientific research would be supported. Before World War II, research was largely done in-house through a privately funded system of immediate rewards and results. No one even thought about separate agencies dedicated to a single science, such as NASA. After the war, public support began to dwarf foundation and other forms of private support.[1] The door was open to a broad-base tax method of funding science and that changed everything.

For science to prosper as it has, various funding sources had to expand: federal and state government, private corporations, and industry, as well as philanthropies such as the Bill and Melinda Gates Foundation. And did it ever expand throughout the postwar years! The number of federal dollars allocated to science continued to increase year after year. With the exception of a few periods of leveling off, and even a few dips in the early 1990s, growth in federal funding has been explosive. The total federal portion for basic and applied research increased from $149 *million* in 1953 to about $35 *billion* in 2004. Daniel Greenberg, who has been documenting the politics of science for forty years and was founding editor of the *Science & Government Report*, notes that "[t]his gusher of money produced innumerable effects, but among them, the two that principally concern us were these: science and technology became attuned to a rhythm of ever-growing financial support, and Congress became increasingly interested in, and querulous about, this suddenly emerged giant in federal affairs" (*The Politics of Pure Science*, 158).

The relationship between science and society was redrawn not only by the amount of money at stake but by the way it was being distributed. In 1938 about 40 percent of all federal support was provided by the Department of Agriculture. By 1962 Agriculture constituted only 1.6 percent. Making up the difference was the Pentagon. During the Cold War the military had become the primary backer of basic research, but as enemies became allies and the Soviet Union fractured from within, a new kind of war was needed to sustain science. If there wasn't one to fight, there was always one to prepare for. Through the 1950s, the Pentagon supported nearly 80 percent of all federal research and development

The most notable change in how science matured is the coinciding shift toward the biological sciences and the infusion of private monies. Sheldon Krimsky, a policy analyst at the Tufts University School of Medicine, notes the university-industry relationship took a major leap in its evolution in the 1980s. A series of federal and state policies established incentives for private companies to invest in university research. In addition, the Supreme Court in *Diamond v. Chakrabarty* (1980) ruled that genetically modified bacteria were patentable in and of themselves, apart from the process in which they are used. As a result multi-year, multi-million-dollar contracts issued by chemical and pharmaceutical firms for biomedical research in the university setting is now commonplace. Likewise, universities and colleges began to place greater emphasis on stand-alone research, as distinct from teaching and research. In 1980 they spent $6.5 billion (current dollars) on research and development (R&D). Twenty years later, the figure rose to $30.2 billion, a 467 percent change. During the same period, the percentage of what industry contributes to R&D of academic institutions rose 875 percent from $0.26 to $2.3 billion (in constant dollars).[2]

The budget for the National Institutes for Health is revealing. The NIH, spread out over 300 acres in Bethesda, Maryland, is a collection of more than two dozen facilities dedicated to research in the areas of cancer, heart disease, mental illness, the human genome, and other biomedical ventures. Funding for the agency stagnated in the mid-1990s at about $11 billion a year. After much advocating by researchers and patients who made their way to Capitol Hill to press their cause and exhibit their suffering, and with bipartisan support from Congress and the White House, funding was pushed to new levels. NIH saw its budget double between 1998 and 2003. It is now at $28.6 billion and holding steady, but still more than the National Science Foundation and NASA combined.

I could continue to throw around figures and budgets but apart from documenting large trends, they should be taken with a grain of salt, and not only because they can be manipulated to reach diverse conclusions but also because they do not tell the whole story. We do not see the entire picture, for instance, if our focus is on federal spending for science. The rapid growth in funding for research and development by industry changes the tone of science. The U.S. biotech industry by itself spent a staggering $11 billion on research in 2000 and employs over 150,000 people. Industrial money is especially attractive because it is *new* money—a fresh faucet attached to a very large source. With the infusion of new money comes the *profit-seeking values* endemic to capitalism.

First appearances can deceive, even if you have found a money trail. Undoubtedly there has been a crossover from military to civilian funding, but the line between the two is just as fuzzy as the demarcation between basic research and applied research. Rockets that carry satellites into space can also position laser guns, yet NASA is officially a civilian organization. Computers designed and manufactured for academic research are a priority for any nation hoping to upgrade its military. The Pentagon's ideas factory, the Defense Advanced Research Projects Agency (DARPA), is sponsoring a competition for the fastest, most powerful, most agile computer design, bar none. Second-phase contracts of $150 million have been let to Sun, IBM, and Cray, who will compete over the next three years to develop prototype designs. DARPA will then fund two companies to move from research to development. The money trail runs from the Pentagon to private universities where a product is developed but there is no definitive line between military, civilian, and industry.

By most accounts science is a unique kind of establishment. It has no coherent mission statement, no centralized administration, no official representatives. No one person or body oversees the individuals and institutions that make up the scientific community, and yet tax funds are appropriated almost on faith with minimal accountability. With a degree of legitimacy, scientists argue they are not corporate leaders with a bottom line or heads of agencies with civic responsibilities or generals charged with defending the nation. They are teachers and researchers motivated by the love of learning and discovery. On the other hand, the sums of money requested year after year are such that science is looking like the rest of corporate America. Daniel Greenberg is forthright about how money has changed science. He traces the beginning of "the new politics of money and science" to early 1960s and made it the subject of *The Politics of Pure Science*. In a sequel book in 2001, *Science, Money, and Politics*, Greenberg describes science as an institution that is well supported, safely walled off, aging into caution-bound institutionalism, moving toward a model of corporate power, seldom venturing into political affairs except to secure additional funding, and only occasionally demonstrating concern for the poor (10).

It's Biology Not Physics, Stupid

The decision of Congress in 1993 not to fund the Superconducting Super Collider marks the passing of an era. Launched in 1986 during the Reagan presidency, the project began with an initial cost of $4 billion. Budget forecast steadily rose until $123 billion was the best estimate. Congress finally closed the door in 1993. It was not only a vote against "big science," it portended something else. Greenberg writes, "The physics community, originally welcomed to Washington for its nuclear knowledge, was dethroned from decades of political influence by the end of the Cold War and the parsimonious politics of the 1990s. The atom was in low repute, if not disgrace, associated with bombs, the Chernobyl and Three Mile Island accidents, unmanageable nuclear waste, and mysterious cancer 'clusters'" (*Science, Money, and Politics*, 403).

The era of physics as king was passing. The future wasn't going to be about more powerful bombs. The science that mattered most would be the transfer of information, a cure for cancer, the secrets of the cell. Whatever remained of the social contract between science and the commonwealth would have to take into account a number of significant changes. We are just beginning to experience the full impact of the biotechnological revolution. In the decades to come a multitude of ethical and political, personal and social decisions will cascade over us and threaten to drown us. The Copernican revolution altered our mental picture of the universe and the Industrial Revolution changed how we understand our role in society. The third fundamental transformation in self-perception is under way. Biotechnology is already providing us with the means to enhance our health, our appearance, our moods, our sexual reproduction, and our intelligence. Factor in the continued revolution in robotics, artificial intelligence, digital information, and virtual reality and you have something more than cosmetic enhancement. The starting line may be about enhancements but the finish line will be about making certain enhancements permanent (the opposite of cosmetic).

The way this will happen is twofold. Some enhancements by their nature will change the culture, just as the Industrial Revolution altered how we tell time.[3] Enhancement drugs, such as the family of Prozac and Ritalin drugs, effectively function as a form of social control. The spectrum of Huxley's brave new world is reflected in a society where misfits are nudged toward an androgynous median personality of social compliance.[4] Second, we will not stop with enhancements when germline intervention—those genes that are passed on to our children—is both easier and permanent. We are not likely to tolerate cystic fibrosis or sickle-cell anemia when it is possible to move beyond genetic screening and eliminate the offending genes themselves. This is the course of events Gregory Stock sets forth in *Redesigning Humans*: as somatic therapies become common they "will smooth the way for a move from screening and selecting embryos to actually manipulating them" (39). The subtitle to Stock's book, "Our Inevitable Genetic Future," should raise more than a passing eyebrow. The most important driving force behind "inevitable" may be the power of the marketplace, for who will dare stand in the way of a parent's right to decide what is best for their child or your right to be the person you desire to be? Let's not presume though what is and is not inevitable. Doubtlessly, science will continue to provide ever more opportunities to alter ourselves. It would be more than ironic and possibly tragic if we allowed technology to shape the future in ways that it becomes our fate.

Biology is now king—or should I say, queen—because the entire matrix of science has shifted from a masculine science associated with men breaking apart atoms to a science with women delicately splicing genes. This is not a pejorative evaluation but a fundamental fact. Physics works by breaking things apart, biology by observing how things are put together. At their very core their differences is the obvious distinction between inanimate and animate. Inorganic matter wants to just be what it is and always has been. A rock is a rock and not much more. Living things move, digest, grow, and are never content with just being. The nineteenth-century popularizer of evolutionary theory Herbert Spencer wrote simply, "A living thing is distinguished from a dead thing by the multiplicity of changes at any moment taking place."

Physicists and biologists inhabit different worlds. Physicists engage in violent disturbances of nature requiring machines that cost millions of dollars. Astrophysicists "see" a cosmos where violence on a very large scale is normal. Whether the probe is deep into the nucleus of an atom or moving across the Martian landscape, their universe is dark, cold, and hostile to life. For physicists the pot of gold at the end of the rainbow is a Grand Unified Law. Physicists often speak of moving toward the final answer but a biologist seldom expresses a similar sentiment. The probings of the biologists are delicate and patient in order to observe without disturbing. Mother Nature, in contrast to Cosmic Nature, has the feel of quality and tells interesting stories of what once was and is still becoming. Because everything is made of atoms, it would seem to follow that living things should fall neatly within the description of atoms except that living things do not just sit there but respond to their ever-changing environment. Viruses and microbes, chipmunks and elephants, plants and trees do it: they change, they evolve, they respond to threats by becoming something slightly different in order to survive. Even something as fundamental as genes react by switching on and off.

There is something up close and personal about the scientific revolution engulfing us. Suddenly it's about us. A sense of unease fills us when the subject of cloning comes up because the thought of looking at an exact double of oneself is troubling. In *The Shattered Self: The End of Natural Evolution*, Pierre Baldi speaks of the eclipse of natural evolution. We are no longer just observing and recording as Darwin did. We are tinkering and engineering with our very own destiny. Leon Kass's little epigram brings home the change: "Engineering the engineer seems to differ in kind from engineering his engine" (*Toward a More Natural Science*, 18). We wonder if we are crossing some kind of Rubicon when life is at stake. What line did splitting the atom cross? Both require human intervention into the natural order with earth-shaking consequences hanging in the balance. The difference is that living organisms have lives of their own. Seeds of a genetically altered plant will propagate without further human intervention. Release a pathogen or change its environment and a form of biological indeterminacy kicks in. As mind altering as splitting the atom was, it was nevertheless impersonal and removed. Biotechnology, on the other hand, offers us ways to alter the way we procreate, and that is as up close and personal as you can get.

The once firm boundary between animate and inanimate is not secure. What do you get when you merge biotechnology, computer technology, and nanotechnology? Does anyone really know? For the moment, nanotechnology is primarily a materials technology belonging to the chemists and physicists. What they make are very small machines on the order of 100 nanometers, or a hundred-billionths of a meter. Scientists at IBM have succeeded in organizing atoms to spell out the letters of their company. But in the realm of the small, nothing is more efficient than living organisms. Imagine living machines with the capability of self-replication and you can begin to imagine self-cleaning window glass or living microbes delivered to your body inside a capsule. Little machines can of course make bigger machines. The best of all worlds or a very bad nightmare, as told by Michael Crichton in *Prey*, is when a cloud of nanoparticles form a cloud of self-sustaining and self-reproducing microrobots. For all practical purposes, it is alive. Where, then, is the distinction between inanimate and animate?

The Gold Standard of Knowledge

At best, science is "a multitude of separated research communities" each with its own "epistemological culture."[5] Nevertheless, those who think of themselves as scientists share a common, but not necessarily uniform, methodological understanding of how to get at the truth of the matter. Because the matter, both animate and inanimate, is so diverse, so is the methodological approach. And even though I will not attempt to define empiricism beyond the common thread of careful observation coupled with some form of verification, it represents the gold standard of how knowledge is procured. The standing test is that knowledge accumulates: we will know more tomorrow than we did yesterday.[6]

Charles Taylor is one of our most respected philosophers and warrants the reflections by another most influential thinker of our time, the philosopher-anthropologist Clifford Geertz. His essay begins with his subject's own confession to be in the grip of an obsession—Taylor is "a hedgehog, a monomaniac endlessly polemicizing against 'the ambition to model the study of man on the natural sciences.'"[7] Taylor has spent a career questioning the dominance of the natural sciences as if the distinctiveness, autonomy, effectiveness, and relevance of other methodologies are suspect. The argument is not only valid but may not even go far enough if technology is a culture on to itself spreading out like an octopus.

Are we justified to think of technology as an ideology? Neil Postman tries to persuade us that the effect of technology is so diffuse, pervasive, and embedded that it totally envelops us and therefore deserves the designation of "technopoly." Along with the French philosopher Michel Foucault, Postman sees technology as "a set of assumptions of which we are barely conscious but which nonetheless directs our efforts to give shape and coherence to the world" (*Technopoly*, 123).[8] Consider the impact the following concepts have had in defining our understanding of reality: space, time, law, causality, verification, force, feedback, indeterminacy, complementarity, relativity, chaos, evolution, speciation, survival of the fittest, ecology, mutation, metabolism, cloning. Let us go one step farther and consider broader concepts such as objectivity, precision, efficiency, speed, innovation, reliability, adaptability, and we find they are "equally applicable to matters of pleasure, leisure, learning, every instance of human communication, and every kind of activity, whatever its ostensive purpose."[9] Taken separately each concept conveys new information about the nature of the universe. Their cumulative impact, however, is of a different kind. Postman believes technology, notably in America, is a worldview or state of mind whereby culture seeks its authorization in technology and finds its satisfactions there (*Technopoly*, 71).

As science flows through technology, it creates is own subcultures. This argument will be explored further in the last two chapters. Whether it constitutes a coherent worldview providing purpose and moral standards is debatable.[10] What can be said for certain is the near monopoly science exerts on what counts for knowledge worth knowing. Jacques Ellul is especially convincing in his analysis that science has succeeded in convincing most of us that everything we need to know about what is true goes no farther than explanations of what is real. By confusing truth with what is real, as if they were identical, there is no place for the spoken universe (word truths) which permits us to go beyond what is real to ask those kinds of question that can only be addressed with language.[11]

Postman cannot justify his claim that technopoly has reached the status of "totalitarian technocracy." He is correct that it is pervasive, barely conscious, and defines what constitutes relevant knowledge. Its dominance is deleterious to the extent that it determines not only what knowledge is valuable but also how we come to know what is true. Science as technopoly may even eliminate alternatives to itself in precisely the way Aldous Huxley portrays in *Brave New World*, not by making them illegal or immoral but unpopular and irrelevant. Postman's logic brings him to the conclusion that two thought-worlds cannot exist at the same time. One must die. The other worldview in the throes of dying is the tradition of religion and the values enshrined in the poetry of Walt Whitman, the speeches of Abraham Lincoln, the novels of Hawthorne and Melville, the philosophy of Emerson and

Thomas Jefferson. The better judgment is to understand science as pushing on the boundaries of traditional beliefs. Contrary to Postman and Foucault, the thought-worlds of tradition and technology have found ways to co-exist. Beginning with the Industrial Revolution, the dominance of science has undercut much that is associated with religion (as Postman asserts). The worldview of tradition, nevertheless, still possess the power to claim and inspire our most worthy endeavors and retains an important role in our daily lives. There is no great ideological war being waged between science and religion in nations of the Enlightenment, not when compared with cultures who have yet to work their way through a period of self-critical examination. While we do not see the withering of religious feelings in America, religions themselves struggle to define their own sources of authority and how to adapt to a scientific, secular culture.

Why does it matter if one model of truth, such as scientific rationality, predominates and wins the respect of the commonwealth? For James Davison Hunter the consequence is a divided society. In his *Culture Wars*, Hunter uncovers two driving forces: "the impulse toward progressivisim" and the "impulse toward orthodoxy." The crucial difference rests with lines of authority. Orthodoxy depends on a transcendent authority which is independent of, prior to, and more powerful than human experience, while the binding moral authority among progressivists resides in personal experience and scientific rationality. Pushing these two alternatives to their extremes, Hunter sees "the institutionalization and politicization of two fundamentally different cultural systems."[12] Hunter does not make the mistake of splitting American culture into two religious camps—on progressive and the other traditional—which happens if one fails to recognize a progressive mentality among religious liberals, and even among some conservative Christians who know better than to ignore science. Yet, there is no way around a cultural divide between those who believe in an ultimate truth divinely revealed and those who are content with a truth self-grounded and constructed, and insofar as this divide exists, the empirical method is the decisive criteria for evaluating the credibility and usefulness of truth that really matters.

When competing ways of knowing are absent from public discourse, the result is a monologue. Keeping in mind the distinction between data and its interpretation, the model of scientific rationality dominates both. When the issue is global warming, science provides both the data and the interpretation. Questions about proper methodology are usually settled among scientists themselves and that is the end of this discussion. The scientific monopoly, however, ends when decisions are made about what to do, for these invariably include values, beliefs, and politics. The telling consequence of one gold standard of knowledge is the difficulty it creates to stand at arm's length and appraise what technology is appropriate and good for us. If science is the gold standard for what passes as knowledge, then it unduly influences the decisions we make concerning how limited resources are allocated.

When our attention is turned to the question of human nature, the full dominance of science is felt. Science weighs in with the data and interpretation of sociology, anthropology, sociobiology, paleoanthropology, and genetics, and together they paint a picture of an evolutionary development that knows only the law of survival and adaptation (see chapter 5 for a fuller discussion). At times the impression is given that this is the only rational approach possible. There is no place for theological truths or a theological way of knowing. When scientists are invited to testify before congressional hearings, the data and its interpretation are received as verifiable and true. When theologians are invited to participate, they are called on as authorities about values and beliefs. What they offer is not an alternative way of knowing, which may be in concert or at odds with science regarding a given question, but an opinion. Their counsel is considered when politicians are concerned about who will be offended and what values are being disrespected. And as important as this may be, what theologians have to say about sin and evil has no standing as true and valid.

Lethal Knowledge, Benign Knowledge

The statement I am about to make is meant to be rhetorical rather than dogmatic, inclusive rather than exclusive. Scientific knowledge is of two kinds, lethal and benign, with variations in between. I am well aware of the two received arguments to the contrary. Basic scientific knowledge is neutral or value-free. Prime examples would be the atomic structure of elements (the Periodic Table) or the constituent parts of a cell. Second, the value of knowledge is ambiguous until developed and put to some human use. The wheel, for example, has one use when part of a wheelbarrow and another when part of a chariot. Does the dual use of knowledge, in this case the wheel, reside in the knowledge itself or its application, or both? Instead of engaging in a lengthy philosophical discussion over what is a thorny issue, I will restrict myself to the era-defining discoveries of splitting the atom and unraveling the mystery of DNA. The distinction between fundamental knowledge and application is becoming less important when the application defines the knowledge. Physicists of the Manhattan Project may have begun with theoretical knowledge of the atom but once they realized what splitting the atom would mean, the science at hand was all about atomic energy. The same thin line or rapid movement from discovery to development is also the story of DNA, but there is a difference.

When the atom is split the result is an out-of-control chain reaction, the dispersion of its energy. The nuclear fission of a nucleus of an element with a high atomic number (e.g., uranium) releases radioactive particles, and in the instance of gamma rays there is no limit to their range in air, though their energy is diminished by half each time they pass through lead 1 cm thick. The potential for death is everywhere present. Atomic or hydrogen bombs arouse our deepest fears of terrible devastation. Emotionally, nothing can dislodge the feeling that here is knowledge too lethal to let loose in a world of dictators and mishaps. The politics of the atom remains one of containment and safeguards. By way of contrast, what is there not to like about the gene? When the gene is the seat of what is wrong with us, it can be altered; when it is seat of what we might become, it can be enhanced. The Human Genome Project inspires a hope of great good. The atom, of course, had its own aura of promise: cheap energy, a new world order. But the history of splitting the atom is one of disappointment and difficult lessons. Why didn't scientists anticipate the environmental catastrophe of radioactive fallout, the intractable problem of radioactive waste, the necessity of building redundant systems to protect the public against meltdown, and the unexpected cost of producing energy from the atom? Scientists might argue that there was nothing wrong with their science, only with the politicians and bureaucrats who would not listen. The politics of the gene modification no doubt will come with its own lessons, but one expects they will revolve around promising benefits.

The science of the atom was traditional in the sense that it was the pursuit of fundamental knowledge for the good of humanity. The knowledge was lethal to be sure but in the spirit of traditional science it was intrinsically good and belonged to no one. The Human Genome Project, on the other hand, began with discussions about market shares and return on investment. And there was nothing traditional about the race between a privately financed for-profit company and a publicly funded organization authorized to share information as soon as it became available.[13] Craig Venter found himself wedged between venture capitalist Wallace Steinberg and a desire to make the "code of life" public and available to all. But the thought never crossed anyone's mind that here is a lethal form of knowledge. Just the opposite, here is information with sky-high potential for making money and helping people. It was a win-win situation except for the fact that from the beginning the Human Genome Project opened the door to a host of other pernicious motives. It could be argued that biotechnology is not the culprit but a victim of the times. But the more likely possibility is that the knowledge itself is just too good not to be exploited.

A Player in the New Global Economy

No one escapes the dragnet of globalization. After months of deliberation President George W. Bush sought to avoid the destruction of new human embryos for research by limiting federal funds to those cell lines created before 9 August 2002. The National Institutes for Health in turn identified ten institutes and companies that together have sixty-four embryonic stem cell lines. The president of the United States can issue an executive order but for it to have any meaning he would need the cooperation of public universities, private companies, international coalitions, and industrial conglomerate all scattered throughout the world. Did you think the cell lines were an American prerogative? Wrong!

Who/Where	Number of lines
Wisconsin Alumni Foundation—Madison, Wis.	5
CyThera Inc.—San Diego (private biotech company)	9
University of California—San Francisco	2
BresaGen—Adelaide, Australia (private company)	4
Karolinska Institute—Stockholm	5
Monash University—Melbourne, Australia (an international coalition of funds)	6
National Center for Biological Sciences—Bangalore, India	3
Reliance Life Sciences—Mumbai, India (part of India's largest industrial conglomerate)	7
Technion-Israel Institute of Technology—Haifa, Israel	4
Gothenburg University—Gothenburg, Sweden	19

Were we naive enough to think science would stand still in face of an executive order issued by the president of the most powerful nation in the world? Perhaps.

> **Dateline *Boston Globe*, 12 August 2004**
> ### Britain Allows Cloning of Human Cells for Research
> The British government yesterday granted a team of scientists permission to begin cloning human cells, the first such license granted in the United Kingdom since the country declared cloning legal in 2001.
> The experiment will clone cells exclusively for medical research, not to create human children (Gareth Cook, A14).

Even if science wanted to escape the tangle of geopolitics, it cannot. Classify this case history under globalization and moral complexity. Professor Rony Swennen has genetically modified banana cells to resist the airborne fungus called Black Signtoka. This disease denies the banana plant the photosynthesis it needs to grow. In Uganda, where bananas are a staple—they eat banana pancakes, banana mash, banana chips, banana bread, and guzzle banana beer—Black Signatoka is a national disaster. The big floppy leaves turn yellow and brown and the crop is considerably diminished. Bioengineered bananas come to the rescue. Since 1994 Rony Swennen genetically modified banana cells have been kept in frozen suspension awaiting the chance to be planted in a test field in Uganda or some other tropical country. Bananas have the distinct characteristic of not producing pollen, eliminating the fear they would run wild in the open. It would seem to be a slam-dunk decision except that Ugandan officials are caught in the crossfire between the United States and Europe over the future of genetically modified foods. The American government and biotech industry are pushing to bring genetically modified seeds to Africa. With markets saturated at home and Africa in desperate straits, it would seem a natural fit. The European Union, where consumers are deeply suspicious of laboratory-altered food ("Frankenfoods"), is urging African nations to adopt their go-slow approach to biotech. Given its fragile economy, Uganda is in no position to ignore the hint that European countries could limit imports from their former colonies if they switched to bioengineered crops. Ugandans themselves ask: If Europeans are concerned, shouldn't we be too? And might American biotechnology be more interested in helping itself than hungry Africans? Meanwhile Professor Swennen nervously bides his time in his Belgium Laboratory of Tropical Crop Improvement hoping to see the fruition of his next project, the development of a plant resistant to the nematodes that eat way at the roots of banana plants.[14]

In his very readable *The Lexus and the Olive Tree*, Thomas L. Friedman entertains what president-elect Bill Clinton should have said at his first inauguration.

> My fellow Americans, my tenure as your President is coinciding with the end of the Cold War system and the rise of globalization. Globalization is to the 1990s and the next millennium what the Cold War was to the 1950s through the 1980s. If the Cold War system was built around the threat and challenge of the Soviet Union, which was dividing the world, the globalization system is built around the threat and challenge of rapid technological change and economic integration that are uniting the world. (*The Lexus*, 355).

Friedman depicts a number of ways to distinguish Cold War systems from global systems. The defining reality of the former was The Wall, the defining document was The Deal. The defining reality of globalization is the World Wide Web, and its primary operation the high-speed transaction. If the Cold War had been a sport, it would have been sumo wrestling; if globalization were a sport, it would be a hundred-meter dash. During the Cold War, the most frequently asked question was, "How big is your missile?" During globalization it is, "How fast is your modem?" The new challenge, as Friedman reiterates, is to figure out what it takes to survive in a world fast dissolving into one borderless market. Science will have to learn to play according to the new rules or return to orphan status.

Globalization is a technology-driven phenomenon with information as its most important commodity. Material goods are still being traded but the new player is technological information. Spies and thieves don't care about the actual hardware, such as computers, but the data codes which run them. Globalization has fueled the race to knowledge. A 1999 United Nation's report on human development succinctly states the interrelationship between the race to claim knowledge and globalization.

> Globalization—and its new rules—is shaping the path of new technologies. Over the past twenty years increasing privatization of research and development, ever-growing liberalization of markets and the tightening of intellectual property rights have *set off a race to lay claim to knowledge, and this has changed technology's path.* The risk is that poor people's and poor countries' interests are being left on the sidelines.[15]

The blush is off the apple and globalization is drawing critics like bees to honey. This new borderless capitalism pits one global village against another.

Cotton subsidies in Mississippi drive cotton farmers in West Africa out of business. When survival of the fittest is the primary economic game to be played, your neighbor is your competitor. The World Trade Organization (WTO) and the World Bank are no longer obscure entities. Protestors at the 1999 Seattle meeting and the 2003 Cancun meeting of the WTO alerted the public to the impact these quasi-transnational institutions have. From positions as different as street protestors to philanthropist George Soros, the prevalent sentiment that "a rising tide lifts all boats" was severely criticized.[16]

It seems that everything is a global problem in need of a global fix, and science is expected to provide the fix. The anthrax attacks that killed five people in the fall of 2001 set off a wave of hysteria. In 2000 President Clinton asked Congress to approve $2.8 billion to prepare for this kind of assault but Congress refused. After the anthrax letters, Bush requested $11 billion and it was approved as part of the November 2002 Homeland Security Bill. Neither President Bush nor the Congress wants to be unprepared for a bird flu pandemic. Unlike in all previous centuries we can do something to prevent a pandemic. Once again millions will be allocated to protect the American people, but to what end if the flu, as it did with AIDS, takes hold on foreign soil? The science we need is not national or foreign. Either we make everyone safe or no one is safe. In an editorial titled "Facing the Threat among Us," Mortimer Zuckerman reminds us that we are threatened by bio*error* as well as bioterror, both the result of two new sciences.

Dateline *U.S. News & World Report*, 1 September 2002

Facing the Threat among Us

Up until the 20th century, the greatest catastrophes were natural disasters—famine, flood, and earthquakes. In the last century, more people died in war or were murdered by totalitarian regimes. In the 21st century, the risk is the perversion of knowledge. We cannot go on any longer avoiding the fact that the downside of science and technology, especially from bioerror and bioterror from both microbiology and genetics, can kill us all. Just what are we going to do? (Mortimer B. Zuckerman, editor-in-chief).

Thus the irony of our situation: we can do something about a pandemic, but we can also cause one.

The World Health Organization is the largest United Nations agency. It has a budget of about $2.5 billion and more than three thousand employees nearly half of whom are health experts. Dr. Gro Harlem Brundtland has been its director for the last five years and reflects upon what has changed.[17] She has seen her role shift from responding to a specific health crisis to moving issues of health onto the political agenda—thus the initiative to establish a Global Fund to Fight AIDS, TB, and Malaria (although President Bush has decided to fund a separate American response to AIDS). In the past, WHO has waged successful campaigns against polio and smallpox, and it seemed that it might tame malaria. But it didn't, and along with tuberculosis and the AIDS epidemic, the health conditions among the world's poor have gotten worse. Malaria kills more than a million people a year, 700,000 of them are children. That many deaths should attract a lot of attention. After trying to eradicate the mosquito, the most hopeful approach is a bed net coated with an insecticide. A change in strategy was prompted by extending the effective life of the nets from six months to five years. With a global demand of 30 million to 50 million nets a year, the question is now cost, manufacturing, and distribution. High-tech science is not always the answer, and in too many instances the pursuit of a knockout solution delays a more effective, low-cost approach.

Globalization deconstructs all notions of pure research conducted in ivory towers. How far does the ethical concern of individual scientists stretch? Do they have a responsibility to rally support, call friends and colleagues, and talk with appropriate senators and representatives? Should Prof. Roney Swennen risk the next grant by becoming politically proactive? Politics is still a messy business, even more so when it is caught between the high expectations of globalization and the stark reality of "immoral man in an even more immoral society" (Reinhold Niebuhr's book is actually *Moral Man and Immoral Society*, because he wanted to highlight the corrupting power of society).

The Profit Motive

In Steven Spielberg's futuristic *A.I.*, the scientist who calls the shots is also a CEO. Researchers need a lot of money and this propels them to garner and manage money. Getting out the latest android model or being the first to patent an important gene is dependent on making a profit to pay the investors who make the research possible in the first place. Scientists today spend an increasing, and many would add inordinate, amount of time on manage-

> **Dateline *New York Times*, 5 March 2004**
>
> ## Companies Facing Ethical Issue as Drugs Are Tested Overseas
>
> Dr. Louis G. Lange, a cardiologist and the chief executive of a small biotechnology company, has a new drug, that if approved will be the first new treatment for angina in a quarter-century.
>
> Like many drug companies, Dr. Lange's CV Therapeutics of Palo Alto, Calif., tested its new product overseas, where studies go faster because it is easy to find patients who are eager to participate.
>
> But the company's testing is nearing its end, and Dr. Lange is faced with an ethical quandary: Is his company obliged to make the drug available to the patients in poor countries like Russia who took part in the studies? (Gina Kolata, www.nytimes.com/2004/03/05/science/ordrug.html?th).

ment, grant writing, accounting, and public relations at the expense of research in the traditional sense of experiments, evaluating hypotheses, writing for peers. It is now possible to ignore the peer review process and its round of scientific scrutiny and concentrate instead on clinical trials leading to a consumer product. Some would say the character of scientific work has changed to the point that research and development is being pulled by a different horse.

Was it ever possible to separate science as research from the need to procure money? Perhaps not. But there were good old days when the amateur scientists dappled in the mysteries of nature for the fun of it; that was when science was relatively cheap and observation with the naked eye was the primary instrument. Astronomer Johannes Kepler was often hired to make astrological charts but he did not see himself as making a choice between astronomy and astrology, empiricism and theology. And this may be the crux of the matter: profit rather than research is driving science. Profit is the horse and research is the cart. Two quite different examples will put some flesh on this bone of an argument.

The military-industrial complex did not pass into oblivion when World War II ended but transformed itself into the medical-pharmaceutical complex. Newspapers are filled with articles about alliances being made between health-care providers, universities, and pharmaceutical companies. Construction has begun for a twelve-story Merck facility in the Longwood area of Boston (home to Harvard Medical School, Brigham and Women's Hospital, Beth Israel Deaconess Medical Center, and the Dana-Fabre Cancer Institute). The Merck facility will employ four hundred scientists with research focused on immunology, diabetes, inflammation, and cancer—all of which happen to be specialties of Harvard Medical School. The dean of Harvard Medical School, Dr. Joseph B. Martin, let it be known that he will not purse the kind of agreement struck between Novartis Pharmaceutical Company and Scripps Research Institute in San Diego. Novartis pays the Scripps Institute $20 million a year in return for first rights to 50 percent of it diagnostic and drug discoveries. Nevertheless, the opportunity will be present for researchers of Harvard and Merck to collaborate and, after all, that is the reason for their proximity. Dr. Martin is fully aware of the danger of selling your research-soul but believes he can walk the fine line between private investments and academic standards.[18] Meanwhile, the new Harvard-Partners Center for Genetics and Genomics is starting up. Partners Health Care brings to the partnership a health-care database of 300,000 individuals dating back to 1977 as well as DNA samples from about 200,000 study participants. Harvard, in turn, will contribute a new academic department of twenty-five faculty members, lab researchers, and administrators.[19]

While compacts between academia, hospitals, and pharmaceutical companies threaten to blur the distinction between research and profit, working for the military is a different kind of horse and cart. A resounding ethical note is struck by Richard Lewontin's observation that "the state of American science and its relation to the American state are a product of war."[20] There has always been a replacement war to employ an army of scientists. In the absence of wars against political enemies, there has been the Cold War, the war on cancer and AIDS, the war on drugs, and now the war on terrorism. Alongside presidents and senators, scientists have learned how to play the political game of "there is a crisis looming and we better deal with it now." There is, though, a fundamental difference when the profit motive is displaced by patriotism. If you work for the military in one of the myriad of offices and departments spread out in a labyrinth of agencies, you have forsworn the incentive of profits. But now patriotism in some form becomes the horse and it can skew one's judgments concerning the value of one's research just as easily. No matter how pure the research is, it is still research in service to the military. It may be that science in most circumstances must serve some master but let's be honest, whether it is profit or patriotism the master you are serving isn't disinterested science or teaching.

Is "pure" research, like innocence, something that never existed? Does it happen when scientists are free to pursue whatever research for the sole purpose of whatever truth? Albert Einstein sitting in his patent office discovering theories of relativity comes to mind. So does the RAND Corporation, where John Forbes Nash spent summers pursuing game theories or the Princeton Institutes of Advanced Study, where great thinkers go to ponder without added duties or obligations.[21] When science is as fundamental as the thought-experiment, research is as pure as it gets. But this is the exception to the rule and the farther one moves away from mathematics and physics and the closer one moves to genetics and biology, the more difficult it is to extract research from compromising motivations.

You Ain't Seen Nothing Yet—Moral Complexity and Ambiguity

Moral issues are cascading over us and tipping our moral lifeboats. Boundaries are shifting and traditional values are under siege. There is no end to the speculation about what the future might bring but this much is certain: during this period of transition to an era of unprecedented biological promise, every value we hold dear will require reevaluating. At every technological turn, a personal decision about which technology to embrace and which to dismiss will ultimately shape postmodern life. Having claimed for ourselves the right to determine our future, the future is now ours to determine.

As we go about tinkering with our own biology, the challenges to our values will be unique. When the mystery of the atom was solved and we understood how to release its energy, the moral issues could be plainly stated. The scientists who had worked for the Manhattan Project had a fairly good idea what to expect. They even had a vision of how to share the knowledge and bring peace to the world. The ethical issues were large, obviously political and international in scope. But now as the secrets of life are demystified, the ethical issues are very personal, incremental, undoubtedly political, and requiring different kinds of responses. There will probably never be a decisive, make-or-break issue. The consensus judgment is that germline manipulation—where we alter the genes in the first cell of an embryo and thus in every cell of a future child, in contrast to somatic gene therapy, which places a modified gene into a target cell—represents a point of no return. That may be true, but there are so many steps leading up to genetically enhancing human intelligence or cloning a human being that we will never know when we have crossed the Rubicon of no return.

A welcome presence in American homes for over twenty years, co-host of ABC's *Good Morning America* Joan Lunden announced that she and husband Jeff Koningsberg are expecting another set of twins from the same surrogate who gave birth just fifteen months ago to the couple's first set, Kate and Max. The surrogate herself, Deborah Bolig, is forty-three and this would be her third time delivering twins. But the truly interesting twist to this story is how the decision was made to have more children. "We had all of these embryos left over," Lunden told *Newsweek*. "Jeff and I have been banking these embryos for a while. It's funny, you pay freezer storage on embryos and I got the 'Do you want to re-up on your freezer storage?' and Jeff and I said, 'Oh, there's a little sibling in there somewhere very, very cold.'"[22] More than one child has been born on such a whim but very few to date because a moral decision had to be made to re-up or not. It causes you to wonder, what else do we have to look forward to in the category of "Why didn't my mother warn me there would decisions like this to make?"

When it comes to deciding which aspects of our lives we regard as too precious to be compromised, there is no objective standard. If we eliminate tradition, wisdom, religion, the civil code, then everything is truly subjective. But we live in a nation, and we are not the exception, where boundaries have been established, where there exists some sense of "this is as far as we should go." If C. S. Lewis were alive to rewrite *The Screwtape Letters*, the Devil would devise a very different lesson plan for "my dear Wormwood." It would include, most assuredly, the advice to tempt others with "don't read the fine print," or "expect a free lunch," and by all means "believe everything you are promised, and be sure to reward yourself often and without reserve." Wormwood would be instructed in the subtle charms of postmodern temptation, namely, it's all in the packaging. But haven't we become savvy shoppers? Some of us even read the fine print and expect a downside, but how will we resist the little voice whispering, "But this product is just what you need"?

Will there come a time when society will once again mobilize and say enough is enough? James Morone's *Hellfire Nation* opens a window of insight into the peculiar way Americans politicize what they regard to be a sin so dangerous that it must be contained. It is fair warning that the pattern will be repeated. Abortion and birth control were issues fought on moral grounds but settled on economic and social grounds. Prior to the Civil War abortion was openly accepted while birth control carried the stigma of licensing casual sex. As the Civil War ended a terrible new sin was discerned. At its 1859 meeting the American Medical Association went on record "against the unwarrantable destruction of human life." Morone summaries: "The AMA had organized an enormous shift in both law and culture" (*Hellfire Nation*, 251). Public sentiment swung from regarding abortion as something of no great harm (especially so prior to quickening in the womb) to one of outrage and disgust. Both abortion and birth control offered women a way to elude motherhood while satisfying their lust for sex. Both encouraged the educated to indulge in sex without consequence while allowing "those foreigners" to breed their way into a majority and bastardize the "pure" race.

Morone is equally perceptive in identifying how the abortion question settled out. The Supreme Court's decision of *Roe v. Wade* did not decide once and for all the question concerning when life begins. Even religious communities do not speak with one voice. The Jewish belief regards the embryo as an ethical concern only forty days after conception. Nor did the question of life's commencement become pivotal for how women actually acted regarding birth control and abortion. What matters most was the push toward gender equality and the role of women in contemporary society. "Outlawing abortion [and birth control]," Morone asserts, "would drive women back to their traditional roles" (*Hellfire Nation*, 491). And the one unalterable political fact was that women weren't going to be enslaved to the kitchen or the bedroom again. So much for moral or theological imperatives. And the same is true for what most Roman Catholics do concerning birth control over against what their church teaches. Traditional values, even when they are undergirded with religious authority, must also answer to the universal drive toward maximum freedom and equality.

There is no way to know if cloning and the like will become the next panic button, subject to the pattern of reaction, legislation, judicial precedents, and a "bureaucratic agency in search of a mission" (*Hellfire Nation*, 257). The trigger might be the sight of a cloned child turned into an idiot, or super-smart children who are incapable of maturing into adults. And what about the scenario where everything goes right and our life expectancy jumps twenty years and women choose to have three children spread out over forty years with robot nannies to do most of the work? Now that would be some kind of population explosion! I don't see the fundamental issues of life, liberty, and the pursuit of happiness disappearing into the woodwork. Nevertheless, Mary Shelley of *Frankenstein* fame knew something that we overlook. We actually do have the technology to create "monsters" that do not know where they have come from or why they were created. Leon Kass is not overreacting when he argues that "the indispensable foundations of a sound family life, itself the sound foundation of civilized community" depends upon "clarity about who your parents are and who your ancestors are, and clarity about who is whose" (*Life, Liberty*, 99–100). Look far enough into the future and the phrase "family of origin" or tracing your genealogy may be a little more difficult.

Boundaries have held together societies and provided the meaning to sustain human relationships. Affixing the word "natural" does not sanctify them, nor should encoding them in religious law make them inviolable. In each instance we must ask ourselves if this boundary is serving the common good, and at the same time acknowledge that it reflects the common sense of humanity and the wisdom of religion. But herein lies the troublesome nature of boundaries. Historically speaking, boundaries reflect the fears of a people at a given time. They are both culturally imposed and, in the eyes of some, divinely given. Their value comes from conserving what is good, but that same inherent resistance to change deters the introduction of new values. The question pressing upon us is whether certain traditional values will remain valid, valid if modified, or just dismissed as irrelevant. What is present and demanding of us is a continuous stream of decisions concerning these boundary questions:

- The boundary between natural and artificial
- The boundary between human and machine
- The boundary between therapy and enhancement
- The boundary between real and virtual
- The boundary between risk and reward.

Natural vs. Artificial—The demarcation between natural and artificial is quickly disappearing and it is happening in two ways: as an absolute distinction and the importance we attach to the distinction. No single reason accounts for the gradual erosion of the boundary between the natural and the artificial but certainly Newton's mechanical model and Darwin's theory of natural selection served to demystify the universe and turn the universe into mere matter. Where once human knowledge and valuation came from connecting ourselves rightly to the significance of what we learn from nature, we now construct knowledge and meaning by using the capabilities of the human mind.[23] The feeling of awe associated with the unexplainable became an attribute of what science explains: "I don't understand how conception works in a Petri dish but I stand in awe of the technology." Generation X and the baby boomers are scarcely aware of a reverential hands-off attitude toward nature because it bears the mark of the divine: created and given and therefore received with gratitude. They have a minimal recollection of a time when no one thought about alternative ways to have babies, or not to have them, or how to enhance food. Breeders knew how to mix and match in order to produce different breeds of animals and different varieties of food, but this was considered cooperating with nature rather than altering what is. For the modern mindset there is nothing sacrilegious in breaking nature apart to see how it works and reassembling it to a meet human need. Knowledge once ascribed to God is simply the fruit of our labor. It becomes our responsibility to use it wisely, but difficulties abound when the demarcation between natural and artificial is blurred.

The consumer fights a daily battle to tell what is natural. We can manufacture diamonds that are indistinguishable from natural ones but we still prefer the latter since they alone carry within them eons of time. The seeds used to grow organic food are likely to be a hybrid of human intervention and invention. The reason we care about organically grown food is not that some violation of natural law has taken place but the distrust of digesting something that is possibly harmful. But demonstrate to us that we are only being sentimentally pigheaded and we will buy and digest what is genetically altered. The bottom line is that we operate from a secular guideline that anything artificial needs to be significantly better than what is natural. Our level of distrust is provoked not so much by artificiality but by a science co-opted by the profit motive and forever maximizing the benefits and minimizing the risks. But there you have it: Whom can we trust when the boundary between those things made and those things given is not valued for itself?

The line between the birth control patch and the rhythm method is symptomatic of this boundary dispute. The Roman Catholic argument goes something like this. Something is morally right if natural, and natural is good because it is ordained by God. Anything unnatural is suspect because you cannot trust human intervention in the same way you can trust God. The birth control patch is immoral because it is unnatural, a human intervention. The Roman Catholic Church is right about human intervention because you can't trust human motivations, but the rebellion comes from another direction. First, nature itself operates by its own set of laws, and the laws are unforgiving, opportunistic, impersonal, uncaring, and set for survival. Second, the good includes not only what is natural but also what humans create to imitate and enhance nature. If given the opportunity, women will choose when and how many children to have and regard it as a good greater than being subject to the whim of nature. The course we have chosen is to take control of our lives, and this means greater dependence on human intervention. The new moral dilemma arises from the good we are capable—doing what nature does, only better—and mixing it with the evil humans are capable—thinking we can create as perfectly as God creates.

Modern forms of birth control make it possible to have sex without reproduction by disrupting the natural rhythm of sex progressing to pregnancy. Women reclaimed their bodies and their place in society beyond mother and housewife. New technologies make it possible to reproduce without sex. Reproduction as a stand-alone procedure will once again move the boundary of what we regard as acceptable. Its psychological and social impact is yet to be fully felt. It will, though, disrupt the natural rhythm of being biological parents. It will bring new meaning to the term "blended." Children will be born with genetic mothers who were never born themselves. This could happen when eggs that are recovered from the ovaries of miscarried or aborted human fetuses become the ingredient for the formation of a new human life.[24] Add the ability to select and enhance genes, and we approach a moment when it matters less who my biological mother and father are and more what genes I have. In a competitive global world, the right genes become very important.

When reproduction becomes a stand-alone event, not all of the consequences are deleterious. On the positive side, if a couple or single parent to be must spend thousands of dollars and endure painful procedures, due consideration is given to why a child is being conceived. When children are the result of natural affections, their very coming into being can be a happy or unwanted happenstance. What difference will it make if children are born in the traditional way, the consequence of an evening of shared loved, or by joining sperm and cell outside the womb? As a child becomes an adult, will it matter to her that her genes are different from her parents? Is it any different from adoption? One lesson we learned from having fathers part of the entire birthing process—from conception through labor and the actual birth—is that bonding comes naturally with nature's way of reproduction. But it also happens when in-vitro fertilization (IVF) is the procedure, because another kind of sharing of pain and joy takes place. The critical value is not whether there is a rigid distinction between natural and artificial, and not even whether reproduction is separated from sexual intercourse, but whether the child to be born is wanted and loved. However children come to us, what matters most is that children are born from the giving and receiving of love for the giving and receiving of love.[25]

Human vs. Machine—In Steven Spielberg's film of artificial intelligence (A.I.) there is a macabre scene where an angry crowd of humans gather for a ritualistic killing of the too-humanlike machines. In a carnival-like atmosphere, one android after another is brought to center ring and destroyed once and for all. The scene evokes a fear of being replaced by robots and androids. Our tolerance for artificiality, and machines in particular, is tempered by an instinctual reluctance to blur the distinction between human and nonhuman. In the world of Philip Dick's *Do Androids Dream of Electric Sheep?* Rick Deckart is a bounty hunter hired to permanently "retire" androids who have gone AWOL and turned against their owners. The new Nexus-6 android seems to possess the one quality all previous androids lacked: empathy. The standard test—an empathy scale measured by eye movements correlated to a series of situational questions (akin to a lie detector test)—is less than unequivocal. Deckart himself goes through an identity crisis when he sleeps with Rachael Rosen, a charming and beguiling Nexus-6, and then is sent to hunt her down as a dangerous prototype. Will he be able to retire someone who can empathize with him? Rachael reacts personally to being hunted down like some animal and goes to the rooftop of Deckart's apartment and throws his beloved goat off the ledge (beloved because it is not an electric one but a real, black Nubian goat). Dick carefully constructs the story in order to throw into ironic relief androids who mourn the loss of comrades and humans who kill without remorse or feeling. Dick left a body of work, including the film *Blade Runner* (adapted from *Do Androids Dream?*), devoted to testing the boundary between technological artifact and human individuality.[26] Living as we do in the twenty-first century, science will compel us to decide whether some absolute distinction is necessary and on what basis.

If androids can think, empathize, and possibly dream, are they human? Perhaps more clarity is gained if we ask whether androids should be baptized. Within an ecclesiastical context, the perfunctory response is "no" because they do not have a soul. But how does one know they do not have a soul? Because they have been created by us and not by God? By definition androids are not human, since only God can "make" a soul. But is the distinction absolute? Humans are created in the image of God, while androids are created in our image. If we are made in the image of God, and we make something in our image will it not be in the image of God? And what does the Christian do with the skeptic's argument that God is nothing but a reflection of our image? But even if the God of Christian worship reflects the worshiper, and it invariably does, the beholder understands human nature to be sinful and consequently can never trust what we construct, knowing that it is sometimes good and sometimes evil.

Perhaps something is learned by asking if androids sin, since sin is integrally related to baptism. To know sin requires that the subject in question exercises free will, a free will intractably joined with knowing that you are not yet the person God created you to be. In other words, to be human is to be accountable for our actions in the context of the disparity between who I am and who I should be. In Spielberg's film the newest prototype is engineered to replace a son who has died. This requires the android to aspire to be sufficiently human to be loved, and this becomes his quest. But since he is not truly biologically human he never experiences what it is to develop from infant to adult, to fall in love and fall out of love, to choose to remain faithful, to repent when unfaithful, to suffer the distance between who he is and who God created him to be. What an android lacks is the same depth of self-awareness born of the pathos of maturing from infant to adulthood. This not to say an android cannot learn and develop, truly reactive to its environment. (Those who build robots know this is the next hurdle to cross.) But is learning to navigate in a human world sufficient? When the pastor asks the adult candidate for baptism, "Do you renounce the powers of evil and desire the freedom of new life in Christ?" there exists the possibility of transformation. The powers of evil on one side and the new life in Christ on the other side constitute the human paradox. We are tempted and fallen; we are redeemed and made whole. Bring to me an android who is self-aware of both his sinful nature and hopeful of his re-creation in Christ and I would consider him/her a candidate for baptism. (This assumes the android is more than anatomically male or female but beset with sexual drives in all their positive and negative dimensions.)

The prevailing judgment is to believe that humans are superior to machines and that machines are merely tools in our service. This is a boundary already tested by machines invested with humanlike intelligence and humans fitted with mechanical parts. The threshold to watch is between incorporation (cyborgization) and fusion (fyborgization).[27] A hearing aid is different from a cochlear implant as a pacemaker is different from a heart transplant, and the deciding factor is the degree of fusion and reversibility. Thus far human beings have voiced a clear preference for separation but the choices will become ever more difficult. Protest as we will our wish to remain biologically independent and distinct, the lure of the bionic person is relentless. It sounds glib to argue that a medical amelioration is illegitimate because it is infused. We do not give a second thought to a surgically implanted pacemaker. Why not a mechanical heart? It took time to realize that we can be the same person with another person's heart. Human desires and feelings of love reside someplace else. The one organ left is the brain and that too will be fitted with electrodes and enhancers. But if no domains are sacred then will humans become hybrids? The most important line that we can draw in the sand does not compromise our identity or allow that identity to be compromised, misused, or appropriated—and this presumes an ongoing conversation regarding human identity.

The process of integration will continue because machines are better at some things and humans are better at other things, and some kinds of amalgamations are better yet. The bionic soldier is presently being designed under a contract with MIT. And someday "it" will take its place on the battlefield along with the increasing use of drones (à la *Star Wars: Return of the Androids*). Such challenges as the exploration of space will require a variety of cyborgizations and fyborgizations. We remain in control as long as we can pull the plug. But the plug is exactly what the astronauts could not pull when HAL of Stanley Kubrick's film *2001: A Space Odyssey* decided it was in charge. And the reason they couldn't pull the plug? HAL, the computer system, is so integrated with the spaceship that to shut down HAL is paramount to shutting down the ship, and that would have meant death to computer and humans.

Rodney A. Brooks, director of the Artificial Intelligence Laboratory at MIT, is a leading authority in the field of robotics. He is not short on optimism, predicting that in twenty years robots will have feelings and consciousness (see his *Flesh and Machines: How Robots Will Change Us*). Brooks's now famous statement that we have "over anthropomorphized humans" is part and parcel of the larger theme that we will accept robots one we give up the notion of our uniqueness. Spoken with the fervor of a true zealot, but most of us will reserve final judgment until Brooks has created a robotic wife and lived with "her" for fifty years. If we choose to relinquish the distinction enshrined in the theology that we alone among the earth's creatures are made in the image of God, then the mold itself is lost and we are free to create a bionic person and marry him or her.

Genetic Therapy vs. Genetic Enhancement—The contentious debate over genetic therapy as distinct from genetic enhancement is already a well-traveled road. Lee Silver, professor of molecular biology at Princeton University, voices the position of most biologists-geneticists that "it is impossible to draw a line in an objective manner." And he is correct, following his own logic. "In every instance, genetic engineering will be used to add something to a child's genome that didn't exist in the genomes of either of his parents. Thus, in every case, genetic engineering will be genetic enhancement—

whether it's to give children something that other children receive naturally, or to give them something entirely new" (*Remaking Eden*, 229). The difficulty with this argument is the conclusion. Silver feels justified to proceed down the path of genetic engineering since there is no meaningful distinction between genetic enhancement and genetic engineering. Bill McKibben, on the other hand, argues that because "the line between repair and enhancement is too murky to be meaningful, the wiser path is proceed with preimplantation genetic screening but abstain from genetic manipulation (*Enough*, 133). It's a boundary issue, but why for McKibben and not for Silver?

Until recently human history was one of living with nature, harnessing nature, and learning from nature. Francis Bacon is credited with introducing a new method of reasoning and discovery so that we can do better than nature.[28] This is a decided shift toward assertiveness and away from passivity, and as more than one feminist has noted, a shift associated with male aggressiveness.[29] Within this paradigm, the only truths that matter are those induced by experimenting and manipulating. The so-called Baconian Project would have us discard truths that are patiently garnered by taking a long and loving look at what is (meditating) or by listening to traditions much older than ourselves.[30] The paradigm shift that took place discounted truths that are given (revealed or known intuitively) while elevating truths of our own making (discovered or constructed). Operating in the background is this old-school versus new-school philosophy regarding truth and the boundaries it establishes. Silver is definitely new school and it shows in his science, which is both aggressive and dismissive of traditional boundaries.[31] McKibben is old school, regarding boundaries as signaling where the slippery slope begins. But what exactly is the downward spiral that might derail the posthuman project?

The distinction between therapy and enhancement is not meaningless, but it becomes subjective, and therein lies the tripping line. Therapy is essentially a remedial procedure. When Leon Kass writes about "a more natural science," he has in mind "wholeness" and "well-working" toward which the body aspires on its own (*Toward a More Natural Science*, 11). Enhancement is a different kind of procedure because it is elective but even that boundary distinction becomes tenuous if a young lady has only one dream, to become an actress, but finds that auditions are next to impossible for someone like herself who is flat chested. Would we say it is morally wrong for her to undergo surgery for a "normal" figure? Here is where subjectivity enters. What is normal or elective and what is normal regarding strength, intelligence, height, or beauty? And where does the ethical boundary fall when there is a genetic "fix" for someone who is very unhappy (depressed to the point of being suicidal)?

Enhancement appears to be a more assertive form of human intervention. The familiar argument meant to erase the distinction between repair and enhancement is to point to the way we have been embracing human intervention for a long time. If we say therapy is partnering with God while genetic enhancement is playing God, we think we have marked a difference in level or quality of intervention. We "play God" every time we inoculate our children against some dreaded disease, use birth control, transplant a heart, or split the atom. Why, scientists ask, is human intervention presumed to be a bad idea? I would concur that creating something new is not inherently sinful nor is assertive intervention, but both open the door to subjective judgments requiring discriminating judgments.

The temptation at our door begins with subjectivity and ends with killing the innocent. An enhancement is not only elective but also driven by subjective discontent. An extreme example has transpired in China and India where the culture's preference for male children has taken a dreadful toll. In the 1990s, when sonograms became widely available, this technology was used to identify the sex of the fetuses so females could be aborted. At one Bombay clinic eight thousand abortions were performed; 7,999 were female fetuses after parents knew the sex of the child.[32] A similar but less dramatic story is the use of human growth hormone (HGH). Originally licensed by the FDA to combat dwarfism, the expectation was of a limited market. Instead, HGH became one of the largest-selling drugs in the country and not because of any great increase in the number of little people but because of the number of parents who wanted to make their slightly short children taller. At four feet one inch, Marco Oriti is about four inches shorter than boys his age and projected to reach a height of five feet four. This was reason enough to prompt his parents to start him on a HGH regimen costing them $150,000 over a four-year period.[33] Driving the "need" to be tall is the subjective feeling that short people are inferior or handicapped. Yet there is little or no research to support the use of growth hormones to improve the presumed psychological impact of being shorter than most of one's peers. Short children, even extremely short children, seem to function quite well in school and social settings in spite of the pervasive attitude to the contrary. What we do know for certain is that individuals who begin hormone treatment do not want to stop, and this in itself creates a psychological need sufficient to support a $2 billion drug industry.[34]

A few may remember the mother who had hired a hit man to eliminate her daughter's rival on the cheerleading team. If this too is part of our genetic makeup, I foresee a genetic one-upmanship, or, don't let my neighbor give birth to a genetically superior child. Thus when Stock answers his own question—"If we could make our baby smarter, more attractive, a better athlete or musician, or keep him or her from being overweight, why wouldn't we?"— the race has begun and it won't be about who has the most toys but the better enhancements. The prognosis Lee Silver entertains seems right. When it comes to human enhancement, the marketplace rules. Who is more powerful than a mother or father who wants the "best" for their child? Certainly governmental regulations will not be allowed to get in the way. After all, who elects our representatives to give us what we want? Silver asks rhetorically: "If it is within the rights of parents to spend $100,000 for an exclusive private school education, why is it not also within their rights to spend the same amount of money to make sure that a child inherits a particular set of their genes?" (*Remaking Eden*, 225). When framed as a matter of rights, money will buy power. When genetic enhancement is framed as a matter of justice, a different answer is called for, and it's about how best to spend $100,000 if I love all the children of the world. But who knows, on the horizon may be a rebellion against the responsibility of determining your child's genetic future. Natural may yet rule the day, "natural" in the sense of before my existence, not of my making.

Real vs. Virtual Reality—Like the grains of sand that turn up everywhere after a trip to the beach, virtual reality will seep into our lives extinguishing the boundary between reality and virtual reality. In the film *Minority Report*, Tom Cruise pops a pill, slips in a CD disk, and relives a memory of his missing son. It is an illicit activity, for reasons not given. Perhaps it is deemed dangerous for the same reasons narcotics are. More likely, virtual reality will become everyone's acceptable "drink after a hard day." The corner Starbucks will host virtual-reality play stations and down the street will be a pleasure center displacing obsolete amusement parks. We can look forward to easing into an armchair, turning out the lights, and enjoying a virtual-reality book where the characters are holograms (almost as good as in the Harry Potter films). This will be entertainment at its addictive best. And where is the sin, I ask again, in dropping into another realm to experience what I desire most?

Placed in the right hands, virtual reality will have its beneficial uses. Teenagers will learn to drive without maiming themselves or the garage door; doctors will be able to practice on virtual patients. Scrapbooks will be more than photographs and faded scraps of newsprint. Virtual reality will allow us to experience what it is like to fly like a bird, swim with the dolphins, and bed the person of our dreams. But will there be any virtue in virtual reality? The virtue of reality is that it teaches us something we didn't want to learn. When one boundary merges with another and the "real" isn't real, the only uncertainties are the ones encoded by the programmer, and every decision is without meaningful consequence. In the final analysis, the reason reality cannot be digitized is its unpredictability—"not in a thousand years would I have thought . . ." How one event influences the next event and so on exponentially constitutes one of life's mystery. Consequently, virtual reality will be of little help in the difficult role of parenting or teaching valuable lessons. It will improve hand-eye coordination and expand one's horizon, but it cannot prepare me to care for a loved one dying of cancer. Albert Borgmann's description of what it means to share a person's mortal illness is all that needs to be said regarding the limits of virtual reality. "Actually to share a person's mortal illness is to feed, clean, and change that person, to suffer the person's bursts of anger and flights of hallucination. It is to see a person suffer deeply and decay. It is to sleep irregularly and poorly and to feel confined and at times resentful. With all that it can be an occasion of grace and gratitude" (*Holding On to Reality*, 191).

Pornography will continue to be the driving force behind this kind of technology, and the reason is quite obvious. Reconstruct your neighbor's wife, dress her up or down as you like, and have an affair with her. No one gets hurt, so where is the sin? The hidden lure of virtual reality rests with the exacerbation of our base desires: those activities we do under the cloak of night or the privacy of a play (pleasure) station. But who is going to stop to ask whether this is a royal waste of time, a virtual siphon of everything I might offer to the world to make it a better place? While love, justice, and mercy could find a place in the realities we construct—though they never seem to—they are only virtuous when practiced in the world of human relations where nothing is simple or easy.

Risk vs. Reward—Everyone who witnessed the first atomic blast knew instantly that here was a technology powerful enough to endanger the entire globe. In many ways biotechnology is its opposite. Fukuyama states it well: "In contrast to many other scientific advances, [biotechnology] mixes obvious benefits with subtle harms in one seamless package" (*Posthuman Future*, 7).[35] After touting the wonderful benefits of a new medication, the advertisement blatantly acknowledges known side effects. It never used to be this way, and pharmaceutical companies do it because they must. You would think it would scare off all potential consumers. It doesn't. Has life become so intolerable? Have our expectations about marriage and work, health and happiness, been set so high that contentment and fulfillment are always out of reach? Or is a different dynamic at work where the benefit is so promising that risk becomes almost inconsequential?

What does it mean when a capsule with breakfast makes a shy person outgoing or a reticent person able to function in the public eye? Peter Kramer's best-selling Listening to Prozac is a highly introspective account of a revolution sweeping through pharmacological science. While the primary use of SSRI medications is to treat depression, they also affect personality in unexpected ways and pay an unexpected dividend. For the sake of the argument consider the moral ramifications of a Prozac-like drug tailor made by your pharmacist in consultation with your doctor-therapist for the purpose of helping you become more assertive or more self-assured. This is precisely the kind of effect Kramer reports in a nonspecific way, but then that was in 1993.[36] What isn't there to like about a pill that draws people toward ordinary and even noble human activities, assuming there are no harmful side effects? Our worst fear, writes Kramer, is whether the cost is hidden within the benefit. In order to feel good about ourselves, we are robbed of what is uniquely human: anxiety, guilt, shame, grief, self-consciousness. Taking a clue from the novelist Walker Percy, Kramer is concerned that we immunize ourselves from the very signals that alert us to what is wrong with ourselves. Percy in turn celebrates those thinkers who paid careful attention to what is wrong with us: Sarte's nausea, Kierkegaard's fear and trembling, Camus's existential anxiety, Freud's unconsciousness, Tillich's angst.

Kramer is also prophetic when he notes: "By observing responses to Prozac, we learn not only about ourselves but about our island's culture" (Listening to Prozac, 297). In other words, we manufacture and prescribe the kind of drug that meets the expectation of the dominant culture. Prozac or a spin-off becomes the drug of choice because American society accepts and rewards those who are bright, alert, flexible, and "on top of it." When American society wanted women at home and on the bottom, the drug of choice was Valium. In discussing the predisposition to prescribe Ritalin for boys who lack the "proper" control of their behavior, Fukuyama calls attention to the gentle nudge "toward that androgynous median personality, self-satisfied and socially compliant, that is the current politically correct outcome in American society" (Posthuman Future, 52).

Are Prozac or methamphetamines different from experience-enhancing, mood-altering drugs, like marijuana or cocaine? The latter encourages self-absorption and opiates the person into a mindless state of "all is right with me and the world." Prozac and methamphetamines, on the other hand, can have the alluring quality of giving pleasure indirectly by increasing feelings of self-worth and lowering barriers to ordinary social intercourse. The "good responders" to Prozac, as Kramer designates them, are released from their fears. But is this substituting stimulation for self-examination, superficial feel-good-about-myself for real (painful) growth? We live in a world that deserves a more complex response than feeling all right. At stake is more than Gerald Klerman's pharmacological Calvinism that whispers to the inner self "that if a drug makes you feel good, it must be morally bad" (*Listening*, 247). A pill may liberate me so that I'm feeling OK, but it also deludes me into thinking everything is OK with the world and me. Medication can do much to stop the hurting, the darkness, the compulsiveness, the loss of control, the days and nights of anxiety and fear. This however is not what it means to be fully human, which includes, not incidentally, feeling and bearing the pain of others.

Psychotropic drugs ensnare us into seeing pills and biological fixes as our salvation. If so, then we have overlooked the theological perspective that our alienation is not only horizontal but also vertical. Guilt and shame are links to an awareness that we have offended another law not written with human hands. Who could imagine Mother Teresa digesting something to deaden the suffering she bore while ministering to lepers in the streets of Calcutta? What she suffered she suffered willingly because of the deeper meaning of her faith. There is no pill that can lead us to see the pattern of sin laid down over a lifetime, because sin is not an emotion or feeling but a transgression. The healing of sin requires confession, contrition, and setting right a wrong I have done. By reducing everything to the level of feelings, medication can delude us still further that the only pain that matters is my own.

As Luke tells the story of the prodigal son, the wayward son does not get up one morning and after a breakfast of oatmeal and Prozac see the error of his ways, realize he has sinned against heaven (God) and humanity (his father), and return home seeking forgiveness. The more likely scenario of a drug-induced repentance would have the son realize life is not so bad and renew his effort to make a name for himself. His moment of self-awareness would come when he understands that he has been given a second chance to succeed. There would be no reason for him to return home for that only represents more pain: confronting a father he believes demands justice and living with his elder brother who hates everything he has done and is.

In the good old days before ethical-review boards and patent lawyers, scientists were not twisted out of shape by the question, "Who do I work for and why am I doing this?" Before conflicting loyalties, composite motives, and multiple paychecks, science was straightforward. Scarcely anything is straightforward when research is done with an eye toward a payoff. You answer to the university but your funding for a particular project comes from a grant with conditions contrary to the best interest of the university. The source of funding may be governmental or private or a combination of both. Sociologist John Ziman explores the culture of science in his book *Real Science* and caustically remarks that "On Mondays, Wednesdays and Fridays, so to speak, they are producing public knowledge under traditional academic rules, on Tuesdays and Thursdays they are employed to produce private knowledge under commercial conditions."[37] Somewhere in this mix the scientist must answer to himself: What are the governing interests, convictions, ethical guidelines, and boundaries which define my integrity? And it will not get any easier, especially if your intentions are honorable.

Patent law will never again be simply about one person's invention. The very nature of what is being protected has changed. The future is not about hardware but software, less about a better mousetrap and inevitably about information. Most inventions did not change the world. A few did, such as Velcro and the telephone, but there was nothing urgent about them. A vaccine for AIDS would be different because it is immediately a matter of life and death for hundred of thousands of humans. The playing field is global and the stakes are enormous. Individuals seeking to patent a good idea are up against transnational corporations. And the number applying is growing at such a pace that it helps to have friends in "high places" to cut through the red tape. In the gold-rush atmosphere unleashed by cracking the genetic code, everyone is scrambling to patent nearly anything that might someday turn out to be profitable. The effect is paralyzing to research. Because the risk-benefit scenario is so pervasive, the most talented scientists and the best research labs are co-opted by the prospect of patents. Otherwise your research is unprotected and your labor unrewarded. Unfortunately, a whole lot of intellectual property (what used to be called research) is either stuffed in file drawers waiting a patent decision or not shareable because it is patented.

Conclusions

A number of conclusions seem unavoidable and together they draw together the various arguments of part 1.

Conclusion # 1—In American and Western societies science *has assumed a dominant position*. It is has grown to be an 800-pound gorilla that sits where it pleases. It's dominance—but not exactly domination—is severalfold. Science is an economic powerhouse, the dynamic that defines progress. When you think of the next big thing, you think technological breakthrough. While the euphemism about aspiring to be a rocket scientist needs to be updated by reference to a molecular biologist, the sentiment is still valid. The methodology of science is the measure by which other truths and methodologies are judged. Science embodies the commonplace notions about hope and progress. If tomorrow is to be better than yesterday, then science will need to lead the way.

As science emerged from World War II, a *dramatic transformation* was already at work. Atomic physicists quickly became acquainted with the politics of power because they were the preeminent doorkeepers to a storehouse of knowledge both lethal and benign. They were courted and given places of honor. The responsibility of what they had created weighed heavily on most of them, and it endures whenever concerned scientists organize to protest or protect. They were motivated to move heaven and earth but their heightened sense of moral responsibility was short lived because it never felt like a good fit. Clearly the good old days of a utilitarian science for useful gadgets or ivory towers of pure research are finished. So much more is expected of science.

The *growth of science* has been phenomenal. When measured against a percentage of our gross national product, research and development is not a budget buster. It accounts for roughly 5 percent of the total federal budget. The figure for the year 2000, including government, universities, and nonprofit organizations, is $264.6 billion for R&D.[38] Compared with other nations, our investment in science is large simply by the virtue of our wealth. Regardless of how large or small the figures are, science is what turned America into the superpower it is—both economically and militarily.

Because science is perceived to be indispensable, it is *more powerful* than its share of the federal budget would indicate. Science is not an industry but without science industry would be stymied. That is why industry now finances over 65 percent of the R&D in America. The twenty-year evolution of telecommunication technology into a $1 billion industry is one of many instances of a new economy thanks to science. The LCD technology so evident in watches and cell phones may be the next big industry, plastering flat screens at every corner and every juncture where the eye comes to rest. But forget the money—if you can—and think about how you felt when the computer(s) was down in your favorite retail store. Remember the panic when the new millennium was about to ring in. We were warned that computers wouldn't be able to adjust for the new century and would shut down or not start up. A sinking feeling of paralysis swept over us: now *nothing* will get done.

What scientists are doing is *newsworthy*. Science is not often headline news but it is news worth reporting on a daily basis. Unlike religion, which is given its due in the Saturday edition, the broader populace wants to keep up with what is the cutting-edge technology or the most current medical treatment available. The headline news for Monday, 11 October 2004 included the death of Christopher Reeve. The lead stories of section B of *USA Today* was a story of a twenty-five-year-old quadriplegic who sits in a wheelchair with wires coming out of a bottle-cap-sized connector inserted into his skull. The wires from one hundred tiny sensors are connected to a computer allowing the man to play the computer game Pong with just his thoughts. Consider the possibilities. And that is why the story is newsworthy, and a little scary. If thoughts can control a computer, then a computer can control thoughts.

Conclusion #2—Something is *qualitatively different* when knowledge is for sale. Sheldon Krimsky's critique of science rings true. He goes farther then decrying the loss of a public-interest science, by naming it as the "most significant loss among the other losses frequently cited—including free and open exchange of information, the knowledge commons, and the norm of disinterestedness" (*Science in the Private Interest*, 215). His argument cannot be accepted at face value, for science has a long history of dependence on patronage of some kind. When a king, a prince, or any benefactor subsidized research, the scientist tended to lose control of the knowledge produced. But as a matter of principle the knowledge in question was considered to be beyond the domain of any one person, even a sovereign. The development of free-standing, independent scientific associations and the move to house scientific research within academia were both extremely significant because science was provided means and motive to pursue knowledge without the encumbrance of patronage. Ken Alder's account of how the universal measure of the meter was arrived at speaks of a different ethos (*The Measure of All Things*). One can only admire the dedication and hardship endured by Jean-Baptiste-Joseph Delambre and Pierre-Francois-André Méchain as they traversed France for seven years in the worst kinds of weather in order to record thousands and thousands of triangulations. Their scientific mission was to derive a fundamental unit of measure from the measure of the world itself. But their self-sacrifice does not distinguish them from scientists toiling away in modern laboratories (uncommon self-sacrifice and dedication may be just an indicator of the unusual scientists in any era). These *savants*, for that is how they were known during the Enlightenment, did not renounce fame and fortune (though those things were by no means guaranteed either). What they did not consider doing and would have found repulsive is the prospect of gaining financial reward by holding a monopoly (patent) on the knowledge itself. But then the opportunity did not present itself, and now it does, and that tells us something too.

Science operates with a set of normative values and norms, and together they constitute its ethos. More than a half-century ago the distinguished sociologist Robert K. Merton identified four norms that distinguish a scientific culture: universalism, communalism, disinterestedness, and organized skepticism.[39] Communalism and disinterestedness refer to the common ownership of the fruits of scientific investigation where information is freely shared without consideration of personal gain. Terms like "technology transfer," "intellectual property," and "university-industry partnerships" describe a different scientific culture, one that stands over against the Aristotelian expression "knowledge is virtue" or "the pleasure of finding things out." The self-interested profiteer has replaced images of the soulless, evil scientist, and this is a very different threat to the social good than blowing ourselves to bits.

The proverbial wall of separation between research and application barely exists. Originally the separation was meant to protect the ideal of pure science from distracting and compromising situations. Whether the separation was by physical location, funding sources, or professional choice, a critical distance was created allowing for second thoughts. The opposite is transpiring. By in large, research today is aimed at a particular development from the beginning. Because science is sensitive to competitive pressures, it cannot allow for second thoughts (recalls of any kind). In the world of biomedicine, everything is pushed forward toward a profitable product, and for the sake of efficiency, research and development become a seamless whole.

If scientists lose their credibility as trustworthy reporters of disinterested information, who will listen to them? No one understands this better than scientists. Yet, science is backing itself into a corner. Every time a conflict-of-interest issue is raised, when a story breaks concerning questionable collaborations between industry and university, the public is given another reason to believe science has sold out. Whatever happened to research done to advance the public welfare or the scientist who places the public interest above his own? We are quickly approaching a crisis requiring a more public statement from scientists of their personal and professional accountability.

Thus far the emphasis has been placed on fiscal transparency and conflict-of-interest disclosures as if they were the panacea.[40] In the fourth century, Hippocrates recognized the need for doctors to swear an oath before the gods. Standing before the human body, weakened by illness, deformed by disease, openly vulnerable (literally "uncovered"), doctors swore to constrain themselves in accordance with virtues appropriate to their science: reverence, discretion, prudence, self-restraint, and justice. "Into whatever houses I may enter, I will come for the benefit of the sick, remaining clear of all voluntary injustice and of other mischief and of sexual deeds upon bodies of females and males, be they free or slave" (Hippocratic Oath).[41] Scientists do not uncover a vulnerable body but they do lay open truths harboring within them the potential for much good and harm. Their obligation is to steward that knowledge as if it were a living thing, for it will indeed take on a life of its own in due time. But stewards are only as trustworthy as the public declaration they make regarding the integrity of their lives. Speaking as both a physician and theological ethicist, Margaret Mohrmann states in the strongest language the significance of making a public profession: It serves as "a virtually unretractable statement about the content, direction, and moral weight of one's life."[42] Is there a better statement of what the commonwealth expects from those who hold life and death in their hands and lead the way into a Genomic Era?[43]

Conclusion #3—If science were not so dominant it would not receive so much critical attention. But it is big and effusive and has attracted a lot of negative attention. A short list of social critics would include Walther Rathenau, Charles Beard, Lewis Mumford, Jacques Ellul, Langdon Winner, Isaiah Berlin, Hans Jonas, and Albert Borgmann.[44] The main thrust of their critique is to warn us of the pervasive power of technology and the serious threat technological systems pose both to humanity and nature. The third conclusion brings to the fore the way science has become *a social problem*.

It did not take long for the world to realize the threat of atomic weapons went beyond human life. The entire biosphere is at risk. No one has set forth the imperative for a postatomic age better than the philosopher Hans Jonas. Jonas depicts the change in this way. Where ethics were once concerned with the interpersonal affairs between human beings, it now finds it necessary to consider the consequences of our actions stretching into the far future. "The containment of nearness and contempaoraneity is gone," writes Jonas, "swept away by the spatial spread and time of the cause-effects trains which technological practice sets afoot, even when undertaken for proximate ends" (*The Imperative of Responsibility*, 7). While traditional ethics concerns itself with the consequences of personal behavior ("Thou shall not steal"), the magnitude of global radiation and the threat inherent in gene splicing requires an added sense of responsibility. More so than ever, the threat to life is not simply outright destruction but transfiguring what it means to be human. But the true irony of our situation, as Jonas grasped so well, is the manner in which science places in our hands the means to direct our own destiny and at the same time rips away the moral ground necessary to steer a wise course (*Imperative*, 22).

Can we imagine atomic physicists engaging in a public discussion at the end of the war about "the shallowness of reductionist programs, the tyrannizing and stultifying effects of bureaucratization in science, the dedicated following of scientific fashion and the attendant loss of the Big Picture and of imagination, the hegemony of Big Science at the expense of Little, the incompetence of the peer review system, the commercialization of science and the attendant ethical and intellectual erosion" (Shapin, *One Culture?* 113)? We have hints of such a critique in the lectures of Oppenheimer in the 1950s but nothing approaching a sweeping critique aimed at the core of science itself. Oppenheimer, like C. P. Snow's famous essay on "The Two Cultures," was primarily concerned with the antagonism between two cultures, one narrowly defined by specialized sciences and the other broadly humanistic. The crisis they predicted would be two cultures speaking two different languages. What happened is quite the opposite. The values of science are so dominant that only the language of truth is empirical. The culture of science is the culture of the most powerful and most prosperous nation in the world.

Science is a social problem because we can't decide whether to embrace or reject it. Our love-hate relationship with technology is almost a daily experience. The frustrating mix of benefits and harm makes an expanding number of decisions more difficult. On the one hand we might regard technical progress to be humanity's supreme achievement but we no longer blindly assume it to be capable of resolving our most profound problems. We who live in developed countries know that we owe our prosperity and position in the world to science. And yet we remain cynical of an overpromising science. The noted historian of science Gerald Holton reminds us of an anti-science sentiment taking root among playwrights, poets, novelists, and philosophers since the Enlightenment. In Holton's view this Romantic rebellion has found new voices—none more prominent or eloquent than the Czech playwright and former president Václav Havel—who strongly resist the modern presumption that the world is "'a wholly knowable system governed by a finite number of universal laws that man can grasp and rationally direct for his own benefit.'"[45]

In the heyday of physics, the great philosophical debate swirled around objectivity. Could the knower know something objective about the universe without undue influence from one's social and historical circumstances? While the debate continues whether empiricism is capable of generating objective knowledge, the pressing concern for us now is whether science is still committed to generating disinterested knowledge. The difference is this: objective knowledge aims to be the antithesis of interested knowledge. What once was an ontological or epistemological question—is there a reality independent of the mind that can be known objectively—has become a moral question—so much so that Feynman believes the integrity of science depends on complete honesty. Advertising, then, is "an example of a scientifically immoral description of products" (*The Pleasure of Finding Things Out*, 108). The moral issues intensify, of course, when scientists choose to engage in R&D knowing that any disinterested motives they have will be shortly compromised by a plan to advertise this knowledge.

For James Robert Brown the crucial question is, to whom should scientists be accountable? "The answer is simple: the public" (*Who Rules in Science*, 212). This straightforward answer immediately gets bogged down in questions regarding who will represent science when science itself is fragmented, and how can the public participate when they know so little. Steve Fuller points out that as each scientist knows more and more about less and less, scientists share in the "sphere of ignorance that increasingly approximates the state of the non-scientific lay public" (*The Governance of Science*, 135). We are left in the unfortunate situation of egalitarianism where only the select few make decisions for all of us. But that is not entirely correct and it is not necessary to surrender the principle of greater participation. Bill McKibben moves this logic one step further by asserting the devil is not in the empirical details but in the basic thrust of technology. "Understanding which chromosomes are responsible for the expression of which protein doesn't give you an added insight into whether designer babies are a good idea, any more than figuring out how to make an atom bomb turns you into an expert on when or where you should drop it" (*Enough*, 182).

The quandary we face is double sided. Science itself is not motivated or equipped to provide direction and moral reasons for much of what it does. We cannot, however, point an accusing finger at science without including the commonwealth. Fuller points to the awe and mystery surrounding science and concludes there has been a "persistent failure of nerve and imagination" on the part of modern democracies to articulate exactly what they expect from science (*Governance*, 102). Nor does it help that modern governments have become so dependent on expert knowledge for so many critical decisions that they are reluctant to demand greater accountability. When government, such as ours, funds R&D through twenty-five departments and agencies, and when private industry plays a growing but hidden role, who can realistically set priorities when no one knows who is funding what? Nothing illustrates better the mixed signals we give science than the clash of values represented by President Bush's decision to restrict federal funding to embryonic stem cell lines already in existence and the popular vote in November 2005 to fund $3 billion for stem cell research in California, an amount substantially more than the entire federal budget for stem cell research. The favorable vote epitomizes what we already know: more and more science is in the hands of private interests (the proposition is the brainchild of venture capitalists hoping California will become the next Silicon Valley for biotechnology), and more and more the promise of radically new treatments for a host of genetic disorders rests with the new life sciences.

On a deeper, more philosophical level, science is regarded as a social problem because we are gradually recognizing that knowledge is neither intrinsically good nor neutral, especially as it passes through human hearts and minds (and, of course, there is no other way we come to know anything). Knowledge is not the problem, humans are. But the two cannot be separated, even though we once thought it possible.

Conclusion # 4—We have backed into an era when science and theology find themselves at loggerheads, situations where one is unable to convince the other regarding the rightness of their understanding. Looming on the horizon are multiple confrontations concerning boundaries, traditional values, and the good of society. The history of their relationship as sibling rivals (who possesses the superior knowledge) predisposes theology and science to see the other as interfering in their domain. On the other hand, a truce has been called and a degree of mutual respect has prevailed for the last century. We should not expect a re-enactment of win-lose battles over grand metaphysical questions. But we should expect believers to take a stand with the intended effect of telling science to back off (enough is enough) or slow down (why the rush?). Scientists, for their part, will not allow themselves to be held hostage by this kind of mentality when a promising line of research is at stake. My fourth conclusion, then, acknowledges the imperative to rethink sin and evil and to see it as an opportunity to rethink the role of theology and science vis-à-vis the common good.

After all is said done, science will proceed very well without the inclusion of a theological understanding of sin and evil. Any mention of sin and evil seems inappropriate and unnecessary. Science is quite content to discount and ignore what theologians have been saying about human nature for thousands of years. (I include the biblical storytellers and writers of *Genesis*.) Christian theologians are no less committed now then in the first century to an understanding of sin as omnipresent. Science is equally committed to a methodology that excludes any explanation dependent on a supernatural explanation. The issue is not so much whether a hidden, supernatural (divine) causation is possible but rather that it is not the kind of explanation that explains something scientifically. The ultimate cause of sin and evil—whether natural or supernatural—is something I have intentionally not taken up in order to avoid making it a point of contention. What matters is whether we deny, ignore, or affirm the reality of sin and evil, and every argument in this book is meant to underscore the consequences of how we understand the perpetual nature of being human.

The profoundly divisive issue of stem cell research exposes the inherent tension between religion's role to conserve and science's need to push forward. Science does not set out to undermine the established norms of society, but science and limits do not mix well. Researchers are inclined to regard boundaries as impediments to truth because they are depositories of superstition, delusion, and gullibility.[46] The matter is immensely complicated when those boundaries carry the weight of "sacred" or "natural," and sometimes both when sexual intercourse between a man and a woman (natural) is sanctified by a religious ceremony. In its restless need to improve on what is, science is well counseled to consider natural and traditional boundaries as measures intended to make us pause long enough to consider the motives of our intrusion and manipulation. Since the consequences of tampering with nature can be so grave, there is something to be gained and little to be sacrificed when an old rule of carpentry is followed: measure twice, cut once. During a time of deconstruction—when the most fundamental reasons for marriage and family are continually challenged—the role of boundaries to safeguard and clarify one's origins and identity (recalling Kass's statement above) is of utmost importance. Science plays its role by challenging the rule of inviolability and the claim for absoluteness. If the values we hold most dear are worthy to guide our future, they should be able to withstand the scrutiny of science while remaining true to our most deeply held beliefs. The wisdom we require to guide us through this twenty-first century is both theological and scientific.

Notes

1. See Harvey Brooks, *The Governance of Science*, 24. Daniel S. Greenberg also has a good discussion of science prior to World War II in *The Politics of Pure Science*.

2. Krimsky, *Science in the Private Interest*, 27–31, 79–81.

3. See Daniel J. Boorstin, *The Discoverers* (New York: Vintage Books, 1983).

4. This theme is developed by McKibben in *Enough*, 44–45, 189–92.

5. This is the verdict of Gyorgy Markus, "Why Is There No Hermeneutics of Natural Sciences? Some Preliminary Theses," *Science in Context* 1 (1987): 5–51 (quotation from 42–43); and Evelyn Fox Keller, *Making Sense of Life: Explaining Biological Development with Models, Metaphors, and Machines* (Cambridge, Mass: Harvard University Press, 2002).

6. Since the publication of books like *The Structure of Scientific Revolutions* (1962) by Thomas Kuhn and Larry Laudan's book, *Progress and Its Problems* (1977), there is no longer a presumption that scientific knowledge is a straightforward linear progression. Nevertheless, I will presume the scientific methodology distinguishes itself by accumulating knowledge in a building-block fashion.

7. Quoted from Clifford Geertz, "The Strange Estrangement: Charles Taylor and the Natural Sciences," in Geertz's *Available Light*, 143. I concur with Geertz that Taylor has turned the natural sciences into a vague and antiquated target (e.g., reducing empiricism to an absolute world of ascertainable fact). Geertz, however, underestimates the powerful *cultural* effect science has had.

8. Foucault, *The Order of Things*, 168. Postman does not cite Foucault to bolster his argument but both concur that two thought-worlds cannot co-exist at the same time. "With the rise of Technopoly," Postman writes, "one of those thought-worlds disappears" (*Technopoly*, 48). The worldview or thought-world that cannot survive is the traditional one of Judeo-Christianity.

9. Langdon Winner, *Autonomous Technology: Technics-out-of-Control as a Theme in Political Thought* (Cambridge, Mass.: MIT Press, 1977), 229. Winner pressed the argument that technology has become autonomous and out of control.

10. In *Competing Truths* (chapter 2), I make a clear distinction between a view of the world and a worldview. We know science changed how we locate ourselves in the universe (a view of the world). I do not think, though, the argument can be sustained that science provided the metaphysical justifications to warrant the designation of worldview. Clearly two views of the world can exist at the same time in one culture. That leaves the arguable question about two worldviews.

11. See the under-appreciated work of Ellul in *The Humiliation of the Word*, especially chapter 1.

12. Hunter, *Cultural Wars*, 128, also 45 and 120. Hunter does not fully acknowledge the liberal Protestant tradition of self-criticism—a tradition that precedes modern science but then defines itself by the way it incorporates experience and scientific rationality into its own religious mentality, a tradition born of the Reformation from Luther through Kierkeggard to Tillich and heir to the historical critical method.

13. For the inside story see *The Genome War* (Ballantine Books, 2004) by James Shreeve. The story of how and why Craig Venter entered the quest for the Holy Grail of science is more complex than the media made it out to be.

14. Roger Thurow, "Seeds of Doubt: As U.S., EU Clash on Biotech Crops, Africa Goes Hungry," *Wall Street Journal*, 26 December 2002, A1.

15. United Nations Development Program, *Human Development Report* (New York and Oxford: Oxford University Press, 1999), 66, emphasis added.

16. George Soros, *On Globalization* (New York: Pacific Affairs, 2002). See also Joseph E. Stiglitz, *Globalization and Its Discontents* (New York: W.W. Norton, 2002) as well as his review of *On Globalization* in *New York Review of Books*, 23 May 2002, 24–28.

17. Based on the interview conducted by National Public Radio, 6 January 2003—"Profile: Tenure of World Health Organization's director general Dr. Gro Harlem Brundtland as she begins her last year in the post." Accessed at www.npr.org/transcripts/story.html.

18. Liz Kawalczyk, "Harvard to Use Caution with Merck," *Boston Globe*, 24 April 2002, C1.

19. Liz Kowalczyk, "$50m Genetics Center Planned," *Boston Globe*, 24 April 2002, A1.

20. Richard Lewontin, "The Politics of Science," *New York Review*, 9 May 2002, 30.

21. See Sylvia Nasar's biography of John Nash, *A Beautiful Mind* (New York: Simon and Schuster), 105–112.

22. Story appeared in *Newsweek*, 27 September 2004, 93.

23. Charles Taylor gives the most complete description of this momentous shift to a modern way of knowing (epistemology) and assigning meaning. See *Sources of the Self*, 144–185, and Coleman, *Competing Truths*, 58–75.

24. Stock in *Remaking Eden* suggests a number of scenarios that stretch to the limit the boundaries of traditional values, 153, 171.

25. See Gilbert Meilaender's chapter on "Cloning and Begetting" in his *Things That Count*, 101–10. Human cloning, he notes, breaks the connection between marriage and begetting children as well as the connection between sexual differentiation. The same is true for artificial insemination and surrogate motherhood. The difference is the all-important question of motivation. If children are begotten of love they are likely to beget their own children in love. But if children are made to be like ourselves—a shaped and willed product—they are likely to have children who love only what they can shape and will.

26. For an independent analysis of Dick's fiction see N. Katherine Hayles, *How We Became Posthuman*, chapter 7.

27. See Stock, *Redesigning Humans*, 24–29.

28. Bacon's *Novum Organon* (1620) was his proposal for a "new instrument" to vex nature until she reveals her secrets. See Zagorin, *Francis Bacon* (Princeton University Press, 1998), 77–89.

29. See for example Carolyn Merchant, *The Death of Nature* (New York: Harper and Row, 1980) and for a more generalized assessment of the aggressive nature of modern

science, see Amos Funkenstein, *Theology and the Scientific Imagination from the Middle Ages to the Seventeenth Century* (Princeton University Press, 1988).

30. For a discussion of the Baconian Project, see Gerald P. McKenney, *To Relieve the Human Condition*, chapter 2.

31. Since Silver's book in 1997 there has been no lack of similar optimistic pictures of how the new technology will enhance our future. See, for example, Ray Kurzweil, *The Singularity Is Near: When Humans Transcend Biology* (Viking Adult, 2005); Ramez Noam, *More than Human: Embracing the Promise of Biological Enhancement* (Broadway Books, 2005); Ronald Bailey, *Liberation Biology: The Scientific and Moral Case for the Biotech Revolution* (Prometheus Books, 2005).

32. McKibben, *Enough*, 22. The British-based medical journal *The Lancet* published a study in January 2006 estimating that Indian women aborted a stunning 10 million girls in the two decades leading up to 1998. See John Donnelly, "Girl Deficit Grows in India," *Boston Globe*, 10 January 2006, A1.

33. Using several sources McKibben pieces together this story in *Enough*, 33. A personal account is reported by Patricia Wen, "Reaching for Growth," *Boston Globe*, 4 October 2005, A1. Nancy Hubbard, the mother of twins, speaks of the contradictory message she gave when they began daily growth hormone treatment. "For years, I told them, 'God made you special. He made you that way.' And now I say to them, 'you need shots.'"

34. Stephen S. Hall, "The Short of It," *New York Times Magazine*, 16 October 2005, 54–59.

35. Kass makes the same observation in *Life, Liberty*, 3, 38. He asks, "But what if the difficulties attending technology are both integral to its very being and inseparable from its benefits—like the other side of a coin?" Prior to both Fukuyama and Kass is Hans Jonas who frequently drew attention to the mix of beneficial and dangerous, for example, *The Imperative of Responsibility*, 20.

36. Kramer overstates the positive affects of Prozac and his "good responders" are the exception. Even with advances made in pharmacology, a "pill" rarely liberates us and makes us feel OK about ourselves. We may feel better but that is not the same since there remains an awareness of "not fully well yet." We should read Kramer, then, with an eye toward future pharmaceutical advances but still wary of reducing wellness and wholeness to a chemical balance.

37. Quoted from Krimsky, *Science in the Private Interest*, 86.

38. The way science is funded in the United States is the epitome of decentralization. If you need to be persuaded, spend some time using the search engines of the NSF, NIH, or science.com. The numbers and statistics are mind numbing. Science is funded in a virtual maze of agencies, departments, and sources. Regardless of what anyone says, science in this country is unregulated and no one knows exactly who is paying whom for what.

39. For a discussion of Merton's normative structure of science, see Krimsky's *Science in the Private Interest*, 73–79, and John Ziman's elaboration in his *Real Science* (Cambridge, U.K.: Cambridge University Press, 2000).

40. See Krimsky, *Science in the Private Interest*, chapter 8, for why he thinks public disclosure (transparency) is not working as a way to remedy conflict-of-interest issues.

41. See Kass's extended discussion of the Hippocratic Oath in *Toward a More Natural Science*, chapter 9. It is also interesting that the longest paragraph of the oath is devoted to preserving the tradition of teaching the art of medicine as an entrusted gift.

42. Margaret Mohrmann, "Professing Medicine Faithfully," *Theology Today* (October 2002): 358.

43. See Gina Smith, *The Genomics Age: How DNA Technology Is Transforming the Way We Live and Who We Are* (New York: Amacom, 2004).

44. Besides the obvious reference to primary sources, a summary of the critique offered by Mumford, Ellul, and Winner can be found in *Does Technology Drive History?* eds. Smith and Marx, 28–35; the critique of Walther Rathenau and Charles Beard in *Human-Built World*, 64–75.

45. Havel in one of his most widely quoted essays, "The End of Communism," quoted in Holton, *Einstein and Other Passions*, 33.

46. No one champions this cause more ardently than Richard Dawkins. See for instance his *Unweaving the Rainbow* (Boston: Houghton Mifflin, 1998).

PART TWO

THE NEW OCCASION FOR AN ORIGINAL TEMPTATION

The first discussion is about science, the second is about sin and evil. In order to connect the two our understanding of sin and evil needs a conceptual overhaul. We begin by disentangling sin from sins, sin from evil, and natural evil from moral evil. On the one hand there is a common sensibility of what sin is. Rousseau's *Emile*, Golding's *Lord of the Flies*, and Stephen King's *Needful Things* highlight a common way to understand sin and evil, but sin of the common variety carries us only so far. We help ourselves immensely if we can find a different approach to reconfigure what is meant by original while maintaining the uniquely Christian understanding of sin. My proposal is to link what is fundamental (and original) about being human—our capacity for self-transcendence—with our evolution. Thus we can say that as we evolve, so does sin. As we become more and more self-aware, we accept more and more responsibility for our behavior. The question that remains nevertheless, and must be answered, is whether we can guide our evolution in such a way that we transcend sin and evil.

The last chapter of part 2 brings together all the parts under the argument that contemporary science is the new occasion for sin. If sin is the desire to know all things and thereby become like God, then a science brimming with unbridled optimism, proned to over-promising, and desperately seeking perfection cannot help but enflame our desire to overreach.

CHAPTER THREE

Sin of the Common Variety: Distinguishing Sin from Evil and Sin from Sins

I used to be Snow White, but I drifted.

—Mae West

How are we to grasp psychologically, socially, the capacity of human beings to perform, to respond to, say Bach or Schubert in the evening, and to torture other human beings the next morning?

—George Steiner, *Errata*, 171

When I say "sin," there is no telling what you see: the stolen candy bar, the rumpled sheets of a bed you shared with someone else's love, a large pipe spilling orange sludge into a once-blue river, a clutch of homeless people sitting around a fire built from trash in a vacant lot between two corporate skyscrapers.

—Barbara Brown Taylor, *Speaking of Sin*, 62

The first two chapters of part 2 will put sin and evil under the microscope. The task of this chapter is to examine sin and evil in our common experience, personal and historical. The next chapter offers a fresh interpretation of the ever-so-difficult task of stating what is unique concerning the Christian understanding of sin. The last chapter asks the intriguing question whether contemporary science creates a new condition for sin and evil by inflating our aspirations and inflaming our willfulness.

What is a discussion of sin—and a fairly lengthy one at that—doing in a book about science and the commonwealth? Sin, after all, belongs to the language particular to the Christian faith and is foreign to science, if not outlawed. Evil, on the other hand, is a word quite acceptable and nearly ubiquitous since the Holocaust. Since September 11th Americans have become reacquainted with evil.[1] With the help of President George W. Bush, evil is back in our national vocabulary. After September 11th evil is a phenomenon Americans can believe in. Just three days removed from that event, Bush said, "Americans do not yet have the distance of history. But our responsibility to history is already clear: to answer these attacks and rid the world of evil." President Ronald Reagan's reference to Russia as "the Evil Empire" made it acceptable for public officials to openly affirm its existence. Bush casts his net farther afield but, like Reagan, evil is what someone else does. By naming it, our mission to hunt down the bad guys is justified. But the language of "sin" is nowhere to be heard. This double disjunction—the antipathy toward sin and the embrace of evil—is telling us something we had best not ignore.

Is It Evil or Sin or Both?

It is no trifle that in both the popular press and academic books a clear distinction is not made between sin and evil. They are commingled, leading to widespread confusion. Here is how I would distinguish the two and why it is important. In the following random listing, mark those associated with sin with an "S" and evil with an "E"; and if neither applies use "N" as neutral:

- poverty
- Nazism
- incest
- Hurricane Andrew
- Tyrannosaurus Rex
- Hannibal Lecter
- communism
- alcoholism
- lying
- young minister in *The Scarlet Letter*
- cancer
- Stalin
- insider trading
- segregation
- looking the other way
- Crusades

- world hunger and disease
- AIDS
- nuclear arms race
- cultural practice of clitoris amputation

The list illustrates the wide range of personal actions, cultural practices, natural phenomena, and social movements we associate with sin or evil. Unless one begins with a firm definition of sin and evil, the terms are used with little discrimination. Yet, there are reasons why one is sinful and another is evil. Most of us make certain reasonable assumptions. Natural phenomena above and beyond any human culpability are not considered sinful or evil. They simply are. While there may be a certain wrongness about the physical universe when it offends *our* sense of the way it should be, we acknowledge the universe as operating according to laws indifferent to our personal well-being. And yet we are reluctant to lump together Hurricane Andrew and the AIDS epidemic because the latter is entangled with personal responsibility. When we consider cancer, AIDS, homosexuality, and alcoholism the range of responses varies, and it varies to the degree we attribute personal responsibility. Only those who are guided by a particular belief system make a causal connection between sin and illness or disease. Cancer and a toothache are not exactly random acts of nature, since we bear some degree of culpability. Some may think of AIDS as an evil, but no one will blame the infant who contracts it from his mother. The line between personal accountability and not-in-my-control is not absolute but the more decidedly we have done something willfully, like lying or smoking a daily pack of cigarettes after the doctor warns us of impending lung cancer, may be sufficient to think of it as sin.

Female genital mutilation is a regular cultural practice among some non-Western societies But is it sinful? What is sinful in one society may not be sinful in another, but follow this logic far enough and nothing is sinful. If the females in question do not experience a particular practice as domination, should we? In discussing a similar issue—that of widows being cremated on their husbands' funeral pyres (the age-old custom of sati)—Miroslav Volf cautions us that "the justice of the dominant is the dominant justice" (*Exclusion and Embrace* 196). Both practices have the feel of male domination justified by a cultural norm of male superiority. Volf counsels that we should make space within ourselves for the perspective of the other and look afresh at our own traditions before judgments are made (213). Whatever judgments we render, they will seem justified to those making them because the standards of assessment are taken for granted. But there is something to be said for the weight of truth when it stands against those who continue a system of domination. At times the better perspective comes from a critical distance of those standing outside this cultural prison.

The demarcation between sin and evil is not absolute but we know evil when we see it. Evil is somehow bigger than sin. It is many sinful people doing a lot of sinful things or it is one person who is rotten to the core. As different as the arms race, segregation, and the Nazis' program to exterminate Jews, we are wont to think of them as evil because they exceed the more familiar boundaries of sin. In his novel *Cast of Shadows*, Kevin Guilfoile sets up an intriguing scenario where Dr. Davis uses his medical skill to clone children for infertile couples (the law permits cloning only if the donor is already deceased), only in this instance his purpose is to find the man who savagely raped and murdered his sixteen-year-old daughter. Using semen from the crime scene, Dr. Davis implants the embryo and then waits to see the face of the killer as the infant becomes a teenager. A colleague who bears the scars of being raped talks about evil in this way.

> "Evil takes up space," she said. "When the men who commit it—and it's mostly men, you know; we can have that discussion another day—when the men who commit evil die, it creates a vacuum, and somebody else gets sucked into it. Killing the evildoer doesn't kill the evil. Another takes his place. Evil is a physical constant. Like gravity. The best we can do is to try to keep ourselves and the ones we love on the right side." (45)

Evil is like gravity, because it is always present. It is a physical constant of the universe and there is nothing you or I can do to kill it or redeem it. Sin is different and even though it is a human universal, parameters can be drawn around it. As Guilfoile's story unfolds, evil is the constant surrounding and energizing human decisions on both sides of good and bad.

Evil is much larger than the individual. It is has a life and synergy of its own. Sin, by contrast, is the discrete act of individuals resulting in some harm or injustice. War and totalitarianism are more than sinful because they magnify and aggravate sinful dispositions and turn them into powers that overwhelm the individual. Evil does not require our cooperation, because it overwhelms even good intentions. We tell personal stories about sin but we write epics and create myths in order to speak of evil. We know we are trying to reference "powers and principalities" when the tragic nature of events have careened out of control. Evil is sin that has gotten out of hand, but evil is not derived from sin. Evil is the ocean; sin is the pond.

Sin is very personal, evil is not. The sins of the day will keep you awake at night but evil wakes you up in a cold sweat. Intentions define sin, evil co-opts them. On those days you have not broken a commandment you are still a sinner. On those days you have not encountered evil, be thankful. Sin is invariably parochial, much like funerals. Evil is invariably borderless, much like bacteria. When sin finds us or we find it, what is required of us is a turning away. In the face of evil, hope and resistance is the best we can do. (President Bush may think we can rid the world of evil, but we can't.)

> **From the Baptismal Covenant
> (The Book of Common Prayer)**
>
> Celebrant: Will you persevere in resisting evil, and, whenever you fall into sin, repent and return to the Lord?
> People: I will with God's help.

Sin makes a realist of anyone; evil makes sinners of all of us. Sin is the daily struggle to do what is right and to be in a right relationship with God and neighbor. At times sin is so subtle you hardly know it has snared you. Sin beguiles you into thinking it's nothing to worry about. Evil is a presence you can smell, touch, even shake hands with.[2] I am at a loss to explain why some people find God in the midst of sin and evil, while others find nothing. This much, though, is true for all of us: we will choose to sin, evil will find us, and we will never be the same.

Sin is a matter of the will: corrupted by power, disposed to indifference, aroused by desire, bent toward greed. Nature knows nothing of this. In his letter to the church at Rome, Paul makes this very distinction: ". . . for the creation was subjected to futility, not of its own will but by the will of the one who subjected it in hope that the creation itself will be set free from its bondage to decay and will obtain the freedom of the glory of the children of God" (Roms. 8:20–21). While nature is incomplete and yearns to be what it is not yet, its lack is not due to a twisted will, and to speak therefore of a natural evil is to sow confusion. Death and decay, randomness and wastefulness—and this is what they are only when seen from a human point of view—do not constitute an ontology of evil. Our universe is the best it can be, because if it were anything else, it would not be. Theology is justified, therefore, in disowning the notion that everything that happens is the will of God. Not everything that happens is intended to make a necessary contribution to the great divine scheme of things or, on a more personal level, is meant to become an occasion for the grace of God. Reflecting on the question, Where was God in the tsunami? David Hart is concise and clear in affirming a "created autonomy that strives against God." His reasoning is both theological and scientific: "For, unless the world is truly set apart from God and possesses a dependent but real liberty of its own analogous to the freedom of God, everything is merely a fragment of divine volition, and God is simply the totality of all that is and all that happens; there is no creation, but only an oddly pantheistic expression of God's unadulterated power" (*The Doors of the Sea*, 91).

Although there is no such thing as a natural evil, this does not constitute grounds to dismiss the theological assertion that God judges and redeems nature, not separately, but as a shared destiny with humanity and all living things. Such is the narrative import of Genesis 3:17. The ground is cursed and together creature and nature will henceforth struggle to exist. The entire cosmos teeters between death and life, order and chaos, existence and extinction. But where to locate the good and evil? On a cosmic scale "evil breeds a contagion of nothingness throughout the created order" (*The Doors of the Sea*, 73). And while the universe is not yet what God intends, it is hardly nothingness or mere futility. In this lacuna of not-yet-free-from-its-bondage-to decay, still waiting for its own ultimate transformation, good and evil contest each other. From this enduring conflict of good and evil—never good or evil or pure good and pure evil but always entangled—we cannot escape, we and no other living thing as far as we know.

Good and evil are entangled because both are original in the sense that they exceed and precede each and every individual. But in what way are they original? The question is difficult to answer when science correctly insists the universe is composed of matter with no propensity toward good or evil. If good and evil are not inherent properties of matter, how are they original with the universe? The only proper way to respond to the question is to focus on the larger picture. The sum is greater than the parts. Good and evil derive their meaning as part of a story line. The true significance of violence, struggle, and waste is not appreciated when seen as solely the engine of evolution. The same can be said of the significance of beauty, creativity, and adventure.[3] Theologians must be careful not to attribute evil intention to natural forces or to see natural disasters as a form of divine punishment, and thereby write a religious narrative. On the other hand scientists cannot justify their argument that since order and chaos, creation, and destruction are in perfect balance, evolution can never be directional. While opposing forces are necessary for this universe to exist,[4] this delicate, mind-boggling balance does not negate the other fact that something has emerged from nothingness and tells a story (and stories) in the process. The universe is more than a precarious equilibrium of countervailing forces, for it were just this and no more, every violence and extinction would be superfluous and of no value whatsoever. Thus a paradox: Not everything is the consequence of divine intention but even violence and extinction are part of a larger story of good and evil.

In the language of Scripture, evil is what frustrates the divine intention for creation. Leaving aside the inscrutable question of the origin of evil, in the priestly creation story (Gen. 1:1–2:3) evil is not defeated but contained by a process of separation and distinction: darkness against the light, the heavens separating the waters above from the waters below. The universe exists as a fragile armistice between forces of disruption threatening to dissolve into nothingness. The goodness of the universe is the gift of God's creating and its original intention. The fullness of that good is frustrated, but not defeated, by nothingness. The image of the lamb and the wolf dwelling together (Isa. 11:6) is emblematic of a universe that does not need to destroy in order to create something new. But for the moment—and it may be a very long moment, extending for billions of years—the lamb is unlikely to meet up with an altruistic lion. The vision of a new heaven and a new earth (read "a new universe") or the positing of a Garden of Eden (read "paradise"), serves to makes us aware that a time is coming where good and evil are separated. Accepting on the one hand the disclaimer from science that good and evil do not refer to opposing forces for which some mathematical formula could be written, good and evil in their more-than-metaphorical import are symptomatic of the entire universe. If we were to encounter extraterrestrial beings, we would expect them to be acquainted with a similar struggle between good and evil. Skeptics, I know, can hardly restrain themselves at this juncture because "good" and "evil" are relative to human life on this planet. What we call "good" another sentient species might call "evil." But isn't it reasonable to expect "good" to refer to what enhances life as they know it? If they see our planet as a nice place to live and humans as good to eat, their good is our evil. But is it necessary to assume or conclude that a struggle for existence, whether personally or cosmologically, is the best the universe can be and the best sentient life can achieve? Are we "made" for nothing more than "top dog rules"? Does evolution have but one goal, survival? We are surrounded by the contrary evidence of the abundance of life in all its fullness. Every extraterrestrial life form has the potential for becoming a mentor in the ways of love and justice. And on that score alone we do not know what to expect of life except creatures who have own history of doing battle with powers and principalities.

Sin is original because the entanglement of good and evil precedes it. Sin reenters into life with the birth of every child, who engages again a history that is not his or her own but at the same time is not so different from what has gone on before. In some enigmatic way the endless struggle between good and evil is writ small just as it is writ large. One is not present without the other, just not in the same proportion. Evil is the context for sin. More and more I am drawn to the conclusion that sin is invariably supported in various degrees by a context hostile to doing the good and can spin out of control creating its own environment of overwhelming evil. The level of atrocities in Rwanda bears little measure against old scores to be settled. When the limbs of children are hacked off before they are killed in full view of their parents, and babies are thrown in the air and then stomped to death, the environment itself has turned evil. When Lt. Gen. Roméo Dallaire received the call to serve as force commander of the UN Assistance Mission for Rwanda, his role was defined as monitoring a peace accord and preventing civil war. Instead, he found himself within a vortex of genocide. In a detailed account of his experience (*Shake Hands with the Devil*), Dallaire does not devote much space to the nature of evil. In one brief passage he writes: "I rejected the picture of the génocidaires as ordinary human beings who had performed evil acts. To my mind their crimes had made them inhuman, turned them into machines made of flesh that imitated the motions of being human" (456). Dallaire notes the factors affecting the toxic extremism leading to civil war and genocide: discrimination and exclusion stemming from colonial rule, personal vendettas, refugee life, envy, racism, power plays, coups d'état, and the deep rifts that embittered Tutsis refugees of the 1959 revolution—sons and daughters raised in the poverty and double standards of Uganda, vengeful Hutus who had been abused by the Habyarimana regime (513). Almost without exception evil begins with the sinful nature of ordinary human beings but something happens to turn ordinary human beings into killing machines. Much has been written concerning the psychology of mob violence but the bottom line is the creation of an environment where goodness is suppressed and evil abounds.

The conduct of a person becomes evil when it exceeds certain limits associated with rehabilitation or forgiveness. Evil is unadulterated sin—the person who is beyond redemption, the unredeemable transgression, the global forces that sweep through history and corrupts an entire nation. Evil is sin that can no longer be constrained by the normal structures of a civilized society (Rom. 13). An evil person, such as Hannibal Lecter or Osama bin Laden, must be locked away forever or executed, because we see no possibility for their redemption.

Among liberal theologians there is a long-overdue acknowledgment of sin that is systemic and corporate. Latin American liberation theologians have been educating North Americans to the sin residing in the systems, structures, and institutions we create. The poverty and marginalization suffered by individuals cannot be countered solely by preaching to individuals to be more compassionate, because when the structures that shape us are inhumane, they too must be transformed. The "powers and principalities" of Romans 8:38 are visible and invisible, earthly and heavenly, spiritual and institutional, and above all else, social and institutional. New Testament scholar Walter Wink is passionately emphatic that Christians greatly underestimate evil when their understanding goes no farther than angelic creatures who have fallen from heaven.[5] "For instance," he writes, "we might think of 'demons' as the actual spirituality of systems and structures that have betrayed their divine vocations. When an entire network of Powers becomes integrated around idolatrous values, we get what can be called *The Domination System* (*The Powers That Be*, 27). Less there be any doubt, this form of evil may begin simply as one person's sin but is transformed into a qualitatively different reality when it turns into a socially shared pathology.

In the checklist above, it is not difficult to identify the species of sin known as "social evils." Being Americans gives us an edge because we know how to politicize sin better than any nation. We have politicized and legislated just about every moral issue: work on the Sabbath, the right to vote, prohibition, segregation, abortion, illicit drugs, various sexual deviations. Social evils invite societal action because to remove one sinful person changes nothing. James A. Morone deftly charts the "cycle of modern moral legislation" as the way Americans have responded to a host of social sins from slavery to birth control. First there is fear, followed by appropriate legislation, judicial precedents, then "a bureaucratic agency in search of a mission" (*Hellfire Nation*, 257 and also 17, 239).

Morone is keenly aware of the distinction and tension between the Puritan vision of a community of model citizens and the broader social vision of the Social Gospel. The Puritan heritage may have faded but its leading precept—Control Thyself—is very much alive. Americans have a sustained history of becoming caught up in the visceral sins of the flesh they fear will get loose and spread like wildfire. Morone's reading of American history may be correct: a series of moralizing outbursts focused on sinners and aimed to prohibit (liquor, abortion), to restrict (birth control, sexual partners), to regulate (drugs, welfare), and to imprison those who cannot control themselves. The politics of sin in America is a series of pitched battles between the virtuous "us" and a sinful "them." From time to time, and only briefly, does American politics come to grip with the social implications of sin: abusing power, squeezing workers, favoring the rich, or segregating children. And so the debate goes on as to whether poverty is the sin of laziness or the evil of economic structures, or both. Jackson Lears is right to fret that Morone never addresses whether "politics inevitably trivializes sin." This is surely the case when sin is barely more than Benjamin Franklin's moralism, William Bennett's virtues, or the violation of community values.[6]

Morone's portrayal overlooks the deeper Augustinian insight that sin is universal and evil is intractable. Lears points out that when Abraham Lincoln rallied a nation to make a stand against slavery, he excused no one of the original sin of slavery and racism. President Harry Truman's inspiration may have come from a different source but it struck at the same Manichaean temptation to divide the world into children of light and children of darkness[7]—"God forbid that I should claim for our country the mantle of perfect righteousness. We have committed sins of omission and sins of commission, for which we stand in need of the mercy of the Lord."

Nowhere is the confluence of sin and evil so manifest than in the ideologies of the twentieth century. It would seem that we crossed some evolutionary threshold as a species. We became rational to the point of believing we could control the present and shape the future. Ideology becomes the tool of tyranny because it accepts and wields the presumption the future is ours to fashion. An individual does not rise to power without an ideology, a means to unify a people under one banner. To believe in a person is to believe he or she knows something that will change the world. All the elements are in place to idolize the leader and the ideology. Together they become the way out, the way up, or, simply, salvation.

Evil is blatant, shameless, and easily portrayed. Sin is subtle, covert, and difficult to expose. Sin is a much "harder sell." The editor of the *Christian Century*, John M. Buchanan, relates an experience that all ministers have experienced. When serving as a pastor he received a phone call from a member of his congregation.

> "I want to talk to you about something I don't like at all about our worship service," she voiced. When he arrived at her apartment she had several worship bulletins in her hand. After I was seated she began to read some phrases from the Book

of Common Worship: "We cling to the values of a broken world. The profit and pleasure we pursue lay waste the land and pollute the seas . . ." "We condone evil, prejudice, warfare, and greed." Then she spoke a common refrain of Christians, "Now really, John, I didn't do all that last week. I didn't lay waste the land and pollute the seas. I didn't have time to do all that. I had a busy week: I went shopping, volunteered at the hospital, saw a movie, went to church. Why do you make me say all those dreadful things every week?"

John Buchanan reports that he did his best to connect the dots between our lives, the corporate nature of sin, our complicity in unspeakable evil even though unintended, but he confesses that alas it was a hard-sell and she probably didn't buy it.[8]

The lenten folder from Bread for the World included a prayer asking us to pray for those who "suffer from the evil of hunger and disease." Across America prayers of confession are offered that make mention of our sin of overconsumption and greed. We eat too much and fret about which diet is best for us, while others have not enough to eat and despair over feeding their children. There is a connection between our sin and the forces of evil but it is always difficult to grasp. How does one add up a collection of individual sins (one cheeseburger and fries we did not need) and equate it with world hunger? Hunger and disease have multiple causes while my eating habits are quite recognizable. But like a storm, which comes out of nowhere gathering momentum and strength, hunger and disease gather up the crumbs of our indulgences and becomes a force of evil. No one person is the indispensable cause but to excuse oneself is to excuse everyone else.

Not every sin becomes an evil, for the former is somewhat contained while the latter never is. The malevolent nature of evil is the way it re-creates itself: the spiral of violence, the cycle of revenge, the perpetuation of abuse until evil creates a world without innocence. "Evil," writes Volf, "generates new evil as evildoers fashion victims in their own ugly image" (*Exclusion and Embrace*, 80–81). Slavery ensnares the captors, the auctioneer, the ship captain, its crew, and financier, and finally the slave owner who perpetuates a system of slavery under the protection of a legal system of segregation and property rights.

When sin and evil are commingled and become theologically indistinguishable, we are on the edge of blunting the force of sin. When we cannot distinguish between sin and evil, the only sin we are prepared to acknowledge is "over there" or that of those who do those "dreadful things." To deny that even a modicum of prejudice or greed in each of us is but a seed waiting to be nourished and harvested is the first step we take on their way to doing the unthinkable. We catch ourselves, or we have been caught, with our hand in the cookie jar and we do not see it is as a harbinger of some monstrous evil. But if we take the cookie jar and keep it for ourselves while others starve, there is a twisting of the soul toward profit and pleasure which lays waste the land and pollutes the seas. The sin we do see bores us, while the sin we cannot see should terrify us.

Evil's New Face

It is difficult to rid ourselves of the nagging feeling that we are witnessing a new kind of evil. Philosopher Susan Neiman is very helpful when it comes to sorting out feelings from clear thinking. She begins with a definition of evil as something that "shatters our trust in the world." From a number of perspectives that is exactly what happened when an earthquake flattened much of Lisbon on All Saints Day, 1755. Lisbon was a busy seaport with a large foreign population, making it "an ideal place from which to broadcast any message to the rest of the world." The quake lasted only ten minutes but turned the sky dark with dust destroying a vast number of buildings and killing thousands of people, many of them attending mass. As terrible fires raged, the port was hit with a series of tsunamis tearing ships from their moorings and drowning hundreds more. It was a catastrophe of fire, wind, and water.

Fifteen thousand died instantly in the earthquake, with a final death toll around sixty thousand. It was a disaster unlike anything else the modern world could remember. The repercussions carried far beyond the physical damage. The calamity was an intellectual shock wave. It was said to have shaken Western civilization more than any event since the fall of Rome, because it shattered confidence in the goodness of God and the moral significance of natural events. "If earthquakes are paradigms of natural evil," Neiman writes, "what kind of moral evil must have occurred to produce this one?" Neiman argues that from this historical juncture a split occurred between *natural* evil and *moral* evil. The former was increasingly regarded as not evil at all. The world is the way it is—full of contingency, bad luck, misfortune, and misery—and none of it is attributable to God. Lisbon marks the decline of a theodicy of natural evil and in doing so marks the beginning of modernity, that intellectual journey where more and more is taken from God's hands and placed in ours.[9]

Moral evil survived—the kind of evil that could be laid at the feet of humanity. No human being is responsible for the earthquake that destroyed

Lisbon. Theodicy survives in the minds of most Christians by way of two tenets: the sovereign God punishes the wicked and rewards the good, and everything that happens happens for a good reason. Neiman is more correct than she may realize, since Christians, Jews, and Moslems hold tenaciously to a faith in the moral justice of God in the face of terrible suffering.[10] It seems there is nothing worse than living in an immoral universe where tragedy and death are meaningless. With Auschwitz, though, every sense of moral good and evil is shattered. In comparing the natural evil of Lisbon with the moral evil of Auschwitz, Neiman concludes:

> The problem of evil began by trying to penetrate God's intentions. Now it appears we cannot makes sense of our own. If Auschwitz leaves us more helpless than Lisbon, it is because our conceptual resources seem exhausted. After Lisbon, one could pick up shattered pieces of worldview and decide to live bravely, taking responsibility for a disenchanted world. After Auschwitz, even our attempts to do this much seem doomed to failure. (281)

Auschwitz, then, represents a different kind of rupture, shattering trust in ourselves. As Neiman develops her argument for a shift in consciousness "so profound that it often remains unnoticed," nothing is gained by comparing Auschwitz with what happened in the gulags or other atrocities. Auschwitz and Hiroshima were death on a scale not known before. Yet, contemporary evil is not about the body count, the technological ease of death, or the depth of cruelty. Even before Auschwitz human beings showed the capacity "for cruelty that words fail to capture." The death camps represent a different kind of evil because they were nightmares of irrationality as much as they were of immorality. People were sent to the gas chambers if they worked hard and if they didn't work at all. Primo Levi, who somehow survived, reports what the guards reminded the prisoners: *"Hier ist kein warum"* (Here there is no "why").[11]

The significance of what happened when children were torn from their parents and put into gas chambers can be measured only against the web of beliefs that held together civilization. Trainload after trainload of men, women, and children dismantled the central tenets of the Enlightenment. Rousseau's optimism embodied the confidence that we could guide our own destiny and become the author of our own happiness. The death camps did more than extinguish bodies. They devastated "the humanistic intellectual skills required to build structures of sense" and left us with no response at all (Neiman, 257). Lisbon generated a century or more of philosophical and theological debate reaching the conclusion that natural calamities have no moral value. But for those who were there and lived to tell of the horror, all attempts to explain Auschwitz are tantamount to blasphemy.

Emmanuel Levinas speaks for a generation of philosophers who view the Holocaust as the end of theodicy, that effort to make God innocent or to make suffering bearable. Remembering Auschwitz, Levinas writes: "This would be pain in its undiluted malignity, suffering for nothing. It renders impossible and odious every proposal and every thought which would explain it by the sins of those who have suffered or are dead."[12] Levinas then refers to Emil Fackenheim concerning the kind of faith that is still possible: "the obligation for Jews to live and to remain Jews in order not to be made accomplices of a diabolical project." Looking to include the wider humanity, Fackenheim continues the plea for a faith to resist the evil that makes victims of all of us: ". . . [A]re we not all pledged—like the Jewish people to their faithfulness—to counter with compassion every form of useless suffering and to do this before the marvelous alterity of the Other has been banalized or dimmed in a simple exchange of courtesies . . . ?"[13]

For Neiman there is another reason to understand contemporary evil as different. The Holocaust also compels us to look at the stubborn fact that Nazi murderers were neither particularly brutal nor cruel but "precisely that, by and large, they were not" (Neiman, 252). When Adolf Eichmann, Hitler's chief administrator of the final solution, was put on trial, it was more than a man who tried to justify himself. On trial was moral evil itself. The world expected a show trial but got instead a testing of the modern legal system predicated upon a scale of intent (murder in the first degree, murder in the second degree, etc.). In her extended analysis of Eichmann's trial, Hannah Arendt writes: "On nothing, perhaps, has civilized jurisprudence prided itself more than on this taking into account of the subjective factor. Where this intent is absent, where, for whatever reasons, even reason of moral insanity, the ability to distinguish between right and wrong is impaired, we feel no crime has been committed" (*Eichmann in Jerusalem*, 277). Eichmann was moved by little more than his desire to please his superiors by doing his job well. The most he could be charged with was ordinary complicity. Eichmann defended himself by arguing that others in his circumstance would have done the same. Was Eichmann less guilty because his ability to distinguish between right and wrong was impaired? Do we retreat from our belief in a hierarchy of wickedness if Hitler and bin Laden are true believers unaware that their evil is a cancer infecting the entire world? Should not the full weight of the law fall upon those who do evil for evil's sake?

Arendt, who was covering the trial for the *New Yorker*, penned the phrase "the banality of evil," and she was widely misunderstood as excusing Eichmann because his actions were only trivially bad. Neiman sets the record straight when she writes: "Her point was not to deny responsibility but to demand that we understand responsibility anew" (*Eichmann in Jerusalem*, 277). It was never Arendt's meaning to imply that the absence of evil intentions mitigates our responsibility. Auschwitz becomes emblematic of contemporary evil by showing us that crimes against humanity are committed by people with motives that are no worse than banal. In his review of Neiman's book, theologian William Placher is quick to point out that there is something sinister and hidden beneath the cover of evil—something nearly imperceptible because it is so universal. He writes: "The chance to torture someone to death would not tempt us, but we might, like Eichmann, be willing first simply to advance our careers by making trains run more efficiently without asking questions about the fate of their human cargoes, and then eventually, many small steps down the road, figure out how to make the process of murdering those human cargoes more efficient too."[14]

Even though we can't always explain it, we know there are degrees of sinfulness and evil. There is evil and there is evil: malignant wickedness (evil for the sake of evil), heteronomous evil (just following orders), and conscientious wickedness. Shakespeare's Richard III is of the latter category because the ancient conflict between good and evil still rages within his conscience. Hannibal Lecter of film infamy is malignantly evil because he *delights* in carving up his victims. Hitler and bin Laden take delight in what they are doing. Given every resource they needed, scientists enjoyed the challenge of making the first atomic bomb. Perhaps this too is a new chapter in the history of evil, as Ron Rosenbaum suggests—turning evil into genocidal art.[15]

When it comes to sin and crime, it makes sense to consider the intention. Does it matter that both Hitler believed and bin Laden believes they are inspired by a noble cause? Bin Laden clearly believes he is on a mission from God. Hitler was a believer too—in the purity and superiority of race. In the final analysis a hierarchy of evil can lead to *reductio ad absurdum*. It matters naught to the victim(s) what you believe. We will not excuse Hitler and bin Laden because it did not seem to matter to them that innocent lives were taken. A dictator who is about to commit mass murder must be stopped regardless of his motivation. He or she may not be any more or less evil than the rapist who mutilates one child, but magnitude matters. In order not to treat every evil as equal, Reinhold Niebuhr used the formula "equality of sin, inequality of guilt" (later rejecting the formula but wanting to make the point in some way). In Matthew 25 a simple standard is laid down and it admits no exclusions. What matters is what you do, and what you should do depends upon seeing every person as bearing the image of Christ. Sin and evil have this much in common: they both deceive. Whatever the justification we proffer, they are part and parcel of our self-delusion, and there is no standing outside of them. The standard of evil must preexist and predate the perpetrator for the same reason you cannot be the presiding judge at your own trial.

Just as Auschwitz calls us to allocate differently our moral responsibility, so does Hiroshima-Nagasaki. The clear lesson of Auschwitz is that we cannot trust ourselves: neither our barbaric nor our civilized selves. The clear lesson of Hiroshima is that we cannot trust ourselves with knowledge, because knowledge corrupts just as power does. Oppenheimer opened the right door when he inferred that to have built such a terrible weapon while "having the best time of our lives" was somehow morally wrong. But unlike the Holocaust it is difficult to say more. The usual litmus test of malicious intent does not fit. And yet, that day in desert when the horizon was set afire there was no doubt a boundary had been crossed from which we would never recover. The atom had been split and making total destruction possible had disturbed the order of the universe. We are reluctant to call this evil—perhaps a little sinful, but not maliciously evil. The actions of the scientists working on the Manhattan Project were motivated by patriotism. The reason we want to excuse death by technology is that it begins with the neutrality of basic research and is extended by the promise of some great good. Those who joined Oppenheimer at Los Alamos knew this wasn't run-of-the-mill research but the kind with the potential for much good and much destruction. This means, as it means with almost every technological advance, that scientists inhale the breath of good intention but exhale the breath of so much that can go wrong. The rarified air of scientific research, however, can be very toxic. There is nothing banal about understanding the universe, for the mysteries of the universe are doorways to power beyond imagination. To open them even with the best of intentions and oblivious to the reality of sin and evil is a new form of culpability.

As a discipline, science was never philosophically inclined to ask whether its accomplishments were a reply to our deepest human questions. Philosophy and theology, however, have occupied themselves with reflecting on the disjunction between the way the world is and the way we think it should be. Science enters the picture with its explanations about the way the world is by rendering all events as one and the same, governed by the same universal laws. It annuls beliefs in a world energized by purposeful forces and so demystifies or de-stories the universe. In such a world suffering and evil become moot—that is, they don't count for anything. But psychologically humans cannot exist without meaning. The more the world is ordered, the less threatening it becomes. Fate, Freud insisted, is our word for untamed nature. Science steps in to satisfy our longing to be at home in the universe by offering to protect us from its uncertainties. It achieves this by radically separating natural evil from moral evil (no "ought" can be derived from an "is") and then renders moral evil irrelevant by telling us to forget about providence and concentrate on progress. While science does not pretend to have a metaphysical explanation for why innocent people die or why there is suffering, it does not leave us idle or hopeless. Birth defects, sterility, and disease, while entirely natural, offend us less when we have a way to ameliorate them. In Nietzsche-like fashion, science would urge us to be more rational by forgoing our beliefs in the way the world should be (grow up and accept that God is dead). For Nietzsche, religious ideals have caused us no end of grief and guilt. If we are seeking the best of all possible worlds, then get down to work and understand how nature works and then do her one better.[16]

Nietzsche was partially correct in his assessment of religion but wrong about the remedy, for nothing will stay us from measuring our days (good or bad) or planning our tomorrows (better than yesterday). What theology has not done is answer the modern challenge of a universe permeated with chance and unmitigated suffering. How can such a world be the best work of a divine and loving Creator? But the question theology throws back at science is this: Why should we believe that anything will change because we become increasingly technologically advanced?

When Christians sanctify suffering by pointing to the atoning death of Christ, they are only partially successful in making narrative sense of senseless suffering. The Christian individual may find consolation by clinging to a theology based on "for everything God works some purpose." But would Christians feel the same if they had suffered an evil as horrific as Auschwitz? A careful reading of the New Testament reveals that not all suffering falls under the umbrella of atonement. For the most part, the suffering Christians are called to take up comes from bearing witness to their faith.[17] If we accept Jean Améry's verdict—"We did not become wiser in Auschwitz . . . more human, more humane, and morally mature need not, I believe, be argued"[18]—the Christian sentiment that God is working out His purposes staggers beneath the weight of evil. For those looking in from the outside, the Christian narrative is too grand and too extended to matter in the short run, and for most of us that is the only way we know how to live.

Auschwitz and Hiroshima reveal a side of human nature we do not want to see. *Homo sapiens*, the rational animal par excellence, is also the irrational animal who knows best how to inflict suffering. Our motives are complex: submerged, sublimated, unconscious, irrational, conflicted, and compromised and this makes us a dangerous, not to be trusted, creature. Surely we are not to be trusted with power. Neither are we to be trusted with knowledge, even when it is "in the service of humanity" or "for the common good." The moral evil we thought we could manage by managing ourselves is but another delusion of Promethean man.

The Narrative Quality of Sin

Our sin is what we remember and forget, what we see and what we are blind to, what we keep for ourselves and what "gifts" of evil we give to the next generation; it is not just whom we love and hate but how we love and hate, what we choose and neglect. Sin (as different from sins) resists quantification because it is woven into the fabric of how we live life. This narrative quality of sin makes it a complicated thing. It is much more than the isolated acts of desire or envy or pride. It is, in addition and more important, the patterns of behavior that are so integrated with who we are that they are inseparable from the persons we have become. Sin has that deceptive quality specified in the First Letter of John: "If we say we have no sin, we deceive ourselves, and the truth is not in us" (1.10).

In his autobiography, *Brother to a Dragonfly*, the Rev. Will Campbell does not talk much about sin, at least not directly. When he does, everyone is indicted. One evening Will, his brother Joe, and newspaperman P. D. East were trying to make sense of the killing of Jonathan Daniel, a student from the Episcopal Theological Seminary in Cambridge, Massachusetts, and Richard Morrisroe, a Roman Catholic priest from Chicago, by the local sheriff as they were leaving a small grocery store with two black students (all had just been released from jail after registering black citizens of Lowndes County, Alabama). P.D. challenges Will to give a definition of Christianity in ten words. After a long agonizing moment Will answers, "We're all bastards but God loves us anyway." Not someone to let anyone off the hook, P.D. presses Will. "Come on, Brother. Let's talk about your definition. Was Jonathan a bastard?" And Will knew his definition would be blown if he said no. "So I said, Yes." "All right," replied P.D., "is Thomas Coleman [the sheriff] a bastard?" With less hesitation Will replied, "Yes, Thomas Coleman is a bastard." P.D. figured he has made his case. "Which one of these two bastards does God love the most? Does He love that little dead bastard Jonathan the most? Or does He love that living bastard Thomas the most?" If Will Campbell had reverted to the theological lingo of his seminary training, he would have said "sinner" rather than "bastard," but that would have cut no mustard with P.D. He offers no intimate knowledge that Jonathan was a sinner, because it is a foundational definition. Nothing more needs to be said.

Sin is normally so subtle and complex that it can only be exposed—seen for what it really is—as the story of a life told. Sin is so tightly woven into the fabric of living that it is nearly impossible to extract it for inspection except when it is scarlet red for all the world to see. This accounts for why most Christians may find it difficult to confess their sinful nature unless it becomes a transgression of a commandment. But a specific sin is only the tip of an iceberg. For the most part sins of commission are black and white; and their consequence is soon to be felt. But the sins of omission are grey and woven into the fabric of life and history. To see what sin is really like requires a self-awareness quite different from self-analysis or introspection (Socrates' "know thyself"). At best, introspection is about a deeper self-awareness but there is a limit to how far insight can go when it begins and ends with you. In trying to illumine why Jesus told parables, New Testament scholar John Dominic Crossan makes a cryptic remark: "One can tell oneself stories but not parables" (*The Dark Interval*, 87). Stories with a moral to teach are always about what one should or should not do. Parables, on the other hand, are blindsided storytelling because you never see it coming, thinking it's a story about someone else.[19] Will Campbell never sees it coming while growing up: how his own goodness blinded him to what that self-righteous goodness was doing to his brother Joe.

While *Brother to a Dragonfly* is a personal reflection on growing up in rural Mississippi during the civil rights movement, it is foremost an introspective look at the relationship of two brothers sharing a childhood together only to experience very different destinies. Both brothers lived through the disturbing nights when their mother thought she was going to die. Will remembers how she kept the family awake at night with her well-timed, programmed bouts of vomiting and screams of agony. The sin is not their mother's illness, as if illness is the consequence of being a bad person. It is closer to the guilt Will feels for not being his "brother's keeper" as Joe gradually sinks into a life of addiction and depression. Why, he wonders, did his mother's illness make him strong but his brother weak? At the age of forty, when life had become too much for Joe, he locked himself in his room and willed a massive coronary. Will reflects on a relationship that begins with Joe as his protector and ends with Will becoming a celebrity in the civil rights movement. Meanwhile Joe sinks deeper and deeper into self-denial and self-hatred. When his brother is gone it is too late to change what has happened, but it's not too late for Will Campbell to understand the turn of events.

> Had he [Joe] been such an idol to me that I had unwittingly, unconsciously set out to turn it around and become his idol? Had he really worshiped the idol he had built and I had let him build and perhaps even helped him to build? An idol who reached idol stature by courting and even flaunting success in the face of the worshiper who had never known success such as he had known? Not success epitomized by the evil of this world's goods, for graven images neither need nor want this world's goods. Epitomized rather by the evility of this world's *goodness*.... An idol who would keep his own clay feet so well concealed that an assumed perfection of the part of the idolator was inevitable. (266)

What sin should Will confess as he kneels at the Communion Table? "O, Lord, I have made an idol of my own integrity and I have deceived myself." In the end, and it is by hindsight, Will Campbell understands how his goodness worked to kill his brother. Most of the time the sins we pass off as hardly worth the bother do not add up to much until they are enfolded into a life lived. We can bring to the confessional, and atone for, the sins we commit, but the sin that is barely conscious and comes to light from looking backward is a subtle undertow dragging us relentlessly into patterns of self-deceit.

Sin Not Sins

With theological acumen we can learn not to commingle sin and sins, but it seems sin is indelibly coupled with personal transgressions. The difficulty with a catalog of sins (cardinal and otherwise) is that they can be expiated with specific penances. With theological diligence we can clean up our language in order to distinguish sins from sin. The Reformation scholar Roland Bainton reminded us that the Puritans believed with Martin Luther that "sins cannot be treated singly because the very nature of man is so perverted that he needs to be drastically remade."[20] Habits can be broken, deficiencies can be remedied, and mistakes corrected, but if original sin speaks to a universal condition, a compulsion that overrides our good intentions, then a twisted soul is in need of divine grace. But a twisted soul is not something the average American is likely to confess, especially when surrounded by a culture that shrinks sin to unhealthy behaviors (drinking, smoking etc.). The Reformation occurred at a time when a blatant cheapening of grace was commonplace (indulgences, etc.). Under very different circumstances we are living in a time when sin has been cheapened. As any good systematic theologian will point out, the doctrine of sin belongs within the doctrine of reconciliation, because it is the miracle of redemption that exposes the true nature of sin. But how often is the grace of God so powerfully preached, or the assurance of pardon so deeply felt, that listeners experience God's amazing grace that "saves a wretch like me"?

"I am a person of unclean lips" and "I dwell among a people of unclean lips," the prophet Isaiah intones (6:5). From year to year, the sin of our human condition is bound together in the stories we can only tell together. The Enron scandal opened a few eyes. "It was an intoxicating atmosphere," said Jeff S. Blumenthal, an Enron tax attorney. "If you loved business and loved being challenged and working with unique, novel situations . . . it was the most wonderful place." They were having the time of their lives and getting rich. Whether mob violence, the heady atmosphere of groundbreaking research, or the corporate environment of "the world's coolest company," the sin we overlook is the sin obscured by bureaucratic structures which make it possible for ordinary people to deny exactly what it is they do.[21]

Sin invariably carries us into the realm of evil, while the sins I commit are contained by the limits of conscience and law. The history of sin is longer than my history of sinning. When sin is carried along by the rivers of emotion and fueled by the winds of righteousness, it is chronicled in history books and told as epics. As far as I know, J. R. R. Tolkien does not tell us who sinned against whom. His stage is one where sin and evil are so entangled that Hobbits, in their innocence, are the saviors. The Ring corrupts virtues far more than it preys on vices so the one chosen to destroy the Ring is the one least enamored by his own virtue. There are many who aspire to carry the Ring: Saruman, Gandalf's fellow wizard who wants to make an alliance with the demonic Sauron for the sake of a benevolent despotism; the warrior Boromir, whose bravery would be used to defend his people; the elf-queen Galadriel, whose beauty blinds all who look upon her (including herself when she sees her own reflection); and even Gandalf, who is pure compassion (almost). What makes Frodo the only suitable keeper of the Ring is his utter lack of ambition or pride; there is little here to corrupt or turn toward the evil in this hairy-footed halfling who does not possess strength or beauty or power. But even Frodo needs an endearing bumbling, sidekick (Samwise Gamgee) to stay the course and finish the race (2 Tim. 4:7).

The race is not only long, for it may present itself in one moment of decision. In the film *Unfaithful*, second thoughts hinging on "what's the harm" lead to one act of indiscretion opening the door to lust, deceit, revenge, and murder. The common expression to explain an uncharacteristic moment of indiscretion is "The devil made me do it." Recourse is made to a power "out there" which enters into my heart. Whether the reality in question is some kind of devil power or not, our moment of sinning has a history of a hundred second thoughts. The "one" discretion has its own history of days and years I would rather not face, but if I did, I would see a thousand faces turning away from that one sin which is everyone's sin.

The September 11th attack on America took away our innocence. We should have never lost it. Lightheartedly, May West confessed that she used to be Snow White but drifted a little. We have all drifted a little, and some more than others, but an inner voice tells us that drifting doesn't explain what happened in the rural landscape of Columbine (Colorado) or the killing fields of Vietnam. We debate intensely whether sin is genetic or environmental, but we know very well that we aren't a clean slate on which we can write anything (just ask any parent). We regard as pure fiction the idea that Rousseau's Emile would turn out just fine if he were just raised in an idealistic rural setting shielded from the evil of urban civilization and taught to listen to his inner voice. If we choose to name this thing we see from the dawning of human life *original sin*, it's because it is indelible, pandemic, and systemic, and we don't know how to make it go away.

The Best We Can Hope For, the Worst We Can Expect

Jean-Jacques Rousseau and William Golding engage us in two worthy thought-experiments concerning what it means to be human. In 1764 Rousseau considered what an ideal education would be, and the result was *Emile, or On Education*. In 1954 William Golding wrote *Lord of the Flies* and asked what would happen if a group of adolescent boys were stranded on an island. Rousseau's is a long treatment of what is the best we can hope, while Golding tells a short story of what is the worst we can expect. As thought-experiments go, these two prove to be perennial.

A word about the authors and their contexts. In *Emile* Rousseau writes that his treatise on education should be considered an extended essay on "the history of his species" (416). He takes up the same theme in the *Dis-*

course on the Origins of Inequality. In the introduction to his translation of *Emile*, Allan Bloom sees Rousseau as struggling with the paradox of how "man was born free, equal, self-sufficient, unprejudiced, and now finds himself in chains (ruled by other men or by laws he did not make), defined by relations of inequality (rich or poor, noble or commoner, master or slave), dependent, full of false opinions or superstitions, and divided between his inclinations and his duties" (3). Nevertheless, Rousseau is hopeful. Entrust to him a child and he will raise up an individual who is independent, self-sufficient, morally responsible, a good citizen, a devoted husband, a person of integrity. This is how Rousseau understood himself. He was born of peasant parents and was educated to be become a priest, as were many indigent boys of France. We would say his education "did not take"; rather than swallowing the whole meal, Rousseau struck out on his own determined to believe what is sensible and honorable. He rebelled against metaphysical discussions that led to nothing. Rousseau never missed an opportunity to argue "[t]he jargon of metaphysics has never led us to discover a single truth . . . ." (274). It is much better to trust our natural sentiments.

William Golding's experiences are thoroughly modern. He was encouraged to be a scientist but, in his own words, after two years he rebelled and continued his education at Oxford studying English literature. World War II interrupted his career as a novelist. He joined the Royal Navy and became a lieutenant in command of a rocket-firing ship, participating in D-Day. The theme of *Lord of the Flies* is described by Golding as "an attempt to trace the defects of society back to the defects of human nature." Both Rousseau and Golding, then, are engaged in a genealogical expedition: where to locate the defect that brings humanity to its knees. Rousseau was living in a time when it was possible to believe a revolution would shortly sweep away the ancient regime and make room for a new world order based upon egalitarian principles. Golding is living through the horror of a war that seemed to spare no one.

Rousseau does not try to enlighten us with theological or philosophical propositions but with a number of commonsense truths beginning with the premise that humans are naturally good. The child must not be constrained. Do not forbid him. "They have to jump, run, and shout when they wish" (86). Children should get what they need but not what they want. The first movements of nature are always right. "There is no original perversity in the human heart" (92). "The love of oneself is always good and always in conformity with order" (213). "As soon as man has need of a companion, he is no longer an isolated being" (214). "Thus, what makes man essentially good is to have few needs and to compare himself little to others" (214).

"Moralizing is the death of all good education" (390). Rousseau never loses his optimism. Even the fires of adolescent, Rousseau counsels, can be a means of consummating and completing an ideal education. If proper guidance is given all will turn out well. Summarizing in a single maxim the ideal education: the parents should strive to do no harm and to let nature take its course.

When Rousseau argues that man is naturally good, he does not mean he cannot be corrupted. But that corruption does not arise from within or from anything innate. It is something that is taught: in schools and churches, by tyrants and well-meaning philosophers, by Christian piety and bourgeois calculations. Rousseau's ideal role model is Robinson Crusoe (his story is the only one permitted for the child to consume), because he knows how to meet his needs without desiring the world. Crusoe lived contently on his island and so should the properly educated individual: self-assured, independent, content with his rank, not easily deceived, skillful, loving the beautiful, doing the good, free from cruel passions, exempt from the yoke of opinion but subject to the law of wisdom (419).

Emile is placed in a garden island where there is no forbidden fruit and if properly educated would know how to resist what would not be good for him. Golding's thought-experiment also takes place on a island where young boys decide what is best for the tribe. One of the very first questions the children of Golding's island ask is who they should elect as chief. When that is done, the next step is the establishment of rules. As good English boys they agree that rules are good. The third element in their effort to remain civilized is the tradition of the assembly and the conch. Whoever holds the conch is permitted to speak and everyone, even Piggy, so nicknamed because he is on the "porky" side, is not denied this right. In a pivotal scene the rules of conduct are the first to break down (83). Ralph and Jack are embroiled in one of their many arguments.

> "The rules!" shouted Ralph. "You're breaking the rules!"
> "Who cares?"
> "Because the rules are the only thing we've got!"
> But Jack was shouting against him.
> "Bullocks to the rules! We're strong—we hunt! If there's a beast, we'll hunt him down."

Thus begins the deposition of their elected chief Ralph by Jack, the fill-my-stomach-with-meat hunter. Near the end of the story when everyone except Piggy has turned against Ralph, a large stone is toppled off a cliff and nearly kills Ralph but does literally and symbolically smash the conch. In the last scene Ralph is running for his life in order not to become the third victim of the unseen but ever-present Lord of the Flies.

The enormous appeal of *Lord of the Flies* (ninety-five printings, seven million copies in print) has more to do with the way it stirs the emotional pot than being a good story. Its power resides not so much in what it answers but leaves open for us to ponder. The boys and children who are isolated on this island have had a proper English education. They know what is expected of them, for they frequently intone, "What will the grownups think?" The breakdown in order is not due to their immaturity, for Golding drops enough clues to let us know that it wouldn't be any different if these were adults. The structures—rules and rulers, rights and traditions—prove to be inadequate because human beings are who they are. They are, as Joseph Conrad so sanguinely depicts in *Heart of Darkness*, savages. When Western explorers were discovering new worlds in Africa and Asia, they brought back with them compelling questions about the distinction between savage and gentleman. *Tarzan* was another thought-experiment pondering what would happen if a human child is raised as an ape and is then reintroduced back into society. It was an explicit argument in story form to show that once a human being always a human being, but Golding is pondering a very different question. What is the nature of this human: gentlemen or savage?

The European experience was repeated as Americans explored the "wild west" and encountered Native Americans. On first impression explorers regarded the natives as subhuman. During their long and arduous expedition, Lewis and Clark come to admire the strength and abilities of Sacagawea, the teenage and pregnant Indian girl who became their interpreter and guide and acted with "equal fortitude and resolution" to that of any of the men. The same could be said of Clark's indispensable slave, York, who did everything asked of him. In spite of this, when the trip was concluded Sacagawea's husband was paid $500.33 for his horse, his tepee, and his service but she got nothing, and Clark would not free York.[22] Even though Lewis and Clark shared President Thomas Jefferson's view of the Indians as noble savages who could be civilized and "to be in body and mind equal to the white man," they could do little, and chose to do little, to change the appointed roles of Indian and Negro.

At a very fundamental level the assumed nature of being human was being challenged. When Jenny the orangutan was brought to London in 1837, she was dressed in child's clothes and appeared on the front page of the widely read *Penny Magazine of the Society for the Diffusion of Useful Knowledge*. A long article assured its readers that despite appearances the fact remains that Jenny lacks "the moral or mental provinces of man." Reassurance was needed because the more that was learned about apes, the more the boundaries became unclear. An acquaintance of Charles Darwin, William Broderip, drew a disquieting notice in his account in the *New Monthly Magazine*. After remarking about Jenny's amiable disposition, Broderip reports an observation from the zoo where she was being kept:

> Her keeper watched as a carpenter worked on her cage. He said: "Come, Jenny, you must leave the carpenter alone," and gently led her away. "Dear me!," said a lady; "Dear me! Does she know what is said to her?" "Yes, she knows her name, Ma'am," was the cautious reply: upon which the lady said "Dear me!" again. (Keynes, *Darwin*, 39–40, and plate 1)

If an orangutan can understand human language, then what separates "us" from "them"? Such might have been the remark of the naval officer as he stepped onto the island, "Dear me," but Golding has him say, "I should have thought that a pack of British boys—you're all British, aren't you—would have been able to put up a better show than that . . ."

The fundamental issues separating Rousseau and Golding have yet to find consensus. Rousseau believed in the natural goodness of the individual as well as the blank-slate presumption of a mind with no inherent structure. The individual, therefore, is infinitely malleable. When the blank slate joins forces with the noble savage (man is born innocent and corrupted by society), they form an alliance which served several generations as the received doctrine that an individual can be anything he or she chooses to be. Rousseau's *Emile* comes full circle with Skinner's *Walden Two*. Skinner's theory was more than stimulus response, for he understood the importance of molding the educational environment. It takes a community to raise a child. Skinner loses nothing of Rousseau's malleability and takes it one step farther. If we can mold the environment, we can construct our own futures. Golding's *Lord of the Flies* repudiates all of it as "pie in the sky." Civilization is no match for humanity's innate barbarism because the former is only a veneer easily marred. Golding's children revert to their base instinct because that is what happens when the constraints of civilization are lifted. In the saying that a bad apple doesn't fall far from its tree, we reveal that we believe it is darn difficult to become something we aren't, to rise above our nature and our nurture. When we try to digest what happened in Rwanda and what is happening in Sudan, we judge that Golding had it about right. There is a savage in all of us and sometimes the savage wears a business suit or carries a diplomatic pouch.

Stephen King Tells Us Something about Sin and Evil

In Stephen King's novel *Needful Things*, the narrator begins enumerating the petty aggravations besetting the good folk of Castle Rock. If left alone these common-enough annoyances wouldn't amount to much. The people of Castle Rock are no more sinful than the folk you know. Everything begins to change the day a new shop opens its door. The sign outside reads: NEEDFUL THINGS. Brian, an eleven-year-old boy, dismounts from his bicycle and enters. He is Leland Gaunt's first customer and he isn't even aware he needs anything. Mr. Gaunt does happen to point out a baseball card. It isn't just any old card but a Sandy Koufax keeper. And by coincidence it is personalized: "To my good friend Brian, with best wishes." Now, I ask you, how can a young aspiring baseball player pass up this opportunity? But Brian only has 85 cents in his pocket. Leland Gaunt assures him a deal can be struck: the card for a favor. There are others, many over the course of weeks who stop in to browse. Nettie Cobb can't take her eyes off a carnival glass lampshade. Hugh Priest can't stop thinking how great the pristine foxtail would look flapping in the breeze as his car cruises down the road. But alas he only has $1.50 in his pocket. Leland advises him that "for the things people *really* need, the wallet is no answer." Hugh agrees and adds, "I'd sell my soul for thus-and-such." "Tell me this," the proprietor of NEEDFUL THINGS responds, "what in the name of all the beasts crawling under the earth would I want with your soul?" "Probably nothing," Hugh Priest sighs. "I don't think it's in very good shape these days." They come to terms and Hugh Priest is only obligated to play a little trick. Even the well-off can't resist. Dr. Everett Frankel spies a dandy of a smoking pipe. He doesn't really need another pipe but the suggestion has been made that it might have once belonged to Sir Arthur Conan Doyle, creator of the great Sherlock Holmes. Meanwhile, back at the ranch the aggravations have escalated. The Baptists, and especially their leader, Rev. William Rose, have no tolerance for the Catholics and their gambling ways (casino night at the Knights of Columbus bugs the hell out of Rose). Father Brigham, on the other hand, is not about to let Steamboat Willie, his nickname for Reverend Rose, rule the roost and cast dispersions upon his flock.

Not everyone in Castle Rock is an easy sell. Quite the opposite. Polly Chalmers is the kindest, most thoughtful person one would ever hope to meet. She also suffers with arthritis. She stops by NEEDFUL THINGS to welcome Leland Grant with a cake (devil's food!). The observant Mr. Gaunt consoles, "It must be difficult to run a sewing shop with that particular disability, Ms. Chalmers. How ever do you manage?" In a short order Polly finds herself wearing a silver charm and, coincidentally, relief from her arthritis. But the hardest sell of all is the county's sheriff, Alan Pangborn. It seems he has no desire to visit Leland Gaunt's shop because there isn't any*thing* he needs. There is, though, something he very much wants to *know*. His wife and son had been killed in an automobile accident, a mysterious one at that. And as Leland Gaunt is fond of saying, "everything, *everything* is for sale."

In King's novel there are no grand Faustian bargains to enter into, only little trade-offs and deals: a baseball card for a little innocent fun (some mud thrown at the clean sheets hanging in the backyard of Mrs. Jerzyck); a silver charm for a letter to be judiciously placed in the barn of Ace Merrill, the very same Ace Merrill the sheriff had sent to Shawshank Prison. From the embers of old scores, ambitions, grudges, closet secrets, pride, and the need to know, Leland Gaunt was fanning a conflagration. With a score to settle with the Catholics, the Baptists are advancing down the road with torches in hand and singing, "Onward Christian Soldiers, Marching as to War." Then there is the real business. "The goods which had so attracted the residents of Castle Rock—the black pearls, the holy relics, the carnival glass, the pipes, the old comic books, the baseball cards, the antique kaleidoscopes—were all gone." In the end the *real* business is always the same. The shape and nature changed with the years, just like everything else, but Mr. Gaunt always sold them weapons . . . and they always bought.

When Polly Chalmers finally finds the courage to rip the charm from between her breasts, she understands just how she and everyone else have been charmed. "I wanted so badly for the pain to be gone, Alan. That was what I wanted, but I don't *need* it to be gone. I can love you and I can love life and bear the pain all at the same time. I think the pain might even make the rest better, the way a good setting can make a diamond look better." Alan too understands that he has bought something after all: the need to know, which Leland turned into a need for revenge. Everything has been built on lies and everyone has been taken in. Mr. Gaunt is about to leave town with a valise full of souls, and so many of the good folk of Castle Rock do not even know theirs are missing.

The true temptation of needful things is not only what we think we need for the wrong reasons and the rationalizations we feed ourselves but also the lies we tell ourselves, believing we need them for the right reason. Living in the Age of Information, is there any greater temptation than the need to know? And who thinks of knowing as sin tied to the coattails of evil? Knowledge, after all, has such a good reputation. In its purest form it is objective and neutral. And if you believe that, then the lyrics of Steve Earle are music in your ears:

> Ladies and gentlemen, attention, please!
> Come in close where everyone can see!
> I got a tale to tell, it isn't gonna cost you a dime!
> (And if you believe that, we're gonna get along just fine.)
>
> —Steve Earle, "Snake Oil"

Notes

1. Written in 1995, Andrew Delbanco's book *The Death of Satan* is a testimony to how Americans lost the language to cope with the reality of evil, and at the same time it reflects a new willingness to publicly talk about evil (but not so of sin).

2. The presence of evil is vividly portrayed in the film *The Exorcist* and in the story told by Lt. Gen. Roméo Dallaire, force commander of the UN Assistance Mission for Rwanda, in *Shake Hands with the Devil*.

3. John F. Haught defines adventure as "the universe's search for continually more intense forms of order and novelty." See his *The Cosmic Adventure* (New York: Paulist Press, 1984), 130.

4. The balance of opposing forces in nature may not be the full story. Common sense along with empirical evidence points to an excess of both order and disorder. That is, there is more violence, death, ugliness, waste, and disorder than is necessary for life to exist. Likewise, there is more beauty, creativity, emergence, and purpose than is necessary for life to exist. Consider the way humans adorn their bodies and decorate their habitats or the lilies of the field, how they grow—all excessive. Isaiah 35 is typical of nature's longing to be restored, and together with the weak and the fearful, "thy shall see the glory of the Lord, the majesty of our God." When theologians speak of a created good, they use the language of blessing and gratuitousness to accent the excess of all that is good, and declare this to be the intention of the Creator.

5. Walter Wink's trilogy is the landmark project to unmask evil as "principalities and powers." See his *Naming the Powers: The Language of Power in the New Testament* (Philadelphia: Fortress, 1984), *Unmasking the Powers: The Invisible Forces That Determine Human Existence* (Philadelphia: Fortress, 1986), and *Engaging the Powers: Discernment and Resistance in a World of Domination* (Philadelphia: Fortress, 1992).

6. Jackson Lears review of *Hellfire Nation* appeared in the *New Republic*, 30 June 2003, 30.

7. Typically, Reinhold Niebuhr does distinguish between the children of light and the children of darkness but then offers a substantial critique of the children of light for

158 ~ Chapter Three

even though they have some conception of a higher law than their own will, they underestimate the power of self-interest among themselves. See Niebuhr, *The Children of Light and the Children of Dark* (New York: Charles Scribner's Sons, 1960), 11.

8. John M. Buchanan, "The Human Condition," *Christian Century*, 27 February–6 March 2002, 3.

9. Neiman, *Evil*, 238–50; and for another provocative account of modernity as the transfer of power from God to man, see O. B. Hardison, Jr., *Disappearing through the Skylight* (New York: Viking, 1989).

10. The reference to Neiman is her observation: "It may be hard to acknowledge God's limits, but its less frightening than denying His goodwill" (*Evil*, 20). This is consistent with her larger observation that modern philosophers came to terms with evil either by understanding God as constrained by the possibilities available to Him or to claim "that all the Creator's actions in fact happen for the best" (21).

11. *Survival in Auschwitz* is Primo Levi's account of his ten months in the German death camp. "To sink," he writes, "is the easiest of matters; it is enough to carry out all the orders one receives, to eat only the ration, to observe the discipline of the work and the camp. Experience showed that only exceptionally could one survive more than three month is this way" (90).

12. Levinas, "Transcendence and Evil," in *The Phenomenology of Man and of the Human Condition*, 163.

13. See *Levinas*, 164–65. See also Neiman, 265–67.

14. William Placher, "Haunted by Evil," *Christian Century*, 5 April 2003, 39.

15. Ron Rosenbaum judges Hitler for the "conscious *artistry*" he employed in crafting his sadistic final solution. Rosenbaum, "Degrees of Evil," *Atlantic Monthly*, February 2002, 68.

16. Neiman's discussion of Nietzsche spills over into my discussion of science. She describes Nietzsche as one who radicalized the modern attempt to take increasing responsibility for the world. Nietzsche urges humankind to take back redemption from God. What better description of science than her statement about Nietzsche: "We cannot get rid of its [religion] power until we get rid of the needs that created it" (218 and 206–27). Exactly the sentiments of Huxley's Mustaph Mond.

17. See Robert Sherman's nuanced treatment of atoning suffering in *King, Priest, and Prophet*, 194–209. Sherman is also cautious about making Christ's atoning work on the cross the prototype for what is required of Christians. The various responses to Mel Gibson's *The Passion* illustrate the two poles of how Christians interpret suffering. Gibson knowingly makes a picture of such graphic suffering because he believes there is a proportional relationship between the terrible suffering of the Lord and the terrible sin of humanity. Trained for the priesthood and now columnist for the *Boston Globe*, James Carroll enters the "passion of Christ" debate from a very different perspective. Carroll argues that by glorifying and sacralizing suffering as Gibson does in the *Passion*, he inadvertently supports violence in all of its sanctified, religious forms, and that Carroll would say is no small matter.

18. Quoted from Neiman, *Evil*, 266.
19. John Shea, *Stories of God*, 182.
20. See Delbanco, *The Death of Satan*, 37.
21. Peter Behr and April Witt, "The Fall of Enron," *Washington Post*, 28 July 2002, A16. Not everyone in the world of business falls into this mold. Larry Page and Sergey Brin, founders of Google, want to keep their priorities straight and have written this into their business plan: "We aspire to make Google an institution that makes the world a better place." And then to state where the danger lies, the company motto is, "Don't be evil."
22. Stephen E. Ambrose, *Undaunted Courage* (New York: Simon and Schuster, 1996), 39, 399, 458.

CHAPTER FOUR

Sin Uniquely Christian: A Fresh Interpretation of "The Fall"

What an ironic drama it is, of man who is a monster in his power, and is a worm in his lack of the power to save himself.

—Reinhold Niebuhr, *Justice and Mercy*

I do not understand my own actions. For I do not do what I want, but I do the very thing I hate. I can will what is right, but I cannot do it. For I do not do the good I want, but the evil I do not want is what I do.

—Romans 7:15, 19

The world is charged with the grandeur of God. . . . Generations have trod, and all is seared with trade, bleared, smeared with toil; and wears man's smudge and shares man's smell.

—Gerard Manley Hopkins

The Christian tradition makes a distinction between general and special revelation in order to separate what is knowable through reason, intuition, and common sense about the goodness of the creation and what we need to know for our salvation solely through divine disclosure (inspiration, revelation, "a small still voice," pattern of events, prophets).[1] General revelation allows for a vertical but limited awareness of God as well as a horizontal but broken awareness of the good.[2] The last chapter is my endeavor to bring to light the kind of knowledge about our human condition available through common experience. In this chapter the underlying premise comes from special revelation: we cannot know the true extent of our sinful nature unless it is disclosed to us. While reason and introspection are helpful, they cannot create a level of self-awareness necessary to bring one to confess, "No doubt about it, I am a sinner." As happens in conversion, something is broken open by an encounter with an*other*. In order to know that I am sinful—to be aware and confess that awareness—requires a disruption that is not of my own doing.

Sin uniquely Christian is an understanding of human nature that stands in sharp contrast to the Enlightenment where the language of error, bad decisions, and immorality predominates. Theologians make such a fuss in defense of original sin because they see how easily all secular discussions regarding the human condition assume some form of perfectibility. The usefulness of sin of the common variety carries only so far. It cannot counter the optimism that we are essentially good, as evidenced by the good we intend.

The Christian understanding of sin is frustratingly difficult to grasp. As a descriptive analysis of the human condition, it defies a straightforward approach. For this reason Walker Percy, who knew how to turn a good story, offers this illustration. Gathered in an auditorium in Aspen is an audience of scientists, philosophers, and ethicists. They have come from near and far to explore the implications of therapeutic cloning for society at large. During one of the presentations, an interloper interrupts the speaker with this announcement: "There is a fire in the building!" Percy notes, "The conferees will be able to distinguish at once between this sentence and all the other sentences which have been uttered from the podium. Different as a bar of music is from a differential equation. . . ." (*The Message in the Bottle*, 138). The conferees will know that here is news that is relevant to their personal predicament. What they need to hear most at this moment is not who had discovered what or what are the ethical implications of therapeutic cloning but instructions on what to do next in order to safely exit the burning building. The situation is even more dire because there are no marked exits in this auditorium. They must trust the bearer of bad news to also provide good news.

The illustration is laden with salient points. The interloper is not one of them and the reason to trust him is the relevance of the news itself. Apart from the situation of fire in the building, the news would be ignored. An auditorium with no exits means the conferees are helpless to find or create an escape route in spite of their considerable expertise. The bad news is given before the good news but if the good news had been delivered first, it would have been ignored as having no immediately relevancy.

Percy tells another story-metaphor equally as powerful and illustrative. The emergency landing of a charter flight has left a passenger stranded on an island. Due to a head injury the individual suffers amnesia. He has the uneasy feeling that he is homeless—not sure who he is and vaguely remembering that he has a family somewhere. Each day in his leisure time, and he has plenty of leisure time, the castaway searches the shoreline for messages sealed in a bottle. It becomes something of an obsession since it is his only hope to end this feeling of hopelessness. Almost each day a new message washes ashore:

> Lead melts at 330 degrees.
> 2 + 2 = 4.
> If water John brick is.
> The Atman (Self) is the Brahman.
> The pressure of a gas is a function of heat and volume.
> In 1943 the Russians murdered 10,000 Polish officers in the Katyn Forest.
> The nucleus from an adult cell can be placed in an unfertilized egg without a nucleus.
> The root of the turnip is edible.
> Being comprises essence and existence.

Some messages readily fall into the category of empirical facts which can be ascertained by careful observation. Others refer to a state of affairs implicit in the very nature of reality (2 + 2 = 4). Some appear to be nonsense (If water John brick is) and others historical.[3] The castaway grows restless awaiting some news about his predicament. One day a bottle washes ashore with the message, "There is fresh water on the far side of the island." This is helpful but it compels a decision whether to leave the beach and miss what he most needs to find out, news of where he came from and who he is and what he must do.

Percy alerts us to some vital distinctions. *News* is a contingent and nonrecurring event peculiarly relevant to the predicament of the hearer. News is also characterized by the fact that "it is a knowledge which cannot possibly be arrived at by any effort of experimentation or reflection or artistic insight" (126). It is very different then from the kind of knowledge "which can be arrived at anywhere by anyone at any time." News is deeply personal but not subjective while information results from excluding what is personal in order to be objective. The castaway is not hopeless about his situation but he knows observation and reflection will not in itself get him off the island. The news the castaway longs to find will not come as island news but as news from across the seas.

The uniquely Christian understanding of sin is nothing short of paradoxical. Because the sinner is incapable of hearing news from across the sea for what it is, news concerning our salvation, something must come to us from outside of ourselves. How can sinners who are not fully aware of their homeless predicament hear and believe they are castaways? The news must be such that it awakens the sinner (there is a fire in the building) and state what must be done; as such it both indicts and calls the person to do something (imperative). The pattern of self-delusion is to believe that useful information will eventually show us how to get off the island and find our way back home. The alcoholic doesn't fully recognize that he is an alcoholic, for this is part of the sickness. So, how does the alcoholic or sinner heed a wake-up moment and understand the direness of his or her predicament? In part, it is when the handwriting on the wall is so vivid that it is hard to miss. The alcoholic who wakes up to an empty house after his family has moved out. The prodigal son wakes up to the fact he has walked away from his father's love and would gladly accept the food he is feeding pigs if someone would offer it to him. When someone yells "fire" (repent for the Kingdom is at hand) your moment of decision has come and it is time to pay attention. Such is the trauma Barbara Brown Taylor has in her sights when she writes, "To measure the full distance between where we are and where God created us to be—to suffer that distance, to name it, to decide not to live quietly with it any longer—that is the moment when we know we are dead and begin to decide who we will be tomorrow" (*Speaking of Sin*, 62).

On the road to recovery the alcoholic must start with two confessions: I cannot help myself and there is a Higher Power to which I must accede. Coupled with the bad news (we're all bastards) is the good news (but God still love us). Because we are inclined to trust our own power of self-rescue, the good news about recovery or redemption is likely to be dismissed. The process of becoming more self-aware is essential to the examined life, but for Christians, the moment of turning or repentance is not the kind of self-awareness we can give to ourselves. The reason Jesus spoke in parables is precisely that parables are the kind of stories we cannot tell ourselves.[4] In other words, they were stories that implicated the listener, and most likely it took some time for the listener to realize the parable he had heard was about himself. The wake-up call that sets the prodigal son on the road home knowing that he has sinned against God and family is not complete in itself. What he discovers in his father's embrace is not what he had imagined. All the way home he rehearses his repentance speech hoping it will soften the old man's heart. But before he crosses the threshold, his father declares his love by killing the fatted calf and throwing a party in his honor. Even though the younger son's project was to "un-son" himself and the older son's to "un-father" himself, the father is not willing to let go of the relationship between them.[5]

The phrase "from across the seas" indicates a transcendent or vertical dimension of the story. Sin spreads out both vertically and horizontally, it offends both God and others, it transgresses both natural and divine limits. What is gained by including the vertical dimension? Medical, psychological, or humanistic models of sin are common enough, but we can tell their inadequacy by the remedy they offer. Any and all efforts to shore up the self—medically, therapeutically, pharmaceutically—may leave the person in better health but with the self still at the center of one's existence. Percy mentions the intensity and increased sound level of the various invitations saying "come"—the Jehovah's Witnesses at your door and the lose-weight-in-four-weeks plan, the Cadillac you deserve, the island vacation you desire. These rescue messages are of two types. Either they omit the bad news or they promise "salvation" through self-awareness and knowledge (it's what you don't know that could save you). The vertical dimension places God as Other at the center of who we are. Grace does not eliminate the self as unimportant but affirms the self as loved by Another. By means of a relationship with God, grace moves the ego out of the center. Luke's story of the prodigal son does not tell us what happens after the son returns home, but we know he is not the same son but a "son-that-was-dead-and-is-alive-again" (Lk. 15:32). The extravagant, unmerited love of the father transforms him, freeing him from his own ego to love the father and others. The very reason for his existence has shifted. Each morning when he begins the day, the motivating question is not, What can I do to advance myself? But, What will I do this day to love others as I am loved by God? His elder brother, on the other hand, has never left home and still awaits his moment of epiphany. It could be a long wait for anyone who has worked so hard to earn his father's affection, because the effort makes him the center of what he is doing when nothing is required except to accept the love already present.

No Exit

It is time for me to speak theologically. We are incapable of redeeming ourselves or of using the language of this chapter; we cannot rescue ourselves from our situation as castaways. The Christian understanding of sin begins and ends with the declaration that "human sinfulness can only be grasped as a reflection of the unmerited advances of the divine lover toward his beloved."[6] The great systematic theologian Karl Barth did not take up the topic of original sin until the end of his multivolume *Church Dogmatics*. His reason was both theological and psychological: humans cannot understand their true condition as sinners apart from the miracle of redemption. At work is a progression of awareness. The greater the gratitude for grace and for growing in it, the greater one's sensitivity or awareness of one's culpability. In Romans 7 and 8, Paul develops the succession as moving from *anomia* (no law) to *nomos* (Law) to thanksgiving for living in the Spirit. At each stage there is a deeper perception of accountability. Carl Braaten comments that "we know lots about lusts, passions, addictions, feelings of worthlessness, depression, anorexia, mental illness, gambling drugs, AIDS, alcoholism, overeating, and we go to doctors, counselors, clinics, and spas for therapy."[7] In other words, utilizing a horizontal model the remedy for the human condition aims to fortify the will, heal the body, exercise, and eat a balanced diet. And to a certain degree and at particular level all of these endeavors are helpful. But there is more to being fully human than health and happiness, more than healing the mind and the body. There is the sickness of the soul, and—interpret the phrase as you like—it always points to the deeper dimensions of life. Even indifference and pride, despair and hopelessness do not comprehend the dismal depth of the human condition. What the medical and educational models do not explain are genocide, cruelty, corporate greed, suicide bombers, the injustice of the rich getting richer while the poor get poorer. When the Christian faith claims that the fathomless depth of sin can only be grasped in the light of the fathomless depth of grace, it counters the precious notion that you can will yourself to love God and others more than you love yourself. What will get you off your island of self-examination is news from across the seas delivered by someone other than yourself.

I laud Scott Peck for sticking his neck out by daring to write about sin. He writes as a psychologist who is able to see into a person's inner life. The historical context is the war in Vietnam and the My Lai incident. In his first, immensely popular, book, *The Road Less Traveled* (1978), Peck defined sin as laziness or the desire to escape the pain one needs to feel in order to grow. In *People of the Lie* (1983), Peck's definition is more radical. He recognizes sin as incredibly seductive, secretive, and delusional. It is also more than simple narcissism becomes he writes of individuals he has tried to help who demonstrate a "malignant narcissism." But Peck seems unsure where to locate this malignant narcissism and so he locates it in various places: the mind, the soul, mental illness, development, a separate evil fore. The telling evidence of Peck's confusion is the hope he offers. The My Lai massacre in Vietnam is presented as an example of "gross intellectual laziness and pathological narcissism at every level." It was all of this but when understood as only this, the remedy can be:

> Children will, in my dream, be *taught* that laziness and narcissism are at the very root of human evil and why this is so. They will *learn* that each individual is of sacred importance. They will come to know that the natural tendency of the individual in a group is to forfeit his or her ethical judgment to the leader, and that this tendency should be resisted. And they will finally see it as each individual's responsibility to continually *examine himself or herself* for laziness and narcissism and then to purify themselves accordingly. (*People of the Lie*, 253; emphasis added)

If it were possible to purify ourselves, if it were possible to teach the children of the world how not to sin, we could have confidence that by human effort alone the next generation would usher in a different future. Since Peck's understanding of sin is something less than ontological (deep down and irreversible), his hope for the future is what so many others have hoped for. Rousseau, Marx, and even Freud are quintessential in their conviction that if humans can see their destructive impulses for what they are, they can effect a change. Everyone, it seems, has a proposal for a particular kind of redeeming self-awareness, just as Peck has become an advocate for self-examination.

The philosophical miscalculation is to presume that an increase in self-awareness leads to an increase in self-determination. Sin is not diminished when self-consciousness deepens, because as awareness increases so do the desires to have all things, to be all things, and to know all things. If we persist in the notion that sin is a kind of defect, the solution will always be in the realm of education, enhancement, or gradual improvement. Jacob Bronowski speaks for every generation that cannot abide Darwin's determination that the "descent of man" is our chief characteristic. Bronowski's *The Ascent of Man* is suffused with the optimism that humanity's destiny is the discovery of knowledge. Edward O. Wilson says as much when he writes, "Science and technology are themselves reason for optimism" (*The Future of Life*, 156). The counter, non-intuitive judgment is rendered by the Christian ethicist Joseph Sittler: "The knowledge of damnation does not of itself generate the powers of redemption."[8] Indeed it does not, nor does knowledge itself or self-knowledge.

The demoralizing critique rendered by postmodernists is meant to cut us loose from the optimism that good overcomes evil. Michel Foucault and

Theodor Adorno love to remind us how the best-laid plans of dictators and ideologues have run amuck. The noblest experiment in democracy enslaved one people (black Africans) and nearly destroyed another (Native Americans). The most cultured nation of modern Europe unleashed an unprecedented holocaust of destruction upon the Jewish people. The endless and repeated "techniques of domination" mean there is no universal history leading from savagery to humanitarianism. Instead, we are confronted by the history leading from the slingshot to the megaton bomb.[9] While not exactly making a counterproposal, Peter Singer and Steven Pinker detect another pattern—an evolutionary pattern—emerging from the dynamics of natural selection and history. Singer offers an attractive argument in his book *The Expanding Circle*. He observes that our capacity for moral awareness has expanded, moving outward from family and village to the clan and tribe, from nation to race, and most recently to all of humanity in the form of universal declaration of rights. Pinker amplifies Singer by speaking of a moral escalator. How else, he inquires, can we account for "the obvious progress that has taken place over millennia." Pinker celebrates that "[C]ustoms that were common throughout history and prehistory—slavery, punishment by mutilations, inquisitions for matters of faith, execution by torture, genocide for convenience, endless blood feuds, the summary killing of strangers, rape as the spoils of war, infanticide as a form of birth control, the legal ownership of women—have vanished from many parts of the world" (*Blank Slate*, 166). The circle of human compassion has grown from including only men to including women, children, prisoners of war, enemy civilians, the dying, the mentally handicapped, great apes, the yet to be born, the ecosystem. Singer and Pinker differ about the source of change in our sensibilities. Singer places his bet on the increase in autonomous reasoning and the freedom it imparts to make moral choices, choices which expanded steadily outward to include ever larger communities. Pinker speculates that human beings posses an emotional repertory for sympathy, trust, guilt, and self-esteem which impels us to see the value of cooperative behavior. "Long ago," he writes, "these endowments put our species on a moral escalator" (168).

Most assuredly we human beings are endowed with capacities and dispositions that allow us to rise above our predatory nature. The evidence is ample that we represent a "leap forward" in the use of reason. But who is to say that we do not use reason to better justify our despicable behavior? Pinker argues that once the "sympathy knob" is in place, it can be cranked up. It can also be turned down, for a host of new justifications. A moral escalator implies that empathetic sensibility runs in only one direction. Along with greater

> Dateline *Boston Globe*, 2 September 2003
> ## School Study Finds Deep Racial Divide
> Almost three decades after Boston's bruising school desegregation battles, nearly half of the white children in the city attend private schools and most minority children remain walled off from suburban school advantages, according to a report released yesterday.
> The report, by the Lewis Mumford Center for Comparative Urban and Regional Research, depicts a region with stark divisions between school districts (Yvonne Abraham and Francie Latour, A1).

sensibility toward the handicapped comes an impulse to eliminate them as a blotch upon progress toward perfectibility. Assimilated into a newfound concern for civilian casualties is an array of technologically advanced weapons that are many times more accurate but many times more destructive. One missed target can translate into the "misfortune" of collateral damage. If history is the measure, then technology "hugely increases the scale of atrocities" (Glover, 409). Perhaps we aren't the barbarians we used to be. We have become sensitive, coat-and-tie statesmen who make one phone call and the sky is filled with ballistic missiles. Husbands may no longer beat their wives with clubs. They just use legal maneuvers or cultural mores to keep them "in their place." I can imagine a day in the future when there exists true equality between men and women. Will it be the end, though, of bitter divorces, custody battles, or love transmuted into hate? There remains the necessity to explain the violence that seems so nihilistic because it is so indiscriminate, and when some rationale is given it still matters naught that children and infants are blown to pieces.

Christian theologians have defended the ontological nature of sin consistently and across denominational lines. Theology and philosophy butt heads over the notion that if we are "saved" epistemologically then we are saved ontologically. The Enlightenment mentality could not tolerate any anthropology where human beings are not capable of rectifying their own condition.[10] Rousseau's belief that we are created essentially good is not theologically unacceptable. Even the conclusion Rousseau advocated is not erroneous: we are rational beings and therefore we can be educated and trained to act morally. Educated and trained to act morally, even armed with a social conscience, we still find new way to segregate, discriminate, and denigrate.

> **Dateline, *Boston Globe*, 2 September 2003**
> ### Israeli Panel Cites Anti-Arab Bias
> A high level commission that investigated the police killing of 13 Arabs at the beginning of the current, three-year armed struggle between Palestinians and Israelis ruled yesterday that the root cause of the deaths was systematic discrimination by Israel against its Arab population.
>
> The unanimous findings of the so-called Or Commission—whose members were Supreme Court Justice Theodor Or, Nazareth District Judge Hashim Khatib, and Shimon Shamir, a veteran Israeli envoy to the Arab world—marked the first time a major institution of the Israeli state has declared the existence of widespread, institutionalized prejudice against the country's Arab minority (Charles A. Radin, A1).

When philosophy is the guiding insight into human nature, the promise of tomorrow always looks brighter. The Christian is given the role of cynic because he has heard it all before, but it does not follow to assign him the role of pessimist. The latter arises from the mistaken presumption that being ontologically sinful means every child is hopelessly consigned to repeat the "sins of the father" (Ex. 20:5 and Num. 14:18). The biblical judgment that our sins reap their consequences to "third and fourth generations of those who reject me" needs to be set along side the largeness of God's "showing steadfast love to the thousandth generation" (Cf. Ps. 100:5). The English-speaking world imbibed both sentiments, though mostly in the form of guilt and revenge as depicted in the King James Bible and Shakespeare, as in *The Merchant of Venice* (5:1). The theological hypothesis that we are simultaneously sinful and redeemed (*simul est justus et peccator*) is not a contradiction, because anthropologically we have existed on the edge of falling toward the good or toward the evil. We are both sinful and redeemable because we are defined not by sin but by our capacity to love and to be loved.

The theological context is not the same as the philosophical one. For theologians, redemption from sin cannot be equated with finding a moral center. Karl Barth resisted every understanding of revelation as the communication of "saving" ideas or doctrines, for the reason that they easily slide into saving tenets of enlightenment or self-awareness.[11] Consider not what revelation brings but what it disrupts—and what it disrupts, fundamentally, is the autonomy of the individual. The holy otherness of the biblical God so ruptures our present assumptions that it is nothing less than a revelation. The disruption is the starting place.

Sin is not epistemic in nature because it is not about engaging a method of knowing, for such an engagement incites our desire and confidence to know all things. Redemption occurs when the possibility of limiting our desires is exercised, and this happens when the self is no longer at the center of our existence. The philosophical shift toward epistemology and away from ontology during the Enlightenment carried with it a denial of sin as ontological and the promise of epistemic salvation. Erazim Kohák bitingly remarks that our confidence in the merely episodic nature of evil may have been convincing "when Victoria was on her throne, Karl Marx sitting harmlessly in the public reading room of the British Museum, and Thomas Alva Edison was busy at work in his laboratory." That confidence was drastically shaken for England by the Boer War, for Germany and all of Europe by two world wars, for America by Vietnam, and for humanity by the Holocaust (*The Embers and the Stars*, 138).

If sin has difficulty holding an audience, then talk of total depravity is a real put-off. Evidence abounds that Christian theologians haven't convinced any skeptic of our total depravity. Of course theologians and preachers may continue to harangue and argue under the assumption that humans don't want to believe something so awful about themselves. And while this is undoubtedly true, the skeptic needs to hear the theological rationale why theologians won't let go of total depravity. Augustine, Luther, Calvin, and Jonathan Edwards found the doctrine to be a bedeviling subject because no straightforward assertion adequately expressed the full truth. The English Puritans who settled in North America knew their Larger Catechism from A to Z, and the answer to the question about original sin states clearly its conveyance "from our first parents unto their posterity by natural generation, so as all that proceed from them in that way, are conceived and born in sin." Apart from endless theological arguments concerning how Adam and Eve's disobedience led to our complete and total corruption, the tenet left its scarlet letter on all who meant to excuse their transgression because of a bad situation or bad ancestry. With torrents of words, preachers of the Great Awakening painted a picture of a fiery Hell waiting to engulf the guilty—and they would underscore that all are guilty before the Judgment Seat—and there was nothing (nothing!) the individual can do to save his sorry ass but to accept the mercy of God Almighty. Original sin, in all its bloody images, became the signature mark among Protestants and denominations claiming the right to call themselves Reformed or Evangelical.

The strong language of total depravity is meant to indicate that sin is all-pervading, affecting all the faculties of being human: willing, thinking, socializing, and all aspects of human relationships, economics, education, politics. Original sin is intended to foreclose any consideration, such as Rousseau's, that we can find a technique for self-redemption. The dire warning that every child is by nature totally depraved and must be born again is one way to put humans in their proper place; but left standing, total depravity obscures the other imperative doctrine that we are created in the image of God, that we have a natural knowledge of good and bad and the freedom to decide for the good or bad. Even those Reformers who would not give an inch on the total effect of sin also asserted not that sin is our essential nature but rather that sin does something to corrupt that nature.

In looking for a way to restore a more balanced picture and find common ground between Christians and non-Christians, Reformed theologian Richard J. Mouw reexamines the doctrine of common grace. Mouw does not want the church to lose the sharp contrast between its understanding about our human nature and the world's inclination to think the slate is not only blank but clean. Yet, he presses the conclusion that if "God is committed both to the election of individuals to eternal life and to a distinguishable program of providential dealings with the broader creation, then it is quite fitting for us to feature a similar multiplicity in our own theologies" (*He Shines in All That's Fair*, 68). From the Christian perspective a doctrine of common grace establishes a meeting place, but just because we gather around the commons does not make all distinctions between humans and creature disappear. As a species we are both terribly bad and wondrously good and most of the time behave with mixed motives and conflicted emotions. What is left unsettled is whether this is a permanent predicament. If it is not permanent then an explanation is required why, for it seems that moments of being wondrously good do not get us where we want to go, much less the Kingdom of God.

The battle with sin and evil will follow us to the grave. For Christians to fall back into the mentality that they are strong enough or righteous enough to make it all the way "home" is a fatal mistake. The answer to sin is not greater effort (I will not do this again) or greater self-awareness (I know my limits). The way home begins with an honest confrontation with human nature and myself. The recovering alcoholic begins his road to recovery with the confession: "I am an alcoholic and I am powerless to overcome my addiction by myself." But this is not a confession made once and forgotten. In order to ensure temptation does not regain a hold over the alchoholic, two things are necessary. The confession must become a daily affair. In both the Roman Catholic mass and the Book of Common Worship, the litany includes the confession, "I am not worthy." To believe that one is worthy is tantamount to the pride that goes before the fall: I am not worthy to heal myself or set the ledger straight, because the plea of Christians is, "Lord, in your mercy, forgive me," not because we have some definable transgression but because it reminds us who we are, deep down and likely to deny. The second necessary step for recovering alcoholics is to ally themselves with a community of recovering alcoholics. Alcoholics attend AA meetings long after they are sober. Likewise, my decision, for good or evil is not nearly as important as the decision whether I go it alone or live in community with other Christians. Holocaust survivor and Nobel Peace Prize honoree Eli Wiesel tells this story to remind us the world will change us unless we keep speaking someone else's truth to ourselves.

> A prophet like Isaiah daily strides up and down the streets of the city, shouting his warning and quietly pleading with his people. But they will not listen and they will not change. But still the prophet strides and implores until one day a small boy tugs at his robe. "Sir," he says, "don't you see that they are never going to change? Why bother? Just forget it." The prophet looks at the boy and then continues on his way. "I do this because even if I never change them, they won't succeed in changing me." (Lecture given at the University of New Hampshire)

Exposition of Genesis 3—You Can't Have It All

My purpose in this exposition is not to revisit the long and controversial interpretation of Genesis 3. Instead, I am interested in what characterizes sin in our time and place and the theological implications for a technologically consuming society.

The ancient story is the ever contemporary history of creatures who are caught up by the desire to gain the knowledge necessary to control their destiny, to then idolize (absolutize) that knowledge as "first principles," which then are twisted by the power such knowledge confers, with the result that we are deceived into believing we know how to handle such knowledge for the good of all. In the words of the serpent: "No! You will not die! It is a good thing for you to be like God who is all-knowing" (Gen. 3:4–5).

> 3:1 Now, the snake was the most subtle of all the wild animals that Yahweh God had made. It asked the woman, *"Did God really say you were not to eat from any of the trees in the garden?"*

Whatever the temptation we face as human beings, it is going to be subtle. It will come as a seducing question rather than a satisfying answer, since the former appeals to the restless nature of our species to transcend limits, while the latter only invites us to stand still and try nothing new. Secondly, as Paul Ricoeur suggests, the snake is already present and so "every individual finds evil already there" (*Symbolism of Evil*, 257). Thus, an anteriority of evil exists before every actualization. The meaning of original sin must therefore include the idea that each person finds and continues while beginning anew a struggle with a cosmic structure of evil and one's own personal history of sinful acts. "From the spectacle of things, from the course of history, from the cruelty of nature and men, there comes a feeling of universal absurdity which invites man to doubt his destination," writes Ricoeur (258). The serpent represents something that is more than what is within us—a desire that can be tempted as well as an ominous past that limits our present freedom.

Notice the way the serpent—the voice of reason but also the voice of deceit—tempts Eve. The serpent begins by posing a metaphysical question about limits: What right does God have to set limits over what you can do and know? "Did God say, 'You shall not eat from *any* tree in the garden'?" Then the serpent deceives by promising, "You will not die because you will be like God since your eyes will be open knowing good and bad" (my translation). Adam and Eve are still very much moral human beings. In order for them to become immortal, they would have to eat of the Tree of Life. God cannot allow a knowing-without-limits creature to proceed, thus they are banished from the Garden, which henceforth is guarded by the cherubim with flaming swords.

> 3:2–3 The woman answered the snake, "We may eat the fruit of the trees in the garden. But of the fruit of the tree in the middle of the garden God said, 'You must not eat it, nor touch it, under pain of death.'"

The fruit symbolizes something desirous. Furthermore, it ferments with explosive potential: Adam and Eve are to keep their distance and not touch it. In the biblical sense, something holy unto God that demands us to keep our distance, for what is holy is from God, and to see God's face or to touch what is divine or to hear God's voice means death.[12] Man and Woman are living in a garden of delights: "Eden" meaning "to delight." Here they are invited to "freely" partake of everything that is "pleasant to the sight" (2:9 and 2:15). Standing tall in the midst of this plenitude is the one delight they are forbidden to taste or to handle. God has identified the poison: the Tree of Knowledge of All Things Good and Bad. Bite of this and you will have bitten off more than you can handle.

Did ancient "man" react as strongly as we do to prohibitions? We seem to take offense that there should be any limits at all, and especially so if those limits concern what we are allowed to know. As heirs to the Enlightenment and the revolution in scientific knowing, we instinctively resist a command, divine or not, that tells us about a knowledge we dare not taste. Insofar as God is understood as the limit against everything (Nietzsche), God's restriction is heard in a patronizing tone. Temptation begins to take hold the moment an inquiry invites us to proceed without consideration of limits. So Oppenheimer said at his trial, "When you see something that is technically sweet, you go ahead and do it and you argue what to do about it only after you have had your technical success. That is the way it was with the atomic bomb."

The snake also questions "who" has established the boundaries they ought not to transgress. "*Who* said you cannot . . . ," the serpent wants to know. The Tempter tempts by casting doubt about this mysterious, unseen divine authority. The relevance is more acute for generations raised on a "God is dead" theology, situation ethics, historical relativism, and a scientific rationality determined to solve any problem without divine assistance. We demand to know more and more because it is our right and nowhere to be found is a God who has demonstrated that he should be obeyed.

3:4   Then the snake said to the woman, *"No! You will not die! God knows in fact that the day you eat it your eyes will be opened and you will be like divine beings who know good from evil."*[13]

We take notice that the initial temptation is about knowing. When your eyes are open fully you can see it all. When you can see it all, you want it all. To be like Yahweh is no less than to see it all. When we see it all, we desire to have it all. As self-transcendent creatures we stand upright, think abstractly, and converse with each other in complex language systems. This is our endowment and because of it we are empowered to name what God has made (Gen. 2:19). But the capacity to distinguish (to name) is also our Achilles heel. If the capacity to transcend the present moment constitutes being made in the image of God (*imago Dei*), then it is likely, or shall we say inevitable, that we will want to remove that very same authority which stands over us. The Greeks immortalized this truth about human nature as they told the Oedipus stories, the Hebrews as they told the story of Adam and Eve.

We find ourselves siding with Adam and Eve wanting to know why the capacity to distinguish good from evil is so wrong. This however misunderstands the meaning behind this Hebrew idiom. The Old Testament scholar Gerhard Von Rad points out that a knowing of good and evil is "a formal way of saying what we mean by our colorless 'everything.'"[14] To speak neither good nor evil means to say nothing (Gen. 31:24), to do neither good nor evil means to do nothing (Zeph. 1:12). In addition, consider that "to know" in the ancient sense implies "being able." The Hebrew root for knowing includes both the knowing of facts and the knowing of relationships. Subtle was the snake when it suggests that God had no right to limit their reach (research).

> 3:6–7 The woman saw that the tree was good to eat and pleasing to the eye, and that it was enticing for the wisdom that it could give. So she took some of its fruit and ate it. She also gave some to her husband who was with her, and he ate it. Then the eyes of both of them were opened and they realized that they were naked. So they sewed fig-leaves together to make themselves loin-cloths.

It was not physical hunger that drove Eve to stand before the Tree of Knowledge reflecting and then deciding to overreach. What satisfies more than bread for the stomach is to be knowledgeable to the extent of being powerful. So Jesus is tempted with the same kind of powerful knowledge that goes beyond mere food to the means of production. In Matthew 4, he is tempted by the offer of *power* to turn stones into bread; the *power* to throw himself off the pinnacle and not be killed; and the *power* to rule the kingdoms of the world. Bread makes us content for the moment—from day to day—but the power of knowledge is to control who will eat. In a postmodern age where knowledge is power and power is knowledge, the need to know drives us to overreach. When science learned the secrets of creating, it became queen of the sciences or queen of knowing.[15]

Something radically different begins to happen when "man" is no longer content to play joyfully in the Garden of Eden and is restless to break nature apart and understand how she creates. Philosopher George P. Grant testifies to where we have landed: "The key difficulty in receiving the beauty of the world these days is that such teaching is rooted in the act of looking at the world as it is, while the dominant science is rooted in the desire to change it" (*Technology and Justice*, 50). "Claiming to be wise," writes Paul, "they became fools, and exchanged the glory of the immortal God for images resembling . . ." (Rom. 1:23; cf. Ps. 115:8). In the movement when temptation becomes actualization, from reflection to deed, an exchange takes place. That exchange is the confusion concerning Creator and creature. Because we know the ways of nature, we assume that we can do what God can do. We have become so creative, such inventive creatures, able to split the atom and unravel the code of life, that we believe we have earned the right to make God-like decisions.

They see (know) that they were naked because they are aware their sexuality has the potential of becoming perverted. That is what happens when your eyes are wide open. You begin to see possibilities you did not see before. With this kind of seeing you desire more. How soon before the woman Eve is not enough, the man Adam is not enough? They no longer trust the other.

Original sin and the Fall of Man have come upon hard times, because as concepts they can no longer be located in a secular culture. If we no longer believe sin is genetically procreated and human beings did not degenerate from a perfect state, then it is perfectly understandable why a "gulf has opened in our culture between the visibility of evil and the intellectual resources available for coping with it" (Delbanco, 3). Our confusion and our ambivalence about Genesis 3 lies in our inclination to equate sin with isolated acts. But in the story of Adam and Eve, which portrays sin dramatically as a single act, what changes is their relationship with God and consequently their relationship to the world and to each other. In the New Testament and especially in the Pauline epistles, the singular "sin" and not "sins" is the overwhelmingly preferred terminology. In one of the better-known biblical passages, the words are "Here is the Lamb of God, who takes away the sin [singular] of the world" (Jn. 1:29.) The biblical preference to speak of sin is an indication of the understanding that Christ comes to heal relationships broken by many willful acts. Part and parcel of the subtlety of the snake's conversation is to offer Eve access to one particular kind of knowledge when in actuality the temptation is to arouse a desire for an omniscient knowledge. Paul Ricoeur's observation is that "a 'desire' has sprung up, the desire for infinity; but that infinity is not the infinity of reason and happiness . . . it is the infinity of desire itself; it is the desire of desire, taking possession of knowing, of willing, of doing, of being" (*Symbolism*, 253). The relationship between creator and creature is not merely strained, it is ruptured.

In a technical sense God did not forbid them to exercise the moral distinction between good and bad. Following a long theological tradition, Ricoeur does not locate the fall in a specific appetite or capacity but in the infinity of desire itself, the desire to take possession of knowledge and in taking possession to break off relationship with the Creator (253). The Enlightenment represents that process of opening the eyes of humankind and then nourishing the belief that we can stand alone and do just fine without God and limits. The independent nature of discovery will always cloud the finitude of being creature.[16] A being who is able to see everything will inevitably seek its freedom in the hubris of absolute freedom. Only as we exaggerate our independence do we see divine limits as vindictive and unfair.

Sin, therefore, must be our situation before God rather than before ourselves. The distinction between Creator and creature is the basis for the distinction between reaching and overreaching. We are not denied our nature to explore, to create, to reach into the unknown—in other words, to transcend. What God cannot tolerate is a creature with a capacity for such self-transcendence to forget from time to time, over and over again, how to transcend wisely, responsibly, and with humility.

> 3:8–21 The man and his wife heard the sound of Yahweh God walking in the garden in the cool of the day and they hid from God among the trees of the garden. But Yahweh God called to the man. "*Where are you?*" he asked.
> Then Yahweh God said to the snake . . .
> To the woman he said . . .
> To the man he said . . .

Yahweh asks a question which he knows the answer. Yahweh has already found Adam and Eve, hiding. What Yahweh wants to know from them is if they think they can hide from God. Do they think or hope God will just go away?

The consequence of their desiring to know everything without limits is that they immediately begin to misuse the power of that knowledge. Once they distort their relationship with God and decide to be gods unto themselves, their relationship with each other, including its sexual dimension, is twisted. They begin to relate to each other in a non-trusting way and so their nakedness becomes an occasion for misusing sex in order to dominate the other (implicit in the naming of his wife in Genesis 3:20, and explicitly in 3:16 where "he shall rule over you").

The bond between human life and the earth ("the Lord God formed man of dust from the ground" 2:7) has now become a source of disharmony ("in thorns and thistles and by the sweat of your face," 3:18–19). Not only does mistrust cloud their judgment, fears distort their actions. The almost benevolent naming of the animals has now become "the fear and dread of you shall rest upon every animal of the earth" (9:2).

When we have something to hide God searches us out with questions: "Where are you?" (3:9); "What is this that you have done? (3:13); "Where is Abel your brother?" (4:9); and "What have you done?" (4:13). Divine questions are meant to open our eyes to the possibility that we have overstepped certain limits (Luther's second use of the law). The theology of Genesis 3 is more akin to understanding revelation as disrupting human smugness with questions we cannot address to ourselves.

> 3:22 Then Yahweh God said, *"Now that the man has become like one of us in knowing good from evil, he must not be allowed to reach out his hand and pick from the tree of life too, and eat and live for ever!"* So Yahweh God expelled him from the Garden of Eden . . .

Their expulsion from the Garden is now made necessary because, motivated by the desire to know all things, this creature will become a real Dr. Frankenstein. The spatial imagery of the Genesis story, introduced in Genesis 2:9, implies that there are limits created into the universe. In the middle of the Garden there are two trees: the Tree of Knowledge of good and evil and the Tree of Life. According to George Aichele, Jr., the spatial separation of these two trees represents the separation or disunity between moral freedom and immortality, between knowledge and life (*The Limits of Story*, 36–46). Human beings desire to have both, for to have both is to be truly divine. Adam and Eve's expulsion denotes a fall from eternity into time—just as the first eleven chapters of Genesis are a universal, mythical account of the world's beginnings,[17] while chapter 12 begins the historical account of how these themes find expression in God's plan for Israel. And simultaneously, it is a fall from play (enjoyment of nature) into work as struggle over nature. The Shalom we lost is what we experience during moments when we fully enjoy creation and our relationships. Such is the value of play and keeping the Sabbath. Nicholas Wolterstorff's discussion of *Shalom* as enjoyment speaks to the what humans are made for: "To dwell in Shalom is to enjoy living before God, to enjoy living in one's physical surroundings, to enjoy living with one's fellows, to enjoy life with oneself" (*Until Justice and Peace Embrace*, 69–72). Life is now a striving and will continue to be such until that time when God redeems *both* nature and humankind (Cf. Isa. 65:21–23 and Zech. 8:10–13). What frustrates community is not simply decay and death but selfishness and pride.

Adam and Eve have lost their home in the Garden of Delight. They are faced with the task of making a new home where thorns and thistles abound. Our attitude toward nature in this regard has been ambivalent. The prevailing Western attitude requires nature to be reshaped into a human environment before it becomes a home for us. American settlers felt obliged to *tame* the West and *clear* the forest before they called it home. The native population had learned how to walk lightly and work with nature. With the introduction of science the human hand that holds the tool is unstoppable. Because we have this urge to design tools and use them, the artificial antipathy between "us and it" escalates. And once nature has been cut open another temptation arises: to improve upon nature by redesigning it to fit our needs and wants. In the biblical vision of Shalom this spirit of frustration is defeated when nature is able to enjoy nature ("the wolf shall dwell with the lamb," Isaiah 11.6), when human beings enjoy nature ("they shall plant vineyards and eat their fruit," Isaiah 65.21), and when nations will benefit each other ("and they shall beat their swords into plowshares," Micah 4.3).

The Blessing and Burden of Self-Transcendence

In the business world it is a neat "trick" to think outside the box. In the survival of the fittest, self-awareness became the neat trick,[18] because thinking outside the instinctual box meant having a leg up. If you could stand outside of your immediate circumstances, if only momentarily, you opened doorways to memory and anticipation. You possessed the advantage of remembering something important and preparing for the future. Food could be stored, a good hunting place revisited, preparations made for the cold season, lessons learned and passed on. Pleasure and distress could be extended in both its remembrance and its expectation. Such a creature would have a higher survival rate and begin to think of life as more than survival.

Self-awareness becomes self-transcendence when another dimension is added, namely that of *other*. Self-awareness does not necessarily include another. At one level awareness happens within the confines of the self: being more aware of abilities, of thoughts, the movement of one's hands and feet, the sounds one can make, recollection of a missed opportunity, or a task to be done tomorrow. Self-transcendence includes an added level of awareness when I see myself against another: what he thinks of me, what she is feeling, what I can do for her, what he can do for me.

As the trick of self-transcendence emerged and planted itself, it eventually was understood as a gift unsolicited. It could not be bought or sold. Some seemed to have it while others not so much. But who was the giver? What was expected in return for the gift? At this level of sophistication the gift is also seen for what it is: a burden. Memory provokes grudges held, revenge sought, remorse felt, or guilt experienced. Given its future orientation, anticipation arouses anxiety, restlessness, fear, greed, or covetousness. While memory recycles what has been, anticipation rehearses what might be. Memory leads to destruction, anticipation to self-destruction. Both will cause us to measure ourselves against what we would take back or do differently: a misspent life, unfulfilled dreams, a love unspoken, an injustice left not righted, a grievance not forgiven. Life is precariously balanced between the two: the gift of standing outside oneself and the burden of the self I am not.

There are many boxes we try to break out of: conceptual boxes which limit the extent of one's horizon, predispositions and heredity which assign us to a certain fate, moral responsibilities which constrain our freedom. And like these boxes, the sin box spoils the day. But unlike the other boxes, sin's deception is subtle and sinister. The splinter in my eye is a log in by brother's eye, and I only see what is in my brother's eye (Matt. 7:2).

Given the fact that we are creatures who mess up much of what we touch and then try to rectify it, is there any hope for us? Will we ever fully do the good we intend? Will we ever act responsibly before amends are necessary? When will we cease to be our own worst enemy? In *The Denial of Death*, Ernest Becker illuminates the paradox of being human without reference to sin.

> This is the paradox: he is out of nature and hopelessly in it; he is dual, up in the stars and yet housed in a heart-pumping, breath-gasping body that once belonged to a fish and still carries the gill-marks to prove it. . . . Man is literally split in two: he has an awareness of his own splendid uniqueness in that he sticks out of nature with a towering majesty, and yet he goes back into the ground a few feet in order blindly and dumbly to rot and disappear forever. (26)

The human paradox is constituted by the fact that we cannot escape our own self-assertion. Wolfhart Pannenberg amplifies the writing of Ernest Becker. All human life is carried out in the tension between self-centeredness and openness to the world (*What is Man?*, 56). With this in mind, *Homo sapiens* is the species that bears the blessing and burden of self-transcendence. The blessing is to be more than a creature of instinct existing for the present moment. The burden is to be accountable for our actions: the tragic results of our misjudgments, the guilt of our misdeeds, the bloody trail of corpses left behind by vengeance. With an eye always ready to scan the historical scene, Reinhold Niebuhr broadens the human paradox: "What an ironic drama it is, of man who is a monster in his power, and is a worm in his lack of power to save himself" (*Justice and Mercy*, 111). With one hand we reach out and with the other hand we overreach.

My theological colleagues point out that overreaching is one among many expressions of sin and may be an inadequate understanding of the biblical witness. But when it pertains to our need to know, overreaching is more fundamental than first impression. What characterizes our time more than our need to know? The quest to know everything about ourselves has begun. Whether we are mapping the human genome or finding a cure for bone cancer, we will not stop until we know how every gene works in concert with every other gene. And so the story goes at every level of science. The pursuit to master quantum computing has begun with seven atoms (*A Shortcut through Time*, by George Johnson). The travel back into time does not end until we know how the universe came into existence and life began. When is it enough to know unless everything is known?

Adam, Eve, and God have triangulated themselves by entering into a covenant, a covenant later formalized with Israel. God will trust them to enjoy the Garden without partaking of the Tree of Knowledge. Their freedom to explore and enjoy is balanced by their agreement not to be greedy. The serpent cozies up to Eve and tempts them by appealing to their need to know—not just to know but to know without limits. Adam and Eve choose to break their covenant with Yahweh in order to infinitely expand their horizon. Their fundamental sin? To break trust with God, to consider their relationship with the Sovereign Other as expendable (the cost to be paid in order to be on their way toward all-knowing). In order to be sovereign in our own right, it becomes necessary to break trust with God and another. Sin is driven by both horizontal and vertical energies; nevertheless, Christians insist the vertical dimension of our relation to God is paramount. "Against thee, thee only, have I sinned, and done this evil in thy sight" (Ps. 51).

Sin has yet another hard sell to make. The horizontal nature of sin is easily appreciated. It spreads out among neighbors and enemies alike. The vertical dimension prompts the skeptic to inquire, What difference does it make?[19] Allow me to illustrate in the person of Albert Speer. As Hitler's chief architect, he was charged with designing what a Nazi future would look like. He worked in a time and place when many of the usual horizontal (civil) limits were weakened and the vertical limit (belief in God) denied. When there is no God, we think ourselves free to act like sovereigns, which is exactly what emperors and dictators do. Without those limits Speer allowed himself to think he was having the best time of his life. In their analysis of what took place, Stanley Hauerwas and David Burrell argue that Speer's self-deception is explained by the lack of a "master story." When Speer writes, "it never even occurred to us to doubt the order of things," it reveals a world closed off to the possibility of a truth from across the sea. Hitler did everything in his power to see that there were no other stories except his, no larger story to frame their particular situation, no paradigm to lift them out of the mission entangling them in the moment. There was, of course, the lower-level excuse that "the ordinary party member was being taught that the grand policy was much too complex for him to judge it." Reflecting on his own ethical failure, Speer writes: "I did not see any moral ground outside the system where I should have taken my stand."[20]

Gitta Sereny's encyclopedic study *Albert Speer: His Battle with Truth* adds another level of analysis to Speer's self-deception. Sereny charts Speer's struggle to face the truth about himself and find atonement. She writes in connection with Speer's relationship with Casalis, an extraordinary pastor and theologian who counsels Speer while he is in prison. As part of his awakening to what Speer had done, Casalis leads him to use language to search for inner meanings. Casalis himself was deeply influenced by Karl Barth and encouraged Speer to read Barth, in the hope that something of Barth's theology of the Word would *disrupt* the shell of justifications Speer had constructed.

The blessing of self-transcendence is the capacity to stand outside ourselves and consider the possibility that our existence does not need to be paramount. This form of self-doubt is the basis for differentiating between good and bad. Speer had the capacity but he did not exercise it. Eugene de Kock, the man whom many considered South Africa's most brutal of apartheid's covert police operatives, knows right from wrong and yet gradually his conscience is stilled by a system that denies what was happening. The Nazis, on the other hand, never denied what they did, only that it was criminal. Even the good-hearted, sincere Will Campbell doesn't see how his goodness devaluated his brother. What they all lack is an operative master story to enable them to step outside the box.

Master stories have fallen victim to the postmodern critique, but there is a limit to how far this critique extends.[21] Lyotard's critique is specifically directed toward such Enlightenment thinkers as Descartes, Adam Smith, Hegel, Marx, and anyone else who believes self-transcendence is how we transcend our finitude. Grand narratives are vicious not only because they legitimize domination, they hide the criteria of truth within the very practice to be legitimized. In examining why Christian nations participated and did nothing during the Holocaust, Darrell J. Fasching is well aware of the problem of placing the criterion of truthfulness in the story but continues by asking how can one see the world truthfully when no master story exists. Fasching's fascinating analysis ends with two conclusions: (1) Christians must cease believing their master story is an exception to the rule, since the Christian story has produced its own forms of self-deceptive accounts, legitimating anti-Semitism and the genocide of the Jewish people, and (2) the Christian story par excellence calls into question every story, even its own. Fasching then makes what I consider to be a foundational statement: "It is difficult to see how there can be anything like self-transcendence without the self transcending itself. The precondition of all conversion is the experience of becoming alienated from oneself" (*Narrative Theology after Auschwitz*, 121). That alienation comes by being confronted by One who is Other and is possible without a capacity for self-doubt. "Doubt," Fasching writes, "reveals the infinite qualitative distance between the self and its story" (121). The edge must given therefore to those master stories that invite self-questioning and warn of self-deception. If I were looking for a master story to help me think or act outside my box, I would want one that is not told by me and one that includes an account of sin.

Because Christians want to proclaim their master story as *the* Master Story, they must be doubly vigilant since a divine storyteller is doing the telling. The very same diligence is required of any religion and its adherent making a similar claim. Insofar as the Christian meta-narrative claims to be a universal story, it wants to claim total allegiance to the point of blindness.[22] On the other hand, what other story of such scope begins with a narrative of sin and evil and then requires that for salvation I first confess that I am a sinner beyond human redemption? What other Savior is not the answer to all questions but the questioning of all answers? As soon as the tension between the now and the not yet is dissipated, the truth of the now becomes the battle cry of fanatics. When God's reign is never fully realized but is always caught in the tension of here and not here yet, the future is not already made but open to the very thing we do not expect of God.

The vertical dimension of sin matters. If you answer to the incomprehensible God, you must continually doubt your own answers. Even for the Christian—and perhaps especially for the Christian and others who profess a Master Story—this is difficult to digest. Pumla Gobodo-Madikizela notes that there were two peculiar features that stood out about the distribution of Bibles to soldiers of the South African Defense Force.

> The first was the gold star-shaped army insignia embossed on the maroon front cover. The second was the inscription in Afrikaans on the first pace, which read:

Message from the State President P. W. Botha

This Bible is an important part of your calling to duty. When you are overwhelmed with doubt, pain, or when you find yourself wavering, you must turn to this wonderful book for answers. . . . Of all the weapons you carry, this is the greatest because it is the Weapon of God. (*A Human Being Died That Night*, 53)

The cynic can be heard carping about what better example to prove that any master story can be twisted and co-opted. So it can, but this wasn't the Christian Story of how sin and evil cling to every story—personal, tribal, corporate, nationalistic. The Bible was being used to justify the meta-narrative of white supremacy told by white men to white men to keep black men and women in their place. It was a story believed because there were many who wanted to believe it. If this isn't sin that became evil, then I do not know where else to look. Nazism and what happened in South Africa were monumental failures of self-transcendence. At times we know when we are allowing ourselves to be deceived, and then allow it to continue. The box being constructed about us is not without a way out. And while there is no exit from a human nature so easily turned to the bad, there are poets and prophets, saints and martyrs, storytellers and watchmen who shake us to the core if only we will listen for a truth not of our own making.

Notes

1. The means of disclosure are varied and the examples here are biblical. For the most nuanced discussion of "God's communication with human beings," see Nicholas Wolterstorff, *Divine Discourse* (Cambridge University Press, 1995).

2. See Gabriel Fackre, *The Doctrine of Revelation* (Grand Rapids, Mich.: Eerdmans, 1997), 53.

3. In chapter 6 of *The Message in the Bottle*, Percy evaluates the different categories of sentences and the meaning they carry, as well as the role faith plays in "dealing with" news from across the seas. For the sake of clarity I have set aside the thorny issues of epistemology or the relationship between faith and reason.

4. See Dominic Crossan's astute insight into the nature of parables as told by Jesus, *The Dark Interval* (Allen, Tex.: Argus Communications, 1975), 87.

5. The language of "un-son" and "un-father" is Volf, *Exclusion*, 156–65.

6. See Braaten and Jenson, eds., *Sin, Death and the Devil*, 40.

7. Braaten and Jenson, *Sin, Death and the Devil*, 104.

8. Sittler, *Essays on Nature and Grace*, 18.

9. See Hodgson, *God in History*, 277, and Focault's hermeneutics of violence, *The Focault Reader*, 83.

10. Even before the Enlightenment and its turn toward reason, Reformation theology was steeped in a mistrust of reason. Using the picturesque language for which he is known, Luther depicts reason as a whore. Reason tempts us to believe we have the capacity within us to know God as God truly is, when faith alone leads us to the God. This is said by a scholar who could reason with the best. But he still did not trust reason.

11. If it is not entirely obvious, I, too, have been influenced by Barth's understanding of revelation and grace as disruptive. See Hunsinger, *Disruptive Grace*. In the introduction he writes: "Grace that is not disruptive is not grace—a point that Flannery O'Connor well grasped alongside Karl Barth" (16). In addition see Graham Ward, *Barth, Derrida and the Language of Theology* (Cambridge University Press, 1955), chapter 7.

12. See Exodus 3:5; Deuteronomy 5:23–26. Saint Paul made his familiar comparison: "For now we see in a mirror dimly, but then face to face. Now I know in part, then I shall understand fully" (I Cor. 13:12). The gift of being resurrected includes seeing God "face to face" and not to die. Cf. Job 19:25–27.

13. Jewish translations, such as *The Torah* and *Tanakh*, render the Hebrew as "good and bad." Christian and ecumenical translations, such as the *Revised Standard Version*, translate it as "good and evil." The juxtaposition of good and bad implies everything in the moral realm; good and evil implies knowledge of everything.

14. Gerhard Von Rad, *Genesis* (Philadelphia: Westminster Press, 1961), 86; also a great Jewish authority J. H. Hertz in *The Pentateuch and Haftorahs*, 10, n. 5. Both think "good and evil" is a Hebraism for "all things." Cf. 2 Sam. 14:17. Hertz also notes that Adam (and Eve) would not have been made in the image of God without possessing the faculty to distinguish what is morally good from wrong.

15. See Coleman, *Competing Truths*, part 1, for a development of the argument that science displaced theology as queen of the sciences.

16. Mary Shelley identifies the autonomous nature of empiricism in her *Frankenstein*. The good doctor who decides to explore the boundary between life and death retreats to the laboratory and cuts himself off from family and friends. The larger issue is what happens when the discipline of science isolates itself from the humanities, or what some scientists regard as second-class science.

17. "Mythical" means something that never was but always is, but it has unfortunately come to mean in the vernacular something that is not true—as if something that never happened (fiction) could never narrate a profound truth.

18. I have in mind the use of the word "trick" in the sense given by Daniel Dennett, *Darwin's Dangerous Idea*, 77–78. A "Good Trick" is a better design or a better adaptation and does not imply something supernatural. Whether a good trick is strictly fortuitous or providential is a different matter.

19. A prime example of human nature without the vertical dimension of the divine is *The Science of God and Evil* by Michael Shermer, editor of *Skeptic* magazine and a monthly columnist for *Scientific American*.

20. See Hauerwas et al., *Truthfulness and Tragedy*, 31–32, 85–88. The authors target their analysis at Speer's own account, *Inside the Third Reich*.

21. See Merold Westphal for a discussion of the differences between the met-narratives criticized by postmodernists and the biblical meta-narrative. Westphal, "Blind Spots: Christianity and Postmodern Philosophy," *Christian Century*, 4 June, 32–35.

22. See the not so minor critique of Christianity as a universal story by John Hick, *Disputed Questions in Theology and the Philosophy of Religion* (New Haven, Conn.: Yale University Press, 1993).

CHAPTER FIVE

Sin's Genealogy: The Emergence of Sin

> If animals can have enemies they can have friends; if they can cheat they can be honest, and if they can be spiteful they can also be kind and altruistic.
> —Frans de Waal, Good Natured, 19

> An honest discussion of human nature has never been more timely.
> —Steven Pinker, The Blank Slate, xi

If sin is to have a place at the table of critical ideals, it will need to satisfactorily respond to three issues: (1) clarify the distinction between sin and sins, and between sin and evil, (2) set forth a new conceptual framework for sin that is biblically sound and relevant, and (3) provide an evolutionary account of sin. The first two issues are discussed in chapters 3 and 4. The thesis developed here is that sin emerged in tandem with the capacity for self-transcendence. I have thought what it would mean to write an evolutionary account of evil, and I find that to be incongruous. Evil has many historical manifestations but its ontological nature is just to be. Sin, on the other hand, is so intimately connected with our humanity that it must have an evolutionary history. Properly speaking, sin is not the actor who is evolving. Human beings, and more specifically their self-awareness, evolved from primitive to highly developed. Sin is our perpetual companion and for that reason it can be said to have a genealogy.

Why do we need an evolutionary account of sin? The short answer is to increase sin's credibility. Reinhold Niebuhr wrote unashamedly of the doctrine of original sin as the one empirical fact no one can deny, an obvious fact of ordinary experience. Realizing the non-Christian public would be a hard sell and especially so if sin is wedded to a literal interpretation of Genesis 3, he sought to locate sin in human experience and history. The effect of reading the opening eleven chapters of Genesis as an actual historical occurrence is to bar an evolutionary account of sin because everything is frozen in time. Adam and Eve's sin is our sin but a veil is thrown over the causal connections except to say that every sin by every human being is somehow connected to the one sin of an original pair. This has all the appearance of being absurd unless Adam and Eve are a representative type—that is, they represent all of us, or sin is genetically inherited. The latter has never been seriously considered because it undercuts the freedom of humans to choose good or evil, and it clearly is not the intended meaning of the writer of Genesis 3. Even those who insist on reading the Bible literally are likely to accept a universe where stars have a history of coming into being, humans grow and mature, tadpoles become frogs, and everything changes by invisible, incremental steps. Everything about sin begins to make more sense when it too has a history.

Catholic theology presents another kind of problem. In 1950 in *Humani Generis*, Pope Pius XII was willing to consider the possibility of evolution but declared emphatically the human soul is not the consequence of evolution. In his 1996 letter to the Pontifical Academy of Sciences, Pope John Paul II acknowledged the theory of evolution to be "more than a hypothesis" but again declared that "if the human body takes its origin from pre-existent living matter, [nevertheless] the spiritual soul is immediately created by God." The underlying presumption is a non-negotiable divide between the spiritual and the material. The human soul, being spiritual, could not be the result of progressive changes in matter. The soul must be conferred on each person by a special act of God. Throughout his theological pronouncements Pope John Paul II felt it was important to clearly distinguish between a God-centered theology and modernistic philosophies that deny the spiritual. I will not venture into the extended debate between Protestants and Catholics on this point except to say that Protestant theology is troubled by the dualism set up by spirit versus matter. Not incidental is the issue of when the soul joins the body, not only biologically but when in the evolutionary development of the human species. Accepting the evidence that *Homo sapiens* first appeared in Africa 150,000 to 200,000 years ago, when can you say definitively God acted? The argument could be made that at the appropriate evolutionary moment God "once and for all" began to endow this not-yet-human species with a soul, but whenever a defining historical moment is identified— whether that be Adam and Eve in the Garden of Eden or an evolutionary lead forward—it runs contrary to an incremental progression of a uniquely human capacity for self-transcendence. And the latter fact of evolutionary history is at the very heart of my argument.

An evolutionary account of sin is needed because so few of us are convinced they are inherently bad or even prone toward evil. In the dusty stacks of seminary libraries are two books that should have settled the issue of original sin. In 1740 John Taylor set forth his ideas in *The Scripture-Doctrine of Original Sin Proposed to Free and Candid Examination*. Trained for the Presbyterian ministry, Taylor found completely untenable the idea that Adam's sin was imputed to us, because guilt is always personal and non-transferable. Both John Wesley and Jonathan Edwards published long treatises against Taylor. In a book that was going to press at the time of his death, *The Great Christian Doctrine of Original Sin Defended* (1758), Edwards minutely dissected Taylor's treatise "in all its parts." With the weight of both Wesley and Edwards coming down squarely upon Taylor, one would have expected this to be the end of the controversy. But Edwards's tortured arguments were not "death to the controversy" but kept the controversy alive for many decades.[1] Succeeding defenders of original sin have not relented for a moment, for nearly every major Protestant theologian since has felt the obligation to mount an apology. Nevertheless, over the centuries detractors have turned into skeptics and have stopped listening. In spite of the in-your-face evidence that it is our manifest nature to screw up, the notion of original sin hasn't sold in the marketplace of critical ideas because no reasonable case has been made explaining how sin that is original with Adam and Eve becomes my sin. The claim to be reasonable needs only bear the weight of "making good sense" in light of what is generally accepted concerning our evolutionary development. And while I do not claim the specifics of my argument are either necessary or complete, the argument itself is necessary and adequate if we are to have a reasonable understanding of human nature. A purely naturalistic explanation, then, is necessary but incomplete, but in saying this I acknowledge this to be something of a pattern by which theologians add on to something scientific in order to make a better (holistic) argument.

The first strike against original sin is the deteriorating authority of Scripture and skepticism concerning the historicity of Adam and Eve. The second strike is the eternal optimist in us who believes that sin, in whatever form of human fallibility, can be gradually purged from our systems. And the third strike is the puzzle of how sin allows for *no* exceptions, not even the exceptional individuals who grace the Roman Catholic calendar of saints. The liberal principle of accountability rules: I am responsible for my own mistakes and not the misdeeds of others and I should not be burdened by the guilt of those near or long dead. However, if I am not as free and self-determined as I would like to think, if my existence is pre-dated by the pre-existence of a sea of evil (metaphorically speaking), if my development as an individual parallels the development of my species, if I am never at rest but always becoming, and if the same pattern of destruction and self-destruction is evident in all of history, then there is something unoriginal about my behavior. To give an evolutionary account of sin is to reaffirm original sin, not in reference to a definable historical moment but to something that is innate and universal.

Everyone can appreciate Genesis 3 as a narrative of the all too human experiences of temptation, transgression, blaming, guilt, and of suffering the consequences. The presence of a talking snake, a Tree of Knowledge, a Tree of Life set within a Garden of Eden transposes the events and personalities into a universal realm where everything takes on cosmic proportions. This is human sin writ large and we find it pulsating within a prologue that begins with the creation, includes the sin of Cain against his brother Abel and the depth of wickedness (Noah), and concludes with the sin of idolatry and the scattering of humans "over the face of all the earth" (the Tower of Babel). Clearly, the rest of the story would not make sense without some account of sin.

The time has come to speak of an evolutionary account of sin, just as the time has come to speak of an incarnated soul.[2] The human soul is the classic ghost-in-the-machine—a non-material substance skyhooked[3] into the body at the time of conception, destined to leave the body at the moment of death. A soul of this type is without a history. It comes and goes but does not develop. A paradigm shift is required and it begins with an understanding of human nature that is both biblically and anthropologically sound[4]—one where body, mind, and spirit are fused together developmentally, historically, and biologically. The soul is not a distinct essence but a dimension of being human. In the language of the pastor-poet Arnold Kenseth, the soul is the meeting place with God. It is the holiness within us. It is the "felt sense that we belong to an order of being beyond this life of clocks and appointments, of minutes and years, and finally of death" (*Sabbaths, Sacraments, and Season*, 23). In the language of a scientist-theologian, John Polkinghorne, the soul carries and expresses the continuity of living personhood. It is "the immensely complex 'information bearing pattern' of life" (*The God of Hope*, 105). Each soul is unique because it has been stamped by each person's identity and that identity is a work in progress.

It is becoming fashionable to trace aspects of human relations back to their genetic roots. Since Richard Dawkins's *The Selfish Gene* (1976) and Edward Wilson's *On Human Nature* (1978), scientists have claimed all human emotions as fair game, including morality and love, aggression and altruism, conscience and spirituality.[5] Theologians, in seeking common ground with science, are also taken with the notion of "the evolution of altruism."[6] If common sense tells us there are genes that endow us with neural systems for shame, anger, empathy, and mysticism, why not study sin scientifically since it is ultimately about human nature? Dean Hamer's anticipated book *The God Gene* is meant to raise the possibility of a biological basis for spirituality. Hamer, a pre-eminent geneticist and researcher at the national Cancer Institute at the National Institutes of Health, is perfectly clear that there is no such thing as a God gene, and a more accurate title would have been "genes that create a predisposition to spirituality." Hamer is willing, nevertheless, to search for specific locators on the DNA spiral and settles on $VMAT_2$.[7] On the one hand science is doing what I expect it to do—produce a naturalistic explanation for personality. True to form Hamer writes: "The one thing we know for certain about spiritual beliefs and feelings is that they are products of the brain—the firing of electrochemical currents through networks of nerve cells" (*The God Gene*, 16). The comparable theological reply is that God cannot be reduced to electrochemical currents in the brain. But having said this, I am intrigued with the way Hamer goes about measuring spirituality. The first step toward linking genetics to spirituality is the identification of specific characteristics. Utilizing a number of existing personality scales, Hamer concentrates on three components: self-forgetfulness, transpersonal identification, and mysticism. The first component measures the predisposition toward being so wrapped up in something that you lose track of time and location. The second marker involves letting go of the "me" in order to identify with someone else, even to the point of personal sacrifices to help others. The third set of traits represent a propensity toward the ineffable or mysterious, a feeling of oneness with the universe and everything in it. In its own way, Hamer's three components describe the saint, the martyr, and the mystic and have much in common with the three capacities I explore (see below). Hamer himself makes the connection between spirituality and self-transcendence, and for good reasons. The golden cord connecting these personality traits is the human capacity to lose or put aside the self in order to be at one with what is other than self. While Hamer is looking at the measurable, what is hardwired and universal, another perspective will find new meaning behind the theological tenet of "being created in the image of God."[8]

The reader will soon see that I have decided not to be fashionable by chasing the empirical tail of science. I do wonder why genes for altruism or self-sacrifice would have been selected in the course of human evolution. It seems self-defeating when the only reality that matters to a gene is its survival. But since arguments are made for why acts of kindness and cooperation work to the long-term advantage of the individual or group, why not include altruism as an evolutionary adaptive behavior? In the end, it does not make a great deal of difference to me which genes code for what trait and how those genes are genetically coded. What does matter is how we account for the sinful nature—this paradox of good and evil—we know to be the core of our human nature. I can even agree with Daniel Dennett's sentiment that in order to explain human nature it must make sense. But here is where I part company with a solely naturalistic explanation. The very genes that give us the capacity for self-transcendence are the very genes that are surpassed when we think and act beyond the historical moment or the immediate needs of the present moment. Does it make sense to claim for ourselves the capacity for self-transcendence and then deny that we cannot, and have not transcended, our genetic makeup?[9] We live in the past as well as for the future; we know both remorse and hope. Our genes do not define who we are, for we have evolved culturally as well as developmentally, and this interplay of nature and nurture is such that we have reached a level of complexity that enables us—the human species—to compose symphonies and live saintly lives of dedicated altruism. Ultimately, because sin (and certainly not evil) is not a personality trait, not a disposition but an aspect of consciousness, it resists being forced into a genetic explanation. And for that reason a genealogical approach (see below) is the best methodological approach, because we know that both biologically and culturally we have evolved to a level of consciousness or self-differentiation that makes it possible to self-doubt, self-sacrifice, and seek the truth (see below).

The question at hand is not the evolutionary development of morality but the more foundational issue of sin. The question is not how we evolved into a moral creature but how consciousness evolved to the point where something besides survival is on our mind. Sin may or may not have been a help-survival technique. Certainly, it was not something our Palaeolithic ancestors gave much thought to. They were much too occupied with surviving the day. But over time they began to give more and more thought to life as it exists in the skin of something else. What is it like to run like the antelope or fly like the hawk? What is it like to give birth? What is my child feeling? And why does life end, and when it ends, is it forever? Balanced against the pain and the struggle are moments of transcendence when I am lifted beyond myself into another place and time.

Sin begins to have meaning when I ask, "Am I my brother's keeper?" (Gen. 4:9). Morality is the endless elaboration of where that responsibility begins and ends, whom it includes, and what sacrifices am I willing to make. While various standards of morality developed in various cultures, sin, or the choosing of good and not-good, has not changed. As we become more sensitive to moral issues, we have not become more or less sinful. Because sin is a function of consciousness, we only become more or less aware of our potential for doing good and harm. Evil, however, is not a function of human consciousness. Evil pre-exists and exceeds life itself. It belongs to a scale much greater than planet Earth.

The daunting task confronting us is to locate sin as it evolved concurrently with an expanding self-awareness. The key words to keep in mind are "concurrently" and "in tandem with." While it is both tempting and logical to make sin a religious thing, this only happened at a latter stage and in various cultural contexts. We did not "get" guilt because we got religion; rather, the experience of guilt predates its ritual expiation. It makes considerable more sense to begin our inquiry in the midst of fundamental needs, drives, and foundational capacities. Common sense directs us to Maslow's hierarchy of needs or the realms of hunting-gathering, birthing-nurturing. We may find that the traditional understanding of sin as an offense against neighbor (other) and God (Other) has an evolutionary basis far deeper and older than its codification as commandments. We will be frustrated only if we expect to find a point of commencement for sin. What matters is that at some point it began to matter: a discomfort with the suffering of another, a feeling of remorse for something done intentionally, a quizzical rumination about why there is something rather than nothing.

As a final preliminary remark, I make this observation. When attempting to trace the origin of sin, the genetic button can be pressed only so hard. Interpret the biblical account, the palaeo-anthropological evidence, the DNA record as you like, sin flies in under the radar screen. Consider what genetic markers have meaning for the Ten Commandments, and the result is minimal. The most that one can hope to lay bare are certain behaviors, such as making graven images, profaning what is holy, dishonoring the elders, cheating, lying, murderous aggression, adultery. The immediate difficulty is the possibility, even likelihood, that these behaviors were survival-adaptive, but if so, when did they become sinful? In addition, all of the behaviors are sinful because they are situated within a social-theological context. Adultery, for instance, only means something within the context of marriage and promise (vow) making. Keeping one day in seven as holy requires an entire framework of holy versus profane, and in the instance of the Hebrews, a cosmology of creating and resting ("and on the seventh day the Lord rested"). Our sinful nature is much more than particular behaviors, whether they are what we do or what we fail to do. Because there are as many ways to sin as there are individuals, any genetic predisposition is only part of the story. The sin that is truly original and perennial is the perversion of something good, the choosing of something not good. We must remember that sin is foremost a theological construct meant to tell us something about ourselves, and that something is a truth we cannot tell ourselves because we are the creature infinitely capable of self-delusion.

The Dynamics of Self-Transcendence

The debate rages on concerning what constitutes our essential human identity. It is customary to define our humanity over against every other species on this planet. The arguments usually turn on the question of a difference in degree or a difference in kind. Anthropologists, biologists, and sociologists minimize the differences and defend the proposition that we differ from animals by degrees—genetically, emotionally, and intellectually—and represent no more than further evolutionary refinements. The theological response will seem to many to be simplistic: we are different and distinct because we pray and worship. We, unlike all the creatures of the earth, were created with the capacity to have a relationship with our creator and our neighbor. For Karl Barth the pivotal distinction is our level of self-awareness that knows we are creatures as distinct from the Creator.

> Of all creatures the Christian is one who not merely is a creature, but actually says "Yes" to being a creature. Innumerable creatures do not seem even to be asked to make this affirmation. Man is asked. But man as such is neither able nor willing to make it. From the very first man as such has continual illusions about himself. He wants always to be more than a creature. He does not want merely to be under the universal Lordship of God. But the Christian makes the affirmation that is demanded of man. . . . (*Church Dogmatics*, III, 3, 240)

In spite of new DNA evidence revealing our ethnic and anthropological origins, it appears that no one is persuading anyone else. The long-argued separation of humans from animals based on our abilities, and their lack of them, is at a standstill. What has changed is the growing body of evidence that we share a genetic and social history. Aside from the controversial question of E. O. Wilson's desire to remove ethics from the hands of the philosophers and biologicize it, sociobiologists took the definitive step toward an evolutionary perspective that includes just about everything. The initial progressive steps of evolution were the same for humans and primates and can account for parallel developments in both moral and social behaviors. Frans de Waal, the Dutch-born zoologist specializing in the study of primate behavior, highlights what he considers requisites for morality: "a tendency to develop social norms and enforce them, the capacities of empathy and sympathy, mutual aid and a sense of fairness, the mechanisms of conflict and resolution, and so on" (*Good Natured*, 39). None of this settles the question whether humans, because they envision a future and tell fairy tales, deserve to be placed in a distinct category, but it does move us a step closer to reckoning with an evolutionary history of sin.

Nevertheless, we cannot shake the feeling that we have abilities that differ in kind. All of the abilities we associate with being human—to think abstractly, to live for the future, to laugh at ourselves, to express ourselves artistically and playfully, to tell stories in order to understand ourselves—depend on a capacity to think reflectively about ourselves. Lurking in the background, so to speak, is an even more basic ability, and because it is so fundamental let's refer to it as a "capacity." The capacity for self-transcendence marks the place in our evolution where we can say to ourselves, "I know that I am not like the other creatures of the earth." I hope that what can be said with a degree of agreement is that over an extended period of time hominids developed a capacity for self-reflection that sets the species apart, and to let it stand at that without asking for a definitive answer to degree versus kind.

The consensus interpretation of Genesis 1:26—made in the image of God—says our peculiarity has little to do with specific human traits but refers to that which makes a God-creature (I-thou) relationship possible. There are limits to how far this can be defended on evolutionary grounds except to point to the fact that here we are, creatures who worship a creator and hear a call to do more than just exist. Systematic theologian Robert W. Jenson cuts through a heap of confusion and verbiage with a straightforward, commonsense statement: "[Adam and Eve] were the first hominid group that in whatever form of religion or language used some expression that we might translate 'God' as a vocative."[10]

During a moment of personal reflection, Philip Simmons found words to describe humanity's particularity. On a cold New England day, when one may wonder why he or she hasn't moved to Arizona, Simmons took notice of "wild things" of nature—the bear that effortlessly bends the bird feeder or the red squirrel that scavenges with a kinetic joy. They are neither innocent nor guilty, neither pure nor corrupt, for these are strictly human categories. He asks what it would mean "to experience our own actions in such a way that the terms 'good' and 'bad' don't apply."

> It would mean living, like animals, without doubt as to our life's purpose. It would mean living in such perfect alignment with that purpose that our every act flowed effortlessly from what was highest and truest within us. It would mean rising each day to forage or feed, to shelter and care for our young, to laze or labor, fight or frolic without distraction, without self-judgment, without taking one step off life's true path. (*Learning to Fall*, 56)

There was a time when *Homo sapiens* was not burdened with guilt and obligations. Now we pay good money to trainers and spiritual guides to show us how to detach ourselves in order to return to a state of immediacy and self-observation without judgment. But we cannot sustain for long the mindless rhythm of running like the red squirrel before an inner voice is heard saying, "You should have bought the other running suit, the less revealing one, because right now there are people scheduling meetings to discuss your thighs."[11]

For their own distinctive reasons, philosophers and theologians have claimed too much for the human capacity for self-transcendence.[12] Philosophers have turned self-transcendence into a methodology for knowing beyond the mundane confines of culture and history. The highest goal of enlightenment would be a science of the mind whereby all subjective notions would yield to objective observation. Theology has been no exception, and one thinks of the liberal tradition of linking self-transcendence with a direct or *a priori* experience of God, such as Friedreich Schleiermacher's "feeling of absolute dependence" or Rudolf Otto's sense of the holy.[13] My understanding of self-transcendence—and here I distance myself from this tradition—does not allow us to circumvent the role language plays in our coming-to-know. In saying this I am affirming the postmodern position that culture and language shape our most basic experiences of the self and world. Thus, there are no unthematized religious experiences. William Placher writes succinctly, "Rather, it is only language that makes any kind of sophisticated human experience possible—and language inevitably shapes the experience's character" (*Unapologetic Theology*, 163). David Tracy and George Lindbeck make a similar argument to the effect that different religions do not diversely thematize the same experience; rather they have different experiences.[14] Just the same, there will be unreflective experiences with immense impact, moments of awe and insight. Some will have a distinctive religious coloring, others a distinctive scientific flavor. In those moments of discovery and self-discovery, the person sees farther and deeper than before, and in some instances than ever before. Such moments of religious creativity or scientific insight do not, however, constitute a transcendent foundation. Peter Berger said it succinctly:

> *Every hierophany is like thunder, and the human beings who hear it must feel that this thunder blots out every other sound in the universe.* . . . The "peace" of which this Koranic passage speaks is precisely the peace of utter certainty. Yet the day breaks. It even broke for Muhammad. And this is the point where reflection must set in. . . . Reflection, by its very nature, always takes place in the cold daylight—on the morning after, as it were. (*The Heretical Imperative*, 82–83)

By identifying self-transcendence as our fundamental capacity, we cannot do better than Roman Catholic theologian Karl Rahner's definition. "We shall call transcendence the subjective, unthematic, necessary and unfailing consciousness of the knowing subject that is co-present in every act of knowledge, and the subject's openness to the unlimited expanse of all possible reality" (*Foundations of Christian Faith*, 20). It must be added, though, that self-transcendence is not equally present in all acts of consciousness. It resides primarily in the capacity to question our existence. For Bernard Lonergan, another Catholic theologian titan, self-transcendence is the stepping-stone of the religious impulse which arises when we are put to the question, that is, when we allow ourselves to be questioned by one who is Other. The question about God becomes the question whether we can find a center that is not self or more than self. Lonergan's argument is epitomized in his statement: "Just as unrestricted questioning is our capacity for self-transcendence, so being in love in an unrestricted fashion is the proper fulfillment of that capacity" (*Method in Theology*, 106). Love is the epitome of self-transcendence since it is the purest act of self-giving and de-centering. Being in love with God is the highest expression of self-transcendence because it is the purest from of exocentricity.

Self-transcendence, then, is a universal and generalized capacity but not strictly a religious way of knowing. Again, it is important to reiterate that self-transcendence is not a thing in itself but those moments of awareness when the self knows something of its finitude and infinitude. In spite of the inclination to identify self-transcendence with intellectual abilities or with a religious way of knowing, self-transcendence is more closely allied with intentionality. I suspect that if we were to look for self-transcendence along evolutionary lines, it emerged as particular abilities were stretched and pressured to work cooperatively. As a dimension of human existence, self-transcendence raises to new heights the different abilities we inherit. For these reasons self-transcendence always becomes operative simultaneously when the self thinks and acts.

The inclination among theologians, notably Reinhold Niebuhr and Wolfhart Pannenberg, is to lay an anthropologically valid foundation before introducing a religious dimension. All human life, Pannenberg would say, is carried out in the tension between self-centerness and openness to the world. As creatures who are open to the world, we will inquire into and beyond everything that crosses our paths (*What Is Man?*, 12). Beginning with the same premise, Niebuhr wrote of the human paradox as the unresolvable tension between the creature who knows the inevitable end is death and yet aspires to the freedom of transcending our mortal nature. A classic Niebuhrism is:

> Man is insecure and involved in natural contingency; he seeks to overcome his insecurity by a will-to-power and overreaches the limits of human creatureliness. Man is ignorant and involved in the limitations of a finite mind; he pretends that he is not limited. He assumes he can gradually transcend finite limitations until his mind becomes identical with universal mind. . . . The religious dimension of sin is man's rebellion against God. . . . The moral and social dimension of sin is injustice. (*Nature and Destiny*, 1:178–79)

In his *The Nature and Destiny of Man*, written while World War II was raging, Niebuhr made a lasting contribution by connecting sin with self-transcendence, and in doing this his book represents the most successful modern interpretation of the Christian doctrine of original sin. Niebuhr did not make the mistake of understanding sin as the loss of, or the misuse of, some human ability. Rather, Niebuhr claimed as I do that sin is that moment of self-transcendence when knowing that we know, we overreach believing we can transcend our human condition of finitude. Following Augustine and especially Kierkegaard, Pannenberg, Niebuhr, and Tillich point to our restless and anxious behavior as indicating an unresolved tension between intention and reality. Augustine said simply that "I can move my hand, but I cannot change my will." The burden and blessing of transcendence is constituted by this bipolar freedom to reach and overreach, and the anxiousness we feel is the price we pay for thinking we can turn the burden into pure blessing.

The debate about human consciousness is ardent and divisive but Steven Mithen proposes a working hypothesis concerning the prehistory of the human mind which makes eminent sense. The specifics are not important to me but the larger picture strengthens the argument for the distinction between specific abilities and overarching capacities. The mind has been compared to a sponge, a computer, and a Swiss Army knife. What these models have in common is the evolution of a generalized intelligence. We got smarter and smarter. The Swiss Army knife model proposes that a number of *autonomous* intelligences developed over time, such as linguistic, musical, logical-mathematical, spatial, bodily-kinesthetic, and social interaction. Mithen argues the mind is too creative and expansive to fit any model based on a single, all-purpose program running separate intelligences. Recall for a moment the way a child will play with an inert doll, investing it with various attributes of a human being. In a moment of play, the child brings together two very different domains, that of inert objects and living things. "A critical feature of that child's mind," writes Mithen, "is not simply that she is able to apply the evolutionary inappropriate rules of psychology, biology and language to play with her inert physical object, but that she is utterly compelled to do so" (*Prehistory of the Mind*, 55). Missing in these models of general intelligence is the evolution of cognitive fluidity, "an integrating mechanism for knowledge that had been previously 'trapped' in separate specialized intelligences" (194).

Mithen's argument for the evolution of cognitive fluidity is depicted by a nave of general intelligence (a central program) connected through open doors to chapels of specialized facilities (figure 5.1). These adaptive specializations include *natural history intelligence* (abilities to understand the natural world essential to life as a hunter-gatherer), *technical intelligence* (abilities for the manufacture and manipulation of tools), and *social intelligence* (abilities for interacting with other human individuals including modules for "reading another's mind"). In some way, linguistic intelligence serves to interlink all of the abilities. What is gained—what is necessary to explain the complexity of the human mind with its ability to solve problems, use analogies and metaphors, empathize, and utilize a unlimited capacity for imagination—is the essential capacity to tap into abilities originating in different domains.

What I propose to take from Mithen's model of a cathedral is influenced by my own distinction between capacities and abilities, and I ask where sin might find a natural home. Capacities serve a broader purpose and engage

Figure 5.1

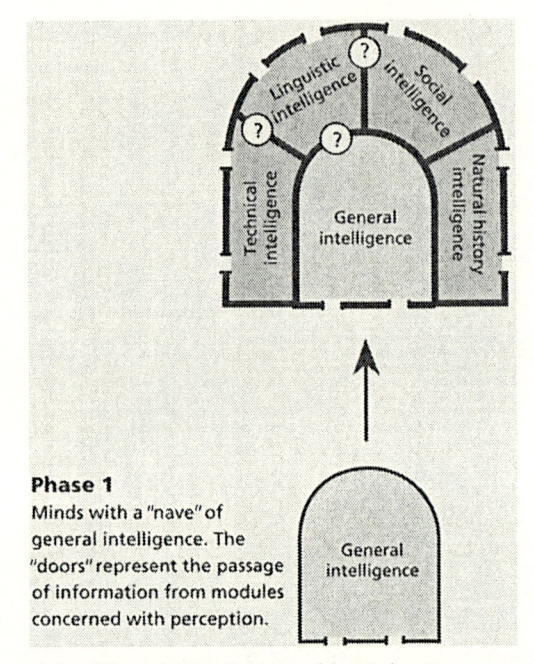

Phase 1
Minds with a "nave" of general intelligence. The "doors" represent the passage of information from modules concerned with perception.

Source: Used with permission of Steven Mithen, *Prehistory of the Mind*, p. 67.

abilities to accomplish those goals. Abilities are more specific and lack flexibility. They are targeted, so to speak, to hit a particular goal such as solving a mathematical problem, building a house, or playing a string instrument. Abilities have a closer association with learned behavior and instinctual drives while capacities are several steps removed. A capacity for love, for example, shows a great degree of adaptability and cultural specificity while the skill to sharpen a knife is specific but generic. The numerous social skills revolving around hospitality, conflict resolution, and proper social greetings and facial expressions are learned behaviors of the larger capacity for social interaction.

Self-doubt puts a dent in our armor of invincibility. Self-doubt means you can feel ambivalence, empathy, shame, be wrong, and make it right. To know that others are looking at you and judging you is the dawn of self-consciousness. Self-doubt is all of the feelings a twelve-year-old has looking in the mirror and weighing what others think of him or her. This capacity generates a host of learned behaviors and coping skills—everything from fussing over the right accessories to returning something you stole, from gossip to making amends.

Self-denial is a nobler capacity inspiring devotion and self-sacrifice. The self is seen over against the non-self. Self-denial cannot begin until self-differentiation takes hold, and the process of self-differentiation has many levels to ascend. The non-self can also be personified, and so there are spirits and spirit worlds. Myths about gods and stories of heroes immortalize the tragedy of life and the great sacrifices demanded of us. In a more mundane setting, self-denial underlies cooperation and altruism. And while this capacity is rarely expressed as a "pure" motive—always a mixture of what I give and what I might get—simple acts of sharing food and taking turns stand as a model of a kind of behavior others can aspire to duplicate.

Human beings are never content with what is. We try to reconcile the disparity between appearance and the way the world is. We exhibit a desperate need to see the other side of the mountain; and while the bear may go in order to find food, we adventure into the unknown because we can't help ourselves, ever treading where angels fear to go. We make tools to gain greater control over the environment, and then we create conceptual tools to enable us to see what the naked eye cannot see.[15] The tools of *truth-seeking* are as varied as the telescope and calculus, as practical as a new method of plowing the earth or as abstract as defining the relationship between energy and mass. And self-transcendence even allows us to use the mind as a tool, which happens when thought alone is used to solve a mathematical problem.

I do not pretend to know if creativity and imagination are separate stand-alone capacities. Certainly they are present and instrumental in the three capacities I have identified and strongly associated with language. Creativity, imagination, and language may have not emerged separately but they made all the difference. Creativity adds pizzazz, color, and style. A simple tune becomes a symphony, a few rhymes become a sonnet, and a pile of stones a cathedral. Imagination enables us to go out from the reality of our lives, to enter other realms and dream of what might be. From language we draw meaning and understanding. Working together they make it possible for the self to free itself from the mortal existence of living and dying.

If in the central nave of our intelligence a general program runs, that program is predicated on self-differentiation. The world begins to make sense if the self is able to make finer and finer distinctions between itself and the world of not myself. As the child matures, as the human species evolves, the depth and breadth of self-doubt, self-denial, and truth-seeking expand outward. In his review of the groundbreaking work of Piaget's theory of cognitive development and Lawrence Kohlberg's theory of moral development, James Fowler charts the progression both morally and spiritually from a me-centered world (stage 1), to an enlarged awareness of the commonwealth of all human beings (stage 6). We begin life oblivious to the experience of others. For a parent to say to a toddler, "Just think how that makes me feel," is to ask the impossible. At the other end of life, Fowler hopes we reach a stage of faith development where we are prepared to be spent on behalf of others because we can renounce the "usual human obsession with survival, security, and significance. . . ." (*Life Maps*, 87–88).

As we evolved, so did sin. It hitched a ride, so to speak, as our capacities for self-doubt, self-denial, and truth-seeking accrued. Self-doubt slides into hardness of heart, remorse, and indifference. Gracious acts of self-denial turn into pride, self-justification, and idolatry. Truth-seeking is corrupted by deceit, lying, and falsifying. What is good and not-good are forever interlocked, never one without the other. In his imagined genealogy of the origins of truth, British philosopher Bernard Williams need only remind us of the obvious: ". . . that while a given person needs correct information, it may well be a good idea for him to keep it to himself" (*Truth and Truthfulness*, 58). Whether driven by anxiety or restlessness, our capacity for self-transcendence is the reason we are our own worst enemy: when we reach we overreach, when we farm we over-farm, when we strip the land we over-strip it, when we create new technologies we over-promise.

To be human is to experience the rift between who we are and who we aspire to be, between life as fate and life as folded into a divine plan (providence), between the world as we think it should be and as we actually experience it. We are never quite at peace with ourselves or at home in the world because of the dissonance between what is and what should be. "When the world is not as it should be," Susan Neiman suggests, "we begin to ask why." On the other hand, "we stop asking why when everything is as it should be," and those are the moments when our experience of the world is so deep that the should melts away (*Evil in Modern Thought*, 320–22). Thus, a schematic emerges to account for philosophy, theology, and science. Metaphysics or philosophy is generated by the need to find and create meaning in a world that seems determined to thwart all such efforts. The impulse to theologize arises from a universe that is created good, mysterious, and sacred. Science arises from the desire to reconcile appearance and experience. Self-doubt is responsible for morality. Self-denial is the occasion for worship, thanksgiving, and humility. Truth-seeking sends us forth to explore, discover, and create. Philosophy is called to do battle with delusion, theology with idolatry, and empiricism with superstition.

Figure 5.2

Capacity	Emotion/response	Abilities	Discipline/corruption
self-doubt	introspection, anxiety	moral discrimination	philosophy/delusion
I am as others see me	empathy, guilt	forgiveness, peacemaking	
self-denial	gratitude/adoration	suspend satisfaction	theology/idolatry
I am as God sees me	humility/prayer	sharing food, joyful dance	
truth-seeking and truth-telling I am what I think	curiosity eureka	story telling rational, abstract thinking	science/superstition

The Emergence of Sin[16]

An evolutionary account of sin is a misnomer because sin is an act of volition, a narrative web we weave, the person we have become, the corporate structures we construct. Although it is useless to look for an evolutionary point of commencement, we can conjecture a line of development whereby our species became sufficiently self-aware to make us morally responsible. Where among the fossils will the paleontologist find a record of the first tear of regret, the first pang of guilt, the first act of self-sacrifice, the first act of reconciliation? The reason we will never find this kind of fossil record is the same reason love and hate, introspection and friendship, forgiveness and worship defy genetic mapping. A gene for treachery, deceit, or prayer? I don't think so. Life is composed of events so merged with other events that their evolutionary course is invisible. The process of becoming human is just that: an indiscernible process of becoming. Everything that "is" has its moment of conception but that does not justify squeezing the entire story of becoming into the behavior of molecules.

Both as individuals and a species, we matured from infantile needs to responsible adults. Somewhere along this trajectory it is possible to speak meaningfully of good and evil, right and wrong. In order to get at the motivations and behaviors behind words like sin and evil, it is necessary to write a genealogical narrative. Bernard Williams employs such a narrative when unpacking what it means to be truthful. Sin, like truthfulness, is best understood by how it functions. "A genealogy," writes Williams, "is a narrative that tries to explain a cultural phenomenon by describing a way in which it came about, or could have come about, or might be imagined to have come about" (20).[17] A genealogy of sin employs the commonsense notion that we can learn much from seeing how sin could have arisen, even if it did not arise that way. Two lines of investigation merge. One is imagined because we do not know the circumstances under which sin emerged. The other is historical. We know that the behaviors and motivations sin describes are observable and universal. The aim is to propose a genealogy that satisfies both the imagined and the known.

Any foray into the realm of cultural psychology ("what did the natives think?") could well be labeled "anyone's guess," and particularly so if speculating about the origin of sin. Nevertheless others do it, so why not theologians? Undoubtedly, sin is a theological construct. The question before us is whether it describes an aspect of human nature more adequately than any other construct. The working hypothesis (genealogical reconstruction) I propose is to think of sin as evolving both horizontally and vertically concurrently with the emergence of self-doubt, self-denial, and truth-seeking.

Working with the premise that in some fundamental respects we are not so different from early modern humans, the following scenario is possible. In the process of becoming human the word "wrong" and its many derivatives became meaningful. In the early stages of cognitive and language development it meant misinformation. You gave me the wrong place or time for the hunt. No morality is involved because no malicious intent was present. But survival being what it is, the time came when I did deceive you willfully. The food I took was stolen because I considered it your food. The lust I felt and acted on was for my own satisfaction with no regard for you. My tribe raided your tribe and a child was taken from his mother. When did these acts become a violation of some unspoken, unwritten law? The distinction between what is mine and what is yours is rudimentary.[18] Very young children naturally develop a strong sense of possession, and with possession comes a struggle for power and nothing good. Can we call it sin when theft and envy are done willfully and maliciously or when they arouse in me something exciting, even fascinating in their execution?

We are social creatures through and through. Did we always hunt in packs, gather around campfires as comrades, seek communal shelter and security, celebrate and mourn together? It is difficult to image us as creatures who did not need and enjoy companionship. Our exocentricity—that drive to move outside of ourselves and to be with others—is as much a part of our evolutionary story as "red in tooth and claw." There was safety in numbers but there were other reasons for us to hone social skills. Instinct and necessity drove us together because we could not survive alone.

Insofar as relationships can be made, they can also be wrecked. In her *Speaking of Sin*, Barbara Brown Taylor comments that we do wrong and we do not do wrong all alone. This is eminently true for the two oldest forms of religion. Ancestral worship places sin within the context of disgracing the honor of one's neighbor and one's ancestors. If you violate me, you violate my descendants. Totemism is usually associated with the practice of attributing human characteristics to animals. According to the famed anthropologist Claude Lévi-Strauss, "animals are not just good to eat but good to think."[19] By this he intended to broaden our understanding of totemism to include humanity brooding on itself and its place in nature. This web of co-dependency, this community of living things, is all we have, both now and then. Barbara Taylor brings us around to the sensible conclusion that "if we want to be saved, then we had better figure out how to do it together, since none of us can resign from this web of relationships" (59).

The evolution of sin is by definition a dynamic, extended process of development. Our predilection is to categorize sin as moving from minor to major, venial to mortal, but this would be naive and literalistic. For sin must be measured against something more fundamental, such as the daily business of living and dying. Wasn't the impulse bound to happen, to defend what is ours and to establish rules lest we trespass where we shouldn't? The logical conclusion is to presume morality evolved in order to bring to expression the implicit rules of behavior already operative.

In her many years of patient observation nothing had prepared Jane Goodall and her associates for the brutal and aggressive attacks of one community of chimpanzees upon another. Around 1973 a single community of chimpanzees separated into two separate communities—the northern Kasakela group and the southern Kahama group. At first the encounters were friendly, but gradually and then suddenly they turned deadly. Through wounding and battering, the Kahama chimpanzees incapacitated their "enemy," leaving them to die of their injuries. Goodall describes a typical attack.

> Humphrey [a male of the Kasakela community] grabbed Godi's leg, pulled him to the ground, then sat on his head and held his legs with both hands, pinning him to the ground. Humphrey remained in this position while the other males attacked, so that Godi had no chance to escape or defend himself. (*The Chimpanzees of Gombe*, 506)

Those observing the attacks were convinced the attacks were both planned and intentional, even when no chimpanzee was killed outright. On several occasions one or more Kasakela males were seen returning to the scene of attack to check if the "victim" was no more. In addition, the pattern of willful attacks was different from those typical of intracommunity mischief. All the males of the Kahama community were killed, both young and old (Godi, Dé, Goliath, Charlie, Sniff), as well as Madam Bee. Two Kahama females may have joined the Kasakela group, or more likely suffered the same fate as Madam Bee. Little Bee, daughter of Madam Bee, did transfer permanently into the dominant group. Goodall concludes by saying, "If they had firearms and had been taught to use them, I suspect they would have used them to kill" (530).[20]

Does Goodall interpret this behavior as cruel? She does. But there is more to the story. Goodall points out that "in order to be cruel, one must have the capability (1) to understand that, for example, the detaching of an arm from a living creature will cause pain and (2) to empathize with the victim" (533). Here the evidence for good and evil coming from the same "tree of knowledge" is explicit. The same capacity for empathy admits cruelty. The chimpanzees of Kasakela recognized that they were doing harm to those who, like themselves, experience feelings of kinship. Goodall remarks that not only were the "outsiders" violently attacked, they were treated "more as though they were prey animals; they were 'dechimpized'" (532). The circle of empathy is complete: to be able to feel another's pain or joy opens the way to cruelty and compassion.

Warfare and cruelty are the product of cultural evolution, so evident in the way they are practiced and perfected by humans. The uncomplicated conclusion is to separate good impulses from the bad and assign them separate etiologies. Goodall however calls our attention to pre-adaptive behaviors. These behaviors include cooperative group living, cooperative hunting skills, weapon use, and the ability to make collaborative plans. Again, the mix of good and not-good is apparent. Cooperative hunting skills and the use of tools will put food on the table *and* shed innocent blood. Good and evil evolved together and should dispel all notions of a linear development of morality—one good deed inspiring another good deed until we became moral creatures. Rather, the morality of cooperation is the same cooperation utilized to make war. The difference is a matter of intention. The truth to be grasped and held is that any good is a hair's breadth from the evil we did not intend.

Is sin and its genesis as simple as "the will to harm"? Even if it is, it would have to be part of a story not so simply told. In *Pearl*, novelist Mary Gordon spins a story revolving around a moment when these words slipped out of

Pearl's mouth: "How can you be so stupid?" Pearl, who is studying abroad at Trinity College, Dublin, has chained herself to the flagpole outside the American embassy and has not eaten for six weeks. She has left a statement stating that her hunger strike is an act of witness, marking the death of a young man in the aftermath of the contested Irish Peace agreement. The young man is the dyslexic son of a friend, and Pearl has been tutoring, encouraging, and in every way giving Stevie hope. But when these words came out of her mouth, like "a snake that traveled from the belly, where it had lain coiled and hidden since when," Pearl knew she had taken the heart out of him, "so that he cared so little about living he was careless of his life." Stevie is struck dead while standing in the middle of a road. The words from Pearl's mouth—"spoken to a boy who all his life had feared precisely that sentence"—came not from an enemy but from a trusted friend. Pearl sees in herself, in everyone around her, and the world itself, this will to harm. She doesn't understand it and explains in some small way why it is so difficult to accept forgiveness, which comes to her when Stevie's mother sends a bouquet of balloons with a note reading, "Dear Pearl. I hope you're fine, I'm fine. I miss you. Wishing you all the best. Let's get together soon, Love, Breeda." When she has recovered the will to live but still "she thinks of her face, what her face must have been like when she said to Stevie, 'How can you be so stupid!' As long as she is alive, she will have it. She is frightened of her own face. Her mother is with her. Her mother can hold her hand. But she cannot take away her face."

Living in a community requires individuals to "bank" a little social capital. Chimpanzees know that a time may come when social grooming translates into social protection. Refuse to groom another, refuse to pay proper respect to elders, especially the male alpha, and you have cashed in your social capital. De Waal must be right in his assessment that in a moral community "it matters not just what I do to you and what you do to me, but also what others think of our actions" (33). The perceptions of others matters, and it matters both for the survival of the individual and the community.

Humans are not the only creatures with language. But once we learned how to speak, there was no shutting us up. Early humans developed a practical language. It was sparse, direct, immediate, and pragmatic. It was a gamut of basic vocalization accompanied with non-verbal signs. It conveyed vital information about the hunt, shelter, and safety. But civilization has miles to go and humans needed a very different kind of language system. At the dinner table Uncle Al can get what he wants with a grunt and the appropriate facial expression, and so can his two-year-old niece. But Uncle Sal and his niece are social beings who need a language to express how they feel. There are matters of the heart, as well as the mind, which make us human. "Me Tarzan, you Jane" won't get you very far, but try, "You Jane, beautiful," or "I think you're nice, Mommy" and you will move ahead of the pack. As long as individuals shared the same needs, a minimal language would do. But once pressure developed to speak and understand the subtly of different desires, nouns needed to be joined with adjectives and verbs needed adverbs. Words came first, syntax later, and Robbins Burling conjectures that while vocabulary needs a lot of cranial storage capacity, "syntax demands some very special cortical circuitry" (*The Talking Ape*, 19). There is the inevitable wrong word at the wrong time, or the right word never expressed, and a train wreck happens. Do we not also need a language of repentance and forgiveness? Obviously we do since we have such a language in a thousand dialects.

A world of meaning needs to be languaged. To know that I am neither the beginning nor the end of myself invites the possibility that there are powers and forces I cannot comprehend. From primitive animism to sophisticated philosophies, language is required to think about and bring to expression the perennial questions swirling around the nature and purpose of life, and our place in the cosmic scheme of things. Can my existence, can the stars and the sun, signify nothing? The two mantras from the *X-Files* television series express a primal stirring: "The truth is out there" and "We are not alone." The narratives we generate to comprehend the mysteries within and without are never without the good and evil. Without the struggle between good and evil life would be insufferably boring and science-fiction writers would have nothing to write.

To do you wrong is sinful because of intention. Intention is a difficult thing to judge. Our judicial system allows us to distinguish between first- and second-degree murder and to take into account one's "state of mind." The religious equivalent is a scale of sinful acts. Venial sins do not endanger your soul, but mortal sins do. Thomas Aquinas divided sins into three domains: (1) those against oneself, such as gluttony and lust, (2) those that harm another, such as thievery and murder, and (3) and those against God, by lack of faith or blasphemy. In *Sin: Radical Evil in Soul and Society*, Ted Peters believes we can "profitably discriminate" in the degree and amount of evil that is produced. He begins with anxiety and travels through unfaith, pride, concupiscence, self-justification, cruelty, and blasphemy. The religious model is not nearly as neat as the criminal code, which weighs the level of self-awareness or intention (carefully planned or accidental) and struggles with how to judge the degree of cruelty (death penalty for some but not for all murders). But then sin and crime are not the same. Every crime may be a sin but not every sin is a crime, and the reason is that criminal acts have nothing to do with the state of your mind unless you act upon those thoughts. Just ask Jimmy Carter about the storm he caused when he acknowledged having lustful thoughts. There are no punishable crimes against God in the Western legal system, yet Judaism and Christianity teach that all sin is ultimately against God. Simply stated, sin includes a more subtle and complex understanding of intention.

Are we sinful because sin is instinctual? There is a long history of identifying sin with crimes of passion, the upsurges of the id, the instinctual drive to strike out if cornered. Are we condemned "to be our cruel, greedy, egotistical, mendacious selves?" George Steiner, novelist and literary critic, asks. It would seem so, with no cessation in sight. But are we not also predestined for love? We do not simply become human. We are literally loved into being human. An unloved child, if she survives, becomes a savage. Steiner is equally eloquent when writing about love: "to shake, in one's inmost spirit, nerve, and bone, at the sight, at the voice, at the merest touch of the beloved; to contrive, to labor, to lie without end so as to reach, to be near the man or woman loved; to transform one's existence—personal, public, psychological, material—on an unforeseen instant, in the cause and consequence of love" (188).

Love makes us crazy. To fall in love is to lose oneself in the other, to willingly sacrifice all for the sake of another. But then reality sets in and the beloved is no longer perfect. He or she is in need of a makeover. The ego boundaries that had melted away like soft butter stiffen, and all is not well.[21] Love, if it is to endure, must become work, a loving *in spite of* what annoys us. What began as something natural beyond words—as easy as falling off a log—is remarkably unnatural when sustained by devotion and faithfulness, or else it slides into resentment, indifference, even hatred.

A sense of morality makes little sense unless humans have the capacity for genuine altruism. Daniel C. Dennett voices a criticism I have anticipated. A Darwinian approach is obligatory, he insists, "because any theory of ethics that just helps itself to a handy set of human virtues without trying to explain how they might have arisen is in danger of positing a skyhook, a miracle that 'explains' nothing because it is can 'explain' anything" (*Freedom Evolves*, 217). Cultural anthropologist and evolutionary philosophers now think there is a place for cooperation and altruism. Altruism, so the argument would seem to go, is self-defeating. In the struggle for existence, good genes finish last because they are sacrificed on the altar of self-denial. Yet, cooperation, reciprocal altruism, and kin altruism make evolutionary sense when they serve the long-term chances of survival even though in the short term they provoke the question "Why bother?" Why not just be selfish and steal what you can and let the weak perish? One reason is that cooperation reinforces its own good behavior. If work and food are shared, notably in dire times, some of the weak may survive who otherwise would have perished and in time prove a valuable asset to the group. This community of cooperators would soon enough "wise up" to the devices of the selfish and exclude them. Altruism strengthens the bond of kinship just as selfishness weakens it, and over time the community that works together survives together.

Genuine altruism, according to Dennett, is treating the welfare of others as an end in itself, where the giving is not contingent on receiving. Acts of courage and kindness would need to become a good in themselves without any thought of *quid pro quo*. But we do not need Dennett's idealistic standard of altruism because our motives are never so pure. Beginning with Dennett's own thesis that freedom evolves, altruism developed as a long series of decisions over a long period of time whereby the self in some aspect is denied for the sake of another. Somewhere in our misty past, in less than genuine forms of self-denial, authentic altruism established a foothold. Random acts of shortsighted kindness and cooperation became a conscious way of life. It was never easy, always an anomaly, an unnatural exploration into the unknown. Who can say precisely where the *oomph* comes from? What is certain, though, is that goodness cannot be sustained by itself. Random acts of kindness are just that, while sustained goodness is lodged in communities where "a cloud of witnesses" and fellow sinners support one another in the marathon to be completed.

Cultural anthropology and biological reductionists do not have a place for the likes of Francis of Assisi. Francis takes altruism too far and turns it into a vow for life. The latter part of his life is an agonizing struggle with those, both from within and without the Brothers Minor, who could not understand someone who enthusiastically embraced simplicity. In a celebrated story, Francis was traveling with Brother Leo to Santa Maria degli Angeli. Knowing that Leo was bothered by the cold and freezing rain, Francis said, "Leo, although we may give sight to the blind, cause the deaf to hear, and even raise the dead—these thing are not the source of perfect joy." For two more miles they walked. Finally, Leo turned to face Francis and asked, "Please tell me the source of perfect joy." Francis replied, "When we arrive at our destination—our cloaks drenched by rain, our bodies shivering with cold, hungry and tired—if we bear all of this with patience, kindness, and love—we will be brimming with joy. In self-conquest is perfect joy" (Sabatier, 165).

To fully understand sin is to know that we are not ruled by our instinctual drives. Evidence abounds that we can makes ourselves larger than we are. Self-doubt prepares us for repentance, which lead to forgiveness. Love lifts us to the level of compassion, when self-denial gives all that one has. Truth encompasses wisdom. Self-transcendence happens in the moments when we rise above the mundane, the expected, the norm, and the predisposed. Falling in love is natural. Loving your enemy is not. Having compassion—literally "to suffer with"—calls us to go where it hurts, to enter into places of discomfort, to be vulnerable in order to be with the vulnerable. To swear a vow of poverty or take upon ourselves the pain of another, especially when that other is not of our kind or kin, is to transcend for the moment our instinct to avoid pain and seek comfort.

From the *New York Times Magazine*, 6 April 2003

One Last Sit-In

Earlier this year Craig Corrie, a Vietnam War veteran, reinsurance company manager, and father of three, faced a quandary. What do you do when you raise a child to care deeply about the world and that child turns into a young woman who cares so deeply that she moves from verdant Washington to desiccated Gaza to become a human shield?

And then, a few days later, Craig Corrie was folding clothes when his wife, Cindy, came running into the laundry room with a cell phone and their older daughter, Sarah, crying through the line. Sarah had just seen it on a television ticker tape: 23-year-old peace activist from Olympia Wash., crushed to death by an Israeli Army bulldozer as she tried to block the demolition of a physician's home in Gaza.

And yet even as the Corries admired Rachel for being so principled, they also were nagged by another feeling: that she cared a bit too deeply for her own good (Deborah Sontag, 80).

The purest act of self-transcendence may be forgiveness. To forgive evil is an extraordinary act. During the years of state-sanctioned apartheid death squads, Eugene de Kock became synonymous with the fear which came in the night and took away loved ones. Paula Gobodo-Madikizela accepted the assignment from the Truth and Reconciliation Commission to interview de

Kock, the man known as "Prime Evil." As a clinical psychologist, she spent forty-six hours with de Kock at Pretoria Central Prison where he is serving a 212-year sentence. "The embodiment of evil," she writes, "stood there politely smiling at me." Gobodo-Madikizela's role was to assess de Kock's state of mind and heart. Was he capable of tears of regret? Had he turned a corner and was he prepared to reenter the human race? Gobodo-Madikizela found herself reflecting on the meaning of forgiveness: forgiveness does not forget and it does not overlook the deed but rises above it. This is what it means to be human, to say, "I cannot and will not return the evil you inflicted upon me." During one interview Gobodo-Madikizela is moved to reach out and touch de Kock, just as Jesus contravenes both social and religious boundaries and touches the lepers and embraces their humanity. But she was not his accuser. She had not suffered by his hand. Another encounter took place between de Kock and the widows of two policemen murdered in the Motherwell bombing. After listening to de Kock's apology, Pearl Faku responded by saying, "I hope that when he sees our tears, he knows that they are not only tears for our husbands, but tears for him as well. . . . I would like to hold him by the hand and show him there is a future, and that he can still change." Together Mrs. Faku and Mrs. Mgoduka answered the question: Was he too evil to be worthy of forgiveness? (Gobodo-Madikizela, 14, 94).

I have delayed the discussion of an apparent link between sin and religion because it is a derivative consideration. More than one hypothesis makes sin concurrent with the emergence of religion, and that in itself confuses religion with religious experience. Various religions appeal to the moral conscience. If we consider morality a latter development, then religion did create a moral consciousness in order to make adherents but provided it with a ritualized formality. When God speaks to Cain, asking, "Where is your brother?" there already exists a sense of violation. A limit has been transgressed. "Who set the limit?" is the wrong question because it assumes religion is the culprit (as Rousseau and Nietzsche presumed). When priests began to establish moral norms, they did not need to create the distance between self and other, between my reason to live and your reason, because it already existed. Religion did categorize sin and its remedy but sin and evil have a deeper, ontological origin.

For early humans to ponder what comes after death may not have been the evolutionary leap we think it was: it may have been a very natural progression on the way toward self-transcendence. To what extent is this hope inextricably joined with belief in the divine? Both lie beyond the realm of sight and touch and require a hopeful extension beyond the fate of decomposition. But belief in an afterlife does not necessitate belief in a God of resurrection since many religions assume a "passing over" into a non-worldly realm with no notion of a bodily re-creation. Guides may be necessary—on both sides of the divide—but resurrection is a specific belief tied to a creating God. At some stage in our becoming we professed that we did not have the power to create life. Life wasn't like fire: a tool to be learned and passed along to successors. Life was wrapped in mystery, likewise death, and the two were chained together.

One trajectory places God as the great Allayer. Once the fear of dying was anticipated, death became a groundswell of anxiety. This of course positioned God on the other side of death. The other trajectory, not mutually exclusive, was to place God at the beginning. This too was a hopeful projection in that it placed all things in God's hands. Since God is the beginning and the end (Alpha and Omega), all of life was hemmed in by the divine presence. Judaism resisted becoming one of the religions of an afterlife, preferring a God who wills creation into being and blesses its continuation. The proper worship of Yahweh is a humble and contrite heart and the future will take care of itself.

I can wrong my neighbor and my God. When these two dimensions—one horizontal and the other vertical—are joined, as they are in Judaism and Christianity, the ante of doing wrong goes up. When I wrong my neighbor, the stranger in our midst, the guest at my table, I have also wronged God. The horizontal dimension of willful wrong has a vertical consequence. Now I have to make peace with my neighbor and with God. Vows exchanged in the presence of God make it a threesome. In the Jewish tradition, the consequence of one's actions spills out to the succeeding generations (the sin of the sons will be visited upon their fathers). In Matthew 5:23, the sin offering you bring to the altar is acceptable only after you are reconciled with the one you are at odds with. Even the communion of saints is offended since time itself does not erase what you have done.

> Most holy and merciful Father:
> We confess to you and to one another,
> and to the whole communion of saints
> in heaven and on earth,
> that we have sinned by our own fault
> in thought, word, and deed;
> by what we have done, and by what we have left undone.
> (*The Book of Common Prayer*, Ash Wednesday Litany of Penitence)

We cannot fully explain what it means to be in the presence of what is holy. Our behaviors are well documented. A shrine is built, a sacred place is defined, shoes are removed, silence is observed, the human form becomes prayerful, lips touch the earth, eye are lifted to heaven. The holy is clean and pure while everything else, when measured against it, is unclean and defiled. Religion ordered the boundaries and priests patrol them, but these are secondary. Primary to sin is the distance between creature and Creator, between the aura of holiness radiated by the presence of God and the earthliness of creatures that can only walk, fly, and swim. As God's holiness within us, the soul signifies a meeting place where the finite and the infinite approach each other and covenants are entered into. Once entered into, our obligations exceed the immediate circle of our family.

When Israel enters into a covenantal relationship with Yahweh, it swears an obligation not to worship idols or mimic what other nations are doing. The Commandments are given to define the requirements of the covenant and in this way the Israelites know what is expected of them. Only a nation committed to obey would be worthy to be called forth (Gen. 12) and given a mission "to be a light unto the nations" (Isa. 42:6). Mutual conditions are consummated: "I will be your God and you will be my people." A new dimension of sin commences. A people are held accountable when they provoke a jealous God (only a loving God is a jealous God), forget the Commandments, transfer their allegiance to false gods, place their trust in sovereign powers, drift away. The sins of the fathers are visited upon their children because the covenant endures from generation to generation.

In Jesus Christ a new ethic is embodied and empowered. The biblical covenant is simplified and intensified. Jesus gives a new commandment to love others as God has loved you (Jn. 13:34–35). What is asked of you is more than loyalty or faithfulness. Surrender your life to God and God will give it back renewed and transformed. This is the paradox Nicodemus could not fathom when he comes to Jesus to see if he has something new to teach (John 3). What Jesus asks of us is more than anyone should ask of us: to share or give away our worldly possessions, to love those who hate us, to forgive in such a way that our oppressors forgive their oppressors, to walk the extra mile and ask nothing in return, and to let love rule our heart. This ethic is the antithesis of Nietzsche's "become what you are," because it offers the possibility of transcending what we are in the cycles of vengeance, hatred, prejudice. It takes the human capacity for self-denial and makes it a way of life. The dynamic of sin—to love oneself as if I am the center of the universe—is countered by the dynamic of self-surrender—to love God and to let that love displace the most natural compulsion to survive above all else. Foremost and last, Jesus is heard asking for a decision about love.

> Whoever loves father and mother more than me is not worthy of me; and whoever loves son or daughter more than me is not worthy of me; and whoever does not take up the cross and follow me is not worthy of me. Those who find their life will lose it, and those who lose their life for my sake will find it. (Matt. 10:37–39, NRSV)

Conclusion

I began this chapter by asking, "Why do we need an evolutionary account of sin?" Without such an account, sin will continue to languish on the sidelines. In the court of intellectual appeals, theologians could use a few allies. It is doubtful that help will come from the new science of the mind. Advocates here construct a potent argument that we are hardwired for some things, such as language, baby talk, and incest avoidance. The ghost that biologists and evolutionary philosophers want most to excise is the idea that we are infinitely malleable. So far everyone is on the same page. The sticking point is the conclusion that throughout history humans exhibit a consistent and persistent nature which is biologically grounded, culturally adapted, and sinful. It makes me wonder what kind of blinders social scientists wear that allow them to overlook the obvious: that human nature includes the nastier traits of indifference, xenophobia, nihilism, cruelty, revenge, concupiscence, covetousness, murder, theft, and so on. Sin is immediately disliked because innateness is associated with determinism. Disdain is heaped on any notion that some "law" of innateness binds us.

Innateness becomes a terrible onus for theologians to bear because it runs counter to the received doctrine that we can construct our own future, which has proven very difficult to dislodge. The political atmosphere of the last half of the twentieth century was dead set against determinism in any form, but especially biological determinism. In his *Blank Slate*, Steven Pinker finds ample evidence for a Western-Enlightenment resistance to anything suggesting determinism. In the discussion of nature versus nurture, Pinker delights in revealing how we invariably favor the power of nurture. The reaction against the book by Richard Herrnstein and Charles Murray, *The Bell Curve* (1994), was swift and virulent, because the authors dared to argue that differences in IQ scores of American blacks and American whites were due to genetic and environmental causes.[22] The American creed will always be defended: no individual should be denied the ultimate right to maximize his or her potential. Baccalaureate speakers are expected to inspire great achievers, and better yet, great achievers against all odds. We are, after all, a people of manifest destiny who wrote a Bill of Rights and defend the right of self-determination.

By saying that sin is innate or natural I am implying the same meaning as when we say sin is original. If sin is our evolutionary partner, then it is natural or inborn. On this front, theologians do have allies. Even if we are hardwired for some things, life is not therefore predetermined. Pinker and Dennett are typical in the way they take us to the brink of biological determinism but then retreat. Whether in a court of law or before God's judgment seat, don't depend on pleading "not responsible" because of heredity or environment. The same argument might be made for sin—we are hardwired for sin but still morally responsible—but this would be theologically deficient. It seems that only the theologically minded can get their minds around the paradox that we are at the same time sinners and justified. And that means sin does not fit neatly into either category of nature and nurture. To say that sin is our nature is only a half-truth—requiring the other half, that we can be redeemed, but not by our own effort.

The advancing frontier of cognitive neuroscience is opening a door that could prove to be grist for the mill. Pinker writes, for instance, that "consciousness and free will seem to suffuse the neurobiological phenomena at every level, and cannot be pinpointed to any combination of interaction of the parts" (*Blank Slate*, 240). The not-so-blank mind, then, is hardwired while manifesting such holistic qualities as self-awareness and free will. Could it be that sin and love are this kind of phenomena? By all accounts, faith, hope, and love transpire at a level of complexity beyond the reach of empirical reductionism. If this is true then there are limits, as Pinker professes, to the reductionism of electrical and chemical signals. Of course neurological signals can be detected when emotions, such as guilt or shame associated with sin, are the subjects under examination. What theology resists is the proposition that a satisfactory account has been given when holistic phenomena are ignored. Once again sin and sins are confused and conflated. Science can choose to restrict itself to an explanation of specific behaviors (what we do when we are in love, what we do when we are bad, what we do when we are feeling spiritual), but from the perspective of theology there is a whole lot more to know.

Notes

1. See the conclusion of H. Shelton Smith's, *Changing Conceptions of Original Sin*, 13–36.

2. See the essays in *Whatever Happened to the Soul?* Brown et al., eds. For an extended and nuanced examination of the soul-body question, see Nancey Murphy, *Bodies and Souls, or Spirited Bodies?* (Cambridge: Cambridge University Press, 2006).

3. See Dennett's *Darwin's Dangerous Idea*, where he uses the term "skyhooked" for a miraculous intervention (83, 145). This, though, is the kind of treatment sin and soul receive when the only theology considered is a stereotype.

4. For an understanding that is biblically sound, see Han Walter Wolf, *Anthropology of the Old Testament* (Mifflintown, Penn.: Sigler Press, 1974), especially chapter 2; Udo Schnelle, *The Human Condition: Anthropology in the Teachings of Jesus, Paul, and John* (Philadephia: Fortress Press, 1966), especially chapter 3; and more generally J. Patout Burns, *Sources of Early Christian Thought* (Philadelphia: Fortress Press, 1981).

5. Following the groundbreaking work of Robert Trivers, Pinker sees no reason not to study the human condition scientifically. See *Blank Slate*, 241. Pinker's references to original sources are quite complete in this regard. See Daniel C. Dennett for more recent resources: *Sweet Dreams: Philosophical Obstacles to a Science of Consciousness* (Cambridge, Mass.: MIT Press, 2005). Also of interest see Matt Ridley, *The Origins of Virtue: Human Instincts and the Evolution of Cooperation* (New York: Viking, 1977); Elliott Sober and David Sloan Wilson, *Unto Others: The Evolution and Psychology of Unselfish Behavior* (Cambridge, Mass.: Harvard University Press, 1998); and Stephen J. Pope, *The Evolution of Altruism and the Ordering of Love* (Washington, D.C.: Georgetown University Press, 1994).

6. See for example Williams's discussion of the evolution of altruism in her *Doing without Adam and Eve*, 125–37. Theologians have a number of different tactics in order to take into account a naturalistic explanation of sin. James M. Gustafson provides a helpful analysis of two important contributions in this regard: Philip Hefner's *The Human Factor: Evolution, Culture, and Religion* (Minneapolis, Minn.: Fortress Press, 1993) and Edward Farley's *Good and Evil: Interpreting a Human Condition* (Minneapolis, Minn.: Fortress Press, 1990). While both strive for an account of sin and evil that is informed by science without allowing science to become determinative, we are uncertain whether science is merely informing theology or is being used to authorize theological claims. See Gustafson, *An Examined Faith*, chapter 3, but especially page 50.

7. Hamer, *The God Gene*, 23–30 and 82–85. Hamer cross-references insights of Robert Cloninger, a psychiatrist and behavioral scientist, and W. N. Pahnke, a physician and theologian, and reduces nine components to three.

8. In his Gifford Lectures J. Wentzel van Huyssteen breathes new life into "the image of God" and other classic theological themes by connecting them to the evolution of Homo sapiens. See Huyssteen, *Alone in the World?: Human Uniqueness in Science and Theology* (Grand Rapids, Mich.: Wm. B. Eerdmans, 2006).

9. In his review of Dennett's recent *Breaking the Spell: Religion as a Natural Phenomenon*, Leon Wieseltier, editor of the *New Republic*, offers the same critique I do of those who take a biological reductionistic approach to human nature by rendering the human capacity for self-transcendence null and void. See Wieseltier, "The God Genome," *New York Times Book Review*, 19 February 2006, 11–12.

10. See Jenson, *Systematic Theology*, vol. 2, 58–59. Robin Collins comes to a similar conclusion: "... I would suggest that 'Adam' should also be understood as having a historical reference, as also representing what could be called the 'stem-father' of the human race. In evolutionary terms, such a 'stem-father' would be the first group of evolving hominids who gained moral and spiritual awareness" (486). Collins has a thoughtful review of the relevant Scripture passages, giving voice to various possible interpretations, but concludes that Genesis 1–11 is "a theological commentary on and partially symbolic reconstruction of primal history using the concepts and stories of the time as raw materials" (488). In this way, Collins wants to hold on to the tension between a historical and theological understanding of original sin. See Collins, "Evolution and Original Sin," in Miller, ed., *Perspectives on an Evolving Creation*.

11. Simmons, *Learning to Fall*, 60. Following Simmons humorous insight, our evolution moved from being buried with implements (as in Neanderthal), to being buried in all one's finery (as in Egypt), to wondering who will come to my funeral and what they will be wearing (modern man).

12. See Davidovich, *Religion as a Providence of Meaning: The Kantian Foundations of Modern Theology* (Minneapolis, Minn.: Fortress, 1993); and Robert D'Amico, *Historicism and Knowledge* (New York: Routledge, 1989).

13. See Ronald F. Thiemann, *Revelation and Theology*. Thiemann is correct that both philosophers and theologians were foundationalists in so far as "knowledge is grounded in a set of non-inferential, self-evident beliefs which, because their intelligibility is not constituted by a relationship with other beliefs, can serve as the source of intelligibility for all beliefs in a conceptual framework" (158, n. 20).

14. George A. Lindbeck also has written decisively against a way of knowing which is pre-languaged. "A religion is above all an external word, a *verbum externum*, that molds and shapes the self and its world, rather than an expression or thematization of a preexisting self or of preconceptual experience." See his *The Nature of Doctrine*, 34, 40, and 43, n. 18. In the same vein, see Tracy, *Plurality and Ambiguity*, chapter 3.

15. I like the way Karen Armstrong differentiates *logos* thinking from mythical thinking. The former "forges ahead, constantly trying to discover something new, to refine old insights, create startling inventions, and achieve greater control over the environment." "A myth could not tell a hunter how to kill his prey or how to organize an expedition efficiently, but it helped him to deal with his complicated emotions about the killing of animals. *Logos* was efficient, practical, and rational, but it could not answer questions about the ultimate value of human life nor could it mitigate human pain and sorrow. Armstrong, *A Short History of Myth*, 31–32.

16. Here begins a running rebuttal of Michael Shermer's *The Science of Good and Evil*.

His stated purpose is to strip away fuzzy logic and metaphysical constructs and in the name of empiricism just describe the way folks are (102–103). Because Shermer never considers the religious experience, only religion, he makes it impossible to look behind the codification of morality. Of course sin is a cultural-theological construct. The issue is whether it is a useful one, even indispensable when examining behavior plus intention.

17. Peter Nozick offers a slightly different way to describe the work of evolutionary genealogy: "We learn much by seeing how the state could have arisen, even if it didn't arise that way." Quoted from Williams, *Truth*, 32.

18. The theme of possession and the fateful consequences it brings is beautifully and movingly portrayed in the foreign film *Summer, Spring, Fall, Winter*.

19. See Mithen *The Prehistory of the Mind*, 165.

20. For an extend analysis and assessment of the ruthless behavior of chimps, and in comparison to Bonobos (a different species of apes), see Frans de Waal, *Our Inner Ape* (Riverhead Books, 2005). Unfortunately, De Waal does not discuss the genetic implications of his observations and directs his conclusions toward the possibility that peaceful behavior can be learned.

21. In *The Road Less Traveled*, Peck has a marvelous section ("Falling in Love") describing what happens to our ego boundaries when we "fall" in love (84–90).

22. Pinker, *Blank Slate*, viii, 301.

CHAPTER SIX

Science as the New Occasion for Sin: When Humans Overreach

> ... The genetic revolution came, so to speak, to cure disease, and stayed to tempt us with the prospect of enhancing our performance, designing our children, and perfecting our nature.
>
> —Michael J. Sandel, *Atlantic Monthly*, April 2004, 62

> The often unexamined arrogance of reason, notably in the sciences, seems to me to cut off ascertainable experience from what may be essential. It is to know everything, but to know nothing else.
>
> —George Steiner, *Errata*, 186

> For the very same movement which put us in possession of powers that have now to be regulated by norms—the movement of modern knowledge called science—has by a necessary complementarity eroded the foundations from which norms could be derived; it has destroyed the very idea of norm as such.
>
> —Hans Jonas, *The Imperative of Responsibility*, 22

For a theologian to write about science as the occasion for sin is both presumptuous and audacious. I do not undertake such an endeavor thinking that theologians are morally superior to scientists. Fairness requires that theology be open to a reciprocal critique by science and if that is to happen, as it has, it must pivot around theology's methodology.[1] Science would not necessarily be in the best position to write about the sin theology knows best, since it doesn't take sin all that seriously. Theologians, on the other hand, know something about sin because it is embedded deep within the theological tradition. The human condition and the biblical account of the world and our place in it are not auxiliary with theologians. Theologians want to know the meaning of human life just as science wants to know how life evolved. Certainly, science has a thing or two to teach theologians about the nature of the universe. The assumption of this chapter is that theology has a thing or two to teach science about the nature of sin, and not I reiterate, because it does not have its own history of instigating the very sin it denounces. It is this clash of perspectives—one discipline content to disregard sin and the other intent to confront it—that makes for the best kind of conversation.

My argument should not be confused with an accusation that science is sinful or evil. Rather, science in its modern incarnation of technological progress is the *precondition* for sin as we know it best in this historical moment. To the extent that science functions as a worldview or universal narrative, it has become the principal precondition of sin. It sets up the internal dynamic of temptation.[2] It is the proverbial snake in the grass whispering, "You are free to know all things and to create whatever you desire in your own image."

Too Much Power, Not Enough Wisdom

When you are immersed in a culture and that culture is omnipotent, the sharpest perceptions will come from a subculture where Wendell Berry occupies a revered niche. In *What Are People For?* Berry tells his story of having a pond built so that he could pasture a few head of stock. On a narrow bench halfway to the top of a slope he hired a man with a bulldozer to cut into the hill. Trees were cleared away and dirt was piled to form an earthwork. The pond appeared to be a success. An extremely wet fall and winter, coupled with the usual freezing and thawing, undid the carefully constructed pond. A large piece of the floor on the upper side slid down into the pond. Wendell sees a lesson. "The trouble was the familiar one: too much power, too little knowledge. The fault was mine." Was his desiring misplaced? Was it wrong to trust the technical advice he had received? The broader lesson Berry draws is this: "Equip a man with a machine and nurture him with an inadequate culture and he becomes a pestilence" (5–8).

Berry is not prepared to speak of sin but of a dominant system of thought—science, technology, and industry—which tempts us to ignore limits and repeatedly engage in arrogant and precipitous behavior. Given the same circumstance, a scientist—an engineer type—would conclude that a mistake has been made and that it can be corrected. You can hear the reassurance, "We'll get it right the next time." Robert Oppenheimer succinctly stated what scientists steadfastly believe: ". . . science is the business of learning not to make the same mistake again" (*Uncommon Sense*, 178). Neither Berry nor Oppenheimer consider a theology of sin and both would be hard pressed to see any reason to do so. Oppenheimer was not oblivious to the considerable distance between correcting empirical mistakes on the one hand and errors of moral judgment on the other. Berry is looking at the bigger picture, the condition of our culture. In his latter years, Oppenheimer addressed the same broader spectrum. The twin peaks that catch our attention are "man"—the nature thereof—and the culture he imbibes. What both see clearly is the symbiotic relationship between the creatures we are and the culture we create. In asking where is the sin, the answer must be pursued within the intersection of human nature and culture. If it is valid and necessary to speak of a creature who knows sin, then it is valid and necessary to speak of a sinful culture. The issue before us is whether science has helped to create a culture where the desire to know all things knows no limits; that is, human nature and culture have come together to give us a history of overreaching.

The discussion concerning human nature has already occupied us in part 2. It is an old theological sawhorse on which many a foundation plank has been cut. I can understand why Oppenheimer and Berry might not want to open this particular door. But the revolution in biological technology has made the issue of human nature imperative and inescapable.

Can there be a more telling indictment than Fukuyama's statement that "science by itself cannot establish the ends to which it is put" (*Our Posthuman Future*, 185)? If Fukuyama is right, and he is by no means alone or the first to make the indictment,[3] we find ourselves in a serious predicament. To the extent that science rules by providing our culture's sole hope to build a better tomorrow, it becomes both the means and the ends. But to what end? If the end is technological progress, the loop is closed and the discussion has no place to go. According to this narrative our genetic constitution and the cultures we create are such that technological sophistication is what we are made for. Fukuyama's statement and Berry's story imply something else. There is an end or purpose we get to choose and the "we" is not just the professional scientist but also the commonwealth.

If science misjudges human nature by thinking our only sin is epistemological (making mistakes due to procedural error), the future will always be amendable. Such was the worldview when the space shuttle *Columbia* disintegrated on reentry and the point men for NASA were quick to reassure the public that any human error would be found and corrected. To err is human. All technological setbacks—such as those plaguing the initial tests of the Anti-Ballistic Missile System—are regarded as part of the natural arc of technological success. "Failure," writes Jack Hitt in his *New York Times Magazine* essay on space warfare, "is just proof that there needs to be more research."[4] But broaden your purview and NASA is found to harbor a culture of isolation bordering on arrogance,[5] and former senator Sam Nunn criticizes the Anti-Ballistic Missile System for becoming "a theology in the United States, not a technology." It is interesting, to say the least, that it is human to err but not to sin.

When the U.S. Congress was debating the merits of human cloning in 2001, Congressman Ted Strickland of Ohio "insisted that we be guided by the best available science, and that 'we should not allow theology, philosophy, or politics to interfere with the decision we make on this issue.'"[6] On one level this is simply a naive statement by the congressman reflecting the prevailing view of a culture dominated by empiricism. We can appreciate Strickland's apprehension that theologians and moral philosophers will muddy the water, for that is precisely what they do. But the reason their opinions are judged unwarranted is the attitude that here are disciplines engaged in subjective beliefs, while a pure science can deliver just the facts. The congressman does not consider the possibility that regardless of how objective the empirical data, it comes packaged in the values of someone's culture, even the culture of one's scientific discipline.

A Methodological Agenda

Empiricism is a methodology with diverse applications throughout various sciences, but just the same it defines science as a distinct tradition. Despite its history of being identified as the method of induction or the method of cognitive progress, empiricism became for all practical purposes the modern project.[7] Bacon's vision of the mastery of nature for the relief of man's estate would have stalled at the starting line were it not for a methodological engine. It was a vision predicated on two unexamined premises: the autonomy of the knower and the neutrality of reality.

Modernity fell in love with the autonomy of the human knower: I am a law unto myself in the sense that I am equipped to apprehend universally valid truth once I have freed myself from the authority of any dominant text or tradition. The goal was objectivity and in order to reach that goal, subjectivity and anything associated with personal preference had to be rejected.

Under the protective canopy of objectivity, scientists claimed the right to pursue knowledge wherever it might take them.

The neutrality of reality—everything is made of matter and matter itself is without purpose or direction—proved to be the perfect match for the objective knower. So perfect was the marriage that it raises the suspicion that it was made for the convenience of a dominant methodology. The marriage of mind and matter, knower and known, granted science a dispensation to proceed with sovereign disregard for other ways of knowing. Under the banner that knowledge is intrinsically good, scientists received the blessing of the public. That science might have a vested methodological agenda was so contrary to the belief in its objectivity that it was considered innocent of all wrong until proved guilty. The fact of the matter is that science operates with its own unique form of moral reasoning. The moral hidden within the method is the premise of goodness. The gift science offers to the commonwealth is the *objective good*. Oppenheimer resolutely declared, "If you are a scientist you believe that it is *good* to find out how the world works; that it is *good* to find out what the realities are; that it is *good* to turn over to mankind at large the greatest possible power to control the world and to deal with it according to its light and its values."[8]

Mapping the human genome was a complex matter. From start to finish it roused all sorts of political concerns. The science of sequencing DNA is itself objective and value free, even more so now that it is largely automated. There is no intrinsic good or evil in the location and function of particular genes. But as a data stream is transposed into useful information, it is likely to become someone's property. Even before the Genome Project was funded, the political nature of the knowledge to be harvested was raised. The Hon. Ralph M. Hall opened the House hearings of October 1989 by asking, "How does the U.S. make sure that the basic research effort . . . is shared equitably among our international scientific partners while recognizing that the nation who leads the applications resulting . . . will have a competitive advantage in pharmaceutical biotechnology and related industries?"[9] At one level everyone recognized the Human Genome Project to be an objective good and wanted the information to be made available to everyone at no cost. Why then did it become so political? Because all knowledge to various degrees has the potential for good and evil. In the case of the map of the human genome, the knowledge is explosive. It is so full of potential that it needs to be protected but who should act as the guardians? That battle is still being fought but no one likes the thought of a jury of one, where the politicians in Washington, private enterprise, the scientists who make the discoveries, or those who hold patent rights constitute the one. The unwritten assumption is that by making knowledge of our DNA available to everyone, the commons would be served. But as the narrative of HGP unfolded, human greed showed its ugly face. The initial effort of the National Institute of Health to seek patents to keep the genomic information within the public domain was subsequently withdrawn, giving the market system free rein. The Genome Project should convince just about everyone that no data that matters stays contained in a cocoon of neutrality for long waiting to be processed by pure science.

Certain elements of Islam do not see Western science as value free. From their perspective it is impossible to separate Western culture from Western science. Whatever we make of these accusations, they do serve to connect science with values and that is something the Western tradition of doing "objective" science has resisted. There comes a point where science shapes and dominates the culture to such a degree that it becomes ideological. The adverse effect of empiricism can be to undermine traditional values, weaken faith, and promote unilateral behavior. A more tolerant understanding of Western science acknowledges the advancements in medicine and agriculture and judges life to be better with than without technology. Science can claim the moral high ground of curing disease, prolonging life, and relieving suffering but must answer the age-old question why the rich and powerful receive the full benefits and the poor and powerless are left out in the cold.

Dateline *Wall Street Journal*, 14 March 2004

Life Is Hard and Short in Haiti Bleak Villages

I only care about whether we can eat. It doesn't matter who's in power. We've never gotten anything from anyone in power (Jeanne Bazard of Haiti).

Unbridled Optimism

In the September 2002 issue of *Smithsonian*, Bruce Watson writes a forty-year retrospective essay on the importance of Rachel Carson's 1962 *Silent Spring*.[10] The world was awash in DDT and hope ran high. The majority of its effects had been positive for it had wiped out malaria in the developed world and drastically reduced it elsewhere. DDT became the promise of a better world through chemistry. The reaction to *Silent Spring* was strongly negative. The chemical and food industries denounced her as overreacting. *Chemical and Engineering News*, the trade magazine for chemical scientists, accused her of "pseudo-science." The National Agricultural Chemicals Association launched a $250,000 campaign to demonstrate her mistakes. On the heels of Carson's "sounding the alarm" came news of Thalidomide, given to pregnant women for morning sickness (its upside) but the cause of widespread birth defects (its downside). Retrospectives of this kind serve to remind us how difficult it is to confess that this "good thing" is not as good as we made it out to be.

Dateline *Wall Street Journal*, 8 October 2003

As Flame Retardant Builds Up in Humans, Debate over a Ban

Five years ago, Myrto Petreas started to investigate how much of the widely used flame retardant had worked its way up the food chain. The results alarmed her.

Dr. Pereas's research is on the forefront of a rapidly escalating debate over PBDEs. Their fire-retardant properties are believed to have saved thousands of lives, but PBDEs have been shown to be harmful to animals in laboratory tests. . . . What is clear is that levels in humans are rapidly building up—apparently doubling every two to five years (Thaddeus Herrick, A1).

Dateline *Wall Street Journal*, 8 October 2003

Chemical Industry Weighs Launching a Campaign to Clean Up Its Image

Dogged by what it considers an unfair reputation for carelessness and coverups, the U.S. chemical industry is considering spending as much as $250 million over the next decade on an advertising campaign aimed at remaking its image (Thaddeus Herrick, B6).

Pierre Baldi is director of the Institute for Genomics and Bioinformatics at the University of California and speaks with considerable authority. No one will dispute his statement that "science has been one of greatest forces driving the evolution of human societies over the centuries." He continues, "In spite of a few hiccups along the way, the majority of its effects have been, overall, positive" (*The Shattered Self*, 158). From a certain dubious perspective Chernobyl, the *Columbia*, Three Mile Island, Thalidomide, and Bhopal (India) could be understood as unfortunate hiccups along the way. Baldi is looking at science as purely technological advance and for him only technological glitches count against it. What Baldi means to argue is that overall positive good outweighs the hiccups. From the same narrow perspective, Richard Dawkins, author of *The Selfish Gene* and *The Blind Watchmaker*, asks, "If all the achievements of theologians were wiped out tomorrow, would anyone notice the smallest difference?" The answer Dawkins is prompting is "no" because the only knowledge that matters is the kind that predicts something or produces something useful.[11] As long as the perspective is sufficiently narrow, our eyes can be diverted from the history of overpromising. Is there something inherently endemic in its methodology that bears watching? Might that be unbridled optimism?

Gregory Stock, who carries equally impressive credentials as director of the Program on Medicine, Technology, and Society at the School of Medicine at UCLA, sounds like an echo. In his book *Redesigning Humans*, he expects "our inevitable genetic future" to be the dawning of a new era. He is not blind to the ethical dilemmas and dangers on the horizon (a subject he explores in *The Book of Questions*–2002). People might turn into biological time bombs, our genetic constitutions might become impoverished, society might fragment, our relationships and values might be distorted, we might lose our spiritual moorings.[12] Being the optimist that he is, Stock counters each pessimistic scenario with a "I suspect it will not be nearly the problem imagined." Everywhere there is a qualification—"In some places, the use of genetic testing might lead to more pernicious forms of racism"— but it is only remotely a possibility. He is confident that we will accept technological advances only when they are safe. "Given the difficulties of broadly implementing these technologies, and given our disinclination to injure our children, it is hard to come up with believable scenarios in which foolhardy uses of these technologies would persist long enough to be as big a health hazard as alcohol, cigarettes, automobiles, lack of exercise, or poor diet" (151–52). Stock assumes that once we see practices that might be damaging, we will censor ourselves or enact restrictive legislation.

The human race Stock is acquainted with may have its foibles and flaws but does not seem to have a history of discrimination and domination. The motivation to give our children the best is the same motivation that will deny that same advantage to other children. What won't parents do to further their genetic pedigree? On what reading of history does Stock base his hope that any society will ensure equal access and make technological advances "cheap enough for everyone to afford"? The lesson from the AIDS epidemic is how industry will protect its profits and how national leaders will deny access for political reasons or simply because of apathy. Alcohol and cigarettes are promoted—regardless of their pernicious and addictive effect—because to do so is profitable. Does Stock know something that I do not? Because on the horizon are drugs and practices that will be even more desirable, addictive, and profitable. The widespread use of medications like Ritalin and Prozac to feel better than we are and the demand for procedures to make ourselves look better than we do demonstrate that there is nothing as addictive as the desire to use technology to alter ourselves. The world would be a different place if we weren't creatures who need immediate gratification and a good return on our investments. Human nature being what it is, isn't it probable that given the opportunity to have genetically embedded "edge," some will choose to do so? And if some so choose, others will follow. It may be harsh to call this the law of the modern jungle, but the instinct to survive and thrive is the same by any name.

Optimism is good, necessary, and often admirably practiced in science. One of the world's most influential scientists, Edward O. Wilson, concludes that we have reached a critical juncture if we are to preserve our planet's biodiversity. Why, I ask myself, do I resist sharing Wilson's confidence that we will make the wise choices? Wilson recognizes the solution cannot be purely technological for science needs to be fortified with foresight and moral courage (*The Future of Life*, 23). He has confidence that a "civilization able to envision God and to embark on the colonization of space will surely find the way to save the integrity of this planet and the magnificent life it harbors" (189). But just because we can envision God does not mean we will *surely* use technology in a wise and just manner. We should be encouraged, as Wilson is, by the growing number of non-governmental organizations devoted to conservation (187). And yet for all the conferences and agreements made by the nations of the world, very little has changed at the level of consumption. Wilson also believes the central problem of the new century can be solved: ". . . how to raise the poor to a decent standard of living worldwide while preserving as much of the rest of life as possible" (189). The necessary resources exist and those who control them have many reasons to achieve this goal. The decrease in population growth in economically developed countries is good news and we can expect further decrease as the standard of living increases. But if everyone shares the same high standard of consumption of industrial countries, the mounds of waste, the harm to the ozone layer, and the appropriation of natural resources will be catastrophic. Raising the standard of everyone would go against the unvarying history of humankind where the poor are the last to receive the benefits of technology. Who is the realist here: the concerned yet hopeful scientist or the concerned but wary theologian? To make an optimist out of me, Wilson would have to show how the world could break the cycle of technological consumerism. The pattern of behavior among all nations and people is to move to the brink of disaster and then try to repair the damage.

Dateline *Boston Globe*, 25 April 2003

Canada Declares an End to Cod Fishing

Faced with the near total collapse of groundfish stocks, the Canadian government yesterday banned commercial and recreational cod fishing off the Atlantic provinces of Quebec, putting an end to the livelihood that for centuries defined much of the region (Colin Nickerson, A1).

Although it is generally assumed that northern cod fell victim of rapacious overfishing, particularly by so-called factory trawlers . . . some scientists believe that subtle changes in the marine environment are equally responsible for the depletion (Colin Nickerson, B1).

No one likes a timid scientist. "Scientists," Stock writes, "are not going to shy away from their role in this grand exploration out of fear that someone might engage in questionable human engineering someday" (47). In our society we reward only the science of great promise. Mishaps and hiccups are part of what it takes to do science. Geneticist Jennifer Puck and her group at the National Institutes of Health were optimistic about building on the results achieved over the last two years by Alain Fischer and Marina Cavazzana-Calvo of the Necker Hospital in Paris. By slipping a new gene into bone marrow cells, they had cured ten children of the "bubble boy" disease (the immune deficiency called SCID). Puck had six children lined up to begin a similar procedure. But then she reports, "We got an e-mail from Alain

Fischer that said, you know, something has come up here that you need to know about." A two-year-old boy in their study had developed a leukemia-like illness with strong indication that it was triggered when the new gene disrupted his DNA. As a result, the Food and Drug Administration wasted no time in suspending three similar trials under way in the United States. A somber Cavazzana-Calvo reflected, "We need to understand before continuing."[13] She might have said, "We should understand before beginning," but that is the catch-22 science cannot avoid: to understand you must begin. But there are many ways to begin. The recurring image is Wendell Berry's man with a machine, nurtured by a culture of The Next Big Thing. An unbridled optimism is just different enough from optimism to push science from reaching to overreaching.

The scientific environment is alive with good intentions, determined optimism, financial remuneration, and a sense of urgency. In comparison with scientific optimism, talk of sin and evil is a killjoy. If the ambience of the former is "reach for the sky," the latter feels like don't try anything new. But before believers in the reality of sin are told to leave the party, it should be noted that we are among the most hopeful of our species. The core characteristic of Christian hope is that, like faith and love, it abides "even in the midst of profound evil, and without ignoring that evil."[14] Technological progress, on the other hand, is tethered to the next technological achievement. Science inspires optimism because it is supremely confident of its cumulative methodological success. It has no doubt that it will take us to the next frontier. And so we "advance" by grasping one promise after another.

Christian hope is not scientific optimism. Hope occurs in situations where optimism would be impossible, even unimaginable. It endures precisely because it is not tethered to a visible or predictable future. Its teleological end is not the transformation of the earth. God's ultimate purpose is not dependent on humankind or planet Earth. That would render God rather small and human beings rather gigantic. Christian hope abides because there is the particular confidence that nothing can separate us from the love of God, including things present and thing to come, life and death, powers and principalities, nor anything else in all creation (Rom. 8:38–39). Lastly, hope is sustained in communities of remembrance, while the light of optimism burns brightly only when something promising is on the horizon.

Desperately Seeking Perfection[15]

It's a chicken-and-egg type of argument. Does science excite the desire for perfection or does desire agitate science to strive toward that elusive end?

This much can be said: the desire for perfection is a methodological hazard for science, a fertile place for sin to incubate. The sworn enemy of perfection is error. Indeed, error is the only problem for an optimistic account of reason. The autonomous, mature, modern self can surely handle error by finding better rational arguments as it moves ineluctably forward toward further enlightenment.

What might happen if we were to achieve the knowledge to create picture-perfect children every time? The real and present danger of biotechnology, as Leon Kass locates it, is desiring perfection in the first place.

> We stand in much greater danger from the well-wishers of mankind, for folly is much harder to detect than wickedness. The most serious danger from the widespread use of these techniques will stem not from desires to breed a super-race, but rather from the growing campaign to prevent the birth of all defective children, and in the name of population control, quality of life, and the "right of every child to be born with a sound physical and mental constitution, based on a sound genotype." (*Toward a More Natural Science*, 62)

Kass continues by quoting geneticist Bentley Glass in his 1971 presidential address before the American Association of the Advancement of Science. His inaugural speech continues: "No parents will in that future time have a right to burden society with a malformed or a mentally incompetent child" (62). What parent would think of burdening society in this way in the first place? Surely we desire a society where every child is free from genetic defects, just as we should seek a world where every child is wanted and loved. This however is a perfection that sin and evil will always frustrate. By seeking perfect babies and making it our sole end, we are willing to risk a trial run of imperfect embryos.[16] Do we consider this just a hiccup on the road toward progress in preventive and remedial medicine? The language of research is always progressing or advancing but never regressing or lapsing, and this obscures the uneven nature of progress. We can hardly think of the Human Genome Project as anything but progressing because of the presumption that it is moving toward such a perfect goal.

Scientists participating in the HGP are sensitive to a link between perfection and eugenics.[17] But this time around eugenics comes with a new postmodern twist. Because of its association with totalitarianism and Nazism, the science that attempted to engineer a perfect race and a perfect society early in the twentieth century fell out of fashion after World War II. The contrast could not be more striking. The proponents of the former eugenics thought in terms of government-sponsored programs dependent on coercion. The new eugenics, as Gilbert Meilaender clarifies, comes "embedded in the language of privacy and choice, and the only two virtues our culture seems to know—compassion and consent."[18] The eugenics of our era proceeds under the saving grace of ridding the world of disease and making it possible for every child to be born with a sound physical and mental constitution. What isn't there to like about preventing genetic disease and relieving suffering?

The skeptic is already thinking this is a typical Christian response. Christians believe suffering is a good thing or at least can serve a good purpose. The Scripture passage lurking in the background is Romans 5:3–5: "And not only that, but we also boast in our sufferings, knowing that suffering produces endurance, and endurance produces character, and character produces hope, and hope does not disappoint us, because God's love has been poured into our hearts through the Holy Spirit that has been given to us." But let us not confuse suffering for the sake of Christ with suffering we do not choose. The first is intentional and excellent because it is chosen, while the second comes to us as a pathogen and is anything but excellent. To embrace suffering is not to be stoic, passive, or fatalistic but trustful that God will bring good out of something that seems only evil.

Christian theology does not associate suffering with imperfection and therefore questions a biotechnology so totally committed to eradicate what is imperfect. The only perfection Christian theology speaks about is "perfect love" (Matt. 5:43–48). Suffering is transformed by embracing it. The very meaning of compassion, "to suffer with," requires us to be "weak with the weak, vulnerable with the vulnerable, and powerless with the powerless."[19] By way of contrast, the perfection science offers will complement what the public is willing to pay for and believes it must have.

In spite of his propensity toward overstating the alternatives in dire terms, Leon Kass locates the moral fulcrum we are most likely to overlook. While his language is not that of a Christian theologian, his arguments have a theological ring to them. If he were to speak of sin, which he doesn't, it would be to understand cloning as another project of our own self-creation. Self-cloning, he writes, "is simply an extension of such rootless and narcissistic self-recreation," personifying our desire "to control the future while being subject to no controls ourselves" (*Life, Liberty*, 144). What it lacks, in part, is an affirmation that sin is not episodic or a sentiment we can educate away.

Cloning and genetic engineering are unique temptations to sin because they beckon us to exercise the power to re-create ourselves in any way that pleases us. Leave aside the notion of sin and ask what is the probability that we will enhance or clone ourselves to be any better than we are now? "Better" is a valuational term but we know well enough the characteristics and virtues we hope our fellow human beings will have. This would be a different ball game if science had a firm grip on the virtues and flaws that make us human, but it doesn't; it is occupied with getting technology to work and maintaining an aura of objective independence. The truth of the matter begins with the recognition that the kinds of individuals who want to clone themselves are the kinds of persons most of us would strongly prefer didn't. Both the philosopher Alasdair MacIntyre and the theologian Gilbert Meilaender ask us to consider whether a world designed by those who enthusiastically embrace genetic engineering would be a place the genetically engineered would want to inhabit.[20] The commodity so glaringly missing is humility and it would go a long way toward tempering the desire to create ourselves in our own image.[21]

In his discussion of germline manipulation Stock places the ethical fulcrum at the point of irreversible mistakes and unpredictable side effects. He mentions such potential risks as impoverishment of the genetic pool, the fragmentation of society into gene-rich and gene-poor individuals, and embarkation upon a road of eugenics, which targets the genetically defective. Stock takes a serious look at these regrettable possibilities, but his trust in science to get the technology right (eventually) and the public's reluctance to accept a technology until it is proven safe is such that he believes science should give the public what it wants (61, 151). A question Stock does not raise is whether we should trust our aspiration, especially when we aspire to re-make ourselves. And wouldn't you know it? The lair where sin hangs out is not the mistakes we might (will) make but the will to power, that is, the power to make the world and ourselves in our own image.

The clash between traditional morality and *the new ethic of willfulness* springs from the discontent aggravated by science. One of the blessings of seeing ourselves as creatures of God is the notion of giftedness. We can love ourselves, others, and the world for what they are rather than how they can be transformed. On the other hand, eugenics and genetic engineering represent something else—"the one-sided triumph of willfulness over giftedness, of dominion over reverence, of molding over beholding."[22] Who among us wants to throw stones of reproach at parents who want their children to be above average? Let's blame the culture for turning us into overly ambitious parents, driven to make ourselves better than well, so discontented with the giftedness of life itself that only perfection will still our longings. But with longings so intense, can we trust ourselves to do what is best for our children, much less their children?

Leland Gaunt [the Devil] in Stephen King's *Needful Things* only needs to dangle before his customers some curio, something the customer wants in his heart of hearts, an enhancement they think they really need to have. Rewrite the story and Gaunt has at his disposal a shop full of genetic curios. If you don't find something for yourself, because you are unusually self-disciplined, there would be something there for your child. When it comes to designing the future, whether as consumers or providers, our subjective desires will give us what we want but not what the world needs.

After a successful career as teacher and author, Henri Nouwen, one of the most honored and best known spiritual writers of our time, chose to become the pastor of the L'Arche Daybreak Community in Toronto where he encountered Adam. Adam was a severely handicapped young man who needed someone to feed, exercise, bathe, and love him. And what could Adam teach this highly educated and sensitive priest?

> Adam offered those he met a presence and a safe space to recognize and accept their own, often invisible disabilities. . . . He seemed to be without concepts, plans, intentions, or aspirations. He was simply present, offering himself in peace and completely self-emptied so that the fruits of his ministry were pure and abundant. (*Adam*, 64)

> I should have known all along that what I most desire in life—love, friendship, community, and a deep sense of belonging—I was finding with him. (*Adam*, 49)

> That, to me, is the final significance of Adam's passion: a radical call to accept the truth of our lives and to choose to give our love when we are strong and to receive the love of others when we are weak, always with tranquility and generosity. (*Adam*, 91)

Adam's *otherness* would frighten most people, awakening the fear that they might somehow, someday become like him. For science, suffering is always a problem to be solved. Within the life of the Christian community, suffering and otherness is a fact of life. St. Paul admonishes the Christians at Corinth to treat with more respect those who were weaker and reminds them that "if one member suffers, all suffer together; if one member is honored, all rejoice together (I Cor. 12:22–25).

Desperation arises because there are no alternatives for science. Progress is nothing if it is not about perfecting. And science, after all, operates with a perfecting methodology.

Summary Thoughts—Runaway Science

"It is interesting," writes Roslynn Haynes in her study of how scientists have been depicted in Western literature and film, "that no screen version has retained Marry Shelley's pessimistic ending" (*Faust to Strangelove*, 102). The 1931 Universal film classic with Boris Karloff as the Monster begins with an announcement of the essential theme: "a man of science who sought to create a man after his own image without reckoning upon God." Although the townspeople set the Monster on fire, the film ends with the celebration of Dr. Frankenstein's wedding to Elizabeth. Evil spreads out no farther than to the Monster, and even this is the result of experimental error rather than Frankenstein's hubris. The implication is that only the experiment had gone wrong, since the brain of a murderer instead of one from a noble person had been surgically implanted. Nothing remains of Shelley's unredeemed and unresolved ending. The suggestion is made that next time, with due precautions, the outcome would be favorable. Haynes conclusion is just as evocative: "It has taken such twentieth-century Monsters as psychoanalysis, nuclear power, in vitro fertilization, and genetic engineering, bursting upon an ethically unprepared world and their dual potential for good and evil, to illuminate fully the depth of meaning in *Frankenstein*" (101).

We may have seen the last of scientists as tragic figures. Dr. Faustus, Dr. Frankenstein, Dr. Jekyll, Dr. Cyclops, Dr. Strangelove are from another era when the practitioners of science are presented as just a little insane. The James Bond series may be the last to portray scientists as mad to the point of plotting to take over the world. The pursuit of knowledge is regarded as a goal far too worthy to be denigrated. We are now too sophisticated to confuse fictional creations with the true titans of science, such as Newton, Einstein, Pauling, and for that matter, every Nobel Prize winner in science. The change in how we view science began when the hubris associated with curiosity was displaced by the sin of not being curious enough (the sin of being intellectually passive).[23] Adam and Eve, Pandora and Prometheus, and Frankenstein could be counseled about overstepping because there were perceived limits. But as those limits were secularized and deconstructed, the only sin left is not realizing one's potential, and who has more potential than a gifted scientist?

Are we to conclude that we live in a time when there are no monsters stirring in the depths of human hearts? In *Jurassic Park*, Michael Crichton introduces something very contemporary. It is not the scientist who "gets loose" but the science itself. Granted, Dr. Henry Wu is a vain man, but he is neither mad nor evil. His mistake is to underestimate nature and overestimate biotechnology. Unlike Frankenstein, he is not hoping to rid the world of disease but to reward his investors and launch a commercially successful theme park. While the idealism of young doctor Frankenstein is not entirely absent from today's graduate students, something else has been added. Knowledge that was once discovered and shared is now constructed and patented. In Shelley's story, honor was a sufficient reward to motivate Frankenstein. With the intellectual shift to knowledge as something that is constructed—the consequence of what the scientist does or adds to a stream of data to make it useful—rather than discovered, the inevitable outcome is the impetus to claim ownership and to turn knowledge into a commodity.[24]

Crichton's *Jurassic Park* is worlds apart from Shelley's *Frankenstein* but one thing remains the same: science still dabbles in knowledge that can get out of control. Even though there are "wild things" chasing after defenseless visitors, Crichton knows the real threat is what is happening in a test tube. What threatens us the most is the deadly smallness of anthrax or a new strain of influenza. Martin Rees, Britain's Astronomer Royal and one of the world's most brilliant cosmologists, gives civilization only a fifty-fifty chance of surviving the twenty-first century. The title of his book says it all: *A Scientist's Warning: How Terror, Error, and Environmental Disaster Threaten Humankind's Future in This Century—on Earth and Beyond*. Among the new terrors Rees mentions are intelligent self-reproducing nanoparticles that could eat us and every other living thing on Earth. We have good reason to be anxious because the science that subdued some of the deadliest pestilences that once roamed the world is the same science that creates new pestilences and seems helpless in the face of new natural pathogens. Anthrax and the bird flu is the assailant we cannot see, and most of us would rather do battle with something we can see, no matter how big.

In Richard Preston's *The Demon in the Freezer: A True Story*, the identified demon is the smallpox virus. It spreads easily, there is no cure for it, and some strains kill 60 percent of their victims. Preston needs to tell but one story to make his point. A tourist just returned from Pakistan lies quarantined in a small hospital in the Sauerland region of Germany in 1970. He has contracted smallpox. One day his symptoms temporarily abate and against the orders of the nurses he cracks a window to smoke a cigarette. Within days seventeen other people who had never been in the same room contract the disease. Later scientists discover the virus can be carried from a patient's breath out a window and into another window and infect people two floors above.

But let us be clear concerning the real demon. It is found in the moral and political decision whether to destroy every vial containing the smallpox virus or to safeguard it for the purpose of research. There are only two declared stocks of smallpox on earth. Suspicion abounds that other nations beside America and Russia have their own freezers with the demon. Science favors the safeguard-and-learn approach with all the usual justifications, but the virus itself is the lesser of two potential evils. It is easier to contain demons in test tubes than demons in the form of knowledge. If a nation or the scientific community decides to get rid of every vial and insists that every nation from North Korea to Iran do the same, it can press the moral case that some knowledge should not be pursued. Before the first atomic bomb test, scientists considered the possibility that the blast would ignite the nitrogen in Earth's atmosphere and incinerate us all. A new arms race revolving around knowledge has already begun, and if it follows the historical pattern, escalation will be the certain outcome.

We are going to modify ourselves and science is going to provide the know-how. This is inconvertible. Previously, we left no stone unturned as we modified the environment. We adapted to the environment by rebuilding our physical surroundings to suit our needs. As a species we did not change because we did not have that choice. We continued to be *homo faber:* tool making, tool using, innovative, creative. We became the creature we have become unintentionally: we did not take an active part in our evolution. But that is about to change as science opens another Pandora's box. Let's note what this means in terms of our evolution. Life begins as a struggle for existence. The meaning of life is determined by self-preservation, the daily grind to secure food and shelter. But as the necessities of life are met, the meaning of life changes (a theme Jared Diamond pursues in his popular *Guns, Germs, and Steel*). We begin to redirect our energies into projects of self-modification. Unwittingly, we enter a race to attain personal fulfillment. Jürgen Moltmann makes the observation that in the midst of this change from a struggle to survive to an "artificial wealth of possibilities" our moral framework changes fundamentally. The conclusion Moltmann draws is jolting: "This makes human life for the first time *de facto* a moral task" (*Science and Wisdom*, 137). In other words, we face a world of decisions about what to do with our lives.

A second inconvertible fact is that science will continue to strive for perfection. Why would we expect anything less? Perfection is what I expect when a surgeon reads the results of an MRI or when the shuttle ferries astronauts to the space station. As rational creatures we should not settle for anything less than the elimination of error. Optimism and progress have been science's chief motivators and together they constitute the confidence that we can make tomorrow better than yesterday. When we bring together the technology to transform ourselves and the striving for perfection, when means and ends come together, the future course of our species seems determined. We will transform ourselves utilizing the model of perfection, a model with no place for sin and evil.

While science is committed to perfection, theology is committed to a peculiar understanding of human nature. Are science and theology then at loggerheads? Science fostering the belief that we can transform ourselves according to our desires and needs, theology holding firm to the truth that our essential human nature is good but perverted. For Christians, there is no human fix for sin. It is and will be our traveling companion. Wherever we go, there sin will dwell. Whatever we create, it will be bear the imprint of one who is tarnished.

Do we think that after a thousand years of human enhancements we will have done anything to fundamentally change human nature? Will we still be the creature who overreaches; the creature who desires too much? The overwhelming scientific opinion is to deny any essential human nature and to therefore bar a discussion of who we are based on who we have been. But there is no argument that there is no end to the pursuit of happiness because there is no end to human desiring. The President's Council on Bioethics demonstrates an unusual level of wisdom by identifying the modus operandi of technology as the pursuit of happiness in a chapter titled "Happy Souls".

> For this reason, the pursuit of happy souls is not simply, in this report, just another case study. At the same time it implicates or points to something final and all-embracing. For it is ultimately our desire for happiness—for the fulfillment of our aspirations and the flourishing of our lives—that leads us to seek, among other things, better children, superior performance, and ageless bodies (and minds). Yet the contribution of those proximate and subordinate ends to the ultimate and supreme end of happiness is partial and indirect.[25]

What does not change and what biotechnology does not transform are the fundamentals of human nature, and nothing is more fundamental than desire itself. And so Paul Ricoeur writes: "it is the desire of desire, taking possession of knowing, of willing, of doing, and of being: 'Your eyes shall be opened, and ye shall be as gods, knowing good and evil'" (*Symbolism of Evil*, 253).

The import of this chapter is the argument that science has shaped our culture and as a consequence has turned the soil for the seeds of sin and evil to find new places to root. Science ignites the quest to know all things and creates an insatiable appetite for the next technological advance. The peculiar character of science is to invest more in means than ends. The creation of the automobile (end) is basically the story of its manufacture (means) and the culture it created. The built-in obsolescence of every new car we drive off the lot, and the reason for its immediate depreciation, is due to the incessant drive to build a better car. When Langdon Winner wrote about passive ends and out-of-control means, he was thinking of the way science becomes caught up in its own problem-solving mentality.[26] Whether it's the auto industry, the razor blade industry, or the military complex, innovation swallows up any appointed goal. For this reason alone science will always tend to be shortsighted and insulated against any vision of the greatest need.

On the surface, science the optimist confronts theology the pessimist. The difference is more basic, as this statement of Robert Jenson highlights:

> Thus what we usually call optimism is a contrary of hope and is a mode of despair. Optimism is the conviction that all we have with which to invoke a better self and a better community and a better world is what we are in ourselves and the insistence that this must be enough. What we more usually call despair is the same conviction and the knowledge that it is not enough. (*Systematic Theology*, 2: 145)

Science does not as a rule inspire us with hope. It does keep us going with the promise of a better tomorrow and a cure for the cancer that is killing me now. The hope for a better tomorrow turns to despair when it becomes always and forever a day away. Sin is not the prophet's instrument to make us doubt ourselves or sink into misery. But sinful as we are, our hope is better placed with the knowledge that what we are in ourselves is not enough.

I do not want to, nor do I think we can, change science. The remedy, if it can be called that, is not to oppose science but to broaden the vision. I have been writing from a Christian perspective pressing the inclusion of sin and evil as realities not to be ignored. The next (and last) chapter will continue this discussion. But while we are still thinking about perfection, it is well to remember the power of perspective. Laurie Zoloth-Dorfman recounts the debate about whether the "blood of the Jews is the same as ours" or if the flat-footedness of Jews makes them unfit as foot soldiers, or the distorted Jewish nose, the unusual Jewish gait, and the unmentionable (circumcision) mark them as having inferior bodies. This mapping of the normal self (read

Aryan body) persists. Every week in her Sunday paper she sees the following advertisement.

A Guide for Cosmetic Enhancements:
A More BEAUTIFUL YOU
Nose Enhancements
Daniel B. Cohen, MD

The advertisement also notes that Dr. Cohen can diminish the size of breasts, lips, and hips—large breasts and hips being associated with Jewish women. Thus, all parts of the offending otherness of a Jewish woman's body can be "literally cut off to fit her into a smaller space in a Gentile world." The public discourse about the human good, Dorfman rightly concludes, "is barren without the perspective of the faith community." If science is the measure of the real self, she warns, "we are addressing a much larger problem than the danger of discrimination . . . we are trafficking in the market of truth criteria." From a Jewish perspective, she adds, this will mean sources science would never consider, such as the *halakhic* codes and *responsum*, midrashic admonitions, and "perhaps most centrally, from the blood and bones and flesh of our history."[27] The broader perspective of which she speaks is no small matter because any lesser perspective threatens to distort what it is to be human.

Notes

1. For example, the scientists who contributed to *Science and Religion: Are They Compatible?* ed. Paul Kurtz.
2. I am making an indirect reference to Niebuhr's terminology in reference to anxiety as the inevitable concomitant of finitude. My argument takes a Niebuhrian form by identifying technology as a new source of anxiety, namely, the insatiable need to know in order to control everything.
3. A similar indictment is made by Leon Kass, *Life, Liberty and the Defense of Dignity*, chapter 1, and more broadly in the writings of Hans Jonas, Jacques Ellul, Langdon Winner, and Albert Borgmann.
4. Jack Hitt, "Battlefield: Space," *New York Times Magazine*, 5 August 2000, 34.
5. William Langewiesche, "Columbia's Last Flight," *Atlantic Monthly*, November 2002, 80–81.
6. Quoted from Fukuyama, *Our Posthuman Future*, 185.
7. See Gerald P. McKenny, *To Relieve the Human Condition*.
8. Oppenheimer, *Letters and Recollections*, 317. Emphasis added.

9. Quoted from Karen Lebacqz, "Fair Shares: Is the Genome Project Just?" in *Genetics*, ed. Ted Peters, 83.

10. Bruce Watson, "Sounding the Alarm," *Smithsonian*, September 2002, 115–17.

11. Richard Dawkins, "The Emptiness of Theology," *Free Inquiry* 18 (Spring 1998): 6.

12. Stock, *Redesigning*, chapter 7, "Ethics and Ideology."

13. *U.S. News & World Report*, 14 October 2002, 34.

14. See Janet Soskice, "The Ends of Man and the Future of God," in *The End of the World and the Ends of God*, eds. John Polkinghorne and Michael Welker, 78. Also, in the same volume, essays by Fraser Watts and Kathryn Tanner contrast Christian hope with optimism.

15. The phrase "desperately seeking perfection" is from an article of the same title by Joel Shuman, "Desperately Seeking Perfection: Christian Discipleship and Medical Genetics," *Christian Bioethics* 5, no. 2 (1999): 139–53. The perfection Shuman has in mind is the elimination of contingency and the maximization of individual freedom. A provocative and insightful examination of science and perfection can be found in Rothman, *The Pursuit of Perfection*.

16. In Alan Nayes's novel, *Gargoyles*, the road toward perfection runs through creating perfectly *im*perfect children.

17. See *Engineering the Human Germline*, eds. Gregory Stock and John Campbell (New York: Oxford University Press, 2000).

18. See Meilaender, "Designing Our Descendants," *First Things* 109 (January 2001): 27; also accessible at www.firstthings.com/ftissues/ft0101/articles/meilaender.html

19. Here I am following the powerful exposition of compassion in *Compassion: A Reflection on the Christian Life*, by Henri J. M. Nouwen, Donald P. McNeill, and Douglas A. Morrison (New York: Doubleday, 1983).

20. For Alasdair MacIntyre's initiating quote, see "Designing our Descendants: Seven Traits for the Future," *Hastings Center Report* 9 (February 1979): 5–7: "If in designing our descendants we succeeded in designing people who possessed just those traits that I have described, . . . what we would have done is to design descendants whose virtues would be such that they would be quite unwilling in turn to design *their* descendants. We should in fact have brought our own project of designing descendants to an end." See also Gilbert Meilaender's essay, "Designing Our Descendants," 25–28.

21. While humility is the virtue par excellence I have in mind, Meilaender's fuller description is worth quoting: "We should want them to be people who do not think the natural world infinitely malleable to their projects; who reckon from the outset with limits to their own knowledge of and control over the future; who respect the equal dignity of their fellows and do not seek to coopt others as means to their own (even if good) ends; . . . who are more disposed to seek wisdom than power. . . ." See Meilaender, "Designing," 27.

22. Michael Sandel, a philosopher at Harvard University and a member of the President's Council on Bioethics, identifies the fundamental issue of our posthuman future as

the Promethean project of willfulness to make the myth of the "self-made man" come true. See his "The Case against Perfection," in *Atlantic Monthly* (April 2004): 51–62.

23. There is no better treatment of how curiosity is regarded and the role it played in the paradigm shifts regarding progress and enlightenment than Hans Blumenberg, *The Legitimacy of the Modern Age*, trans. Robert M. Wallace (Cambridge, Mass.: MIT Press, 1983).

24. See Corynne McSherry, *Who Owns Academic Work?* 46–50. This subject is taken up again in the next chapter.

25. See chapter 6, section 1 of the President's Council on Bioethics, "Beyond Therapy: Biotechnology and the Pursuit of Happiness," released October 2003; accessed at www.bioethics.gov/reports/beyoundtherapy/index.html.

26. Langdon Winner wrote often and persuasively that technology proceeds independent of any well-thought-out direction. "But while the ends have become passive in the face of technical means, the reverse is not true. Indeed, the nature of the means requires that the ends be precisely redefined in a way that suits the available technique" (*Autonomous Technology*, 229).

27. Laurie Zoloth-Dorfman, "Mapping the Normal Self: The Jew and the Mark of Otherness," in *Genetics*, ed. Peters, 180–97.

PART THREE

SCIENCE AND THEOLOGY IN COUNTERBALANCE

As this twenty-first century begins, we are disheartened by historical events but nevertheless optimistic about the future we can create. The critical issue is what can we *realistically* expect of ourselves on the verge of taking evolution into our hands. Religion is usually expected to raise the red flags, while science is impatient with ancient and irrelevant restraints. There are other ways of understanding how science and religion serve the common good. If each discipline—science and theology—does what each does best, then each will speak of truths that counterbalance the other, truths the other is not prepared or equipped to propose and defend. The challenge for theology, hopefully met by this book, is to raise human awareness that we cannot fully trust ourselves.

CHAPTER SEVEN

What Can We Expect? So Much Depends on How We Answer

The passion of greed is so powerful that to become rich without injustice is impossible.

—St. John Chrysotom

Secularity is the unreflective world setting its own agenda.

—Rowan Williams, Archbishop of Canterbury

For the healing of the nations, God, we pray with one accord; for a just and equal sharing of the things that earth affords.
   All that kills abundant living, let it from the earth be banned; pride of status, race, or schooling, dogmas that obscure your plan. In our common quest for justice, may we hallow life's brief span.

—Hymn, "For the Healing of the Nations," Fred Kaan, 1967[1]

We begin with a summing up and a few conclusions. The world that shaped the science Oppenheimer and Bohr knew is a relic. Along with the Cold War, the era of atomic physics has been displaced by globalization and biotechnology. Not much of the original implied contract between science and the commonwealth survives except for mutual expectations. Science offered its expertise for the common good in exchange for fiscal security and the right to chart its own course. But as science became a major player in war, possible wars, and the gross national product, it was subjected to legislative oversight and political pressures. Along the way science turned into this quasi-institution we both love and hate.

We sense that something has changed as the shadow of the bomb recedes. On the flats of Alamogordo a select number of scientists witnessed the awesome destructive power of what knowledge can create. The world would soon learn that something as small as an atom contains the energy to annihilate a city or power it for decades. The something new, we have come to realize, is the sheer reach of our technology for good and evil. The report of the President's Council on Bioethics, released in October 2003, is several hundred pages long but never loses sight of what is fundamental to our own era: "For the age of biotechnology is not so much about technology itself as it is about *human beings empowered by biotechnology*."[2] Biotechnology is more than a tool to remedy incurable diseases. It will create its own culture and shape human aspirations, just as the atomic bomb did, though we cannot see clearly the details of that future. What is becoming very clear is the unavoidable confrontation with ourselves. Whether the task is designing a human-like robot or selecting the preferred genetic makeup of a sperm or egg donor, the one doing the creating is no other than the human self looking in a mirror. We will undoubtedly learn a great deal of what it means to be human as we re-create human life.[3] The question left unasked is whether sin and evil are part of our evolutionary cultural heritage just as much as the language we learn to speak and are hardwired to learn.

My final arguments pivot around expectations. What can we expect from technology? Are we looking forward to a future where we control the means by which we engineer our biological-robotic destiny? Or will our worst fears come to pass and something go terribly wrong (accidents will happen, you know) or a lethal new technology fall into the hands of a rogue scientist or a rogue state? A different line of thinking prompts the question what we should expect from science and religion. Both are vital to the common good we seek for the commonwealth but both are assigned very different roles. By situating religion and science vis-à-vis culture, we can ask another question. What can the commonwealth reasonably expect of science and religion as creators and protectors of the common good, and more specifically, how will science and theology play off each other? Everything it seems boils down to the straightforward question whether we can trust ourselves. It may well be that scientists and theologians have very different expectations, and that in turn reaches back to a decision about the reality of sin and evil.

A sidebar concerning terminology is called for. Throughout this book, and as the arguments have unfolded, science and theology have been the dialogue partners rather than science and religion. There are several reasons for this pairing. Religion is multifaceted, generalized, rich in its variegated traditions but, like Jell-O®, difficult to hold and say, "Now I've got you." In comparison, theology is an academic discipline practiced for the most part by professionals (those who have the proper credentials and are paid to theologize). Theology can be self-critical as well as critical of religion, while each religion insulates itself against self-criticism. Science becomes the parallel discipline when it is self-critical and historical. Science and theology are disciplines with a past relationship. Theirs has been a conversation alternating between hostility, rivalry, and collaboration. When their engagement is going well each sees the other as a truth-seeker, even as "intellectual cousins under the skin."[4] Religion, on the other hand, does not exactly have a separate existence apart from the religious beliefs held by scientists or theologians. But it is religion that is embodied in and by culture, just as science is embodied by way of attitudes and values.

To Transcend or Not to Transcend

In his book *Radical Evolution*, Joel Garreau lays out three possible future scenarios: Heaven, Hell, and Prevail. His arguments represent a good place to begin our inquiry into human nature. Of course, the future will be Heaven, Hell, or something in between. What interests me about the Heaven scenario is the language of progression or acceleration. Garreau argues forcefully that we are on the brink of something big—a quantum leap forward in our evolution—and the sciences of genetics, robotics, information, and nanotechnology (GRIN is Garreau's acronym) will be the catalyst. This does not mean that all will go well, and this is why Garreau thinks the Prevail scenario is the most realistic. Nevertheless, Garreau is fascinated by the curves of exponential change. Among the best-known doubling theories is Gordon E. Moore's observation that the minimum cost of semiconductor components has been doubling once a year, every year since the first prototype was introduced. Numerous variations sprouted, and so Moore's Law is about the doubling of information technology every eighteen months, for as far as the eye can see. Something similar can also be said of the other three GRIN technologies. You get the picture. As such this has little to do with the human condition but then Garreau turns his attention to the Curve of human evolution.

> To get from the formation of the Earth to the first multicellular organisms took perhaps 4 billion years. Getting from tiny organisms to the first mammal took 400 million years. Getting from mammals to the first primitive monkeys took 150 million years. Getting from monkey to hominid species such as chimpanzees took something like 30 million years. Notice how the pace accelerates? Getting from

hominids to walking erect took 16 million years. Getting from walking erect to humans painting on cave walls at Altamira, Spain, took 4 million years. (58)

The rest is history, except that something new begins. Humans learn how to pass information from one generation to the next and the learnings of the past become the footstool for the future. Thus the beginning of cultural evolution—and just as genetic evolution reaches a plateau, cultural evolution begins to accelerate. Advances in the sciences, arts, and economics rise exponentially. "Four thousand years to the Roman Empire, 1,800 years to the Industrial Age, 169 years to the moon and 20 more to the Information Age" (58). If not excited yet, then consider the likelihood that we are engineering our own evolution. And this does seem to be the natural outcome of cultural evolution. As humans began to seize the day and change the environment in order to survive in hostile habitats and so spread out across the globe, our tool-making abilities began to take precedence over instinctual drives. It was not our genes that adapted but our ability to make ever more sophisticated tools. Something else was happening. *Homo sapiens* as opposed to *Homo erectus* began to ask deep and fascinating questions about the world about and the self within. As John Polkinghorne points out, the processing of information is clearly an advantage in the struggle for survival while proving Fermat's last theorem is not. No doubt kin altruism and reciprocal altruism "shed some Darwinian light on aspects of human behavior," but the notion of Darwinian survival as providing the sole engine behind human development is anemic when trying to explain the mental world of mathematics or Mahler's Ninth Symphony. The curve of human development, as distinct from the curve of genetic evolution, is dependent on "these noetic realms of rational skill, moral imperative and aesthetic delight to draw out and enhance human potentialities."[5]

When self-proclaimed student of culture Joel Garreau writes about the "steep ramp of cultural evolution" or the "ramp of human connectedness," I am reminded of Peter Singer's expanding circle of human empathy and Steven Pinker's moral escalator (introduction). The theme here is that we are getting better and we are following a natural curve of progression. It is an argument that makes sense only if we take into account the distinction between human evolution and cultural evolution. A number of grids are possible, such as human rights, literacy, self-determination, respect for life, democracy, environmental awareness, or international law. Graph, for instance, dignity and autonomy and you find a trajectory from the revolutionary proposition that "all men are created equal in 1776 through the abolition of slavery, women's suffrage, laws against racial discrimination, the censoring of politically incorrect language" (Garreau, 213). Sam Harris, who takes dead aim at the clash between reason and belief, says it is time for us to admit that not all cultures are at the same level of moral development, and he shows no hesitation in contrasting those societies "whose moral and political development—in their treatment of women and children, in their prosecution of war, in their approach to criminal justice, and in their very intuitions about what constitutes cruelty—lags behind our own" (*The End of Faith*, 145).

All of it is arguable—this notion of cultural and moral development—and yet it rings true. The atrocities of the past, such as slave ships and chemical warfare, are no longer tolerated in a growing number of societies. What can be argued with certainty is that we are more self-aware of our actions. Nurture, as Rousseau devoted his life to show, makes a difference, and there is little doubt that as a global civilization we have made progress in taming base instincts. I am still troubled, just the same, by the supposition that some curve of human evolution is moving us inevitably in the direction of Heaven and that we can do something to speed it along.

The Hell scenario has a different take on human behavior. It warns that we are dangerously close to releasing the genie from the bottle only to discover there is no going back. What the optimist conveniently forgets is that people are evil and make mistakes. Add into the mix some really lethal ideas (creating things that can make more of themselves that might not be eradicable) and wrong suppositions (technology always produces positive social outcomes), and the Heaven scenario is almost laughable. History is littered with technologies that promised much, and in many cases delivered much, but left behind a legacy of appalling consequences. The pesticide DDT was very effective at killing insects but lethal to birds and many other living things. CFCs are great coolants for refrigerators and air conditioners but destroy the earth's ozone layer. The introduction of genetically altered seeds and plants has been a godsend for humans on the brink of starvation, and yet individuals and nations have stubbornly refused to embrace the change. In fact, an entire global business of organic foods has taken hold. A simple rule is operative: the greater the technological innovation, the greater it will impact on complex social and cultural relationships. It may be more than science fiction entertainment to foresee a deeply divided society. Not only are humans pitted against each other, human are up against androids and cyborgs (the films *Blade Runner* and *The Terminator*) and machine intelligence (*The Matrix* film).

Garreau's Heaven is populated with geeks and wizards, prognosticators and innovators par excellence, such as the radically optimistic Ray Kurzweil (*The Age of Spiritual Machines* and *The Singularity Is Near: When Humans Transcend Biology*), the guru of nanotechnology Eric Drexler (*Engines of Creation: The Coming Age of Nanotechnology*), the grand old man of artificial intelligence and co-founder of the MIT Artificial Intelligence Lab Marvin Minsky and the herald of robotics Rodney Allen Brooks (*Flesh and Machines: How Robots Will Change Us*), evolutionary biologist Lee M. Silver (*Remaking Eden*), and the not-afraid-to-try-anything researchers at the Pentagon's Defense Advanced Research Projects Agency (DARPA). You haven't heard of DARPA? It is an agency of the Defense Sciences Office of the Pentagon funded for the purpose of creating better humans—that is, better soldiers, better defense weapons. If that isn't a little scary, consider that DARPA invests 90 percent of its sizable budget outside the federal government, mainly in universities and industry.[6]

Garreau's Hell scenario attracts a very different kind of non-geek expert: naturalist Wendell Berry, doomsday prophet Martin Rees, political analyst Francis Fukuyama, conservative moral philosopher and former chair of the President's Council on Bioethics Leon Kass, outspoken and politically active environmentalists Bill McKibben and Jeremy Rifkin, and, last but not least, Hell scenario's most celebrated spokesperson, the Edison of the Internet William (Bill) Joy. The Heaven scenario is not without its literary masterpieces by such luminaries as Sr. Francis Bacon, Jules Verne, H. G. Wells, B. F. Skinner, and Arthur C. Clarke, and they stack up against the likes of Aldous Huxley, George Orwell, Mary Wollstonecraft Shelley, and Michael Crichton. Garreau categorizes many of the latter as the Naturalists. Unlike the Laggards, who are simply suspicious of any change and are so poor that they have no choice, the Naturalists prefer to keep it simple, keep it pure, take it slow, and mobilize others to resist certain technologies. The Naturalists and the Laggards may be technologically handicapped but they counterbalance those who are believers in curves of exponential change.

Garreau is my kind of realist, who weighs "the promise and the peril of enhancing our minds, our bodies." I, too, like to think we will somehow persevere in spite of ourselves. My hope, though, is little more than a trust placed in common sense. Common sense, after all, is the better part of the common good, and it does have a way of eventually prevailing. Science will help us live longer and healthier lives, enhancing both mind and body while preserving what is essentially human. What I cannot abide, though, is talk about transcending ourselves, as if this is a mission we should be undertaking at all due speed. In the hands of technophiles, transcendence refers to a quantum leap—to rise above, surpass who we are, until mind is no longer bound by human flesh. Garreau concludes his book with a chapter devoted to the implied consequence of scientific progress ever accelerating. He asks whether these GRIN technologies can change the basics of the human condition. "Can we imagine them changing the way we shape truth, beauty, love or happiness? Can we imagine altering the seven deadly sins—pride, envy, gluttony, lust, anger, greed and sloth" (240)? By asking so many excellent "can" questions, we are apt to overlook the absence of any "should" questions. The difference between "can" and "should" requires the will not to do something we can do.

Garreau is more optimistic than say Wendell Barry and Bill McKibben, or Leon Kass and Francis Fukuyama. Barry and McKibben are in the camp of the Naturalists (so is Jeremy Rifkin) and when asked how we resist being overrun by technology, they respond that we will pick and choose the technologies that will do us the most good while doing the least harm. Because they are immersed in the politics of government, Kass and Fukuyama find hope through regulations and international agreements. They rightly point to the places and times when we have shown self-restraint by self-regulating. Writing as a theologian, I see our future as a continuation of what it already has been. We are creatures who exist within the paradox of choosing both good and evil with extraordinary compassion and unthinkable cruelty. This is our future as far as the eye can see. Absent the notion of sin and evil and we will jump to the conclusion that we are the masters of our destiny.

For those who contemplate the future, let them not confuse sin with error. If to err is human, why isn't it human to sin? The reason why one does not follow the other is our human propensity to place the errors of technology into a different category. Simply stated, they are correctable. And they are amendable, because of the upward curve of scientific knowledge. If an engineer makes a mistake, he or she is expected to learn from that mistake and not make it a second time. Perfection is the goal and nothing less will do. In the Heaven versus Hell debate, critics focus on what can go wrong with this or that technology, and the rebuttal about how it can be made right.[7] Sin and evil, on the other hand, are not a function of rationality. The ancient tradition of assigning different physical locations for different passions retains a certain legitimacy. The "heart" is the seat of certain desires quite apart from the "mind." When we say, "the heart wants what the heart wants," we acknowledge a certain lack of willpower. Even though we *know* better, the heart leads us down paths only a fool would go. If only the consequences of sin were correctable or the energy of evil reducible. Of course I know something of repentance, forgiveness, and atonement. It's the language for sin but hardly a technological fix.

What makes anyone think there is scientific fix, a way to exponentially evolve to a higher state of mind and body? And why is transcending the human condition always a better future? Going down this path would mean overcoming a built-in catch-22. If we transcend the human condition, we would no longer be human. Aren't we forgetting that in this universe there is only one kind of existence? Science fiction writers understand this. When they project the future thousands of years and galaxies far out, the universe is populated with species who consider our technology to be primitive. But the universe is still no kinder, everyone still needs to survive, and the choosing between good and evil goes on and on.

Let's blame technology or science for advancing too fast for our own good. But the lesson of the last century is that murder, maiming, and torture arise from the primitive steel of a machete as well as the sophisticated wiring of a smart bomb. The greatest evil flows from the twisted logic of egomaniacs rather than the idealism of well-meaning scientists. In reaching for the "apple" of knowledge, Dr. Frankenstein created a creature he did not understand and could not control (the monster could think for himself), but it was society who disfigured him into an object of hate and fear. This does not mean technology itself (the gun not the gun owner) is not ensnared by its own dual use of good and evil. It cannot claim the mantle of innocence. Technology and the knowledge it embodies is its own temptation, but in the end it is the human mind that directs the hand, the heart that wants what the heart wants.

Since sin is a component of self-awareness, it isn't going anywhere as human awareness expands and deepens. It will be our enduring traveling companion to the horizon of the universe and the limits of human intelligence. Because sin is the consequence of a dovetail-like fit between nature and nurture, the only way we might transcend sin is to transcend it both biologically and culturally. But how likely is that? It matters little which is first or most important so long as both instinct and culture are given their due and are not segregated.[8] At a fundamental level, the capacity for self-transcendence is both genetic and learned, and each has its own particular evolutionary history. Consequently, humans learn two kinds of behaviors and are biologically predisposed toward good and evil. Children teeter on the brink of good and evil. And "Fall" they will, pushed by their societies' prejudices and fears. Yet inspired by saints and geniuses, they will strive and thrive to be better than might otherwise be. Protected from themselves by a history of laws and customs, they are yet driven by instincts to do the wrong they know is wrong. On either side—as we make our choices—we both respond to base instincts and answer a higher calling. It matters not if I am remade super intelligent or super strong, the temptation of seven deadly sins is ever before me. So if we prevail—if compassion and sacrifice and endurance win the day—we will not find that we have transcended to a higher level of existence. We will be no less human, and therefore no less defined by the human paradox of good and evil.

What Can We Expect? Science and Theology in Counterbalance

Jürgen Moltmann captures a prevailing sentiment when he writes: "Einstein once said that earlier, people had perfect purposes but highly imperfect means of achieving them; today we have perfect means and immense possibilities but confused purposes" (*Science and Wisdom*, 20). The same refrain is heard in various contexts. We are adrift without a compass in a sea of technological innovation. The overall impression of science may be turning sour because scientists seem more preoccupied with revenue-sharing contracts than a social contract for the good of the commonweal. The diffused way science is funded, its quasi-institutional character, the way it has burrowed its way into our daily lives make it extremely difficult to separate science from the culture we live in or the future we hope to secure. So everyone is frustrated over how to induce science to be more sensitive to the will of the people. There is always the political system and in democratic societies the ballot box. But how do we vote science out of office? How do we say "yes" to some forms of technology while saying "no" to others? While we no longer go to bed at night anxious that we might radiate most of our planet with a few hydrogen bombs, we face the much more subtle prospect of biologically enhancing ourselves into a society we would hardly recognize and certainly would not have chosen.

If we don't know what to do with a science of "immense possibilities but confused purposes," we also have ambivalent feelings about the role of religion. A short time after September 11, a nighttime host of National Public Radio conducted an on-air poll. We were invited to cast a call-in vote whether religion, on balance, was a detriment or a benefit to world peace. While this kind of poll would have been highly unlikely before September 11, the mixed emotions so evident now have been brewing for a long time. A more erudite assessment is equally divided. Jonathan Sacks, chief rabbi of the United Hebrew Congregation of Britain and the Commonwealth, argues that contrary to all expectations the world's religious communities "have emerged in the twenty-first century as key forces in a global age" (4). Admitting religion's part in fostering a tribal mentality, Sacks counters with his conviction that "the supreme religious challenge is to see God's image in one who is not in our image" (*The Dignity of Difference*, 60). Writing as an ethnologist-sociologist, Alan Wolfe is of a different mind. After surveying the wide diversity of religious expressions in America, Wolfe concludes that democracy has nothing to worry about. Religion has become a tiger whose teeth have been removed by a secular culture. Believers of every faith, so Wolfe asserts, "have found their own comfortable niches in American society" and instinctively avoid strategies that would disturb the status quo (*The Transformation of American Religion*, 254). So much the better for democracy, Wolfe maintains, because our nation has been delivered from rabid defenders of the faith who sow seeds of dissension. Stated more succinctly, we have all become mainstreamed just trying to keep up, unable to swim against the current. What separates Sacks from Wolfe is more than the breadth of their surveys or the depth of their religious commitments. There is nothing deeply troublesome for Wolfe when religion becomes enculturated. The world is a better place, a safer place, when religion loses its sharp edges by losing its absolutes. Sacks too is troubled by absolutes but at the same time he is not afraid of diversity born of deeply held beliefs. Sacks would have us revel in our diversity and embrace different standards of truth-knowing since there are many ways to know and worship God.[9] Probe a little deeper and you begin to see the need for a fresh evaluation of religion's role vis-à-vis culture.

It seems obvious to me that human problems require solutions that are moral, scientific, and political. Equally uncomplicated is the observation that we do not need further ideals but communities that embody the ones we have. We do not need more visions of utopian futures but visionaries who know our past record. We do not need further moral insight but stronger moral convictions. On all fronts—including no less scientists, theologians, and people of all religious faiths—we need to shore up the common good and make it a political priority.

Since that night when Robert Oppenheimer stood to address his colleagues who had literally released the most powerful scientific discovery known to humankind, nothing has changed and everything has changed. Oppenheimer foresaw a dangerous world made even more dangerous by a most potent knowledge. The war drew to an end, the task of rebuilding began, and science accepted its responsibility to make the world safe from itself. During the intervening years the public's expectation of science expanded far beyond what Oppenheimer could have imagined. But then a peculiar thing happened to that expectation. Optimism turned into postmodern skepticism. "The West's dominant belief system," writes Leo Marx, "turned on the idea of technical innovation as a primary agent of progress." There was nothing in that Enlightenment world picture, Marx continues, which prepared its believers for the horrors and disasters linked to modern technologies. Chernobyl and the *Columbia* could be written off as human error but not so the Holocaust, Hiroshima, the nuclear arms race, acid rain, global warming, or ozone depletion. No less than an ideological shift was required: "*It entailed the atrophy of the Enlightenment idea of progress directed toward a more just, republican society, and its gradual replacement by a politically neutral, technocratic idea of progress whose goal was the continuing improvement of technology.*"[10] This clarifies as well as any explanation why we find ourselves living "in the shadow of unwanted, built-in, automatic utopianism" (Hans Jonas). More than any previous philosopher Jonas provided substance to "the utopian dynamics of technical progress" and the magnitude of responsibility it imposes on us. Nearly twenty-five years ago Jonas reckoned: "We need wisdom most when we believe in it least" (*The Imperative of Responsibility*, 21). One is naturally led to inquire who should assume the role of returning science to the service of moral and political ends.

Theology is justified in asking why should anyone be surprised by the perversion of high ideals given the sinful condition of humanity. While the question begins to define theology's responsibility, the issue at hand is whether science should care about the direction technology takes. After a surge of social responsibility and political action, scientists of the postwar era settled into their comfort zone of problem solving and knowledge accumulation. At the end of her *A Peril and a Hope*, Alice Smith sounded a skeptical note (as did Oppenheimer). After noting the gradual return of atomic scientists to work as usual, she acknowledged the reality that scientists do not make good agents of change. In light of this history, doesn't it make sense to let science be what science is—a rather aimless enterprise except for the business of understanding the laws and principles that govern matter and life? And yet, there are strong indicators the public does expect science to serve the common good, and while the nature of that good is not well defined, it includes honesty, fairness, trustworthiness, openness, equity.

A reasonable expectation summons scientists to be good stewards of the knowledge they mine. The stewardship of knowledge becomes their most important responsibility.[11] Stewards exercise a form of protectorship over what they do not own. Since Hiroshima most scientists have understood the fate of the world rests with the kind of knowledge they bring to light, the kind of knowledge that is too dangerous to let loose indiscriminately. The perplexing issue for modern science is where its responsibility begins and ends. The standard response is that some knowledge is so fundamental and without immediate application that it belongs to everyone. No one owns the law of thermodynamics or the double-helix design of DNA.[12] But there is also a history of extending the rights of ownership to those who discover something new with the prospect of some new practical application.[13] Also involved is the factor of one's employment. Individual scientists may see themselves as public servants or employees for hire. Working for the military is its own conundrum of contradictions. What a sense of stewardship does or does not straighten out, it can serve to underscore an indigenous knowledge present in what existed long before any of us came along.

All of this is changing as the global economy becomes a marketplace for the exchange of knowledge. Corynne McSherry appropriately begins her study of intellectual property rights with a case study (also known as property tales). In the case of *Pelletier v. Agouron*, a young postdoctoral researcher brought suit to recover the intellectual property she claimed was hers, including experimental procedures, charts, data, creative inspiration, financial investment, and her status as a researcher in the scientific community. All of this Pelletier argued was "stolen" when researchers at Agouron Pharmaceutical published a paper covering the same research in *Cell*, the leading journal in the field. Pelletier had cooperated with two senior biochemists, Krust and Wilson, and fellow graduate student Michele McTigue. McTigue was married to Jay Davis who managed Agouron's research team. Pelletier brought suit because she felt betrayed.

This and many other property tales convinced McSherry that legal precedents are rapidly becoming the primary means of sorting out useful application from a data stream, expression from initial discovery, and even the meaning of academic freedom. The invocation of copyright and patent law is one way for authors and researchers to protect what is theirs, and this is the intent behind these laws. What is a professor to do when he discovers a student has sold his lecture notes to an Internet website? What recourse did Pelletier have when she felt her proprietary rights had been violated?

As a public institution the university has a long tradition of anchoring the commons. The traditional raison d'être of the university is the free inquiry of disinterested reason. As the primary site of not-for-profit intellectual curiosity, the university serves to provide knowledge for the sake of the common good. Scientific research is intentionally protected from "interested" production in order to provide the larger public with knowledge that is unbiased and disinterested. In his comprehensive vision of postwar science, Vannevar Bush (*The Endless Frontier*) argued adamantly for the separation of basic research (pure science) and applied science. The former should only be carried out in a university or research setting where scientists can work in an atmosphere free of commercial pressure. To the degree that universities have altered their mission away from the public interest and toward "a piece of the action," Bush's worst scenario has come to pass.

The philosophical-theological premise behind disinterested knowledge is an understanding of the universe as God given, or at the very least, not mine. Those who read the Book of Nature did so as stewards of the commons. Academia operated on the basis of a gift economy. In exchange for honor and prestige, scholars revealed knowledge in order to gift it to the greater good. We have a heightened awareness today that reading the Book of Nature requires the expenditure of money. Facts don't fall off trees like apples. But is there no sense of stewardship and gifting left except as the uncommon scientist demonstrates it?

Market forces threaten the public domain—the common pool of knowledge that is meant to be shared and used for the common good—where it matters greatly if you are information rich or information poor. Public universities and private colleges find themselves in an awkward place. Being rich with information and creativity places them in the midst of a competitive market. Everyone wants to be a knowledge owner rather than a knowledge worker. After reorganizing itself around the image of "excellence," academia finds itself in the business of knowledge transfer as its raison d'être. As knowledge becomes a commodity, presidents and deans must make daily decisions about whether to enter into third-party contracts, how to structure those contracts, and how to protect the autonomy and freedom of the university.[14] By enabling universities to claim entitlement to inventions made with the support of federal funds, the Patent and Trademark Amendments Act of 1980 (Bayh-Dole Act) accelerated the commercialization of knowledge. The Freedom of Information Act was meant to restore some balance by requiring federally funded researchers to make public all data produced with those funds, essentially to return it to the public domain. It hasn't happened and won't until the communal sense of ownership is restored and the eroding nature of market forces is countered.[15]

Dr. Richard Horton wants to know if "science, and especially biomedical science, is now hopelessly compromised by its apparent dependence on industry."[16] Universities and hospitals are open to the same skepticism for

> **Dateline *Boston Globe*, 26 January 2004**
> ## MIT's Technology Matchmaker
> By marrying the assets of one of the nation's top research universities to the resources of venture capitalists, Lita L. Nelsen has quietly become the gatekeeper to MIT's technological riches and a builder of the technology-business ecosystem that is key to the economic growth in the Boston area.
> The role of Nelsen and her technology licensing office . . . looms large for inventors seeking to commercialize their science and investors hoping to capitalize on it.
> Last year alone, the office managed 484 new inventions from MIT labs, received 152 patents from the U.S. government, and collected royalties of $26.8 million, according to figures released last week (Robert Weisman, A1).

similar corrosion of values. In one well-documented case, Nancy Olivieri, a researcher at the University of Toronto and the City's Hospital for Sick Children, was overseeing a drug to treat a rare blood disorder called thalassemia. The Canadian Medical Research Council and a pharmaceutical company called Apotex sponsored her research. When she discovered the drug was not as effective as the company had hoped and even appeared to have very serious side effects, Olivieri indicated her wish to publish her findings. Apotex threatened her with legal action. The hospital fired her and the university ostracized her. The hospital and the university, which should have been the first to offer her protection, were the last to defend either her right to publish or her duty to her patients. While all of this was going on, the University of Toronto was itself lobbying the Canadian government on behalf of Apotex and discussing with Apotex a $12.7 million donation to the university.[17] These are the kinds of tangled webs science seems unable to avoid. And they result from research that is driven not by curiosity or the desire to contribute to the common good but an immediate economic payoff.

The diminution of the public sphere comes at a moment most unfortunate, because now more than ever knowledge is an ethical responsibility. The development and use of the atomic bomb opened the barn door and let loose a technology that was greater than the bomb itself. To think of technological knowledge as neutral because it is objectively procured by a disinterested rationality goes beyond naiveté; it is dangerous to a frightening degree.

If we do not return knowledge most beneficial and dangerous to the public domain, then certain interested parties will use it for private, personal, monetary, and evil purposes. The quandary is this: patent and copyright laws were intended to grant the inventor-author-discoverer a limited reward in return for making public something that is original and beneficial, but the balance between these two "rights" has been tilted to the detriment of the common good. The reason is obvious. Those with the most power are the ones who are already knowledge rich and they will do what is necessary to benefit themselves.

Utilizing good Lockean logic, the little red hen declares, "Now I'm going to it eat it myself."[18] We empathize with her because, after all, she had planted the seeds, watered the plants, harvested the wheat, ground the flour, and baked the bread. The substance of Locke's theory consists of the principle that something becomes "mine" rather than simply being available for general use when I mix my labor with available resources. Being both a moral philosopher and a student of human behavior (the best combination), Locke included two necessary provisos: (1) all should have an equal opportunity to mix their labor with raw resources and (2) a person may not appropriate the only water hole in the desert and charge what he will. But modern science is never so simple. Whether it is Edison's light bulb, Linus Pauling's vaccine, or Watson and Crick's double helix, everyone's research is dependent on a legacy of research by others. Nancy Wexler's groundbreaking research on Huntington's disease depended on the participation of an entire village in Venezuela.[19] The technological and organizational complexity of modern research is such that Locke's notion of "mixing" is obviously shortsighted. The bread the little red hen ate is reminiscent of stand-alone economies quickly disappearing across the face of the globe.

The little red hen could claim it was all hers because only she had worked to produce the bread, but what if the others did not participate because they did not have the skills or governmental support or the luxury (time away from just surviving) to pursue biological research? Doing good science runs counter to the premise that there is only one watering hole which can be owned, because good science requires a process of public verification and the free exchange of ideas. When the watering hole is information and your labor is added to make it into something specifically useful, and you claim that you are going to eat all of it yourself, you have essentially turned your back on the human family by privatizing knowledge. Where is the justice or the compassion when a corporation or university declares it is theirs, at least until the patent runs out? Sin has a corporate face and the healing of the nations is frustrated whenever information that can save lives and restore health is withheld because the price isn't right.

In the last fifty years we have witnessed a subtle transfer of responsibility. The effects of splitting the atom were too gruesome to be ignored. In this context atomic physics was understood as negative science, the source of all that could go terribly wrong. The decisions that had to be made eventually were crafted into international treaties. On the other hand, biotechnology is essentially a positive science. Every frontier is seen as leading to health and happiness—so much so that Bill McKibben asks us to consider what kind of future will we create if everything goes right (*Enough*, 36). With so much riding on the manipulation of genes and stem-cell research, scientific responsibility is becoming more imperative and more personal. Biotechnology is opening so many new ethical doors that it has enlisted the help of ethicists and ethical review boards. It seems that each new trial must first be scrutinized for its legal and ethical ramifications. What is our responsibility for those not yet born? What are the known and unknown side effects? What are the likely consequences if a particular technology, such as the pre-birth selection of gender and newborn testing for genetic disorders, is promoted as the next big thing? The feature article of the 24 January 2004 issue of *Newsweek* explored "The New Science of Sex Selection" and asked "How You Can Choose, But Should You?" At least in the area of biotechnology, the individual no longer has the luxury of being a passive consumer. Making a place for moral responsibility is usually a role assigned to religion, but on what basis should we exempt science from matters of justice? The old litany is hollow: science deals with objectivity. Scientists do not make good politicians and they should not be diverted from their primary mission of pursuing universal truths. But something has changed. Now knowledge most valued is knowledge about us, and that kind of knowledge must not be separated from matters of justice and compassion. The practical truth lies somewhere in the middle. We may not want scientists running for public office any more than we want pastors asking for our vote. But neither do we want them silent when it is a matter of protecting the common good.

When the issue of responsibility is probed it leads back to the exercise of reasonable stewardship. When can the scientist in good conscience say, "It is now out of my hands"? Certainly not when a patent or license is granted. Ownership conveys both benefits and responsibilities. When a name is legally attached that person can be sued, but sued for what? The usual grounds include deception, falsification, misrepresentation, and errors of omission but not sins of commission. It would be a novelty if a patent included a provision regarding the intended purpose and the possibility of criminal or civil suit if that purpose is subverted. Of course this is not the real world. When scientists "release" information, others must be responsible for their own actions but that does not mean the inventor-creator should not care what happens to his or her "baby." Neither science nor scientists shoulder the full responsibility for weapons of mass destruction but they make them possible. That other hands and minds actually fashion the end result—a militarized world—does not absolve science. To rightly speak of sin and evil requires us to implicate the human heart. Sins of commission and omission—"Most merciful God, we confess that we have sinned against thee in thought, word, and deed, by what we have done, and by what we have left undone"—come together and accuse us in such a way than no one is absolved. Stewardship requires us to distinguish between real need and perceived need, between what we desire from what the commonwealth requires. This distinction contains an implied principle of justice: no one should get what is desired until everyone is provided with what is needed. Human desires that are tied to our hopes and dreams have a way of getting beyond us and when they become excessive, we need words like "greed" to identify and "sin" to condemn them.

The original question was whether science should be trusted with the common good if it is compromised by immense possibilities but confused purposes. Some argue there is no inherent conflict between knowledge for sale and knowledge for the common good.[20] If proper safeguards are in place, a healthy and symbiotic relationship can exist between science and the private sector. Even if we conceded as much, the argument is self-serving, and when has it been a good idea to let the fox guard the hen house? Might we also ask at this junction if theology should play a role by reminding us of things we dare not forget? Society can expect only so much from science. Freeman Dyson is not out of line when he chides science for making technological toys for the rich. But is he being realistic when he asks for a reversal to take place so that "technology is guided by ethics" (*The Sun, the Genome*, 61)? Science is ill equipped and hardly motivated to make social and economic justice a high priority. The fundamental reason science is not so prepared is the way empiricism looks straight ahead in order to solve the next technological problem or undertake the next research project. Scientific rationalism makes it a principle to exclude theological type questions which do not presume to pass the test of experimental verification. Bear in mind that empiricism is the methodology that gave us a universe where causation is blind and matter is pointless. This is not an argument for the superiority of theology—

quite the contrary, because theology is hemmed in by its own methodological limitations.

Once theology is introduced into the mix we are confronted with a subsidiary problem. Is theology up to the task of providing meaning and purpose where science chooses not to go? The wisdom theology might bring to the table is compromised by secularism, relativism, and pluralism, in ways science is not. The integrity of science is most susceptible to the intrusion of market values. Theology (read "religion"), on the other hand, is hapless against the rising tide of relativism, secularism, and pluralism. Unlike science, which wears an aura of objectivity and universality, theological speech is dismissed because it can neither shake the stigma of subjectivity nor rise above its own divisiveness. To listen to theologians is to hear endless disputes, though they be of the highest caliber, and to observe a clashing of absolutes—too many voices claiming too much.

The common threat born of these forces is an "unreflective world setting its own agenda" (Archbishop Rowan Williams). While our expectations of science are modest regarding purpose and meaning, the same is not true of theology. The responsibility theology bears is to speak with a prophetic voice, and in order to do that its voice must be sufficiently distinctive to save it from sounding like a Republican or Democrat campaigning for public office, or the moral voice of Catholicism, or the liberal voice of Protestantism. Here the distinction between theology and religion is critical. When Alan Wolfe speaks of a toothless tiger, he is referring to religion when it "goes along in order to get along." His criticism is not new and was articulated by H. Richard Niebuhr in his classic study of religion and culture, *Christ and Culture*. Niebuhr framed the fundamental tension in its broadest outline: "For Christianity, whether defined as church, creed, ethics, or movement of thought, itself moves between the poles of Christ and culture" (11). Niebuhr then proceeded to probe five possibilities. Bounded on the left by "Christ *against* culture" and on the right by "Christ *of* culture," the center is composed of three models: "Christ *above* culture," Christ and culture *in paradox*," and Christ the *transformer* of culture." At the extremes, the Christian faith either brings radical confrontation to culture or blends faith and culture as mutually supportive. At its core, Christianity neither rejects nor flees from the culture around it. In seminal ways, the New Testament calls Christians to be *in* but not *of* the world. The tension between Christian community and culture never dissipates because commitment to the Center (Christ) bestows a freedom to resist or affirm what is Christ-like in the culture at any particular moment.

For those who are uneasy with assigning to religion the role of supporting what is good in American culture, two leading Christian thinkers, Stanley Hauerwas and William H. Willimon summon Christians to be "alien residents." Christians will always have fundamental quarrels with the powers that be, for theirs is a faith of redemptive suffering for the sake of the powerless. Since Hauerwas and Willimon believe the role of the Church is not to transform American culture, they have sharp words for those congregations who busy themselves with making America a better place in which to live. The faithful church—the confessing church—will find itself confronting "the world with a political alternative the world would not otherwise know" (*Resident Alien*, 41).

Old Testament scholar Walter Brueggemann begins with a similar assessment: "The contemporary American church is so largely enculturated to the American ethos by consumerism that it has little power to believe or to act" (*The Prophetic Imagination*, 11). In the story of Daniel, the choice is between going along with Nebuchadnezzar's three-year training program, which includes a table of rich food fit for a king, or remembering *who* he is by remembering *whose* he is. Daniel chooses to engage in counterculture tactics by refusing the imperial diet and existing on vegetables and water (*Finally Comes the Poet*, chapter 4). Those who choose to be alien residents in a culture aimlessly pursuing limited goals may find that their only recourse is to resist and hope.[21]

The argument I put forward is that theology is singularly equipped and motivated to do what science is not. The strength of religion lies with its ability to create communities which embody collective judgments of what is sacred and thus uniquely valuable. Science has nothing comparable, not even close, to communities of faith which tell meta-stories of sin and redemption and instill them through liturgy. "The power of the great world religions," writes Jonathan Sacks, "is that they are not merely philosophical systems . . . they are embodied truths, made vividly real in lives, homes, congregations, rituals, narratives, songs and prayers" (158). By defining sacred spaces and sacred times, religion resists a world that is continually shaping humanity into its mold (Rom. 12:1). For their part, people of faith must first demonstrate among themselves how different standards of truth can enrich the collective heritage of humankind. Such is the import of Sacks's book, winner of the 2004 Grawemeyer Religion Award. But Sacks does not really wrestle with how ardent believers can be at the same time tolerant of others whose beliefs they regard as untrue. He escapes the clash of different truths by claiming there are no universal religious truths because there is no universal standard of truth, but try telling that to a fundamentalist.[22] Whether there are absolute fundamentals or not, communities and even nations war with each other over the particularities of their religion and culture, and often the two are fused into one belief system. The best kind of religious authority emanates from faith communities that embody what they believe without imposing those beliefs on others. The public says, "Show us the difference faith makes, and we will listen to what you have to say."

Both theology and science speak from traditions that generate truths that are relevant and enduring. Thus far we have discussed their roles as if they were independent of each other. Since the 1960s, a renewed interest has taken place in finding areas of common ground. Theologians and scientists have sought to break lose from their "separate ghettos of knowledge" in order to explore points of contact and shared understandings.[23] The conversation between science and theology has a number of significant hurdles to overcome. Scientists still harbor a deep-seated fear theology will pollute empiricism with speculation, metaphysical abstractions, and supernatural explanations. Theology cannot understand why science is not more amendable to correction by other methodologies which seek a "thicker," more holistic explanation.[24] Putting aside notions of bitter warfare and separate but equal domains, the time has come for theology and science to do better than just coexist. Science and theology will better serve the commons by understanding themselves as counterweights to the other.

For all the ways science and theology enrich culture, each brings its unique excesses: science's fascination with perfection and addiction to an unbridled optimism, religion's slide into intolerance and fanaticism. In this bent to inquire without understanding, to create without purpose, to reach without looking, science is out of balance and a threat to earth and humanity. Reaching the same conclusion, Sherwin B. Nuland, clinical professor of surgery at Yale, asks hopefully if "the moment has finally come when society might reconsider whether the curiosity and enthusiasm of scientists alone should determine the direction of research into certain technologies."[25] Skeptics will complain that theology is a stale witness to a past that is itself irrelevant. But let us not be too quick to dismiss the past. Those who know that we repeat the past are skeptical of a future that always looks promising.[26] History may be a burden we would rather not bother with—too many bodies and too much blood—but ignore it and soon enough the future is your worst nightmare. Caricatures these certainly are, but in both theory and practice, science and theology complete what the other neglects.

Einstein's familiar epigram—"Science without religion is lame, religion without science is blind"—stated that the best one could expect was a reciprocal relationship between disciplines with well-defined functions. The year was 1946. The value of what each could offer to the other depended on clearly established boundaries. For Einstein, the exchange entailed a balancing of weaknesses. The lameness of science is amended by purpose and morality; the blindness of religion is corrected by the rationality of science. But to understand the relationship in this manner, even as the late Stephen J. Gould defended it in *Rock of Ages* (1999), turns theologians and scientists into defenders of their domains. Most theologians are dissatisfied with artificial barriers because the complexity of the universe and life requires explanations that are many layered, or "thick," in order to do justice the richness of the universe.[27] Einstein's overriding conclusion still stands. Science's contribution to the commonwealth is hobbled without moral direction. The more science provides the goods society wants (including military hardware), as it is increasingly inclined to do, the more it needs to listen to a voice declaring that "man does not live by bread alone" (Matt. 4:4). And religious assertions are blind when all authority is assigned to the past. And yet Einstein and Gould followed a well-trodden path without examining the alternative—that in doing what each does *best*, science and theology counterbalance their inherent deficits. It does not fall to religion or theology to tell humans to be less curious. But knowing that we are creatures who are going to overreach should make us a little more cautious. Science will be there to direct our curiosity and theology will be there to remind us of our perpetual history of sin.

Can We Trust Ourselves?

The ponderous and complex issues of a new century are distilled by the question of whether we can trust ourselves. So much depends on the answer. If we cannot trust ourselves, we should be wary of what we might do to our planet and ourselves. If we can, there is little we cannot do. In this book I have asked the reader to rethink sin and evil, and to give it an evolutionary history, and so armed with that understanding to address the growing public debate about what it means to be human. My concluding task is to see how this plays out.

As heirs of an enlightened optimism, we have learned three lessons well. The first is to separate what we can do from what we should do. The second is to reduce truth to its lowest common denominator. And third is to construct political, social, and economic theories dependent on optimistic presumptions about human nature.

Whatever the reasons, philosophy drove a wedge between our ability to do something and our capacity to be responsible. Immanuel Kant may have been the last modern philosopher to posit an immeasurable distance between God and humans. Throughout his three *Critiques*, he seldom misses an opportunity to remind us of everything that God can do and we cannot.[28] Earlier philosophers may have understood the finitude of human knowledge as a problem, Kant did not. But those who followed Kant saw in human reason a stepping-stone to heights heretofore unattainable. They thought its only gain was to assume the responsibility to design our own purposes. Reason is sufficient to establish ends worthy of our striving. Steven Weinberg's forthright conclusion to his survey of what physics can tell us about the cosmos is well known. "The more the universe seems comprehensible, the more it also seems pointless." Weinberg, however, does not step into complete nihilism. Science should be pursed not because we will find purpose written into the universe but because science gives life a purpose. "The effort to understand the universe is one of the few things that lifts human life a little above the level of farce, and gives it some of the grace of tragedy" (*The First Three Minutes*, 154–55). In many respects this is the sum total of modern rationality—a rationality that has no place for sin and evil and no purpose beyond the purpose we create. Consequently, we are left alone to make our way in this universe, and the way we have made thus far does not speak well for our species.

The historical divorce between modern science and theology accounts in large measure for the partition between fact and value, as if facts are without value and value has nothing to do with fact.[29] As modern science grew more confident of its own prowess, it resisted all attempts to admit anything that looked like a supernatural explanation. The divorce between science and religion, signed and sealed by Darwinism, allowed science to be as amoral as it pleased. When theology conceded the factual universe to science,[30] it was left to oversee metaphysical questions of matters increasingly irrelevant to an industrial-atomic era. Time has shown the disastrous result. Isolated into separate domains, religion promulgated moral imperatives but with no relevance to matters scientific. Science grew in stature, assuming the role of queen by laying down the rules governing what counts as knowledge. It may only be perception but it seems the more we are empowered by science, the farther we move from the cautionary restraints of self-knowledge measured against One who is unknowable. The skeptic may ask why it matters, if we answer only to ourselves. Perhaps it would not matter greatly if the "I" or the "we" in question did not have such a grandiose view of himself. But such is not the case and the evidence is a history of doing whatever is possible and believing that it will turn out for the better.

There is no way to put a happy face on this picture, as philosophers have done, with the process of reducing truth to its lowest common denominator. The argument running from the premise that the best truth is a verifiable one effectively reduces what counts as rational.[31] When all truth claims must submit to the test of verifiability, then only those claims with an empirical pedigree have any hope of serving as the common denominator for public agreement. Using this scorecard, scientific rationality is privileged because it is not relative (i.e., culturally determined), while theological language is irrelevant because it is speculative and subjective. Although the claim for a culturally free science is an argument that is increasingly difficult to defend,[32] the lowest common denominator in practice is knowledge with the claim of being *urgent*, *necessary*, and in the *public interest*.

The prestigious *New England Journal of Medicine* does not usually take an editorial stand of a political nature. It did so in the 17 July 2002 issue. Writing for the editors, Jeffrey M. Drazen, M.D., revealed a growing impatience with the non-vote taken by the U.S. House of Representatives and Bush's 2001 executive order limiting stem-cell research to a few already existing lines of cells. "It is reasonable to regulate the technology of somatic-cell nuclear transfer . . . but it is unreasonable to prohibit using this technology." Two reasons are given for lifting federal restrictions inhibiting stem-cell research. One appeals to the urgent need to provide the best possible care for patients. The second refers to the inevitable (necessary) march of science. If not here in the United States, embryonic stem-cell research will be advanced somewhere else. And sure enough, scientists in South Korea announced 12 February 2004 that they had successfully cloned a human embryo and extracted viable stem cells from it (erroneously, we learned later). The moral issue, as Drazen asserts, is the missed opportunity to do the technologically sweet thing for the welfare of the commonwealth. In this short, one-page editorial, Drazen does not raise any further ethical issues, and we can only surmise his reasons. Waiting backstage is a host of professional scientists ready and eager to press on. Researchers do not want to wait for a divided Congress to come to some compromised decision. They are anxious to proceed because theirs is a noble and necessary cause. Consider for a moment, though, the ramifications if scientists in North Korea had made the breakthrough announcement. The question that bothers us most about this scenario is not whether scientists of North Korea are capable of doing good science but whether their motivation and values are acceptable. In this instance urgent, necessary, and relevant seem like a pretext to do what is good for North Korea with little or no regard for anyone else. And as it turns out, pressure and pride to succeed overwhelmed even the best intentions of Hwang Woo Suk and his colleagues.[33]

By asking if we can trust ourselves to do the right thing, we have come full circle to the issue of our human nature. "In various guises and at various times," Matt Ridley observes, "philosophers have argued that man is basically nice if he is not corrupted, or basically nasty if he is not tamed" (*The Origins of Virtue*, 252–62). Thomas Hobbes came down on the side of nastiness. Writing *Leviathan* in the 1650s during a century of interminable religious and political wars, Hobbes saw nothing noble in the savage actions of individuals, governments, or religion. Writing a century later in a very different age, Rousseau held out the hope of living in harmony with nature unless corrupted by the evils of culture. Basically nice and basically nasty are two ways to sum up the human capacity for good and bad but neither is theologically adequate. Christian theology has steadfastly pointed to the human condition underlying all human situations. The reality of sin and evil shuts the door we open every time we think tomorrow will be a better day in the life of humanity. It makes no difference whether we are living in age of dismal failure or great promise, no difference whether we play children's games on an island or come to save them on a warship.

The Enlightenment, with all of its hopes for a rational and sane world, ended with the Holocaust. Contemporary evil, as Susan Neiman so forcefully argues, defies explanation and plays havoc with every presumption that we are rational beings who can progressively plan our future. This is a new century and what makes it new is the ascendancy of biotechnology. No one seems to be drawing the conclusion that genetic engineering is an antidote to evil. But history repeats itself because sin repeats itself. We will most likely ignore the lesson of the atomic bomb: the more we bury our heads in the doing, the less likely we are to ask if we should. To think ethically and to act responsibly means asking *should* we *before* we begin. But that isn't going to happen, neither then nor now. The decision to proceed with the atomic bomb was not devoid of moral considerations but no one fully anticipated the political and social fallout. With hindsight we see the litter of industrial toxins, stockpiles of radioactive waste, more bombs than we know what to do with. We cannot foresee the future but expect more unforeseen, unintended consequences from genetic engineering. Because the doing is always so exhilarating, the chances are very good that we will again choose not to ask about a worse case scenario.

C. S. Lewis's Devil would have much to teach Wormwood about the confluence of science and human nature. Let them build one _____, he would advise, because one will never be sufficient. Nor, as it turned out, would science be content with anything less than a super (hydrogen) bomb. It wasn't science alone. It never is. Political circumstances make it seem necessary for men with dangerous toys to prove their theories correct and their political judgments shrewd.

Dateline *United Church News*, January–February 2004

UCC Members to Commemorate 50th Anniversary of "Bravo" bomb

At least seven United Church of Christ representatives . . . will be among those in the Marshall Islands on March 1 to mark the 50th anniversary of the U.S. government's 1954 detonation of a 15-megaton hydrogen bomb—the largest ever tested.

Known by its codename, "Bravo," the bomb left a mile-wide, 240-foot deep crater and produced a radioactive cloud that reached 20 miles into the atmosphere.

In its wake, the explosion—five time greater than the government had projected—left thousands of first-, second-, and third-generation survivors [Marshall Islands] ill from radioactive effects.

Science and politics only become allies when power is involved. Scientists shun it, and politicians seek it. Where the two meet is during the "handoff." Scientists are not powerless, not any more. They have the information everyone wants, not the least those in political power. The maneuvering to come will make the machinations of atom splitting look crude. The game has become more subtle, but it hasn't changed. Let scientists "play" in their laboratories but when all is said and done, just hand over the goods.

Until just more than a century ago, the medical community was content to cure disease and ease human suffering. But just as one bomb was not enough, neither will one enhancement be enough. A growing number of individuals make their way to a doctor's office dissatisfied with what nature and their own DNA have given them. In their book, *The Pursuit of Perfection: The Promise and Perils of Medical Enhancement*, Sheila and David Rothman warn that we are entering an era when "there is no holding back" the history of enhancement we are now writing. Health is no longer enough. The desires of the heart require hormone replacement therapy, Botox® injections, breasts implants, or growth hormones. Even without science present to overpromise or physicians willing to please, humans are the kind of creature who desire the moon and will not stop until they get it. The power to manipulate genes and the body's chemistry is itself intoxicating, but when coupled with human desires, there is no reason to believe humans will not overreach.

The human nature we cannot fully trust includes the very quest for knowledge. We would not be human without the itch to go "where no man has gone before." If we weren't discontented with the way the world is, restless to the point of wanting to be where we are not, forever creating and discovering something new, the malignant forces of entropy would quickly leave us drowning in the disorder of what transpires when we do nothing. Science is better at scratching that itch than keeping a firm grip on its hubris or amnesia. In our culture's romance with science, curiosity cannot get a bad rap. A time long ago religious authorities warned that unchecked curiosity could lead to no good. Luther and Calvin were inclined to regard scientific curiosity as speculative and secondary. In almost no time at all the religious indictment included the invasion of God's sovereign right to the secrets of his creation. The modern age, so Hans Blumenberg detailed in *The Legitimacy of the Modern Age*, is no less than the legitimatization of theoretical curiosity. We can understand why science challenged the Church's role of conservator of all truth worth knowing but then mistakenly presumed religion is against knowing as such. No less a thinker than St. Thomas Aquinas acknowledged that "the soul has an urge to know about all things," but continued, "which needs to be laudably tempered, lest we stretch out to know beyond due measure" (*Legitimacy*, 332). Today we stumble over "the due measure," because who among us takes to heart St. Augustine's correction that knowledge of the world is of limited value apart from one's salvation? Knowing is a good thing, but when humans make it an end in itself, they corrupt it because they are corruptible.

Is there any human activity more shortsighted and self-invested than politics? There is no end to the ways political theories underestimate or overestimate human nature. In civil matters, the legacy of Hobbes, Locke, and Jefferson includes a good dose of mistrust concerning power and authority and therefore an admonition to write checks and balances into the ordinances of government.[34] The framers of our Constitution made sure to erect fences between state and religion because they were wise enough to know that even God-fearing intentions can lead us astray. Once again in Rwanda and the Sudan we learn that government is needed to tame our nastiness, only to learn it can turn even nastier. In spite of all evidence to the contrary, we dearly hold onto the hope that we are basically good. But what separates Augustine from other political and moral philosophers is the belief that basic goodness is a gift from God, in stark contrast to the goodness of our own doing. The former will keep us humble; the latter will inflate our ego.

Has there ever been an ideology that wasn't optimistic? Even if one does exist, the rhetorical question still serves its purpose. The insidious nature of social and economic ideologies is how they lead us by the nose to the Promised Land when we should know better. The politics of utopia are nothing without the promise of progress. We fall for it every time: there is no today or yesterday, only tomorrow leading to a better tomorrow. Alive within us is a propensity to hope that goodness will return goodness and that self-interests can be balanced against each other. Adam Smith and Karl Marx did not exactly take the high road of human nature. They understood humans to be primarily motivated by self-interest. Smith's guiding belief was that even though individuals were driven by making themselves better off, the aggregate outcome was a collective gain. Smith was right in his realistic assessment: "I have never known much good done by those who affected to trade for the public good." Capitalism succeeds where communism fails because you can count on individuals to diligently work for themselves but not necessarily for the good of the state. But even if there is an "invisible hand" to "promote an end which was not part of his intention," the net result is not a straight road to economic justice for all. Reinhold Niebuhr's assessment of Marxism as only *provisionally* pessimistic holds across the board. A classless society, really! The withering of the state! Give me a break! Based on what reading of human history or human nature did Engels and Marx draw this conclusion? Both were astute readers of the past but their hope for the future was overly optimistic because they had a vision of how human nature could be re-made. And that is what you get, every time, when sin and evil are not worth the bother to consider.

So, what understanding of human nature drives the ideology of globalization? The prevailing optimism is that when market-generated growth and free-market democracy are paired, they will lift everyone's economic boat. What actually happens, according to Yale Law School professor Amy Chua, is a violent backlash against *market-dominant minorities*. And who exactly are the market-dominant minorities? They are the Chinese in Burma and Indonesia, the white descendants of Dutch and French Huguenots settlers in

South Africa, the white commercial farm owners in Zimbabwe, the entrepreneurial Lebanese in Sierra Leone, the well-educated Tutsis in Rwanda. No one is saying globalization will right these long-standing historical wrongs; but at work is an implied faith that if you give an individual the opportunity to work and vote, a kind of equilibrium will be reached. As Chua reads recent history, developing countries are consumed by ethnic violence because when indigenous people see the injustice of their situation, they demand the interlopers and exploiters get out. What is unexplained is why payback time takes the form of such terrible atrocities. "Consider, for example, the brutal takeover of Sierra Leone by diamond-hungry, limb-chopping rebels; or the confiscations of land in Zimbabwe; or the anti-Chinese riots in Indonesia" (*World on Fire*, 263). In each instance the subsequent economic situation grows much worse and poverty increases. What leads anyone to think globalization will tame greed, crony capitalism, or corruption when the players change places? Is there anything about a free-market economy or democracy that ensures profit sharing, generosity, and kindness? Every ideology heightens expectations and leaves matters of justice to take care of themselves. It doesn't work that way because human nature is what it is, and the outcome is not the best we had hoped for but the worst we did not anticipate.

When things go badly, it is naive to place all the blame on the individual. Sin and evil inhabit economic systems just as well. Because no economic system is value neutral, every system must be subjected to moral scrutiny. Adam Smith understood why the law of self-interest must operate under conditions of honesty and fairness; otherwise the temptation to cheat will be too great. Western democracies went the next step and instituted networks to redistribute wealth, such as national health insurance, unemployment benefits, minimum wage laws, antitrust laws, progressive taxation, pension plans, and estate taxes. Democracy, too, is a complicated mix of different branches of government to counteract each other, and all of them under the scrutiny of a free press, public assembly, lawful access to information, constitutional protections of minorities, an independent judiciary, and the ballot box. All of this requires a substantial investment in the common good, lest society fall prey to the jungle law of "me first." So when Chua speaks of a "world on fire," we need to interpret this to mean indigenous people incited by an ideology promising a glory yet to come and greater than anything seen before.

The renewed discussion of dignity and rights as way to define and protect what is human is an admirable move. *Dignity* uncovers "a universally shared participation in morality," and rights solidify what we agree to guarantee as a civilized people. (Kass, *Life, Liberty*, 16). The language of human dignity and rights captures the good we are capable of and should expect of each other. Both concepts are helpful but problematic in what they disregard about human nature. The exemplary declarations of universal rights set forth what we should expect of ourselves as human beings. At the same time by ignoring the reality of sin and evil, as the rhetoric of dignity and rights talk is inclined to do, we equivocate a side of human nature we would rather not look at. Unfortunately, this century has already written a history of blatant and brutal disregard of both human dignity and rights. Yet few are inclined to see in this something fundamental and innate about human nature.

The *idealism* built into the Universal Declaration of Human Rights, adopted and proclaimed by the General Assembly of the United Nations in 1948, leaves the impression that a dawning of a universal morality is right around the corner. No matter what standard of justice one employs, there is no basis to presume that every society or nation can move forward from the present state of affairs, when every present is hobbled by past injustices. This is the experience of South Africa and every nation that suffers atrocities. Universal declarations of human rights guaranteed by nation-states are a starting place, but the cycle of revenge is not so easily satisfied. Such declarations overemphasize positive human characteristics to the neglect of destructive ones. Look closely at what is being said and you find a hidden supposition that we cannot be entirely trusted as a species. Our impulses persistently exceed our self-control and our idealism does little to restore justice.

Fukuyama gives two compelling reasons to resurrect the concept of natural rights and return to a pre-Kantian tradition: (1) "the language of rights has become, in the modern world, the only shared and widely intelligible vocabulary we have for talking about human goods or ends," and (2) the language of human rights serves as "our principal gateway into a discussion of the nature of justice and of those ends we regard as essential to our humanity."[35] Both Fukuyama and Kass are to be commended for countering the entrenched philosophical premise that human nature is so religiously ambiguous, politically contentious, conceptually bankrupt, and lacking in empirical observation that any thought of making it a principal mainstay of one's anthropology should be rejected. But that is exactly what philosopher John Rawls does by sidestepping any discussion of human nature. His theory of justice requires that we blind ourselves to who is getting what goods, but that is patently something we cannot do.[36] So much of the Ten Commandments is premised on what the eye cannot keep from desiring (idols or another person's wife or goods). Moslems more directly remove from the eye what might be tempting. A theory of justice based on fairness and equity is reminiscent of the liberal social contract with its implied principle of trading certain rights for our cooperation in upholding the laws of the land. Fukuyama could not be more correct in his assertion that in spite of the renunciation of all notions of a persistent human nature, philosophers "end up reinserting various assumptions about human nature into their theories" (*Our Posthuman Future*, 120). The bone I am picking is slightly different. How can we talk realistically about justice or fairness without taking into account the evil humans perpetuate while claiming for themselves the high ground of intending to do the right thing?

Under the umbrella of human rights and dignity, much good is protected, but biotechnology and eugenics will bring a different kind of rain. In the West, we have become quite proficient at sheltering the rights and dignity of individuals. Our minds are attuned to ethical protocols and strict procedural guidelines, and progress has been made to protect patient and donor. But what slips under politically correct fences are "the dehumanizing hazards of a Brave New World."[37] We can guard everyone's dignity and violate none of their universal rights while selling them the prospect of a healthier, longer, and more beautiful future with no thought of others who have no future. By making private choice our god, we also make it possible (read "likely") that the suffering we relieve and the science we pursue will benefit those with the highest standard of living. Wisely, Western societies have made the decision to include a broader sense of the common good than the religious. The issue is not only whether religion should be a moral gatekeeper, because it should. This is what religion contributes toward the common good. The role of the theologian is more countercultural: their biblical mandate is to be a distinctive voice, not moralistic per se, but pointedly theological and prophetic.

We are now at that historical moment where we possess the means to shape who we will become. But is this not a phantom, a figment of our overreaching? Anyone who believes sin and evil are here to stay also believes science will do nothing to change human nature. Insert a few genes here, remove a few there, and you do not have a new creature. You may have humans who live longer and healthier lives but continue to do what they always have done, only with more vigor for a longer duration. Science will find a chemical concoction to reduce violence but there will be a price to pay. Along the way we may discover that we have made life very dull and have traded away our self-determination piece by piece. And while we move forward redesigning human behavior, let's include a remedy for envy, lust, avarice, jealousy, pride, and apathy. Even if we have the will to tame our desires, which I thoroughly doubt we do, what makes us think human nature is pieced together in separable parts? What leads us to believe our good intentions and bad intentions can be isolated and worked on independently? Faster than it takes to get a doctor's appointment, goodness can become badness, love can turn to hate, altruism can be corrupted by greed. One slides into the other sometimes without a conscious decision being made, and the mystery of being human lies beyond the reach of a genetic surgeon.

In discussing the deeper sources of sin as we know it today, R. R. Reno looks to acedia rather than pride. Given that acedia has slipped out of our everyday religious vocabulary, Reno describes how we experience it. "Most of us just want to be left alone so that we can get on with our lives. Most of us want to be safe. We want to find a cocoon, a spiritually, psychologically, economically, and physically gated community in which to live without danger and disturbance."[38] I am being cynical but for no reason beyond the fact that it takes more self-discipline than most of us can muster to leave our gated communities of acquaintances to attend to the welfare of total strangers. I empathize with those who think we are basically good. Most days I think the same. But being a good person is not the epitome of what Christ expects of us. Whenever St. Paul speaks of the fruits of the Spirit—and they include love, joy, peace, patience, kindness, goodness, faithfulness, gentleness, and self-control—they are the consequence of a life dead to our past and raised in newness (Rom. 8:4, Gal. 5:22, Col. 1:10). In other words, these fruits are the natural result of a seed planted and nurtured until it reaches maturity.

Paul Sabatier, the first modern biographer of the St. Francis, gives an account of the saint's stages of conversion. Harder than turning his back on evil—a life he no longer found meaningful—was learning to love the unlovable.

> It is far indeed from hatred of evil to love of good. They are more numerous than we think who, after some severe experience, have renounced what the ancient liturgies call "the world," with its pomps and lusts. But the greater number of those who have renounced the world have not at the bottom of their hearts the smallest grain of pure love. (*Road to Assisi*, 16–17)

No longer is it simply a matter of survival—though it remains that for millions who die unnecessarily—but of surviving with style. We should not be too quick to mock style; it is an essential part of how we distinguish ourselves as a species. Style is braiding ribbons in one's hair, adding spices to food, dressing up for special occasions, decorating a home, cultivating flowers, following the fashion of the day, spreading a carefully prepared picnic beneath a tree. We are told by anyone under the age of twenty, "If you ain't got style, you ain't got nothing." Style trumps survival. But along with style comes the siren call to overdo. Because style is so much more interesting than survival, matters of necessity are neglected. Our priorities get turned around and we chase after *needful things* until all that matters is looking better than we ought. Even "better" may not be enough when expectations are raised to ever higher levels. While we are primping and adorning ourselves, the world can go to hell in a handbasket.

The biogenetic gold rush is on and it will consume more research dollars than keeping ourselves safe from weapons of mass destruction. We will continue to rob survival to pay for style and neglect one of the most important moral questions we face: How far will our excessive desires take us? Style becomes excessive when a player is paid millions to hit a ball while a family of five lives on four hundred dollars a year, or when luxury cars are sold with seats that can be cooled as well as heated while children scavenge for enough firewood to cook a meal. Hunger now kills more people in two days than the first two atomic bombs killed. Standing as we do at this crossroad where the choices we make will determine the culture we create, we may yet find the will to feed and shelter every human being but it will require deciding whether technology serves substance or style.

Dateline *Boston Globe*, 8 February 2002

At MIT, a Low-Tech Plan to Save Lives

Nine graduate students from MIT returned from Nepal this week carrying inventions that they hope someday may save tens of thousands of lives by purifying poor people's drinking water.

While some MIT engineers are trying to send a $15 million rocket to Mars, these engineers arriving in Room 1-047 have been trying to build a better water filter for $5 or less.

In Nepal alone, the annual death toll from dirty water is 44,000 children, according to Murcott. So the challenge has been to build a contraption with indigenous materials that will cost $3 to $5, the maximum that Nepali women say they can afford for such a device (David Arnold, B8).

What does the individual do with a surplus of *goodness*? How does one go about investing an excess of compassion, good will, hospitality, or concern for the environment? By excess I mean more goodness than the immediate family-tribe needs with an eye toward the greater good. We look to hospitals, churches, service clubs, school boards, environmental organizations, public service, and institutions like the United Nations. In their various configurations, these institutions function to bank and redistribute goodness. Their stated purpose is not to combat evil but to channel the impulse to do good; however, when evil threatens to overwhelm the goodness of the human heart, standing steadfast are institutions we have created.

What is goodness if it seeks to be seen? The evening news focuses our attention on sin made so visible it cannot be ignored. Good deeds usually go unreported because it makes us feel better to hear how bad off someone else is. For the most part goodness is so ordinary not to call attention to itself, but fail to practice it and its absence is immediately noticed. Like sin, it is woven into the pattern of life we know as character. In Sabatier's biography, the young man Francis was at first content to be a hermit. One day a priest came to the little chapel of Portiuncula and read the words of Jesus speaking: "As you go, proclaim the good news, the kingdom of God has come near. Cure the sick, raise the dead, cleanse the leper, cast out demons." The very next morning St. Francis went to Assisi and began to preach his message of repentance and simplicity. He was astounded that so many stopped to listen. The world would soon be astounded that a love so pure could light so many fires. Sabatier offers an explanation and at moments when cynicism, even nihilism, threatens to overtake us, it rings true.

> It is not easy to realize how many waiting souls there are in this world. The greater number of people passes through life with souls asleep. Yet the instinct for love and for the divine is only slumbering. The human heart so naturally yearns to offer itself up, that we have only to meet along our pathway someone who, doubting neither himself nor us, demands it without reserve, and we yield it to him at once. (45)

Notes

1. Kaan's widely published text was first sung at a service of worship marking Human Rights Day in 1965 and was used for the twenty-fifth anniversary of the United Nations.

2. The report of the President's Council on Bioethics, "Beyond Therapy: Biotechnology and the Pursuit of Happiness" (October 2000). Accessed at www.bioethics.gov/reports.beyondtherapy/index.html.

3. The brief history of artificial intelligence is instructive. The first attempts to build a human-like robot separated mind from body and used the computer as a bridging model. Ann Foerst, with degrees in theology and computer science, recounts why this was a mistaken approach and explains why researchers found it necessary to reframe the question by asking a different question: What can we learn about what it means to be human as we go about building a more human-like robot? The mistake was to miss the fact that for humans knowing is embodied. See her *God in the Machine*.

4. John Polkinghorne, *Science and Christian Belief*, (London: SPCK, 1994) 47.

5. Polkinghorne, "Beyond Darwin," *Christian Century*, 15 November 2005, 26–27.

6. Garreau provides a lengthy description of DARPA in *Radical Evolution*, 22–44.

7. Some of Kurzweil's most ardent critics sound off and Kurzweil replies in *Are We Spiritual Machines? Ray Kurzweil vs. the Critics of Strong AI* (Discovery Institute Press, 2002).

8. While recounting the history of the nature-nurture controversy, Matt Ridley makes good sense in giving both instinct and culture their interactive due. See his *The Agile Gene*.

9. Miroslav Volf has written a more theological book on the same issue of toleration by those who live by deeply held beliefs. See his *Exclusion and Embrace*.

10. Leo Marx, "The Idea of 'Technology' and Postmodern Pessimism," in *Does Technology Drive History?* 241. Italics are mine.

11. Cf. Hans Jonas, who makes a similar assessment in *Imperative*, 7–8.

12. What better indicator, though, of what is different now than the virtual war waged by those who fought to keep the decoding of the human genome public and open and those who could not refrain from keeping it private and for profit? Those who think Craig Venter perfectly illustrates the latter miss the intense struggle he lived through, being pulled in both directions. Read James Shreeve, *The Genome War*.

13. The accent should be placed on what is *new*, for this is a guiding principle behind patent law. See Sheldon Krimsky, *Science in the Private Interest*, 58–66.

14. See Derek Bok, president emeritus of Harvard University, *Universities in the Marketplace: The Commercialization of Higher Education* (Princeton, N.J.: Princeton University Press, 2003).

15. This entire discussion of the shrinking public domain is indebted to Corynne McSherry's *Who Owns Academic Work? Battling for Control of Intellectual Property*.

16. Richard Horton's review of *Science in the Private Interest*, by Sheldon Krimsky, *New York Review of Books*, 11 March 2004, 9.

17. See Krimsky, *Science in the Private Interest*, 45–47.

18. Karen Lebacqz introduces the story of the red hen in her excellent essay in order to raise the possibility of an alternative paradigm for justice, namely that we think in terms of "sharing burdens" rather than "fair shares." See Lebacqz, "Fair Shares: Is the Genome Project Just?" in *Genetics*, 88.

19. Lebacqz, *Genetics*, 99.

20. The dean of Harvard Medical School, Dr. Joseph B. Martin, is taking a cautious

approach with Merck & Co. Construction of the twelve-story Merck facility has begun, located in Boston's Longwood Medical Area. The close proximity to Harvard Medical School, however, is no accident. Dr. Martin had a hand in bringing the first major drug company to Longwood and everyone is expecting a fruitful synergy.

21. From a different perspective, David Tracy, a Roman Catholic theologian, sees no alternative except for Christians to live a life of resistance and hope. See his *Plurality and Ambiguity*, 110. Resistance and hope may be the best we can do when one knows he cannot prevail against evil.

22. For a very different approach see S. Mark Heim, who argues that tolerance and understanding result from the appreciation of the *particularity* of another's truth. See Heim, *Salvation: Truth and Difference in Religion* (Maryknoll, N.Y.: Orbis, 1995), and *The Depth of the Riches: A Trinitarian Theology of Religious Ends* (Grand Rapids, Mich.: Eerdmans, 2001).

23. Ted Peters, ed., *Science and Theology: The New Consonance*, 1.

24. John Polkinghorne, scientist and theologian, is the most vociferous proponent of "thicker" accounts. He is by no means the only theologian who advocates a more holistic approach to a coherent universe since it is almost universal among those interested in a renewed conversation with science. See his *Science and The Trinity: The Christian Encounter with Reality*, chapter 4, "Theological Thickness."

25. Sherwin B. Nuland's review of *The Pursuit of Perfection: The Promise and Perils of Medical Enhancement*, by Sheilia M. Rothman and David J. Rothman in the *New York Review of Books*, 13 February 2004, 35.

26. Archbishop Rowan Williams serves up a theological approach to history but there is nothing anachronistic about the reasons he gives for why we need to study history. See his *Why Study the Past?* (Grand Rapids, Mich.: Eerdmans, 2005).

27. Polkinghorne and Welker in *The End of the World and the Ends of God*, 11.

28. See Susan Neiman for her discussion of Kant, *Evil*, 57–84.

29. The philosopher Hilary Putnam takes issue with the idea that while factual claims can be rationally established, value claims are wholly subjective. See his *The Collapse of the Fact/Value Dichotomy* (Cambridge, Mass.: Harvard University Press, 2002).

30. Quite some time ago Langdon Gilkey stated clearly and frankly the moment when religion could no longer compete with science when it comes to objective facts. For Gilkey that moment was 1830, the publication of Charles Lyell's *Principle of Geology*. See Gilkey, *Religion and the Scientific Future* (New York: Harper and Row, 1970), 14.

31. Amartya Sen is one of the few economists who care about the justice of economic theories. He has also written one of the best discussions of what is wrong with narrow notions of rationality. See his first chapter in *Rationality and Freedom* (Cambridge, Mass.: Belknap Press, 2002).

32. See *The One Culture?* eds. Jay A. Labinger and Harry Collins.

33. The Korean stem-cell scandal must be seen against the backdrop of a government that provided $65 million to encourage Hwang's promising research. It should be noted that it was other Korean scientists who were the first to question the results.

34. See Mark Ellingsen, *Blessed Are the Cynical: How Original Sin can make America a Better Place* (Grand Rapids, Mich.: Brazos Press, 2003).

35. Fukuyama, *Posthuman*, 108; cf. Kass, *Life, Liberty*, 15–22.

36. See his *A Theory of Justice* (Cambridge, Mass.: Harvard University Press, 2001) and *Justice as Fairness* (Cambridge, Mass.: Harvard University Press, 1971).

37. See Kass for his discussion of this topic in *Life, Liberty*, 17–22.

38. Reno, "Fighting the Noonday Devil," *First Things* 135 (August–September 2003): 32.

Selected Bibliography

Aichele, George Jr. *The Limits of Story*. Philadelphia: Fortress Press, 1985.
Alder, Ken. *The Measure of All Things*. New York: Free Press/Simon and Schuster, 2002.
Ambrose, Stephen E. *Undaunted Courage*. New York: Simon and Schuster, 1996.
Anderson, Gary A. "Necessarium Adae Peccatum: The Problem of Original Sin." In *Sin, Death and the Devil*, edited by Carl E. Braaten and Robert W. Jenson. Grand Rapids, Mich.: Wm. B. Eerdmans, 2000, 22–44.
Angell, Marcia. *Science on Trial*. New York: W. W. Norton, 1996.
Arendt, Hannah. *Eichmann in Jerusalem*: New York: Viking, 1963.
Armstrong, Karen. *A Short History of Myth*. Edinburgh: Canongate Books, 2005.
Baldi, Pierre. *The Shattered Self: The End of Natural Evolution*. Cambridge, Mass.: MIT Press, 2001.
Barth, Karl. *Church Dogmatics*, vol. 3. Edinburgh: T&T Clark, 1961, 3.
Becker, Ernest. *The Denial of Death*. New York: Free Press/Macmillan, 1973.
Behr, Peter, and April Witt. "The Fall of Enron." *Washington Post*, 28 July 2002, A16.
Berger, Peter. *The Heretical Imperative*. Garden City, N.Y.: Anchor/Doubleday, 1979.
Berry, Wendell. *What Are People For?* New York: North Point Press, 1990.
Blumenberg, Hans. *The Legitimacy of the Modern Age*. Translated by Robert M. Wallace. Cambridge, Mass.: MIT Press, 1983.
Borgmann, Albert. *Holding On to Reality*. Chicago: University of Chicago Press, 1999.
Braaten, Carl E., and Robert W. Jenson. *Sin, Death and the Devil*. Grand Rapids, Mich.: Wm. B. Eerdmans, 2000.
Brooks, Harvey. *The Government of Science*. Cambridge, Mass.: MIT Press, 1968.
Brown, Donald E. *Human Universals*. New York: McGraw-Hill, 1991.
Brown, James Robert. *Who Rules in Science?* Cambridge, Mass.: Harvard University Press, 2001.
Brown, Warren, Nancey Murphy, and H. Newton Malony, eds. *Whatever Happened to the Soul?* Minneapolis, Minn.: Fortress Press, 1998.
Brueggemann, Walter. *Finally Comes the Poet*. Minneapolis, Minn.: Fortress Press, 1989.

———. *The Prophetic Imagination*. Philadelphia: Fortress Press, 1978.
Buchanan, John. "The Human Condition." *Christian Century*. 27 February–6 March 2003, 3.
Burling, Robbins. *The Talking Ape: How Language Evolved*. Oxford: Oxford University Press, 2005.
Campbell, Will D. *Brother to a Dragonfly*. New York: Continuum, 2000.
Chua, Amy. *World on Fire*. New York: Anchor Books/Random House, 2003.
Collins, Robin. "Evolution and Original Sin." In *Perspectives on an Evolving Creation*, edited by Keith B. Miller. Grand Rapids, Mich.: Wm. B. Eerdmans, 2003, 469–501.
Crossan, John D. *The Dark Interval*. Allen, Tex.: Argus Communications, 1975.
Dallaire, Roméo. *Shake Hands with the Devil: The Failure of Humanity in Rwanda*. Toronto, Canada: Random House, 2003.
Davis, Nuel Pharr. *Lawrence and Oppenheimer*. New York: Da Capo Press, 1986.
Dawkins, Richard. *Unweaving the Rainbow*. Boston: Houghton Mifflin, 1998.
de Waal, Frans. *Good Natured: The Origins of Right and Wrong in Humans and Other Animals*. Cambridge, Mass.: Harvard University Press, 1996.
Delbanco, Andrew. *The Death of Satan*. New York: Farrar, Straus & Giroux, 1995.
Dennett, Daniel C. *Darwin's Dangerous Idea*. New York: Simon & Schuster, 1995.
———. *Freedom Evolves*. New York: Viking, 2003.
Dick, Philip K. *Do Androids Dream of Electric Sheep?* New York: Ballantine Books/Random House, 1968.
Dyson, Freeman J. *Disturbing the Universe*. New York: Harper & Row, 1979.
———. *The Sun, the Genome, and the Internet*. New York: New York Public Library and Oxford University Press, 1999.
Ellingsen, Mark. *Blessed Are the Cynical: How Original Sin Can Make America a Better Place*. Grand Rapids, Mich.: Brazos Press, 2003.
Ellvl, Jacques. *The Humiliation of the World*. Grand Rapids, Mich.: Wm. B. Eerdmans, 1985.
Fasching, Darrell J. *Narrative Theology after Auschwitz*. Minneapolis, Minn.: Augsburg Fortress Press, 1992.
Feynman, Richard. *The Meaning of It All: Thoughts of a Citizen Scientist*. Reading, Mass.: Addison-Wesley, 1993.
———. *The Pleasure of Finding Things Out*. Cambridge, Mass.: Perseus, 1999.
Foerst, Anne. *God in the Machine*. New York: Dutton/Penguin, 2004.
Foucault, Michel. *The Foucault Reader*. Edited by Paul Rabinow. New York: Pantheon Books, 1984.
———. *The Order of Things: An Archaeology of the Human Sciences*. New York: Vintage/Random House, 1994.
Fowler, Jim, and Sam Keen. *Life Maps: Conversations on the Journey of Faith*. Waco: Word Books, 1978.
Friedman, Thomas L. *The Lexus and the Olive Tree*. New York: Farrar, Straus & Giroux, 1999.

Fukuyama, Francis. *The End of History and the Last Man*. New York: Free Press/Macmillan, 1992.

———. *Our Posthuman Future: Consequences of the Biotechnology Revolution*. New York: Farrar, Straus & Giroux, 2002.

Fuller, Steve. *The Governance of Science*. Buckingham/Philadelphia: Open University Press, 2000.

Garreau, Joel. *Radical Evolution*. New York: Doubleday/Random House, 2004.

Geertz, Clifford. *Available Light: Anthropological Reflections on Philosophical Topics*. Princeton: Princeton University Press, 2000.

Glover, Jonathan. *Humanity: A Moral History of the Twentieth Century*. New Haven: Yale University Press, 1999.

Gobodo-Madikizela, Pumla. *A Human Being Died That Night*. Boston: Houghton Mifflin, 2003.

Golding, William. *Lord of the Flies*. Biographical and critical note by E. L. Epstein. New York: Capricorn Books, 1954.

Goodall, Jane. *The Chimpanzzes of Gombe*. Cambridge, Mass.: Belknap Press of Harvard University Press, 1986.

Gordon, Mary. *Pearl*. New York: Pantheon Books/Random House, 2005.

Gould, Stephen J. *Rock of Ages*. New York: Ballantine Publishing Group, 1999.

Grant, George P. *Technology and Justice*. Notre Dame, Ind.: University of Notre Dame Press, 1986.

Greenberg, Daniel S. *The Politics of Pure Science*. New York: New American Library, 1967.

———. *Science, Money, and Politics: Political Triumph and Ethical Erosion*. Chicago: University of Chicago Press, 2001.

Gregersen, Niels Henrik, and J. Wentzel van Huyssteen, eds. *Rethinking Theology and Science: Six Models for the Current Dialogue*. Grand Rapids, Mich.: Wm. B. Eerdmans, 1998.

Gustafson, James M. *An Examined Faith: the Grace of Self-Doubt*. Minneapolis, Minn.: Fortress Press, 2004.

Hamer, Dean. *The God Gene: How Faith Is Hardwired into Our Genes*. New York: Random House/Anchor Books, 2004.

Harris, Sam. *The End of Faith*. New York: W. W. Norton, 2005.

Hart, David Bentley. *The Beauty of the Infinite: The Aesthetics of Christian Truth*. Grand Rapids, Mich.: Wm. B. Eerdmans, 2003.

———. *The Doors of the Sea. Where Was God in the Tsunami?* Grand Rapids, Mich.: Wm. B. Eerdmans, 2005.

Hauerwas, Stanley. *With the Grain of the Universe*. Grand Rapids, Mich.: Brazos Press, 2001.

Hauerwas, Stanley, Richard Bondi, and David B. Burrell. *Truthfulness and Tragedy: Further Investigations in Christian Ethics*. Notre Dame: University of Notre Dame Press, 1977.

Hauerwas, Stanley, and William H. Willimon. *Resident Aliens*. Nashville: Abingdon Press, 1989.

Hayles, Katherine N. *How We Became Posthuman*. Chicago: University of Chicago Press, 1999.
Haynes, Roslynn D. *From Faust to Strangelove: Representations of the Scientist in Western Literature*. Baltimore: Johns Hopkins University Press, 1994.
Herken, Gregg. *Brotherhood of the Bomb. The Tangled Lives and Loyalties of Robert Oppenheimer, Ernest Lawrence, and Edward Teller*. New York: Henry Holt, 2002.
Hershberg, James G. *James B. Conant: Harvard to Hiroshima and the Making of the Nuclear Age*. Stanford: Stanford University Press, 1993.
Hertz, Joseph H. *The Pentateuch and Haftaroths*. 2nd ed. London: Soncino Press, 1961.
Hitt, Jack. "Battlefield: Space." *New York Magazine*, 5 August 2001, 31–63.
Hodgson, Peter. *God in History*. Nashville: Abingdon, 1989.
Holton, Gerald. *Einstein, History, and Other Passions*. Reading, Mass.: Addison-Wesley, 1996.
Horton, Richard. Review of *Science in the Private Interest: Has the Lure of Profits Corrupted Biomedical Research?* by Sheldon Krimisky. *New York Review of Books*, 11 March 2004, 7–9.
Hughes, Thomas P. *Human-Built Word: How to Think about Technology and Culture*. Chicago: University of Chicago Press, 2004.
Hunsinger, George. *Disruptive Grace: Studies in the Theology of Karl Barth*. Grand Rapids, Mich.: Eerdmans, 2000.
Hunter, James Davison. *Culture Wars: The Struggle to Define America*. New York: Basic Books/HarperCollins, 1991.
Huxley, Aldous. *Brave New World*. New York: HarperCollins, 1998.
Jenson, Robert W. "Introduction: Much Ado about Nothingness." In *Sin, Death and the Devil*, edited by Carl E. Braaten and Robert W. Jenson. Grand Rapids, Mich.: Wm. B Eerdmans, 2000, 1–6.
———. *Systematic Theology*. 2 vols. Oxford: Oxford University Press, 1999.
Johnson, George. *Shortcut Through Time*. New York: Alfred A. Knopf, 2004.
Jonas, Hans. *The Imperative of Responsibility: In Search of an Ethics for the Technological Age*. Chicago: University of Chicago Press, 1984.
———. "Toward a Philosophy of Technology." *Hastings Center Report* 9, no. 1 (February 1979): 34–43.
Kanon, Joseph. *The Good German*. New York: Henry Holt, 2001.
Kass, Leon R. *Life, Liberty and the Defense of Dignity: The Challenge for Bioethics*. San Francisco: Encounter Books, 2002.
———. *Toward a More Natural Science*. New York: Macmillan, 1985.
Keller, Evelyn Fox. *Making Sense of Life: Explaining Biological Development with Models, Metaphors, and Machines*. Cambridge, Mass.: Harvard University Press, 2002.
Kenseth, Arnold. *Sabbaths, Sacraments, and Season*. Amherst, Mass.: Windhover Press, 1982.
Keynes, Randal. *Darwin, His Daughter and Human Evolution*. New York: Riverhead Books, 2002.

King, Stephen. *Needful Things*. New York: Penguin Books, 1991.
Kohák, Erazim. *The Embers and the Stars*. Chicago: University of Chicago Press, 1984.
Kramer, Peter D. *Listening to Prozac*. New York: Penguin Books/Viking, 1993.
Krimsky, Sheldon. *Science in the Private Interest*. Lanham, Md.: Rowman & Littlefield, 2003.
Kurtz, Paul, ed. *Science and Religion: Are They Compatible?* Amherst, N.Y.: Prometheus Books, 2003.
Labinger, Jay A., and Harry Collins. *The One Culture? A Conversation about Science*. Chicago: University of Chicago Press, 2001.
Langewiesche, William. "Columbia's Last Flight." *Atlantic Monthly*, November 2003, 58–87.
Lears, Jackson. Review of *Hellfire Nation*, by James A. Morone. *The New Republic*, 30 June 2002, 27–32.
Lebacqz, Karen. "Fair Shares: Is the Genome Project Just?" *Genetics*, edited by Ted Peters. Cleveland: Pilgrim Press, 1998, 82–107.
Levi, Primo. *Survival in Auschwitz*. New York: Collier Books/Touchstone, 1958.
Levinas, Emmanuel. "Transcendence and Evil." In *The Phenomenology of Man and of the Human Condition*, edited by Anna-Teresa Tymienicka: Dordrecht, Holland: E. Reidel, 1983.
Lewontin, Richard. "The Politics of Science." *New York Review*, 9 May 2002, 28–31.
Lincoln, Brue. *Holy Terrors*. Chicago: University of Chicago Press, 2003.
Lindbeck, George A. *The Nature of Doctrine*. Philadelphia: Westminster Press, 1984.
Lonergan, Bernard. *Method In Theology*. Minneapolis, Minn.: Winston Press, 1979.
MacIntyre, Alasdair. *Whose Justice? Which Rationality?* Notre Dame: University of Notre Dame Press, 1988.
Marx, Leo. "The Idea of 'Technology' and Postmodern Pessimism." In *Does Technology Drive History?* edited by Merritt Roe Smith and Leo Marx. Cambridge, Mass.: MIT Press, 1994, 237–57.
McKenny, Gerald P. *To Relieve the Human Condition*. Albany: State University of New York Press, 1997.
McKibben, Bill. *Enough*. New York: Times Books/Holt, 2003.
McSherry, Corynne. *Who Owns Academic Work? Battling for Control of Intellectual Property*. Cambridge, Mass.: Harvard University Press, 2001.
Meilaender, Gilbert. "Designing Our Descendants." *First Things* 109 (January 2001): 25–28.
———. *Things That Count*. Wilmington, Del.: ISI Books, 2000.
Migliore, Daniel L. *Faith Seeking Understanding*. Grand Rapids, Mich.: Wm. B. Eerdmans, 1991.
Mithen, Steven. *The Prehistory of the Mind*. New York: Thames and Hudson, 1996.
Mohrmann, Margaret E. "Professing Medicine Faithfully: Theological Resources for Trying Times." *Theology Today* (October 2002): 355–68.
Moltmann, Jürgen. *Science and Wisdom*. Minneapolis: Fortress Press, 2003.

Morone, James A. *Hellfire Nation: The Politics of Sin in American History*. New Haven: Yale University Press, 2003.
Mouw, Richard J. *He Shines in All That's Fair*. Grand Rapids, Mich.: Eerdmans, 2001.
Neiman, Susan. *Evil in Modern Thought*. Princeton: Princeton University Press, 2002.
Niebuhr, H. Richard. *Christ and Culture*. New York: Harper and Brothers, 1951.
Niebuhr, Reinhold. *Justice and Mercy*. New York: Harper & Row, 1974.
———. *The Nature and Destiny of Man*. vol. 1 and 2. New York: Charles Scribner's Sons, 1941.
Nouwen, Henri J. M. *Adam: God's Beloved*. Maryknoll, N.Y.: Orbis Books, 1997.
———. *The Return of the Prodigal Son*. New York: Doubleday, 1992.
Nouwen, Henri J. M., Donald P. McNeill, and Douglas A. Morrison. *Compassion: A Reflection on the Christian Life*. New York: Doubleday, 1983.
Nuland, Sherewin B. Review of the *Pursuit of Perfection: The Promise and Perils of Medical Enchancement*, by Sheilia M. Rothman and David J. Rothman. *New York Review of Books*, 13 February 2004, 32–35.
Oppenheimer, J. Robert. *Letters and Recollections*. Edited by Alice K. Smith and C. Winer. Cambridge, Mass.: Harvard University Press, 1980.
———. *The Open Mind*. Edited by G. C. Rota, N. Metropolis, and D. Sharp. New York: Simon & Schuster, 1955.
———. *Physics in the Contemporary World*. Cambridge, Mass.: MIT Press, 1947.
———. *Some Reflections on Science and Culture*. Chapel Hill: University of North Carolina, 1960.
———. *Uncommon Sense*. Edited by N. Metropolis, G. C. Rota, and D. Sharp. Boston: Birkhäuser, 1984.
Orr, Allen H. Review of the *Blank Slate: The Modern Denial of Human Nature*. *New York Review of Books*, 27 February 2003, 17–20.
Pannenberg, Wolfhard. *What Is Man?* Translated by Duane A. Priebe. Philadelphia: Fortress Press, 1970.
Peck, Scott. *People of the Lie*. New York: Simon & Schuster, 1983.
———. *The Road Less Traveled*. New York: Simon & Schuster, 1978.
Percy, Walker. *The Message in the Bible*. New York: Farrar, Straus and Giroux, 1954.
Peters, Ted, ed. *Science and Theology: The New Consonance*. Boulder, Colo.: Westview Press, 1998.
Peters, Ted. *Sin: Radical Evil in Soul and Society*. Grand Rapids, Mich.: Wm. B. Eerdmans, 1994.
Pinker, Steven. *The Blank Slate: The Modern Denial of Human Nature*. New York: Viking, 2002.
Placher, William C. Review of *Evil in Modern Thought* by Susan Neiman. *Christian Century*, 5 April 2002, 38–40.
———. *Unapologetic Theology*. Louisville, Ky.: Westminister/John Knox Press, 1989.
Polkinghorne, John. "Beyond Darwin." *Christian Century*, 15 November 2005, 25–28.

———. *The God of Hope and the End of the World.* New Haven: Yale University Press, 2003.

———. *Science and the Trinity.* New Haven: Yale University Press, 2004.

Polkinghorne, John and Michael Welker, eds. *The End of the World and The Ends of God.* Harrisburg, Pa.: Trinity Press International, 2000.

Postman, Neil. *Technopoly: The Surrender of Culture to Technology.* New York: Vintage Books/Random House, 1993.

President's. Council on Bioethics. "Biotechnology and the Pursuit of Happiness," October 2000. Accessed at www.bioethics.gov/reports/beyondtherapy/index.html

Preston, Richard. *The Demon in the Freezer.* New York: Random House, 2002.

Primo, Levi. *Survival in Auschwitz.* New York: Touchstone/Simon & Shuster, 1958.

Rahner, Karl. *Foundations of the Christian Faith.* New York: Seabury Press, 1978.

Rees, Martin J. *Our Final Century: A Scientist's Warning: How Terror, Error, and Environmental Disaster Threaten Humankind's Future in This Century—on Earth and Beyond.* London: Heinemann, 2003.

Reich, Robert B. *The Future of Success.* New York: Alfred A. Knopf, 2001.

Reno, R. R. "Fighting the Nooday Devil." *First Things* (August–September 2003): 31–36.

———. *In the Ruins of the Church.* Grand Rapids, Mich.: Brazos Press, 2002.

Rhodes, Richard. *The Making of the Atomic Bomb.* New York: Simon & Schuster, 1986.

Ricoeur, Paul. *The Symbolism of Evil.* Boston: Beacon, 1967.

Ridley, Matt. *The Agile Gene: How Nature Turns on Nurture.* New York: HarperCollins, 2003.

———. *The Origins of Virtue: Human Instincts and the Evolution of Cooperation.* New York: Viking, 1997.

Rothman, Shelia M., and David J. Rothman. *The Pursuit of Perfection: The Promise and Perils of Medical Enhancement.* New York: Pantheon Books, 2003.

Rorty, Richard. *Truth and Progress.* Vol. 3 Philosophical Papers. Cambridge: Cambridge University Press, 1998.

———. *Truth and Progress.* Cambridge: Cambridge University Press, 1998.

Rosenbaum, Ron. "Degrees of Evil." *Atlantic Monthly*, February 2002, 63–68.

Rousseau, Jean-Jacques. *Emile, or on Education.* Translated and introduction by Allan Bloom. New York: Basic Books, 1979.

Sabatier, Paul. *The Road to Assisi: The Essential Biography of St. Francis.* Edited and introduction by Jon M. Sweeney. Brewster, Mass.: Paraclete Press, 2003.

Sacks, Jonathan. *The Dignity of Difference.* London: Continuum, 2002.

Sandel, Michael J. "The Case against Perfection." *Atlantic Monthly*, April 2004, 51–62.

Schweber, S. S. *In the Shadow of the Bomb: Bethe, Oppenheimer, and the Moral Responsibility of the Scientist.* Princeton: Princeton University Press, 2000.

Sereny, Gitta. *Albert Speer: His Battle with Truth.* New York: Alfred A. Knopf, 1995.

Shea, John. *Stories of God: An Unauthorized Biography.* Chicago: Thomas More Press, 1978.

Shelley, Mary. *Frankenstein*. Edited and an introduction by Maurice Hindel. New York: Penguin Books, 1992.
Shermer, Michael. *The Science of God and Evil*. New York: Henry Holt, 2004.
Shreeve, James. *The Genome War*. New York: Ballantine Books/Random House, 2004.
Shuman, Joel. "Desperately Seeking Perfection: Christian Discipleship and Medical Ethics." *Christian Bioethics* 5, no. 2 (1999): 139–53.
Silver, Leo M. *Remaking Eden: Cloning and Beyond in a Brave New World*. New York: Avon Books/Hearst, 1997.
Simmons, Philip. *Learning to Fall: The Blessings of an Imperfect Life*. New York: Bantam Books/Random House, 2002.
Singer, Peter. *The Expanding Circle: Ethics and Sociobiology*. New York: Farrar, Straus & Giroux, 1981.
———. *One World: The Ethics of Globalization*. New haven: Yale University Press, 2002.
Skinner, B. F. *Walden Two*. New York: Macmillan Paperbacks, 1962.
Smith, Alice K. *A Peril and a Hope: The Scientists' Movement in America, 1945–47*. Chicago: University of Chicago Press, 1965.
Smith, Gina. *The Genomics Age: How DNA Technology is Transforming the Way We Live and Who We Are*. New York: AMACOM-American Management Assoc., 2005.
Smith, Shelton H. *Changing Conceptions of Original Sin*. New York: Charles Scribner's Sons, 1955.
Sontag, Susan. *Regarding the Pain of Others*. New York: Picador/Farrar, Straus & Giroux, 2004.
Soskice, Janet. "The Ends of Man and the Future of God." In *The End of the World and the Ends of God*, edited by John Polkinghorne and Michael Welker. Harrisburg, Pa.: Trinity Press International, 2000, 78–87.
Soyinka, Wole. *Climate of Fear*. New York: Random House, 2005.
Steiner, George. *Errata*. New Haven: Yale University Press, 1997.
Stock, Gregory. *Redesigning Humans: Our Inevitable Genetic Future*. Boston: Houghton Mifflin, 2002.
Taylor, Barbara Brown. *Speaking of Sin: The Lost Language of Salvation*. Cambridge, Mass.: Cowley, 2000.
Taylor, Charles. *Sources of the Self*. Cambridge, Mass.: Harvard University Press, 1989.
Thiemann, Ronald F. *Revelation and Theology: The Gospel as Narrated Promise*. Notre Dame: University of Notre Dame Press, 1895.
Tickle, Phyllis A. *Greed*. New York: Oxford University Press, 2004.
Volf, Miroslav. *Exclusion and Embrace*. Nashville: Abingdon Press, 1996.
Ward, Graham. *Barth, Derrida and the Language of Theology*. Cambridge: Cambridge University Press, 1995.
Watson, Bruce. "Sounding the Alarm." *Smithsonian*, September 2002, 115–17.
Weinberg, Steven. *The First Three Minutes*. New York: Basic Books, 1977.
———. "Physics and History." In *The One Culture?* edited by Jay A. Labinger and Harry Collins. Chicago: University of Chicago, 2001, 116–27.

Weisskopf, Victor F. "The Privilege of Being a Physicist." *Physics Today* (February 2003): 48–52.

William, Rosalind. "The Political and Feminist Dimensions of Technological Determinism." In *Does Technology Drive History?* edited by Merritt Roe Smith and Leo Marx, 217–35. Cambridge, Mass.: MIT Press, 217–35.

Williams, Bernard. *Truth and Truthfulness*. Princeton: Princeton University Press, 2002.

Williams, Patricia A. *Doing Without Adam and Eve: Sociobiology and Original Sin*. Minneapolis, Minn.: Fortress Press.

Wills, Garry. *Saint Augustine's Sin*. New York: Viking/Penguin, 2003.

Wilson, Edward O. *The Future of Life*. New York: Alfred A. Knopf, 2002.

Wink, Walter. *The Powers That Be*. New York: Galilee Doubleday, 1998.

Winner, Langdon. *Autonomous Technology: Technics-out-of-Control as a Theme in Political Thought*. Cambridge, Mass.: MIT Press, 1977.

Wolf, Alan. *The Transformation of American Religion*. New York: Free Press, 2003.

Wolterstorff, Nicholas. *Until Justice and Peace Embrace*. Grand Rapids, Mich.: Wm. B. Eerdmans, 1983.

Zagorin, Perez. *Francis Bacon*. Princeton: Princeton University Press, 1998.

Zoloth-Dorfma, Laurie. "Mapping the Normal Human Self: The Jew and the Mark of Otherness." In *Genetics*, edited by Ted Peters. Cleveland: Pilgrim Press, 1998, 180–97.

Subject Index

Atomic bomb: new opportunity, 46, 48; President Truman, 50–51, 55–57, 68; protests, 50, 52, 55; Trinity test, 48, 50
Atomic Energy Commission, 63–64

Biotechnology: different from physics, 83–86; dominant position, 6, 79, 83–86, 113–15; globalization, 91, 95; as positive science, 90, 264; profit motive, 95–98
Boundary issues: human vs. machine, 103–6; natural vs. artificial, 101–3; real vs. virtual, 109–110; risk vs. reward, 110–13; therapy vs. enhancement, 106–9

Conclusions, 21, 65–75, 113, 217–18, 242–43, 245–50, 278–79
Creation, goodness of, 29, 135, 157n4

Desire, 16, 167, 175, 177, 179, 235, 241, 274; to know all things, 2, 10, 173, 179, 224–25, 242; for perfection 233–34

The end of fate, 5–6, 8, 13
Evil: cosmic, 134, 149, 195; degrees of, 143; evil not sin, 130–36; good and evil, 29, 134, 136, 208; Lisbon earthquake, 22, 140–44; modern (Auschwitz and Hiroshima), 22, 141–46, 272; natural vs. moral, 21–22, 40–41; nature not evil, 133–34; powers and principalities, 137

The 'Fall' (interpretation of Gen. 3), 25, 173–80
Federation of Atomic Scientists, 52, 63; Bulletin of Atomic Scientists, 63, 65
Frankenstein, 238. *See also* Shelley, Mary; Haynes, Roslynn

Globalization, 91–95, 249, 253, 260, 275–76
Grace, common, 29, 172; God's grace, 134, 165–66
GRIN technologies, 251; curve of evolution, 252; geeks and naturalists, 254

Human Genome Project (HGP), 61, 69, 227, 234; DNA lines, 91, 227–28
Human nature: altruism, 3, 14, 24, 193–94, 211–12, 252; blank slate, 8, 154; capacity as different from abilities, 197–202, 205; capacity for self-denial, 203; capacity for self-doubt, 184, 202; capacity for truth-seeking, 203; cognitive fluidity, 201; genetic determination, 7–8,

13, 19, 24, 27; overreaching, 2, 229, 233, 241; philosophies of, 7, 170.

Knowledge: benign and lethal, 89–91; dual use, 62, 89, 256; good and evil, 61–62, 89–91, 256–57; intrinsically good, 60–62, 73, 227; responsible stewardship, 65, 117, 264

Manhattan Project, 50, 53, 57, 63, 65, 68, 71, 72
Moral complexity and ambiguity, 98–101
Moral escalator, expanding circle, 13–14, 168, 252

Original sin, 3, 21, 29, 39n24, 134–36, 162, 171, 174, 191, 200

President's Council on Bioethics, 241, 250

Religion, 8, 10; enculturated, 258, 266; guardian of, 4, 9, 28, 274, 278; not paired with science, 250–51, 266; skeptical of, 257; strength of, 101, 267
Revelation: being put to the question, 178–79, 184, 199; as disruptive grace, 162, 171, 179, 183, 186n11; general vs. special, 161; as news from across the sea, 162–66

Shalom, 40n28, 225
Science: curiosity, 4, 238, 245n23, 268, 269, 274; desperately seeking perfection, 233–38; disinterested knowledge, 97, 115–16, 119, 260–61; ending of an era, 83; globalization, 91–95; growth and change, 5, 79–83, 113–15; intellectual property rights, 260; knowledge for sale, 115, 265; profit motive, 95–98, 262; proper role of, 67, 69, 121; as social problem, 117–20; unbridled optimism, 228–33, 242, 269

Science and government: implied contract between, 47, 63–64, 68; replacement war, 81, 97; shift in funding, 80–83, 92–94, 114; wall of separation, 80, 83, 90, 116
Scientists: autonomous but beholden, 63–65, 67; self-conscious, 48–51, 66; optimist, 60, 106, 254–55, 259; and politics, 80–83, 92–95; socially responsible, 51–54, 70; visionary, 54–59, 258, 261
Self-transcendence, definition, 3, 180, 196, 199; as blessing and burden, 180–83, 200; capacity for, 175, 191, 194, 197, 198–99; transcending ourselves, 251–57
Sin: Augustine's understanding of, 20, 40n33, 274–75; corruption, 29, 149; innate (biological), 23–24, 26, 193, 211, 217–18 (*see also* human nature, genetic determinism); narrative quality, 146–48; ontological and not epistemological, 169–71; politicized, 137–38 (*see also* Morone, James); as self-deception, 182–83, 196, 215; sin not evil, 130–40; sin not sins, 20–21, 38, 148–50; total depravity, 171–73; uniquely Christian (no exit), 165–73; vertical dimension, 112, 161, 165, 182–83, 206, 215
Soul, 166, 190–92, 216, 219n2

Theology: common good, 28; methodology, 4, 10, 24, 37n2; proper role, 28, 266–69
Theology and science: common good, 9; in counterbalance, 120–21, 241, 257–59, 265; at loggerheads, 120–21, 241, 242; separate domains, 29, 268–70; sibling rivals, 9, 120; rapprochement, 9, 268

Author Index

Arendt, Hannah: on Eichmann, 142–43

Bacon, Francis, 6, 107; Baconian Project, 107, 124n30
Baldi, Pierre, 230
Barry, Wendell, 224–25, 254
Barth, Karl, 37n2, 166, 170, 183, 186n11
Berger, Peter, 5
Blumenberg, Hans, 274
Bohr, Niels, 46, 54–56, 67, 69, 72
Borgmann, Albert, 110, 117
Brown, Donald: human universals, 38n8
Bush, Vannevar, 54, 68; *The Endless Frontier*, 261

Campbell, Will, 146–48, 183
Chua, Amy: *World on Fire*, 275–76
Coleman Richard, 28, 37n3, 49, 122n10, 123n23, 186n18
Crichton, Michael, 86, 239
Crossan, Dominic, 147, 185n4

Dallaire, Roméo: *Shake Hands with the Devil*, 136
Dawkins, Richard, 125n46, 193, 230, 244n11
de Wall, Frans, 197, 209
Delbanco, Andrew, 157n1, 177

Dennett, Daniel, 13, 27, 186n21, 194, 211, 218
Dick, Philip, 104
Dyson, Freeman, 51, 71, 265

Eichmann, Adolf. *See* Arendt
Ellul, Jacques, 87, 117

Fasching, Darrell, 183–84
Feynman, Richard, 70, 119
Foucault, Michel, 167
Friedman, Thomas, 93
Fukuyama, Francis, 13, 225, 254–55, 276–77; *End of History*, 5–6, 15–16, 39n15; human rights 277; *Our Posthuman Future*, 110, 111

Garreau, Joel: *Radical Evolution*, 4, 251–55
Geertz, Clifford: on Taylor, Charles, 86
Golding, William: *Lord of the Flies*, 14, 23, 150, 152–55
Goodal, Jane, 207–8
Greenberg, Daniel, 65, 70, 75n8, 81; *The Politics of Science*, 83; *Science, Money, and Politics*, 77n27, 79, 83
Gustafson, James 37n2, 219n6

Hamer, Dean, 193
Hart, David, 134

Hauerwas, Stanley, 23; Burrell and, 183; on Albert Speer, 183–84
Havel Václav, 11, 118–19, 125n45
Haynes, Roslynn: on *Frankenstein*, 238
Holton, Gerald, 38n5, 118
Hunter, James: *Culture Wars*, 88
Huxley, Aldous: *Brave New World*, 30–32
Huxley, T. H., 7, 30–32

Jenson, Robert, 24, 197; and Braaten, 185n62
Jonas, Hans, 117, 24n35, 223, 259

Kass, Leon 16–17, 85, 100, 124n4, 124n35; human dignity, 15–22, 276; *Life, Liberty and the Defense of Dignity*, 17, 27, 235; *Toward a More Natural Science*, 107, 230, 234
King, Stephen: *Needful Things*, 16, 21, 155–57, 237
Kramer, Peter: *Listening to Prozac*, 111–12
Krimsky, Sheldon, 81, 115, 282n13

Lebacqz, Karen, 227, 282n18

MacIntyre, Alasdair, 24, 236
McKibben, Bill: *Enough*, 4, 107, 119, 254–55, 264
McSherry, Corynne, 260
Meilaender, Gilbert, 123n25, 235–36, 244n18
Mithen, Steven: *The Prehistory of the Mind*, 201
Moltmann, Jürgen: *Science and Wisdom*, 240, 257
Morone, James: *Hellfire Nation*, 99–100, 137–38
Mouw, Richard 172

Neiman, Susan, 21, 39n15, 189, 200, 272; on Arendt, 142–43; modern evil, 140–42, 272; natural and moral evil, 22; on Nietzsche, 158n16

Niebuhr, Reinhold, 95, 37n2, 143, 157n7, 189, 243n2; *Nature and Destiny of Man*, 23–24, 38n6, 200
Niebuhr, Richard, 266
Nietzsche, Friedrick, 21, 145
Nouwen, Henri, 237

Oppenheimer, Robert, 48, 50, 53, 55, 73, 118; farewell speech at Los Alamos, 46–47, 56, 59, 118, 277; knowledge as intrinsically good, 59–60, 227; sin, 2, 19, 37n149, 51, 70, 225; vision, 56–58, 63, 67, 69, 71, 72
Orr, Allen, 15, 38n13

Pannenberg, 200
Percy, Walker, 111; *Message in the Bottle*, 162–65
Pinker, Steven, 12; *Blank Slate*, 12, 14, 27, 217–18; moral escalator, 13–14, 168, 252
Polkinghorne, John, 252, 283n24
Postman, Neil: *Technopoly*, 86–87

Ricoeur, Paul, 174, 177, 241
Ridley, Matt, 6, 7, 272
Rousseau, Jean–Jacques, 7, 35, 169; *Emile*, 21–23, 150–55

Sabatier, Paul: St. Francis biography, 279–81
Sacks, Jonathan, 257–58, 267
Schweber, S. S.: *In the Shadow of the Bomb*, 50, 53
Shelley, Mary: *Frankenstein*, 17, 30, 33–35
Shermer, Michael, 187n22, 220n16
Shuman, Joel, 244n15
Silver, Lee, 6, 106–7, 109, 124n31
Simmons, Philip: *Learning to Fall*, 197–98
Singer, Peter, 13–15, 168
Skinner, B. F.: *Walden Two*, 22, 32–33, 154
Smith Alice, 51, 65, 259
Sontag, Susan, 15

Spielberg, Stephen, 95, 103
Stock, Gregory, 84, 109, 230–32, 236

Taylor, Barbara, 129, 164, 207
Taylor, Charles, 86, 101, 123n23
Teller, Edward, 48, 53, 54, 59, 76n11
Thiemann, Ronald, 220n13
Tracy, David, 199

Venter, Craig, 90, 282n12
Volf, Miroslaw, 131, 139

Walker, Percy, 11, 162–63
Weinberg, Steven, 61, 76n17
Weisskopf, Victor, 48, 72
Williams, Bernard, 204, 205
Williams, Rowan, 266, 283n26
Wilson, Edward, 167, 193, 197, 231
Wink, Walter, 137
Winner, Langdon, 117, 242
Wolfe, Alan, 258, 266
Wolterstorff, Nicholas, 40n28, 179, 85n1

About the Author

Richard J. Coleman is a minister in the United Church of Christ, having served as the teaching minister of a university church, the pastor of a small-town congregation, and the director of an interdenominational inner-city Christian center. A graduate of Johns Hopkins University and Princeton Theological Seminary, he has published a wide variety of topics as well as books on the dialogue between Evangelicals and Liberals (*Issues of Theological Conflict*) and between science and theology (*Competing Truths: Theology and Science as Sibling Rivals*). Selected to participate in the pastor-theologian program sponsored by the Center of Theological Inquiry at Princeton, he is now a local group leader.